**palgrave advances in
william blake studies**

Palgrave Advances

Titles include:

Phillip Mallett (*editor*)
THOMAS HARDY STUDIES

Lois Oppenheim (*editor*)
SAMUEL BECKETT STUDIES

Jean-Michel Rabaté (*editor*)
JAMES JOYCE STUDIES

Frederick S. Roden (*editor*)
OSCAR WILDE STUDIES

Nicholas Williams (*editor*)
WILLIAM BLAKE STUDIES

Forthcoming:

Robert Patten and John Bowen (*editors*)
CHARLES DICKENS STUDIES

Peter Rawlings (*editor*)
HENRY JAMES STUDIES

Anna Snaith (*editor*)
VIRGINIA WOOLF STUDIES

Palgrave Advances
Series Standing Order ISBN 1–4039–3512–2 (Hardback) 1–4039–3513–0 (Paperback)
(*outside North America only*)

You can receive future titles in this series as they are published by placing a standing order.
Please contact your bookseller or, in the case of difficulty, write to us at the address below
with your name and address, the title of the series and the ISBN quoted above.

Customer Services Department, Macmillan Distribution Ltd, Houndmills, Basingstoke,
Hampshire RG21 6XS, England

palgrave advances in
william blake studies

edited by
nicholas m. williams
indiana university

palgrave
macmillan

First published 2006 by
PALGRAVE MACMILLAN
Houndmills, Basingstoke, Hampshire RG21 6XS and
175 Fifth Avenue, New York, N.Y. 10010
Companies and representatives throughout the world

PALGRAVE MACMILLAN is the global academic imprint of the
Palgrave Macmillan division of St Martin's Press LLC and of
Palgrave Macmillan Ltd.
Macmillan® is a registered trademark in the United States,
United Kingdom and other countries. Palgrave is a registered
trademark in the European Union and other countries.

ISBN-13   978–1–4039–1599–3 hardback
ISBN-10   1–4039–1599–7 hardback
ISBN-13   978–1–4039–1600–6 paperback
ISBN-10   1–4039–1600–4 paperback

This book is printed on paper suitable for recycling and
made from fully managed and sustained forest sources.

A catalogue record for this book is available
from the British Library.

Library of Congress Cataloging-in-Publication Data
Palgrave advances in William Blake studies / edited by Nicholas M. Williams.
p. cm. — (Palgrave advances)
Includes bibliographical references (p.) and index.
ISBN 1–4039–1599–7 — ISBN 1–4039–1600–4 (pbk)
1. Blake, William, 1757–1827—Criticism and interpretation. I. Williams, Nicholas M. II.
Series.

PR4147.P35 2005
821'7—dc22

2005048774

10   9   8   7   6   5   4   3   2   1
15   14   13   12   11   10   09   08   07   06

Printed and bound in Great Britain by
Antony Rowe Ltd, Chippenham and Eastbourne

contents

list of illustrations

notes on contributors

Helen P. Bruder is an independent scholar and author of the feminist study, *William Blake and the Daughters of Albion*. She is currently editing a compendium of reflections, which will show the varied ways which women artists have responded to Blake's verbal and visual art.

Angela Esterhammer is Professor of English and Comparative Literature at the University of Western Ontario. Her publications include *Creating States: Studies in the Performative Language of John Milton and William Blake* (1994), *The Romantic Performative: Language and Action in British and German Romanticism* (2000), and several edited collections, the most recent of them being a volume of international and comparatist essays on *Romantic Poetry* (2002).

Nelson Hilton is Professor and Head of English at the University of Georgia. His *Literal Imagination: Blake's Vision of Words* was published in 1983. A second book, *Lexis Complexes: Literary Interventions* (1994) and his 'Blake Digital Text Project' are accessible from his homepage: <www.english.uga.edu/nhilton>.

John H. Jones is an Associate Professor of English and director of the Honors Program at Jacksonville State University in Alabama. His publications include articles on Blake's idea of self-annihilation and poetic inspiration and on *The Book of Urizen* and print culture. He is currently working on a study of self-annihilation, language, and authority in Blake.

Edward Larrissy is Professor of English Literature at the University of Leeds. Among other books, he is the author of *William Blake* (1985), and the editor of a volume of essays, *Romanticism and Postmodernism* (1999).

Andrew Lincoln is Senior Lecturer in the school of English and Drama, Queen Mary, University of London. His publications include *Spiritual History: A Reading of William Blake's Vala, or the Four Zoas* (1996).

Mark Lussier is an Associate Professor of English and Director of the Ph.D Literature program at Arizona State University. His last book, *Romantic Dynamics* (1999), examined major poetic works of the period through the critical lens of contemporary physical theory. He is the author of several essays on Blake and is now working on a book-length study entitled *From Romanticism to Buddhism*.

Saree Makdisi is Professor of English at the University of California, Los Angeles and the author of *Romantic Imperialism* and *William Blake and the Impossible History of the 1790s*.

Peter Otto is Professor in the English Department at the University of Melbourne. He is author of *Blake's Critique of Transcendence* (2000) and co-editor of *Gothic Fictions*, a large microfilm collection of Gothic novels and chapbooks (2002–04).

Stephen Prickett was formerly Regius Professor of English at the University of Glasgow, and is now Margaret Root Brown Professor and Director of the Armstrong Browning Library at Baylor University, in Waco, Texas. He has published one novel, nine monographs, seven edited volumes, and over eighty articles on Romanticism, Victorian Studies and related topics. He is currently editor-in-chief of a multi-lingual anthology of European Romanticism.

David Punter is Professor of English and Research Director of the Faculty of Arts at the University of Bristol. His publications include *Blake, Hegel and Dialectic* (1982), *William Blake: Selected Poetry and Prose* (ed. 1988) and *William Blake: The New Casebook* (ed. 1996).

Christopher Strathman is an Assistant Professor of English at Baylor University. His book, *Romantic Poetry and the Fragmentary Imperative: Schlegel, Byron, Joyce, Blanchot*, is forthcoming from State University of New York Press in 2005.

Nicholas M. Williams is an Associate Professor of English at Indiana University. He is the author of *Ideology and Utopia in the Poetry of William Blake* (1998).

chronology

a note on the text/list of abbreviations

Unless otherwise noted, references to the works of William Blake come from *The Complete Poetry and Prose of William Blake*, edited by David V. Erdman, with commentary by Harold Bloom, newly revised edition (Garden City: Anchor/Doubleday, 1988). In keeping with the conventions of criticism on Blake, verse works are cited with plate and line numbers, followed by a reference to the page in the Erdman edition (indicated with the letter 'E'). For example, plate 10, line 20 of *Jerusalem* (on page 153 of the Erdman edition) is cited as follows: *J*10.20, E153. The following abbreviations are used for Blake's works:

A	*America a Prophecy*
ARO	*All Religions are One*
BA	*The Book of Ahania*
BL	*The Book of Los*
BT	*The Book of Thel*
BU	*The Book of Urizen*
E	*Europe a Prophecy*
FZ	*Vala or the Four Zoas*
J	*Jerusalem: The Emanation of the Giant Albion*
M	*Milton a Poem in 2 Books*
MHH	*The Marriage of Heaven and Hell*
NNR	*There is No Natural Religion*
SIE	*Songs of Innocence and of Experience*
SL	*The Song of Los*
VDA	*Visions of the Daughters of Albion*
VJ	*A Vision of the Last Judgement*

1
introduction: understanding blake

nicholas m. williams

In 1818, at a time when William Blake, age sixty, had finished almost all of the works by which he would subsequently be known, the great poet and critic Samuel Taylor Coleridge was given a copy of *Songs of Innocence & of Experience* by C.A. Tulk, an acquaintance of both men. Coleridge responded to the volume strongly, writing to another friend, Henry Cary,

> He is a man of Genius – and I apprehend, a Swedenborgian – certainly, a mystic *emphatically*. You perhaps smile at *my* calling another Poet, a *Mystic*; but verily I am in the very mire of common-place common-sense compared with Mr. Blake, apo- or rather ana-calyptic Poet, and Painter.[1]

Allowing himself this joke of calling Blake more a concealing than a revelatory poet, Coleridge nevertheless appreciated the excellences of the volume, and his choice of favorites – 'The Tyger', 'London', 'The Sick Rose', 'The Lamb', 'The Divine Image' – comes oddly close to today's appraisal of the book's high points. What is strangest about the episode, however, is the fact that Blake, in the last decade of his life, was here being introduced to Coleridge as an artist of whom the latter never had heard. Coleridge himself had been notorious in the periodical press of the nation since at least the late 1790s, first as dangerous Jacobin, then as author of *The Rime of the Ancient Mariner*, and finally as public lecturer and editor of his own experimental periodicals. But to this man at the heart of his country's literary culture, Blake's now most popular volume was unknown, even more than twenty years after its initial publication.

The reasons for Blake's obscurity, even late in his life, are many, and they reveal much about the cultural system of the time. That it was C.A. Tulk who served as a 'go-between' for Blake and Coleridge itself says much about Blake's position in society. Tulk was a lawyer with philosophical interests, who, more importantly, followed the teachings of Swedish mystic and prophet Emmanuel Swedenborg. Tulk's father had belonged to a Swedenborgian church of which Blake had also briefly been a member in the 1780s, his only flirtation with organized religion. What this means practically is that C.A. Tulk was an emissary to Coleridge from a world of which the poet would have had little knowledge, a world beyond the pale of Coleridge's rational Enlightenment universe. Both Blake and Coleridge experimented with unorthodox religious thought and both had broadly republican political sentiments (at least Coleridge did in his youth), but the differences in their contexts forms a partition between them. The usual way of describing the generally working-class religious atmosphere from which Blake emerged is to label it 'enthusiastic', by which is meant a dissenting Protestant, spiritualist, irrational (even if the members of the movement would not have used this word) and, from the point of view of the respectable middle class, somewhat suspect religious excitability. Even if placing Blake in this context does not entirely explain his propensity to visionary experiences, having, according to report, first seen God through his window at the age of four, it does suggest that he was not entirely alone in his experience of powerful, inward spiritual events. And since the apparatus of publication and artistic exhibition was largely in the hands of men for whom this enthusiasm was an alien and inexplicable milieu, this context also partly explains how Blake's work could have remained so inaccessible to the mainstream of British readers and critics.

Related to Blake's religious background in an explanation of his relative obscurity during his lifetime is his vocational background. The son of a London hosier, Blake received only a limited formal education. Although his parents seem to have supported his interests and talents, Blake by necessity commenced training for the life of work quite early, sent to Henry Pars' Drawing School at the age of ten and then apprenticed to engraver James Basire at fourteen. It is indeed impossible to understand Blake fully outside of his status as engraver, since that profession helped form his highest artistic aspirations. Highly skilled professionals, engravers belonged to an anomalous social formation known as the artisanal classes. On the one hand, they required extensive training, such as Blake's drawing tutorship and apprenticeship, and possessed a great familiarity with the techniques of the fine arts. After his apprenticeship and as he was beginning his professional career, Blake attended classes at the Royal

Academy Schools, practicing life drawing and painting next to students preparing for the most rarefied and exalted careers as independent artists. But at the same time that engravers shared this knowledge of the techniques and products of the artistic tradition, their craft was regarded as lower in the hierarchy of artistic methods and unworthy of representation among the members of that same Royal Academy. In spite of the finely honed talents required by engraving, establishment artists regarded it as merely a reproductive technique (as it would, indeed, increasingly become), not meriting the name of art. Although engraving, and Blake's other main occupation, the selling of prints, was becoming quite lucrative at the time, due to England's pre-eminence in these fields, Blake's reliance on them for income distinguished him from the more famous poets and artists of the period, whose independence of means (or reliance on more 'respectable' professions) gave them an appearance of superiority to economic need. The artisanal class would, however, in both the United States and England, be the source of much artistic innovation and political radicalism, precisely for the way its members were unable to look past the brute fact of labor. Blake's pervasive meditations on work processes form a significant part of this class's new concerns and expand the subject matters for literature.

But if Blake's enthusiastic religious background and vocation as an engraver partly explain his relative obscurity during his life, the central factor is certainly his means of producing texts, a technique largely invented by Blake and now called relief etching. Although this technique will be treated at greater length elsewhere in this volume, it can be considered here as a crucial factor in Blake's lack of broad reception in his own time. Relief etching was difficult and time-consuming, and the resultant texts were more expensive than many potential readers could afford. Blake's intentions in employing this mode of production have been much debated, but there's reason to think that he believed, at one time, that relief etching could become a viable means for reaching a large audience, and that he didn't intentionally limit himself to the small number of copies of each of his works which resulted.[2] To understand why Blake chose this laborious and unremunerative mode of production, one must see the verbal and visual elements of his illuminated works as an integral whole, neither taking priority over the other, and both necessary for the full impact Blake intended. Blake's pictoral designs don't merely 'illustrate' the texts they accompany, in the sense of replicating verbal significance by visual figure: instead, they frequently serve as counterpoint to the verbal text, or set out in directions unanticipated by the words on the page. What's more, in Blake's hands these words themselves begin to take on the properties of visual art, as they sprout tendrils, release birds, or simply extend themselves across the page as indices of Blake's work upon the copper plate. In short, the reader of Blake's illuminated page will understand that among the 'Satanic Mills' his works set out to criticize – those regimented, standardized and oppressive systems for destroying human imagination while maximizing production – must be numbered conventional typography itself. The price for rejecting standard type in favor of relief etching is high, in terms of the size of the potential readership, but to do otherwise would have dramatically changed his artistic intentions and achievements.

And so we are left with the image of Blake in the twilight of his career, surrounded by an appreciative group of young painters who called themselves 'the Ancients', but little known outside of this circle, and, if known, known as an engraver rather than a poet. The history of writerly reputation takes many shapes, however. If some posthumous reputations might be graphed as jagged up-and-down lines, reflecting great variation in different periods (Percy Shelley and John Donne might be thought of in these terms), others appear as steadily downward plummets, as fame during a poet's lifetime gives way to posthumous disregard (Robert Southey comes to mind). For Blake, the line of reputation traces a steadily upward progress, the course of which it will be the job of this introduction to describe. Since it is the task of the chapters which follow to treat contemporary approaches to Blake, this brief overview will end at around the middle of the twentieth century with two groundbreaking pieces of Blake criticism which influence everything that follows them.

out of obscurity: nineteenth-century responses

Given the paucity of responses to Blake during his own lifetime, as noted above, those few which do exist take on added importance. First among these is an unusual book by a schoolmaster named Benjamin Heath Malkin, entitled *A Father's Memoirs of his Child* (1806). The subject of the book is Thomas William Malkin, the author's son who died at the age of six, but in the course of an introductory letter Malkin turns to the designer of the book's frontispiece portrait of the boy, William Blake. The best speculation is that Malkin and Blake were introduced by Robert Hartley Cromek, an engraver and publisher who had given Blake some engraving commissions but whom Blake would later disparage as a 'Petty sneaking knave' (E509), on the suspicion that Cromek had stolen his idea for an illustration of the Canterbury pilgrims. Malkin's account is partly useful for its providing of details of Blake's biography otherwise unavailable, evidence that the men knew each other well. Beyond that biographical detail, however, Malkin also provides texts for several of the *Songs of Innocence and of Experience* (including 'Laughing Song', 'Holy Thursday', 'The Divine Image' and 'The Tyger'), as well as 'How sweet I roam'd from field to field' and 'I love the jocund dance' from *Poetical Sketches*. He displays a sympathetic understanding of the reasons for Blake's lack of popular success, claiming that '[t]he skeptic and the rational believer [. . .] apply the test of cold calculation and mathematical proof to departments of the mind, which are privileged to appeal from so narrow a tribunal' (xxiii). If this appraisal rings of Blake's self-justifications, Malkin yet shows independence of mind in criticizing his efforts at epic (the prophetic books are no doubt intended) as 'wild' and 'pass[ing] the line prescribed by criticism to the career of imagination' (xl–xli). This gesture of praising the short lyrics while passing over the prophetic books would continue throughout the nineteenth century, even among Blake's most enthusiastic readers. Of the lyrics, however, Malkin is an astute reader, as evidenced by his identification of echoes of the book of Revelation in the Innocence 'Holy Thursday' (xxx). On the whole, Malkin's response is remarkable for both its earliness and its sensitivity: he strikes a claim of appreciating Blake's uniqueness at a time when the artist was otherwise little known.

This fact of being little known, even at the time of his death, would shape much of the initial response to Blake, since much of it would take the form of biographical introductions of this unusual figure to a larger public. John Thomas Smith's biographical sketch, part of his *Nollekens and His Times* (1828), supplies important details from the early part of Blake's life, particularly his association with the bluestocking circle surrounding Harriet Mathew and her husband, which was of great assistance in publishing his first book, *Poetical Sketches* (1783). Smith's bias leads him to see Blake's poetry as an inferior accompaniment to the designs, leading him to dismiss even the *Songs* as 'wild, irregular, and highly mystical' (477). This tendency to divide Blake's corpus into distinct parts also characterizes Allen Cunningham's more widely read life of Blake in *The Lives of the Most Eminent British Painters, Sculptors, and Architects* (1830–46). As this general title indicates, Cunningham's focus, like Smith's, is mainly on Blake the painter and engraver, and Cunningham goes so far as to divide Blake's productions into the sensible work of the day and the mad excesses (mostly poetic) of the night. He focuses on the visionary nature of Blake's experience and relates a fascinating story of Blake's vision of Satan: '[i]ts eyes were large and like live coals – its teeth as long as those of a harrow, and the claws seemed such as might appear in the distempered dream of a clerk in the Herald's office' (174). When he turns to Blake's illuminated page, however, he sees greatness 'worthy of Michael Angelo' (161) in the designs, combined with the frustrating obscurity of the text: 'meaning seems now and then about to dawn; you turn plate after plate, and read motto after motto, in the hope of escaping from darkness into light. But the first might as well be looked at last' (160–1). An addendum to the second edition of the sketch softens the judgment of the verse, at least for *Songs* (the prophetic work still meriting only disdain), but the overall effect remains still that of a brilliant visual artist compromised by his eccentric experiments in verse.

A more important resource for gaining access to Blake's opinions and day-to-day life is to be found in the materials gathered by Henry Crabb Robinson, a journalist and acquaintance of Blake, as well as of Wordsworth, Coleridge, Charles Lamb and others prominent in the period. Robinson first learned of Blake from Malkin's *Father's Memoir* and subsequently attended the 1809 exhibition of Blake's paintings located (pitifully) in his brother James's hosiery shop. Crabb Robinson was struck by the catalogue Blake had written for the exhibition and impressed enough by the paintings to write an article on Blake for a German magazine. The two men finally met in 1825 and the diary accounts, letters and reminiscences in which Crabb Robinson recorded some of the details of their handful of meetings represent the most vivid description remaining to us of the living (though aged) Blake. These materials, understandably, don't possess the polish of Smith's and Cunningham's formal biographies (and were only published piecemeal over the following hundred years), but they offer a more direct picture of Blake in exchanges with his often bemused interlocutor. Indeed, one of the main pleasures in these accounts for today's students of Blake lies in Crabb Robinson's tendency to misunderstand the fullness of Blake's comments, taking for inconsistency insights which reveal further depths to those familiar with Blake's thought. For instance, when Blake charges John Locke with atheism (largely due to the philosopher's empiricism), Crabb Robinson objects that Locke endorsed 'the evidences of Xnity [Christianity] & lived a virtuous life' (8), pleased that Blake can say nothing in reply. A reader of *The Marriage of Heaven and Hell* (which Crabb Robinson probably was not) would suspect, however, that a Christianity subject to rational proof or a virtue based on abstract moral codes would go no way with Blake in refuting his charges of Locke's atheism. In another instance, when Crabb Robinson is trying to gauge Blake's orthodoxy by asking him his opinion on the divinity of Jesus Christ, Blake responds '*He is the only God*', but then adds (in a manner Crabb Robinson neglects to comment on), 'And so am I & so are you' (3, emphasis in original). The tendency of Blake's comments to exceed the boundaries of Crabb Robinson's questions suggests the authenticity of the latter's records and does credit to his value as a memoirist, even when he seems unequal to his subject's observations. Like Smith and Cunningham, Crabb Robinson is torn between ideas of Blake as 'Artist or Genius – or Mystic or Madman' (2), but his honesty as a diarist guarantees the value of his work.

This group of largely biographical appraisals (along with further materials from the group of painters surrounding Blake in his last decade, only published towards the end of the century) could reasonably be expected to emerge shortly after the death of such an unusual figure as Blake, and their appearance didn't dramatically alter his renown. Alexander Gilchrist's full-length biography, *Life of William Blake, Pictor Ignotus*, published in 1863, did, however, and it represents the first substantial uptick in Blake's reputation and the first period of intense interest in his works. As Gilchrist's subtitle indicates, Blake could still be approached at this period as an 'unknown' entity, and it is in those terms that the author describes texts and paintings with which most of his audience is unfamiliar. Gilchrist's strengths, and the reasons for the enthusiastic response his book elicited, lie in the thoroughness of his treatment of the life (drawing upon earlier biographies as well as sources unknown to them) and his persuasive conviction of his subject's genius. Of his first reading of the *Songs of Innocence*, Gilchrist writes, 'the effect was as that of an angelic voice singing to oaten pipe, such as Arcadians talk of; or as if a spiritual magician were summoning before human eyes, and though a human medium, images and scenes of divine loveliness' (71). In addition to the enthusiasm of passages such as this, it is the sheer volume of biographical detail, recording all the main phases of Blake's life, which here establishes him as a major figure, beyond risk of slipping back into the night of obscurity. In spite of Gilchrist's general praise, however, he remains as immune to the appeal of Blake's more difficult texts as earlier commentators. To his credit, he does offer descriptions of every major work, including descriptions of the plates, but he often throws up his hands in despair at the meaning of the texts, falling back on extensive quotation. Of *The Marriage of Heaven and Hell*, he says 'to seek any single dominating purpose, save a poetic and artistic one [a synonym, for Gilchrist, of vagueness], in the varied and pregnant fragments of which this wonderful book consists, were a mistake' (78); *Milton* 'has no perceptible affinity with its title, [and] the designs it contains seem unconnected with the text' (240); with *Jerusalem*, 'the eyes wander, hopeless and dispirited, up and down the closely-written pages' (228). That an ingenious and compelling Blake can still emerge from such negative appraisals is a testimony to Gilchrist's high praise for the artist's visual designs and his relish of Blake's unique ideas and character. Although the verdict of Gilchrist's chapter, 'Mad or Not Mad?', is for the latter, the figure traced here is the eccentric, charming, childlike and wildly imaginative genius who continues to dominate the popular conception of Blake today.

Shortly following Gilchrist's acclaimed biography, and initially intended to be published with it, is Algernon Swinburne's book-length, *William Blake: A Critical Essay* (1868), the first study which can be said to attempt to come to terms with the fullness of Blake's poetic output. Swinburne's style of expression, his language always pitched at the height of rapturous enthusiasm, can be wearying, but his unhesitating plunge into the texts yields palpable results. He rejects out of hand Gilchrist's (and others') tendency to value only the visual element of the prophetic books, instead suggesting (in line with a poet's bias, perhaps) that 'each [is] a poem composed for its own sake and with its own aim, having illustrations arranged by way of frame or appended by way of ornament' (206). And if he seems to echo earlier commentators when he admits that '[i]f any one would realize to himself for ever a material notion of chaos, let him take a blind header into the midst of the whirling foam and rolling weed of this sea of words' (207), he later claims of this textual welter that '[c]haos is cloven into separate elements; air divides from water, and earth releases fire' (211). As one might expect from the author of *Laus Veneris* and numerous other works designed to scandalize a respectable Victorian audience, the Blake Swinburne salutes as comrade and prophet is not a retiring Christian exemplar but rather a rebel unswervingly committed to the gospel of art: 'Once let art humble herself, plead excuses, try at any compromise with the Puritan principle of doing good, and she is worse than dead' (101). As for an ethic that Blake might have followed, Swinburne suggests, 'his creed was about this: as long as a man believes all things he may do any thing; scepticism (not sin) is alone damnable, being the one thing purely barren and negative; do what you will with your body, as long as you refuse it leave to disprove or deny the life inherent in your soul' (105). Given these statements, it's perhaps not surprising that, for Swinburne, *The Marriage of Heaven and Hell*, 'gives us the high-water mark of his intellect' (227). That work's propositional audacity, caustic satire of high-mindedness, and gnomic vigor make it stand out for Swinburne as a key document in the counter-cultural tradition of amoral art he's interested in tracing (the concluding pages enlist Walt Whitman in the same cause). Although the longer works don't elicit from Swinburne this degree of excitement – of *Jerusalem*, he fears that 'one cannot imagine that people will ever read through this vast poem with pleasure enough to warrant them in having patience with it' (307) – he does comb through them for the same antinomian perspective he values in *The Marriage*. In the final analysis, Swinburne's own interests in aestheticism and in well-delivered insults to bourgeois respectability (interests partly echoed in some twentieth-century accounts of Blake, such as Georges Bataille's in *Literature and Evil*) might be seen as unduly influencing his views on Blake, but there's no question that his perspective underwrites a productive encounter with the earlier poet.

Gilchrist's biography, then, ensures Blake's place among recognized literary and artistic figures, while Swinburne's essay begins the long work of interpreting his poetry. Along with the attempt by William Michael and Dante Gabriel Rossetti to establish a stable body of Blake texts, published as a second volume with Gilchrist's biography (and largely unsuccessful in its editorial goals), these works represent Blake's definitive inclusion in the main stream of English literary history. (One close-to-hand measure of his emergence at this moment is George Eliot's use of two Blake poems as epigraphs in *Middlemarch*, published between December 1871 and December 1872.) It only remains, to close out the nineteenth-century portion of this survey of writing on Blake, to turn to the work of yet another poet, William Butler Yeats, and his collaborator, Edwin John Ellis. In 1893, the two Irishmen came out with an enormously ambitious edition of *The Works of William Blake, Poetic, Symbolic, and Critical*, which attempted to gather everything then known as the work of Blake. The texts themselves are fairly corrupt and not of much use for a modern reader, but the 'Works' occupy only the third of the publication's three volumes, the first two being called, respectively, 'The System' and 'The Meaning'. The use of the word 'system' in reference to Blake – a word that he himself used, most famously in Los's statement that he must 'Create a System, or be enslav'd by another Mans' (J10:20, E153) – indicates much about Yeats' and Ellis' approach, one that would be very influential for subsequent decades of work on Blake. Rejecting summarily any notion of Blake's madness, the two insist that it is rather the perfect coherence of Blake's work which has hitherto puzzled readers, and they claim in the present volumes to have 'shape[d] the master-key that unlocked all the closed doors of the poet's house' (I:ix). That 'key' comes, in large part, from a tradition of mystical thought including the Kabala, Jacob Boehme, Emmanuel Swedenborg and Yeats' favorite theosophical works. Mysticism, for the pair, is no realm of cloud and shadow, however, but instead a highly structured system of metaphysical meanings, a grid upon which poetical symbols can be laid. From Swedenborg, they draw the crucial premise that human beings possess a physical, an intellectual and an emotional aspect, each of them utterly distinct from the others and related only by symbolical 'correspondences' rather than by a sharing of essence. On this foundation of three aspects, along with a fourth aspect of 'the mirror' or 'the imagination of God' (I:246), Yeats and Ellis build up the entire four-fold symbolism of Blake's prophetic work, including the four Zoas, the realms of being, compass points, body parts, elements, and so on (much of it laid out in schematic charts). In the second volume, this system is then returned to individual works, which are then interpreted in its light. The fact that Blake freely admits his debt to many of the mystical thinkers mentioned by Yeats and Ellis, and that the later prophecies include an element of cosmic schematizing similar to the critics' four-fold charts, suggests that their approach does yield insights into Blake's corpus. The impulse to 'figure out Blake's system' is indeed a powerful one, and one that would be pursued in the following century. Where a modern reader might object to this approach, however, is precisely in its claim to have the one true 'master-key' to the texts, as if their richness could be adequately reflected in one of the book's fold-out graphic devices. Related to this weakness is the sense that the approach drains Blake's texts of their contemporary political and social significance, in the drive to fit them into the mystical system. It is, indeed, those poems which have little or no explicit mystical apparatus, such as many of the *Songs of Innocence and of Experience*, which present Yeats and Ellis with their most difficult cases. Seeing them read 'The Little Black Boy' entirely in terms of the relations of the temporal and eternal worlds, with no reference to the colonial slave system (II:9–10) is ample indication of the blind spots of their method. The gains of their approach are palpable: they present a thoughtful and capable Blake uninfected by madness and possessed of insights unknown to his poetic contemporaries. The loss they risk, however, is cutting this Blake off from the stream of history and confining him to the purely mental world of mystical meaning, where his poems almost don't need to be read to be understood.

Yeats and Ellis can serve well as the sentries standing beside the door leading to twentieth-century considerations of Blake, since their call to 'system' would meet both with many sympathetic responses and, eventually, with oppositional voices suggesting that Blake can't be understood systematically. This struggle, between forces which we might too hastily call 'the systematizers' and 'the historicizers', could indeed be seen as the main debate in work on Blake in the first half of the twentieth century. That debate would issue, as we shall see, in the publication at mid-century of two works of Blake criticism which make debtors of all subsequent writers on Blake: Northrop Frye's *Fearful Symmetry* and David Erdman's *Blake: Prophet Against Empire.*

system and history: 1900–54

Due to Blake's increasing popularity at the turn of the century, and to the proliferation of studies of him (spurred in part by the appearance of the first reliable edition of Blake's poetical works (1905) under the hand of John Sampson), it is impossible to describe in detail all of the criticism which emerges at this time. There are new biographies – one by John Ellis (1906), another by Arthur Symons (1907), the prominent proponent of the *symboliste* poets, a third by Mona Wilson (1927) – as well as the enormously useful *Bibliography of William Blake* (1921), compiled by Geoffrey Keynes. Yeats continues to be influenced by Blake in his poetry and also publishes two essays on Blake in his 1903 collection *Ideas of Good and Evil* (the title itself drawn from Blake). T.S. Eliot, in *The Sacred Wood* (1920), praises Blake's 'profound knowledge' of human emotion, while lamenting his seeming need to cobble together a philosophical system (154, 156). As a way of organizing the growing critical literature on Blake, however, one might identify two strands of thought culminating in the masterful achievements of Frye and Erdman. On the one hand, the systematizers tend to focus on Blake's work as internally coherent and consistent, its arcane images explained partly by cross-reference to other Blake texts, partly by reference to the mystical tradition he consciously invokes. From this perspective, Blake's poetic goals are the highest imaginable: to describe humanity's relationship to the divine (a relationship in which the two terms are not entirely distinct), to diagnose the nature of the fallen condition in which we find ourselves, and, to the extent possible, to prescribe a method for rectifying that condition and accessing the Eternal. These largely non-literary goals distinguish Blake from other writers, from the systematizers' point of view, making him a figure of sage wisdom and prophetic knowledge, rather than just a versifier. In their handling of Blake's texts, these critics can sometimes seem to suggest that nothing changed in Blake's thinking over the course of his life, that the vision was entire at its beginning and only needed to be expressed in the succession of works which occupied some three decades. Similarly, this approach sometimes seems to suggest that Blake's message bore little relation to the time in which it was recorded, that it has more connection to the deep tradition of mystical thought than to the issues and seismic political upheavals of the late eighteenth and early nineteenth centuries. For their part, the historicizers, gaining strength in the wake of systemic critics, strive to open Blake's system to the external world of political and social influence, to suggest that Blake's work is a message to his own time and that, rather than remaining locked in his mystic tower poring over Boehme and Swedenborg, he lived in a recognizable London among people who shared many of his beliefs and concerns. Historicizers, reading specific Blake works, refer images and habits of language outward to the political debates engaging the nation at the time, rather than inwards towards the internally coherent Blakean system. Uncovering largely forgotten movements and historical actors, the historicizers seek to create a contemporaneous context for Blake, peopling a world in which his works could conceivably emerge. These two directions for work on Blake don't, of course, have to be mutually exclusive: historicizers can recognize the systematicity of Blake's thought and systematizers can locate Blake historically. There has been a tendency, however, to pursue one track or the other, and the tension between these two approaches continues, in some sense, to the present day. The work of the first half of the twentieth century can thus usefully be organized as flowing in two separate streams, towards Frye and Erdman at the headwaters of the mid-century.

Of first importance for the development of the systemic view of Blake is S. Foster Damon's *William Blake: His Philosophy and Symbols* (1924). This work, along with the *Blake Dictionary* (1965) he would publish forty years later, represents one of the major contributions to twentieth-century scholarship on Blake. In keeping with the systemic view, Damon focuses more on the coherent message of Blake's entire corpus than he does on the literary form of particular examples, going so far as to claim that '*Blake was not trying to make literature*' (63, emphasis in original), and that '[h]e wanted to rouse with thought, not to lull with beauty' (xi). In contrast to Yeats and Ellis, with whom Damon actually has much in common, this view reveals a rather impoverished view of poetry, since it suggests that poetic form is a mere ornamental addition to conceptual content, rather than an inherent medium of mystical truth, as Yeats and Ellis claimed. What Damon shares with Yeats and Ellis, however, is the firm belief that Blake is the expositor of mystical truths and it is only in this sense that Damon sets out to describe, in a somewhat too rational-sounding phrase, Blake's 'Philosophy': 'The key to everything Blake ever wrote or painted lies in his mysticism' (1). Although mysticism begins, for Damon, in an ecstatic monism of vision (and Damon carefully traces Blake's visionary experiences as crucial turning points), it issues in a highly ordered system of stages and insights. Borrowing from Evelyn Underhill's transhistorical study of mystic experience, Damon identifies five stages in Blake's biography – 1) awakening to divine reality; 2) purgation of the Self; 3) enhanced return of the Divine; 4) the 'Dark Night of the Soul'; 5) the complete union with Truth – which he then maps on to Blake's works, each representing one or another stage of the mystical process. As indicated by Damon's reference to a 'key' to Blake, he believes, as did Yeats and Ellis, that the five-stage mystical experience exhaustively interprets Blake's work, with no need of supplementary or divergent interpretations. What's more, he sees that mystical experience as essentially the same in all ages, directed towards subjective experience rather than to engagement with the outer world: 'The experience is always the same, no matter in what land or level of civilization it occurs' (2). The expression of the experience does indeed vary (and Blake is praised as one of the most communicative of mystics), but since the kernel of the work lies in the experience rather than in its outward form, the texts largely seem a veil to be penetrated, an allegorical husk to be cracked. Damon does make a gesture towards historical contextualizing, in a chapter entitled 'The Temporal Blake', but what is most striking about Damon's treatment of the Industrial Revolution, the rise of radicalism, the abolition debate, the spread of Methodism and other 'enthusiastic' religions, is how little Damon sees them affecting Blake, who seems a solid pillar withstanding the storm of history. Damon's usefulness in explicating the symbols of the paintings and poems is inescapable (especially in his lengthy appendix of line-by-line commentaries on the poems), but, as with the other systematizers, one must first access the outermost frame (here, the five-stage mystical experience) which inflects everything which is placed within it.

Another work which must be mentioned in this context, but which it would be a mistake to assimilate entirely to the systemic school, is J. Middleton Murry's *William Blake* (1933). Murry shares with the systematizers the sense that it is Blake's doctrine rather than his literary techniques which is the most valuable object of study: 'Blake was not at all concerned to be an artist, in the accepted sense of the word' (7). Unlike Damon, and Yeats and Ellis, however, his entry to that doctrine lies not through mystical tradition nor through a highly structured account of mystical experience, but rather through a sensitive reading of Blake's texts and a finely honed ability to isolate the philosophical issues at play there. For Murry, Blake's thought begins with the recognition that there is a 'sense beyond sense' (14), a way of experiencing the world not limited to the repertoire of physical senses which forms the foundation of empiricist psychology. The distinction between empirical sense and the 'sense beyond sense' ultimately gives rise in Blake to a distinction between two notions of the individual, the limiting Self and the liberating Identity. The story of Blake's work, according to Murry, is the putting off of Self (as in the 'self-annihilation' of *Milton*) and the putting on of Identity. What charms in Murry's account is his sense that this achievement is available to everyone sporadically (and only sporadically to anyone), not requiring arcane knowledge, even if the expression of it in language is necessarily obscure. Murry also attempts to connect this quest for Identity to Blake's engagement with radical politics, seeing political activity as the necessary complement of the purgation of psychic limitations: 'The happening of the inward revolution brings with it inevitably, the expectation of a revolution in the world of men' (54). This formulation, of inner revolution preceding outer revolution, is at least as old as Friedrich Schiller's *Aesthetic Education* and it no doubt suffers from a mentalist bias (not to mention that the history it engages remains largely abstract), but it does represent a serious attempt, largely avoided by Damon, to connect the 'temporal' and the 'eternal' Blakes. All in all, although Murry's account suffers some of the methodological weakness of the systematizers (such as the tendency to draw on later Blake works to gloss the earlier ones), his sincere brand of radical Christianity (which he would expound in a number of books) makes him an unusually insightful critic of Blake.

With the invocation of the mystical tradition in explanations of Blake going back as far as Yeats and Ellis, it was virtually inevitable that critics would eventually turn to a more detailed exploration of this material. Two books, Helen C. White's *The Mysticism of William Blake* (1927) and Milton Percival's *William Blake's Circle of Destiny* (1938), do just this. White's book suffers from a somewhat rigid notion of mysticism, but its goal of specifying what might be meant by the rather vague claim that 'Blake was a mystic' is a worthy one. Her conclusion – that Blake is, in fact, 'not a great mystic' (245) – has limited explanatory power for his work as a whole, but the care with which she evaluates this common claim is salutary. Percival's account has broader significance for an understanding of Blake. His catalogue of sources for approaching Blake includes '[t]he Orphic and Pythagorean tradition, Neoplatonism in the whole of its extent, the Hermetic, Kabbalistic, Gnostic and alchemical writings, Erigena, Paracelsus, Boehme, and Swedenborg' (1), which serve as an illuminating backdrop for a careful overview of the entirety of Blake's work. In keeping with the systematizers, Percival stresses the coherence of the entire Blakean corpus, admitting that he 'take[s] the prophetic writings as a single entity' (12) and, in the recurrent phrase of this school, that '[t]he same key unlocks them all' (5). For Percival, that 'key' is an interpretive scheme that distinguishes between the outer (rational, passive, temporal, feminine) and the inner (imaginative, active, eternal, masculine) realms, as well as the four-fold scheme familiar from Yeats and Ellis, here broadly characterized as 'the intellectual life, the emotional life, the creative life, and the sensuous life' (8). Like Murry, Percival attributes to Blake an insight that 'man must be paradisical within before an outer paradise can be secured' (12) and the prophetic works are glossed as the story of that triumph, the 'Circle of Destiny' by which fallen experience arrives at the eternal. Almost necessarily, this interpretive stance abstracts Blake from his historical world – Blake 'would have been more at home in the Alexandria of the third century than he was in the London of his own time' (3), Percival claims – even while it gives a much fuller picture of the mystic tradition so often identified as an inescapable source in the earlier criticism. Within the heuristic limits of the systematic school's assumptions, then, limits which tend to idealize the object of study, not allowing for progress over the course of a career nor for the deep influence of historical and social conditions, Percival gives readers the fullest picture yet of the arcana upon which Blake drew.

Against the background of this rich body of work on Blake's system, and as if obeying the Blakean dictum that 'Without Contraries is no progression' (*MHH*, E34), there gradually arose a distinct school of interpretive thought with its own assumptions about his work. Jacob Bronowski's *William Blake: A Man Without a Mask* (1943), Mark Schorer's *William Blake: The Politics of Vision* (1946) and David V. Erdman's *Blake: Prophet Against Empire* (1954) each begin with the idea that Blake was passionately involved with the debates of his own time, political, religious and social. Since these works are amply discussed by Andrew Lincoln in his chapter on 'Blake and the History of Radicalism', along with their continuing influences on the critical projects of today, I'll keep my treatment of them brief, stopping only to point out their most salient differences from the earlier work on Blake's system. First, and perhaps most importantly, the Blake they describe lives in a material and temporal world. The Blake of the systematizers was, for the most part, a reader of 'forgotten lore', a journeyer through the reaches of mystic inwardness. For this new group of critics, he is the working engraver, participant in radical conversation circles, eager reader of broadsides and newspapers, strident advocate of 'Republican Art'. Although earlier studies included sketches of the world in which Blake lived, they tended to treat him as a stranger in it, remarkable precisely for the way in which he was unmarked by his times. As Lincoln argues in his discussion of

Erdman's groundbreaking work, such detailed historical considerations of Blake go far beyond a mere contextualization of his work, changing the very way those works are read and interpreted. In Erdman's hands, the obscurities of Blakean prophecy are not merely to be set against the political and social debates of his time: they are themselves maps of those debates, pervasively referencing specific figures and events of their historical era. Such an approach shines a light on aspects of Blake's works left largely unexamined by the systematizers, on references in his work to real historical figures – Newton, Bacon, Voltaire, Rousseau – and to persons contemporary with Blake but largely lost to history: Robert Cromek, a commissioner of engraving work; John Scofield, the soldier who accused Blake of treason and who appears as a Satanic conspirator in *Jerusalem*; William Hayley, second-rate poet and condescending patron of Blake. As such, the historical school of Blake criticism (which stands as the dominant school at the present time) offers as counterweight to the atemporal mystical Blake of the systemizers, a temporal Blake whose opinions change over the course of his life (even as his quest for liberation persists), whose works should not be read as a single epic but as separately engaged with their separate historical moments. Erdman, in particular, stands as the invaluable resource for this approach to Blake, who, however his conclusions or emphases may be disputed, must be consulted for his story of Blake's engagement with his times.

If, however, as noted above, the historical line of critics springing from Erdman continues to dominate much current work on Blake, it's nevertheless fitting to end this survey of early criticism by turning to the single greatest example of the systemic school and still the most useful introduction to the poet, published seven years before Erdman: Northrop Frye's *Fearful Symmetry: A Study of William Blake* (1947). John E. Grant's extravagant claim in a 1982 review of the state of Blake criticism – that Frye's is 'the one book we can most confidently recommend to the Blake scholar of 2100 A.D.' (440) – perhaps best expresses the esteem in which it is still held long after its publication, a status relatively rare in the critical literatures on major figures. Before assessing its particular strengths and limits, one might first note some important respects in which it differs from the assumptions of the systemic school. First of all, Frye rejects the notion, which had been current since at least the time of Ellis and Yeats, that Blake should be considered primarily a mystical poet: 'Mysticism is a form of spiritual communion with God which is by its very nature incommunicable to anyone else, and which soars beyond faith into direct apprehension. But to the artist, *qua* artist, this apprehension is not an end in itself but a means to another end, the end of producing his poem'

(7). For Frye, mysticism is too cloudy a term to describe the care, the vigor, above all the *consciousness* with which Blake undertook his works, which, for Frye, should not be mistaken for the 'automatic' writings of recently returned visionaries or spiritual travelers frustrated with the inadequacies of language, but instead as carefully crafted works of art. This latter point – that Blake should be considered primarily as an artist – forms of course a second point of distinction in regard to the systemic school and is the linchpin of Frye's whole approach. Unlike Damon and Murry, who had claimed that Blake was on the trail of far bigger game than merely art, to the extent that he was attempting to describe or even to initiate an ecstatic mystical experience, Frye characterizes Blake as primarily an artist or, even more strongly, as the paradigmatic case of the artist. The influence of Frye's work, its power in creating an image of Blake which reserved his place, once and for all, in the literary canon, as well as establishing Frye himself as one of the pre-eminent literary critics of the twentieth century, has everything to do with the emergence of a particular notion of literature in mid-century North American academic culture, a notion of literature for which Blake was now a key exhibit. For by claiming Blake for literature rather than mystical experience, Frye was certainly not denigrating him, but rather finding a new way to raise him to the pinnacle of cultural importance.

These extravagant sounding claims can be supported by tracing the ties between *Fearful Symmetry*, Frye's first book, and his even more famous second book, the widely read theoretical work, *Anatomy of Criticism* (1957). The latter, with its 'Four Essays' and its four-fold system of interpretation (borrowed in part from medieval theories of polysemy), reads like a reconfiguration of the systemic school's four-stage accounts of Blake or like Blake's own accounts of Golgonooza, the city of art built on a principle of four, and the Four Zoas who revolve around it. Frye's immensely influential theory of literature can thus be seen, and the author himself admits something of this in his account of the genesis of *Anatomy* in the book's preface (vii), as the gospel of literature according to (Frye's) Blake. What is it, though, that Frye takes from Blake, and why is Blake thus positioned as the Messiah for a revalued notion of the literary? A large part of the answer lies in Blake's superlative need for interpretation, and the role it plays in the American post-war English Department's dissemination of a powerful new expertise in interpretive techniques, open to all those willing to learn. While the mythic grandeur of Frye's discussions can seem far afield from the detailed treatments of balance and paradox purveyed by New Criticism's main proponents, he shares with them a sense of the dignity and importance of interpretive activity.

Indeed, one might say that it's Frye who provides the sublime element of dignity to an otherwise technical craft, for if Brooks, Warren and Ransom provided New Criticism its methodology, then Frye, through the vehicle of Blake, would seem to have provided its metaphysics, its theology. Although he draws a clear line between Blake's artistic genius and the mystical aptitude claimed by Yeats and Ellis and the other systematizers, Frye nevertheless invests interpretation with an almost holy significance: as the initiate passes through the four stages of reading, from a literal construal of letters on the page, to a sense of formal unity, then on to the identification of universal archetypes, and the final perception of all-in-all in the anagogic phase, the result is an almost religious calm, a purging of self in favor of perceptions of global and transhistorical meaning. That magisterial calm, that sense of one's part, as interpreter, in establishing the ultimate significance of literary art, formed the core of authority of English as a discipline in the post-war period, until its desublimation by deconstructive and historical/material critique.

This is, of course, to take a bird's-eye view of Frye's emergence, and Blake's along with him, in the mid-century context. To get a full sense of Frye's importance to the understanding of Blake, one must dig into the masterful readings of individual works in *Fearful Symmetry*. The mark of the book's strengths is that it provides many of the terms and concepts – the Orc cycle, the notion of Satanic Parody, and so on – in which subsequent discussions would be carried on. One of the time-honored rhetorical devices of literary criticism is the depiction, usually early in an essay, of a critical authority, seeming to stride like a Colossus over the scene, but, in reality, carefully positioned in order to be taken out at the knees or betrayed by a banana peel planted by the mischievous author. Within Blake studies, Frye repeatedly plays the role of the rhetorical fall guy, a testament to the power of his formulations. A common target of critique is Frye's version of the systematicity of Blake, something he carries over from earlier systemic critics and carries to perfection. In Frye's hands, Blake's system doesn't even require the outside reference of mystical experience or theosophical arcana, but rather possesses an artistic unity unto itself. Polysemy, the medieval interpretive system upon which Frye bases his approach, although its name makes it sound like a device for proliferating meanings, is actually carefully organized in its structure of expanding frameworks of interpretation, and Blake's system, as Frye lays it out, possesses a pleasing wholeness, seemingly complete in each of its parts and in each stage of Blake's career. Although Frye does detail Blake's place in intellectual history and his contentious relationship with earlier thinkers – the first chapter is entitled 'The Case

Against Locke' – his strong sense of system renders these encounters mythically titanic rather than minutely detailed, with Blake seeming utterly fortified in mental battle by his fully realized vision of art. When the view of Blake's system gets extended, in *Anatomy of Criticism*, to a general theory of literature, it can seem as if Blake's cosmic vision opens wide its jaws to swallow all the artistic traditions of the world, along with the histories of philosophy and religion. In a critical climate that emphasizes difference, cultural specificity, historical detail, the political and ideological dimensions of literature, Frye can seem a worthy but necessary opponent.

Like Innocence and Experience, like the 'true friends' who are at their best in opposition and whom it is a grave error to try to reconcile, the mythic systemic approach of Frye and the encyclopedic historicizing approach of Erdman must each be given their due. As one traces the cross references in Blake's work, the re-used lines, the reappearing figures, there *does* seem something system-like about what he acheives, much as Los claims to 'Create a System' for his own salvation. But that system is rooted in such contingency, in the vagaries of language, in the recalcitrance and splendor of the body, in mud and blood of war and history, and the chaos of personal reference woven into the works, as to sometimes make the systemic structure totter (perhaps with Blake's full permission) beneath the materiality of its references. Maintaining these contraries, acknowledging the complex existence of the literary text and of Blake's text in particular, is the challenge taken on by the very best criticism, of Blake and others. As the following chapters amply show, Blake has continued to exert a powerful force over readers who wish to face these challenges, in the wake of Frye and Erdman, a force which shows no signs of weakening in a new millennium.

notes

1. This episode is recorded in Richard Holmes, *Coleridge: Darker Reflections 1803–34*, 473–4. Coleridge and Blake would meet eventually and, according to second-hand reports, enjoy each other's company.
2. The issue of whether or not Blake desired or could reasonably have hoped for a large audience has been a topic of critical contention. Joseph Viscomi, suggesting that Blake's notion of audience bears a greater resemblance to the modest ambitions of painters than those of conventional publishers, suggests that 'Blake appears to have advertised primarily to connoisseurs, collectors, and other artists' (174). Jon Mee, on the other hand, situates Blake in an early-1790s context (John Boydell, Thomas Macklin, Robert Bowyer) which had high hopes for the commercial potential of mixed-media works.

works cited and suggestions for further reading

Bronowski, Jacob. *William Blake: A Man Without a Mask*. London: Secker and Warburg, 1943.

Cunningham, Allen. 'William Blake' from *The Lives of the Most Eminent British Painters, Sculptors, and Architects*. 2nd ed. London: 1830–46. II, 143–88. Reprinted in *Nineteenth-Century Accounts of William Blake*. Ed. Joseph Anthony Wittreich, Jr. Gainesville, Florida: Scholars' Facsimiles and Reprints, 1970. 149–94.

Damon, S. Foster. *A Blake Dictionary: The Ideas and Symbols of William Blake*. New York: Dutton, 1971.

——. *William Blake: His Philosophy and Symbols*. Gloucester, Massachusetts: Peter Smith, 1958.

Eliot, T.S. *The Sacred Wood: Essays on Poetry and Criticism*. 7th ed. London: Methuen and Company, 1950.

Ellis, Edwin J. *The Real Blake: A Portrait Biography*. New York: McClure, Phillips and Company, 1907.

Erdman, David V. *Blake: Prophet Against Empire*. 3rd edn. Princeton: Princeton University Press, 1977.

Frye, Northrop. *Fearful Symmetry: A Study of William Blake*. Princeton: Princeton University Press, 1947.

——. *Anatomy of Criticism: Four Essays*. Princeton: Princeton University Press, 1971 (1957).

Gilchrist, Alexander. *Life of William Blake with Selections from His Poems and Other Writings*. Yorkshire: EP Publishing Limited, 1973.

Grant, John E. 'Inside the Blake Industry'. *Studies in Romanticism* 21 (Fall 1982): 436–43.

Holmes, Richard. *Coleridge: Darker Reflections 1803–34*. New York: Pantheon, 1998.

Keynes, Geoffrey. *A Bibliography of William Blake*. New York: 1921.

Malkin, Benjamin Heath. *A Father's Memoirs of His Child*. (London, 1806), pp. i–xlviii. Reprinted in *Nineteenth-Century Accounts of William Blake*. Ed. Joseph Anthony Wittreich, Jr. Gainesville, Florida: Scholars' Facsimiles and Reprints, 1970. 3–50.

Mee, Jon. *Dangerous Enthusiasm: William Blake and the Culture of Radicalism in the 1790s*. Oxford: Clarendon Press, 1992.

Murry, J. Middleton. *William Blake*. London: Jonathan Cape, 1933.

Percival, Milton O. *William Blake's Circle of Destiny*. New York: Octagon Books, 1970.

Robinson, Henry Crabb. *Diary*. Reprinted in *Nineteenth-Century Accounts of William Blake*. Ed. Joseph Anthony Wittreich, Jr. Gainesville, Florida: Scholars' Facsimiles and Reprints, 1970. 55–108.

Sampson, John, ed. *The Poetical Works of William Blake*. Oxford: 1905.

Schorer, Mark. *William Blake: The Politics of Vision*. New York: Henry Holt and Company, 1946.

Smith, John Thomas. 'Blake' in *Nollekens and His Times*. 2 vols. London: 1828, 2, 454–88. Reprinted in *Nineteenth-Century Accounts of William Blake*. Ed. Joseph Anthony Wittreich, Jr. Gainesville, Florida: Scholars' Facsimiles and Reprints, 1970. 112–46.

Swinburne, Algernon Charles. *William Blake: A Critical Essay*. London: Chatto and Windus, 1906.

Symons, Arthur. *William Blake*. New York: E.P. Dutton and Company, 1907.

Viscomi, Joseph. *Blake and the Idea of the Book*. Princeton: Princeton University Press, 1993.

White, Helen C. *The Mysticism of William Blake*. New York: Russell and Russell, 1964.

Wilson, Mona. *The Life of William Blake*. London: 1927.

Yeats, William Butler. *Ideas of Good and Evil*. New York: Russell and Russell, 1967.

Yeats, William Butler and Edwin J. Ellis, eds. *The Works of William Blake*. 3 vols. London: Bernard Quaritch, 1893.

part one
textual approaches

CHAPTER TWO
textual approaches

2
blake's production methods
john h. jones

Recent studies in print culture and the history of the book over the last twenty-five years have made readers acutely aware of the variety of consequences that the medium of print has for literary production, dissemination, and reception. As Nicholas Hudson, for example, reminds us, a writer and his or her manuscript are only small parts of a vast industry involving an intricate series of transactions among writers, booksellers, printers, typesetters, stationers, learned societies, bankers, and readers, and all of these factors play crucial roles in the way a book is produced and understood as a cultural artifact (85). Students of William Blake, of course, have realized at least some of these complications for quite some time, because as is well known, Blake not only wrote his own poetry but, for the most part, illustrated, printed, colored, bound, and sold his work using mainly his own methods and working at odds with the conventional book selling industry – an industry of which he was also very much a part. While other writers of his day, like Wordsworth and Coleridge, understood the issues surrounding the publication of their work and made efforts to control them (Boehm 469), no writer has ever controlled so much of the process himself, nor has any writer been so self-conscious about the process of making books. The many references to book production and the power of books in Blake's work include the description of the printing house in Hell in *The Marriage of Heaven and Hell* (E40), the making of Urizen's 'books formd of metals' in which he writes his 'iron laws' (E72, 81), and the poet's reference to printing in his call to the reader in *Jerusalem* (E145). As Mark Greenberg has noticed, self-consciousness of medium also appears in the frequency with which Blake uses the word 'book' in his titles and in the fact that the words 'book(s)' and 'print' each appear 130 times in the complete works (163). Accordingly, Blake scholars have been prompted to examine Blake's book

25

making processes and question why Blake chose to operate against a burgeoning print industry and consider what effects that choice had. While much has been accomplished in the areas of recreating the actual etching process and understanding Blake's confrontation with the print industry, several areas require further exploration, in particular those having to do with textual and bibliographical issues, the effects of book production on interpretation, and the way book production reconfigures the reader's role in the literary exchange.

Since Blake was an engraver by trade and since engraving is central to his book making process, an understanding of the printing and engraving industry of the eighteenth and early nineteenth centuries is crucial to understanding Blake.[1] Compared to publishing standards in Europe in the first half of the eighteenth century, English printing practices were crude at best with little or no logic or standard. The type was often old and worn, and proofreading was only cursory. Title pages were often cluttered and disorganized. Illustrations, while perhaps charming for their rustic quality, rarely displayed professional skill. Even the paper and binding were inferior. Any book that did show superior characteristics usually benefited from the help of foreign craftsmen. Adding illustrations to a book was especially cumbersome and expensive. While the process of transposing a writer's verbal ideas from paper to print was fairly straightforward, the process of recreating a design onto a copper plate was excruciatingly laborious and could cost a bookseller as much for one engraving as for all other non-illustrative costs combined (Bentley, 'The Great' 59, 62–3). For this reason, plates printed and sold separately, such as those reproducing works of art, were the dominant mode of engraving in the eighteenth century and were the means by which most of the English public had access to works of art, since travel was limited, no galleries were open to the public, and no public exhibitions of contemporary art took place until 1760 (Alexander and Godfrey 1). Because engraving was so time-consuming and unsystematic, compared to typographical print, it came under a great deal of pressure to keep pace with printing (Eaves 188).

By 1775, new techniques and better ways of managing older ones helped to speed the production of engravings and reduce their labor costs. Mezzotint, the first main form of graphic reproduction using copper plates, involves the use of a multi-toothed rocker to cover the entire plate with ink-holding indentations, and then some of the indentations are flattened with a scraper to produce the white spaces. This process creates chiaroscuro effects that closely resemble those of oil painting, but the mezzotint plates were not especially durable, being able to produce only 100–200 good impressions. With William Hogarth, line engraving, which involves cutting lines into a copper plate with a steel tool called a burin, came into vogue. The engraved plates were more durable for printing, but the process, the most systematized of all the engraving forms, was much more difficult to learn and more time consuming to produce (Alexander and Godfrey 1, 6–7). Because line engraving translated visual images into a system of lines and crosshatchings, an engraver had to learn elaborate linear codes to produce effects of color and light. The systematization, however, allowed for an assembly-line approach whereby several workers could each focus on a particular element or technique. In the words of Robert N. Essick, 'Whether grass, stone or the human form, all is dominated by the system of lines which constitutes an eighteenth-century engraver's technique' ('Blake and the Traditions' 61). Although line engraving would remain dominant through the end of the eighteenth century, processes known as stipple and aquatint, which like mezzotint, were faster and produced the tonal effects of painting, would appear at the end of the century. Stipple uses tools with spiked wheels of various sizes that dot the copper to produce shadings. Aquatint is a form of etching that imitates watercolor (Alexander and Godfrey 7–8).

Because of the difficulty of their training and work, line engravers felt superior to those practicing mezzotint or stipple, but they still never achieved equal status with the painters and sculptors whose work they reproduced. Indeed, the mechanization of line engraving does not ordinarily permit original work but usually requires a model, most often a sketch of a painting or sculpture, to reproduce. The work of the line engraver is, therefore, always subordinate to that of the painter or sculptor, and so is their status in the hierarchy of printmaking. While artists, especially painters of portraits and history like Joshua Reynolds, could take advantage of the financial benefits that separate prints of their work would bring them, the engraver, no matter how great his skill, was always seen as a craftsman and not an artist. Indeed, the Royal Academy excluded engravers from membership and did not show their work (Alexander and Godfrey 1). While some viewed the mechanization of engraving as a way to cut costs and improve profits, others saw it as a cheapening of both the quality of the work of engravers and of the engravers themselves (Eaves 154). William Blake, of course, held the latter view.

In some respects, Blake's apprenticeship and experience as a commercial engraver helped to position him on this side of the debate.[2] Blake entered into a seven-year apprenticeship in 1772 at the age of fourteen with James Basire, an antiquarian line engraver whose specialty was the accurate representation of old buildings and monuments and whose style was much like the styles of Dürer and Marcantonio, which heavily emphasized line over shading, a style antithetical to the predominant one exemplified by Reynolds (Bentley, *The Stranger* 33). While copies of prints that Blake collected as a boy show the same old-fashioned taste, Basire was certainly influential, teaching Blake not only his version of line engraving – a mixed method of engraving that relied on etching a copper plate in an acid bath prior to the actual line engraving to speed up the process – but also careful attention to scale, the clear rendering of every detail, and, perhaps most importantly, accurate delineation of outlines (Essick, *William Blake* 4, 34–5, 60).

Upon the completion of his apprenticeship with Basire in 1779, Blake set out not to engrave others' designs for publication but to achieve success as an original artist whose art form was engraving. His direction was not without precedent, considering that William Hogarth achieved great success and fortune in the same medium. Contemporaries of Blake's who had similar success included John Hamilton Mortimer, Henry Fuseli, and James Barry, all of whom Blake admired. While none worked primarily as an engraver, they each executed some plates and developed interests in the same high Renaissance style (Essick, *William Blake* 41–3). While Blake began his career as an artist-engraver, he actually made his living with the commercial engraving of book illustrations, most of which were after designs by other artists. According to Charles Ryskamp, about half of Blake's engravings through 1806 were published by Joseph Johnson, and many of those were of the work of Thomas Stothard, one of the best illustrators of the day (19–23). As Bentley notes, Blake's most ambitious commercial work, his original illustrations and engravings for Edward Young's *Night Thoughts* to be published by Richard Edwards, was in direct competition with the work of the most important illustrated book publishers of the day, John Boydell, Thomas Macklin, and Robert Bowyer, but while it gave Blake some notoriety, the work was never completed ('The Great' 67, 79–81, 89). While not necessarily important for understanding Blake's iconography, some of these commercial projects helped to reinforce the ideas learned during his apprenticeship, and others gave him opportunities to experiment with new techniques that would prove useful to him in engraving his own designs (Essick, *William Blake* 45). Yet despite his *Night Thoughts* designs and despite the artistic liberties he often took when engraving others' designs, Blake's commercial work would never elevate him above the status of craftsman in the eyes of his contemporaries, who viewed the work of most engravers as mere copying and not original art.

In an effort to achieve the status of artist, Blake turned to a form of engraving called relief etching.[3] Most commercial engraving on copper plates, including Blake's, was intaglio engraving; lines are cut into the copper with a burin or with acid etching enhanced by the burin, the method Blake learned from Basire, as noted earlier. If the plate is to be etched first, an acid-resistant material, called stop-out varnish, is applied to the surface of the copper, and the engraver then scrapes away portions of the varnish where the lines of the image, the blacks, are to appear. The acid eats into copper where the varnish has been scraped away, and these lines are enhanced by the engraver's burin. Once the plate is cleaned and inked, the ink fills the depressions made by the acid, and the press, using great pressure, transfers the ink to paper. In relief etching, however, the lines and letters are applied in stop-out varnish to a clean plate, and acid is used to eat away the surrounding portion of the plate, the whites, leaving raised letters and lines, which are then inked and pressed onto paper. Blake was not the only one looking to relief etching as an alternative to intaglio engraving, since as Essick describes, relief etching of texts offered considerable advantages of economics and independence that mechanical type could not provide, and Blake was one of a number of individuals looking for these advantages through the eighteenth century and into the nineteenth century (*William Blake* 112–19). Despite the fact that market conditions were such that Blake could only have supplemented his income with relief-etched, hand-colored illustrated books – a reality he seems to have understood – there still was considerable demand for such books, as he also would have recognized (Viscomi xxv).[4]

The advantages of relief etching for Blake were both economic and artistic. Economically, it eliminated the huge investment that conventional illustrated book publication required. Normally, a conventional publisher would incur an enormous labor expense, because of the addition of the painters and engravers to the process. During the wars with Napoleon, trade to the Continent was also cut off, which eliminated a significant potential market for illustrated books. Moreover, because of close government regulation to prevent sedition, libel, and blasphemy, conventional publishers would be unlikely to consider anything inflammatory. The publisher, then, could only take on a project that gave him a considerable expectation of profit. Indeed, the profit motive forced some of the finest illustrated books of the time to be produced by means other than conventional publication, including John Thornton's *Temple of Flora*, John Flaxman's *Iliad* designs, Thomas Bewick's *British Birds*, and of course Blake's illuminated books. All were published either by the authors themselves or with the help of friends and relatives, not by conventional publishers.[5] With relief etching, however, an individual engraver could execute and print the plate, both text and illustration, alone, thereby saving the costs of the additional labor and making the whole process relatively cheap and quick (Bentley, *The Stranger* 101, 103). Another advantage is that unlike conventional type that has to be broken down and reset, the relief-etched plates were entirely portable and could be used many different times, with even years between printings. While two thirds of the copies of Blake's illuminated works were printed between 1789 and 1795, he continued to print them from time to time until his death, and some copies of his works were even printed after his death in 1830 and 1831 (Bentley, 'What Is the Price' 623).

From a conventional publishing standpoint, the relief-etched prints would appear crude compared to regularized typesetting and intaglio line engraving and, therefore, be considered a disadvantage. From the point of view of the engraver attempting to elevate his craft to the level of art, however, the primitive appearance could be seen as an artistic advantage, since it stands in sharp contrast to the polish of commercial print. Blake's earliest illuminated books, *All Religions Are One* and *There is No Natural Religion*, are especially rudimentary, partly because the plates are so small and also because the thickness of the etched lines is considerably greater than in intaglio work. In the *Songs of Innocence*, Blake more than tripled his plate size, which allowed him to include more detail, like the vegetation, the folds in clothing, or the indications of wood grain. The larger plate size makes the lines seem smaller by comparison, and Blake's work continues to evolve in this direction (Essick, *William Blake* 137, 140). Even so, his work always achieved a handmade look rather than the perfection attained through mechanization.

Another artistic advantage of relief etching is that since the engraver-artist can work alone, he can control the entire production process. Hudson explains that once a book leaves the hands of its author, events like pirating or simply the process of compositing and editing can cast doubt on the reliability of any information conveyed from the author through the press (84). In relief etching, not only is the author in control of the entire printing process, but the medium itself allows for a much closer unity of text and design. Blake does produce whole plates of text and full page illustrations, but his illuminated works are famous for the way he manipulates text and design so that the two intertwine and interact with each other. While the plates themselves were relatively stable compared to moveable type, they could still be altered, either with engraving tools or etching, and Blake did so sometimes years after a plate was originally etched. Taking further advantage of having complete control over the entire process, Blake could make each copy of each book unique not only by altering plates but by shifting plates, including at times text plates, into different positions within each copy, thereby creating new and interesting juxtapositions and, therefore, new reading experiences. As Eaves explains, illuminated printing represents for Blake 'an autographic medium close to drawing, responsive to the hand and thus to the "melodious accents" of a single mind and imagination' (185).

To take the idea of eliminating the fragmenting mechanization of book production a step further, Blake's relief-etching process may very well have allowed him to compose directly on the copper plate, thus unifying conception and execution and eliminating the intermediary original design that caused engraving to be considered secondary and subordinate. Blake himself says in his 'Public Address' that his engraving is 'Drawing on Copper as Painting ought to be Drawing on canvas [. . .] & nothing Else' (E572). By itself, this statement could be understood figuratively, as Viscomi implies when he says, 'Blake eliminated the grounds for valuing one medium over another. [. . .] Reducing all art making to drawing was Blake's way of leveling the playing field, of removing the taint of craft from his works as printmaker' (qtd. in Kraus 169). But statements made by people closer to Blake's time, like his friends John Linnell and J.T. Smith, attest to Blake's literally drawing and writing the text of his poems backwards directly on the copper with stop-out varnish.[6] Even so, scholars of Blake's engraving process have had a difficult time accepting the idea that Blake would have written all the text of his illuminated books, including the 100-plate *Jerusalem*, backward, and for about forty years in the middle of the twentieth century, the reigning theory, argued most prominently by Ruthven Todd, was that Blake must have used a transfer process, which Todd, along with Joan Miró and S.W. Hayter, attempted to replicate in the print studio. Working from the only known example of one of Blake's relief-etched plates, a small fragment of a canceled plate from *America, a Prophecy*, Todd claims that Blake must have written his text in stop-out varnish on paper coated with gum arabic, laid the paper on the plate, and applied pressure to achieve the transfer. Once the paper was removed, the lettering of the text would have appeared in reverse on the plate, requiring only a small amount of touching up. The designs were then drawn directly on the plate in stop-out varnish. Documentary evidence does, indeed, exist that shows Blake knew and used transfer processes for intaglio engraving (60, 62).[7]

The problem with the transfer theory is that it puts an intermediary step between composition and execution, thereby undermining long held assumptions about Blake's efforts to overcome division artistically and perpetuating the eighteenth-century assumptions of the secondary nature of engraving. Of course, practice does not always live up to theory, but the painstaking historical, visual, and experimental analyses by Essick and Viscomi make a convincing argument that in this case it does. In *William Blake: Printmaker*, Essick points out that all the writers arguing for the transfer method ignore not only the comments by Blake's contemporaries but also the fact that engravers were normally trained in reverse writing. He also points to the lack of extant detailed preliminary designs, which may not prove that Blake did not use a transfer process but certainly does raise some doubt (89–90). Viscomi goes further, pointing to several objections to the transfer theory. First, he notes that Blake would have had plenty of time to do his reverse writing, since most of the illuminated books were done during 1789–90 and 1793–95, when Blake had few other professional commitments, and his 100 plates of *Jerusalem* were composed over a sixteen-year period. Also, the transfer techniques available in Blake's time would not work in illuminated printing, and the ones that would work were not available until later. The available techniques involved graphite or chalk being transferred from paper to the plate – the transfer process used in intaglio engraving – and would not work in relief etching, because the stop-out varnish, which would have to be applied over the transfer in reverse anyway, would not adhere to the greasy-textured graphite or would come off with the chalk, which had a tendency to flake away from the copper. Finally, while transfers may work for single plates, they would be extremely cumbersome for whole works. If transfers were done, Blake would have had to arrange all the text and images beforehand, and since no two plates of any illuminated book are the same size, the whole process of working the book out in advance would be extremely difficult (20–1). From these points and from experimentation with techniques and materials likely available to Blake, Viscomi concludes, '[W]hat is imagined to have occurred on paper in the form of the "preliminary drawing," or mock-up, did occur, but it occurred on copper and only on copper' (25). By composing directly on copper, Blake was able to take existing processes and materials to fashion a new art form, marking a radical departure for engraving by eliminating the key division between conception and execution.

The same argument about process and theories of conception and execution carries over into the coloring of Blake's books. Early in the printing of illuminated books, Blake and his wife, Catherine, hand colored the finished monochrome prints. The Blakes were simply participating in a rather fashionable market for hand-colored prints, one that started as a small cottage industry but grew to a major commercial enterprise. To speed the process of hand coloring, the major publishers divided the labor among several colorists, each one being responsible for a particular color or area of the image (Essick, *William Blake* 121). By 1794, however, Blake developed a process for color printing his illuminated plates, whereby he applied the colors directly to the plate and printed it in much the same manner as printing a monochrome plate. Several of Blake's illuminated works seem to have been designed exclusively for color printing, including *The Song of Los, The Book of Los, The Book of Ahania*, and possibly *The Book of Urizen*, since the only monotone print of *Urizen* was done some time around or after 1818. All of the color printing seems to have been done between 1794 and 1796, since Blake returns to monochrome printing for his later epics, *Milton* and *Jerusalem*. With color printing, Blake is able to unite the coloring process with the printing process, thereby eliminating another mechanical division (Essick, *William Blake* 125, 147, 149).

As the issue of transfers versus direct composition in relief etching raises questions about just how unified Blake's process really was, so does the debate over the particulars of Blake's color printing. The question arises whether Blake did the color printing in one or two runs, or pulls, through the press. Several critics argue for the two-pull process, with Michael Phillips's work being the most articulate.[8] According to Phillips, Blake printed the monochrome plate first, removed the plate from the press to clean it, applied the opaque color pigments to the areas of the plate where the design would be colored, and returned the plate to the press for a second time. He argues that Blake's process is a combination of the *à la poupée* method of color printing, in which all colors are applied to a single engraved plate, and the multiple plate technique, which uses a series of plates each engraved and inked for one of the colors and printed successively to produce one multi-colored image (95–7). This process would be especially difficult, though not impossible, because in printing the page twice, Blake would have to take extra care to register the page to the plate exactly through both pulls.

While there is evidence that a few color prints were done in two pulls (Essick, *William Blake* 127), Essick and Viscomi argue, again rather convincingly, that Blake's common practice must have been a one-pull procedure. First of all, the two-pull process would be more time consuming and, therefore, unnecessary if a one-pull process could work. Second, if Blake did use two pulls, there would be visible evidence, and in most cases, there is not. Third, historical precedent is against the two-pull method. The standard at the time for color printing was *à la poupée* (which Alexander and Godfrey, interestingly, refer to as 'the usual English way of inking the plate' for color printing (8)), since it was faster and cheaper than using multiple plates, which no one in England was using in the 1790s. Where Blake departs from standard practice is in the printing of both surfaces of the plates, both the raised letters and lines and the etched-away background. The shallow relief surface of Blake's etching process allowed him not only to ink the raised surfaces but also to apply his thick coloring pigments, made most likely from carpenter's glue, to what would normally be the white surfaces. The thick, sticky pigments pull away from the paper, leaving a mottled or reticulated effect, giving the printed image not only color but texture, as well (76–8). The two-pull hypothesis, therefore, seems unlikely and works against Blake's attempts to overcome division in his art. In the words of Essick and Viscomi, 'Blake's color printing, even more than relief etching, fully realized Blake's objective of combining in one seamless process printmaker, poet, and painter' (100–1).

Blake's experiments with color printing culminated with the twelve sets of large color prints of 1795. With these prints, like *Newton* and *Nebuchadnezzar*, Blake produced works of art that went even further than the color printing of the illuminated books in their innovation and effect. While it is difficult to ascertain the process, Blake seems to have painted thick pigments onto millboard, pressed the pigments onto paper, and finished the print with watercolor and pen-and-ink outlines. He apparently was able to make three impressions from each pigmented design with each successive print being considerably lighter than the previous one.[9] The fact that the millboard of the large color print is unetched, unlike the copper plates used for the illuminated books, makes controlling the transfer of pigment to paper more difficult and causes considerable accidental variation from print to print. Since the conventional print industry aims to turn out vast numbers of identical prints from a single plate, Blake's small editions of large color prints are arguably his most radical departure from commercial printing. According to Essick, '[Blake's] evolution of new techniques out of old could progress no further without leaving printmaking altogether' (*William Blake* 135).

Although Blake would never leave print making, he would later devote more time to painting, as with the series of works he called 'frescos' and the watercolors he did on biblical subjects for his friend and patron Thomas Butts. Of course, oil painting was considered superior to watercolor, but according to his earliest biographers, he disliked the muted nature of the colors and the inability to achieve a definite line with oil paint (Tatham, qtd. in Bentley, *Blake Records* 515; Gilchrist 1.369). Not only did Blake diverge from the standard by choosing to work in watercolor, he also diverged in his materials and practices, as Ann Maheux explains. Like most watercolorists of the time, he ground his own colors, but rather than using a gum for the binder, as was common, Blake most often chose carpenter's glue, which has less of a tendency to crack over time and, once it dries, is insoluble. New washes, therefore, would not dissolve the previous ones, keeping the work from blurring. He also relied heavily on pen and ink for outlines and used washes more for developing form, rather than for deepening color, which he applies in smaller strokes and in more detail (124–6). The frescos also use carpenter's glue, but the application is much thicker than with the watercolor. In Joyce H. Townsend's description of the process, Blake began by drawing in pencil or ink upon, most often, a stretched canvas. Over that he applied a thick priming of glue and whiting. Blake would then apply colors in carpenter's glue in thick layers to add depth without losing transparency. On top of this he applied another coat of glue and sometimes a coat of natural resin. Because new layers would not dissolve old layers, the result was a painting that had the clarity of watercolor without losing the density of oil. Unfortunately, this particular medium using the thicker applications of carpenter's glue did not age well. Most of Blake's frescos have turned brownish with age, much worse than oil, and exhibit extensive cracking (66, 68). The point is, though, that taken together, all of Blake's work, the relief etchings, the color printing, and the watercolors and frescos, shows a continuous sense of innovation with each medium having influence on the others, whether it is in commonality of underlying materials, like the carpenter's glue, the consistent preference of line and form, or the continuous effort to raise a subordinate medium to the level of art.

In the last twenty-five years much has been accomplished in the study of Blake's book production. The improved understanding of the late eighteenth-century publishing industry, the very close examination of Blake's own books, the careful research of the historic availability of materials and techniques, and the faithful attempts to replicate the processes in the studio have gone far in settling several vexing questions. Along the way, however, new questions and new ways to look at old questions have emerged. These new questions and approaches center on the way in which Blake conceived of the book as a part of a transaction between himself and an audience in the context of social conventions and economic realities of his time. Jerome McGann's words from 1981 about Blake's books still serve as a challenge to Blake scholars today:

> Each of these texts is the locus of a process of artistic production and consumption involving the originary author, other people (his audience[s], his publisher, etc.), and certain social institutions.

Blake's special way of creating his works emphasizes the presence of these impinging social factors precisely because Blake strove so resolutely, even so obsessively, to produce work that was wholly his own. (275 6)

The study of Blake's illuminated books in particular and his artistic output in general needs to be understood as a focal point for a broad matrix of social, political, and economic interactions. When asked in a 2002 interview about the future of Blake studies, Essick projects that the next development will examine

context (political, religious, social) in the direct service of interpretation and explore the interconnection among Blake's methods of writing, drawing, etching, printing. The ideological implications of graphic technologies, as it were, coupled with the ways Blake's texts and images were both shaped bv and point toward their methods of production and their producer's social context. (qtd. in Kraus 146)

The fact that Essick's words echo McGann's twenty-one years later suggests that now that we have a better understanding of the process of making illuminated books, we can begin to explore the larger cultural implications of that process.

One important issue that needs to be explored further has to do with Blake's unit of production. Perhaps the longest held notion about Blake's process claimed that because demand for his work was limited and because the plates could be easily stored, Blake tended to print copies of his books only when he had a buyer for them. Thus, the unit of production, from this point of view, is the book.[10] This assumption leads to certain conclusions about dating the individual books throughout Blake's career and to the idea that the variations in the individual books could be so significant as to be even connected to the prospective buyer. Viscomi's work, however, makes very clear that such a printing practice would be highly impractical. Setting up the studio to print any particular work requires an enormous investment in preparing the press, the ink, and the paper, and all other work comes to a halt. The practicalities of book production indicate that Blake's unit of production, like most any printer's unit of production, would be the edition, the printing of at least several copies of an individual book in one session. Furthermore, edition printing raises different possibilities about the dating of the prints and the significance of their variations (xxiv–xxv). In terms of the dating, Viscomi's work has shown that Blake did almost all of his illuminated printing in relatively brief periods, as noted earlier, and that significant variations appear across editions rather than from copy to copy. The implications of this change in perspective need further exploration, in terms of both individual books and the relation of the illuminated books to the other elements of Blake's career.

The issue of the variations in the copies of books is especially significant. Contrary to the norms of commercial printing, Blake's production methods invite accident and difference at just about every phase, changing the aesthetic landscape. Because Blake managed each step of the process, he could alter plates, change ink and pigment colors, and change the order of plates. The methods themselves created variation, as well, since the shallowness of the relief etching and the way that color pigments behave under pressure often create unexpected results from impression to impression. The difficulty, then, lies in deciding first whether a variation among copies creates a significant or meaningful difference and then upon how the difference, if it is significant, impacts our understanding of the work. Essick and Viscomi have strongly cautioned readers against seeing the variations as producing signifying differences among copies. In the essay 'How Blake's Body Means', Essick argues that since the vast majority of variants are accidents of the production process beyond the print maker's control, the variability of Blake's work has more to do with the subversion of commercial standardization, signifying systems, and conventional notions of authorial intention than with the development of an alternative symbol system (207, 211). Viscomi concurs, saying that the notion that the variations are intended to make each copy a separate version of a book misunderstands the mode of production (167). But surely, the alteration of a plate or changes in the order of plates within a book or, perhaps, different colorations suggest some change in the attitude toward the work, and even if a variation is accidental or if intentionality is always questionable, each of the variations will produce some effect at least from the standpoint of the reader. As Stephen Leo Carr argues, omitting from consideration even the subtle differences misses some of the most remarkable aspects of Blake's work, since this 'radical variability [. . .] always enters into the verbal-visual exchanges generated with each page' and 'challenges aesthetic beliefs deeply associated with conventional modes of producing books and prints' (182). What Blake's books do, as Greenberg claims, is to 'beckon or even demand an active role for the reader confronting his book', asking him or her 'to reimagine not only existing texts but to associate the material form in which texts are produced and received with their themes and with the particular historical conditions attending their production' (161–2). While a limited amount of work has been done on the shifting of text plates in *Urizen* and *Jerusalem*,[11] the nature and effect of the full range of variation in Blake's books needs much more scrutiny, and it seems unlikely that any treatment of any illuminated book would be considered full unless it took into account the many variations among copies.

Examining variations among copies can be difficult, especially since original copies are scattered in collections on both sides of the Atlantic and because access, at times, can be difficult. It would be technically and economically impractical, perhaps impossible, to reproduce each copy of each of the illuminated books in print form, since most of the nineteen illuminated books exist in more than one copy and since each of the copies has its own history and idiosyncratic features. A number of very good print facsimile editions do exist, but even the best ones, like the Blake Trust/Princeton UP series, can only offer a limited approximation of the originals. A better substitute has emerged in recent years, however, in the form of the electronic William Blake Archive at <www.blakearchive. org> and edited by Eaves, Essick, and Viscomi. Their editorial principles are designed to take the best advantage of the electronic medium, which allows for multiple copies of individual works, text and image searching capability, and better reproductions than print versions, along with up-to-date bibliographical and contextual material. The Archive, of course, does have its limitations. For example, because of limits in storage capacities, monitor capabilities, and other concerns, only the image itself is reproduced and not the whole page on which the image is printed. Such variations as irregular plate sizes and misregistrations are, thus, edited out, limiting one's experience in comparison to viewing the original. Nevertheless, the images are so faithful to the original that an examiner can detect whether 'something has been erased from the paper, added to the print, or altered in pen and ink', details that were previously undetectable without the originals (Viscomi qtd. in Kraus 149). This advantage of technology will certainly become increasingly useful as more materials continue to be added to the Archive.

The Blake Archive itself, however, raises at least one more issue for further consideration. In conjecturing on the future value of the Archive, Essick states, '[Its] influence in the long term may have more to do with the issues it raises, in terms of editorial theory and concepts of representation, than its utility in support of traditional types of textual and iconographic research' (qtd. in Kraus 171). The irony to which Essick alludes is that as Blake's illuminated books both critique and provide an alternative to conventional print, so too do they resist reproduction in conventional print, or even in electronic media. They continually remind us that the choice of production methods and the illuminated book's distinct material features have a profound impact on how we understand their creation, their history, and the way we read them now. As recent studies of how Blake's own books were made are reconsidered along with new studies in print culture and the history of the material book, new ways of addressing some vexing issues will emerge, along with, no doubt, new questions.

notes

1. Many histories of the print industry and engraving are available, but an especially concise example is Alexander and Godfrey, *Painters and Engraving: The Reproductive Print from Hogarth to Wilkie*. Another useful background source is Joan M. Friedman, *Color Printing in England, 1486–1870*. For a thorough treatment of the debates within the engraving industry and how they shaped its development, see Morris Eaves, *The Counter-Arts Conspiracy: Art and Industry in the Age of Blake*. See also Robert N. Essick, 'Blake and the Traditions of Reproductive Engraving' and G.E. Bentley, 'The Great Illustrated-Book Publishers of the 1790's and William Blake'.
2. See Essick, *William Blake: Printmaker* for the most complete description of Blake's career. Chapter Two is most impressive for its description of the painstaking work an engraving apprentice would have had to endure (8–28). Bentley, *The Stranger from Paradise*, the most recent and most thorough biography, includes many important details. See also Bindman, *The Complete Graphic Works of William Blake* and Ryskamp, *William Blake, Engraver*.
3. Currently, the two most important works on Blake's relief etching are Essick, *William Blake: Printmaker* and Joseph Viscomi, *Blake and the Idea of the Book*. Other major contributions include Michael Phillips, *William Blake: The Creation of the Songs from Manuscript to Illuminated Printing* and Ruthven Todd, 'The Techniques of William Blake's Illuminated Printing'.
4. Bentley shows that despite Blake's claims about profits from illuminated printing in a letter to his brother dated 30 January 1803 (E726) and despite what earlier biographers may have thought, Blake could never have made a profit with his work and, indeed, could only have incurred a loss. He notes the absurd figures Blake quotes and relates them to contemporary prices ('What Is the Price' 622).
5. See Bentley, 'What Is the Price' 619 and 'The Great' 60–2, and Bindman 10, 13.
6. See for example, Bentley, *Blake Records* 32–3, 460, 460 n1, 472–3, 486.
7. Todd's work has had many adherents including Anthony Blunt, *The Art of William Blake* 45–6; Bindman 13, 15; Friedman 16; Jean Hagstrum, *William Blake, Poet and Printer* 4; Raymond Lister, *Infernal Methods: A Study of William Blake's Art Techniques* 67–8; and Ryskamp 30–1.
8. Others favoring the two-pull process include Martin Butlin, 'The Evolution of Blake's Large Colour Prints of 1795' 113 and *The Paintings and Drawings of William Blake* 1.156, and Lister 61.
9. See Butlin, 'The Evolution', Lister 59–61, and Essick, *William Blake* 131–5.

10. The many scholars that support this view include David Erdman in his Textual Notes to the *Complete Poetry and Prose* (E786); Butlin, 'The Evolution' 110; Lister 75; Friedman 16; and Essick, *William Blake* 124–5.

11. On the shifting of text plates in *Urizen*, see John H. Jones, 'Printed Performance and Reading *The Book[s] of Urizen*: Blake's Bookmaking Process and the Transformation of Late Eighteenth-Century Print Culture'. For *Jerusalem*, see Vincent A. De Luca, 'The Changing Order of Plates in *Jerusalem*, Chapter II' and R. Paul Yoder, 'What Happens When: Narrative and the Changing Sequence of Plates in Blake's *Jerusalem*, Chapter 2'.

works cited and suggestions for further reading

Alexander, David, and Richard Godfrey. *Painters and Engraving: The Reproductive Print from Hogarth to Wilkie*. New Haven: Yale Center for British Art, 1980.

Bentley, G.E., Jr. *Blake Records*. Oxford: Clarendon Press, 1969.

——. 'The Great Illustrated-Book Publishers of the 1790s and William Blake'. *Editing Illustrated Books: Papers Given at the Fifteenth Annual Conference on Editorial Problems, University of Toronto, 2–3 November 1979*. Ed. William Blissett. New York and London: Garland, 1980. 57–96.

——. *The Stranger from Paradise: A Biography of William Blake*. New Haven: Yale University Press, 2001.

——. 'What Is the Price of Experience? William Blake and the Economics of Illuminated Printing'. *University of Toronto Quarterly* 68 (1999): 617–41.

Bindman, David. *The Complete Graphic Works of William Blake*. London: Thames and Hudson, 1978.

Blunt, Anthony. *The Art of William Blake*. New York: Columbia University Press, 1959.

Boehm, Alan D. 'The 1798 *Lyrical Ballads* and the Poetics of Late Eighteenth-Century Book Production'. *ELH* 63 (1996): 453–87.

Butlin, Martin. 'The Evolution of Blake's Large Colour Prints of 1795'. *William Blake Essays For S. Foster Damon*. Ed. Alvin H. Rosenfeld. Providence: Brown University Press, 1969. 110–16.

——. *The Paintings and Drawings of William Blake*. 2 vols. New Haven and London: Yale University Press, 1981.

Carr, Steven Leo. 'Illuminated Printing: Toward a Logic of Difference'. Hilton and Vogler 176–96.

De Luca, Vincent A. 'The Changing Order of Plates in *Jerusalem*, Chapter II'. *Blake/An Illustrated Quarterly* 16 (1983): 192–205.

Eaves, Morris. *The Counter-Arts Conspiracy: Art and Industry in the Age of Blake*. Ithaca and London: Cornell University Press, 1992.

Essick, Robert N. 'Blake and the Traditions of Reproductive Engraving'. *Blake Studies* 5 (1972): 59–103.

——. 'How Blake's Body Means'. Hilton and Vogler 197–217.

——. *William Blake: Printmaker*. Princeton, Princeton University Press, 1980.

Essick, Robert N., and Joseph Viscomi. 'An Inquiry into William Blake's Method of Color Printing'. *Blake/An Illustrated Quarterly* 35.3 (2002): 74–103.

Friedman, Joan M. *Color Printing in England, 1486–1870*. New Haven: Yale Center for British Art, 1978.

Gilchrist, Alexander. *Life of William Blake*. 2 vols. London: Macmillan, 1863.

Greenberg, Mark L. 'Romantic Technology: Books, Printing, and Blake's Marriage of Heaven and Hell'. *Literature and Technology*. Research in Technology Studies 5. Ed. Mark Greenberg and Lance Schachterle. Bethlehem, London: Lehigh University Press, Associated University Press, 1992. 154–76.

Hagstrum, Jean H. *William Blake, Poet and Printer*. Chicago: University of Chicago Press, 1964.

Hilton, Nelson, and Thomas Vogler, eds. *Unnam'd Forms: Blake and Textuality*. Berkeley and Los Angeles: University of California Press, 1986.

Hudson, Nicholas. 'Challenging Eisenstein: Recent Studies in Print Culture'. *Eighteenth-Century Life* 26.2 (2002): 83–95.

Jones, John H. 'Printed Performance and Reading *The Book[s] of Urizen*: Blake's Bookmaking Process and the Transformation of Late Eighteenth-Century Print Culture'. *Colby Quarterly* 35 (1999): 73–89.

Kraus, Kari. '"Once Only Imagined": An Interview with Morris Eaves, Robert N. Essick, and Joseph Viscomi'. *Studies in Romanticism* 41 (2002): 143–99.

Lister, Raymond. *Infernal Methods: A Study of William Blake's Art Techniques*. London: G. Bell, 1975.

Maheux, Ann. 'An Analysis of the Watercolor Techniques and Materials of William Blake'. *Blake/An Illustrated Quarterly* 17 (1984): 124–9.

McGann, Jerome J. 'The Text, the Poem, and the Problem of Historical Method'. *New Literary History* 12 (1981): 269–88.

Phillips, Michael. *William Blake: The Creation of the Songs from Manuscript to Illuminated Printing*. Princeton: Princeton University Press, 2000.

Ryskamp, Charles. *William Blake, Engraver*. Princeton: Princeton University Library, 1969.

Todd, Ruthven. 'The Techniques of William Blake's Illuminated Printing'. *Print Collector's Quarterly* 29 (1948): 173–81.

Townsend, Joyce H. 'William Blake (1757–1827), *Moses Indignant at the Golden Calf*, c. 1799–1800'. *Painting and Purpose: A Study of Technique in British Art*. Ed. Stephen Hackney, Rica Jones, and Joyce Townsend. London: Tate Gallery, 1999. 66–9.

Viscomi, Joseph. *Blake and the Idea of the Book*. Princeton: Princeton University Press, 1993.

Yoder, R. Paul. 'What Happens When: Narrative and the Changing Sequence of Plates in Blake's *Jerusalem*, Chapter 2'. *Studies in Romanticism* 41 (2002): 259–78.

3
blake's composite art

peter otto

Speaking and seeing, or rather statements and visibilities, are pure Elements, *a priori* conditions under which all ideas are formulated and behavior displayed, at some moment or other.

Giles Deleuze, *Foucault* 60

1

Blake's composite art is an obvious exception to Foucault's claim that in 'Western painting from the fifteenth to the twentieth century [. . .] verbal signs and visual representations are never given at once. An order always hierarchizes them, running from the figure to discourse or from discourse to the figure' (*Pipe* 32–3). As W.J.T. Mitchell observes, Blake's 'composite art is, to some extent, *not* an indissoluble unity, but an interaction between two vigorously independent modes of expression' (*Composite Art* 3). Readers/viewers of Blake's composite art are therefore presented with a conundrum. Although 'Blake's poems need to be read with their accompanying illustrations', it is far from self-evident 'in what precise sense [his] poems "need" their illustrations, and vice versa' (3).

It is commonplace to construe poetry and painting, word and image, as contrasting 'modes of expression': the first being an art of time, the second of space. As Lessing argues in *The Laocoön*, 'in its imitations painting uses completely different signs than does poetry, namely figures and colors in space rather than articulated sounds in time'. As a result, the subject-matter proper to each art and the way in which they engage their audiences are different. While painting solicits the eye, poetry addresses the ear through the medium of an actual or implied voice (rhythm, rhyme, sequence, and so on). 'Accordingly', Lessing argues, 'bodies with their visible properties are the true subjects of paintings [. . .] [and] actions are the true subjects of poetry' (78). More broadly,

42

poetry and painting provide 'representations of the basic modalities in which reality [is] apprehended – space and time, body and soul, sense and intellect, and, in the realm of aesthetics, *dulce et utile*' (Mitchell, *Composite Art* 30).

Difference does not necessarily mean incommensurability. Lessing, along with writers such as Burke and Shaftesbury, was writing in opposition to the long tradition of *ut pictura poesis* (as is painting, so is poetry), which represents the differences between poetry and painting as kinship. On the one hand, despite their different media, painting and poetry are assumed to be mimetic arts, similar in that they both aim to represent nature, whether visible or ideal (Hagstrum, *Sister Arts* 134). On the other hand, although painting and poetry rely on and address different senses, those senses, and by implication the arts they enable, are united by their origin in the human body. These twin grounds suggest that poetry and painting are complementary, the one adding what the other lacks. In the words of Simonides of Keos (as recounted by Plutarch), 'painting is a mute poetry, poetry a speaking picture' (Lee 3).

In the 1970s, Blake's relation to the tradition of *ut pictura poesis* was the subject of a debate between Mitchell and Jean Hagstrum, which has become the most important point of departure for work on Blake's composite art. This debate turned on the quandary mentioned above, namely, how does one make sense of 'verbal signs and visual representations' which belong together and yet remain 'vigorously independent'? In the pages that follow, I argue that for Hagstrum this quandary doesn't appear in its full force because word and image are ordered by an 'ideal' reality, and that for Mitchell, it soon fades away: word and image 'dramatize the interaction' of what are only 'apparent dualities' in our experience of the world. Disjunction embodies its opposite, 'the strivings of those dualities for unification' in the human imagination or the human form ('Composite Art' 62). In contrast, through a reading of plates from *There is No Natural Religion* (c. 1788) and *Jerusalem* (1804–20), I suggest that the struggle between word and image (and the closely associated struggles between mind and body, time and space) in Blake's illuminated poetry should be understood as a primary, unresolved element of both the Imagination and the Human form divine. Indeed, it is the struggle to return such dualisms to a primordial unity that for Blake is constitutive of the Fall.

2

The term 'composite art' was first used to describe Blake's illuminated poetry by Hagstrum in his *William Blake: Poet and Painter*. By borrowing this phrase for the title of his own monograph, Mitchell signaled Hagstrum's influence on and role as antagonist for *Blake's Composite Art*. A composite is, of course, a whole composed of disparate elements. Mitchell and Hagstrum disagreed on the point in relation to which the elements of Blake's art could be drawn into a unity. Their debate was first publicly rehearsed in 'Blake's Composite Art' and 'Blake and the Sister-Arts Tradition', essays published in *Blake's Visionary Forms Dramatic*, edited by David V. Erdman and John E. Grant. Mitchell's essay was later elaborated as *Blake's Composite Art*.

According to Hagstrum, pictorialists 'in general' agree that poetry and painting 'should combine forces in order to lead the beholder beyond themselves to nature, or nature's God, or the mind of man'. Although he rejects the first and the second, Blake endorses the third of these 'traditional aims of composite art': 'His forms are displayed in order to bring us to what his predecessors called "ideal" reality and what he himself called the "Intellectual" or "Mental"' ('Composite Art' 90). Blake therefore belongs within the tradition of *ut pictura poesis*. Indeed, Hagstrum judges him to have 'molded the sister arts, as they have never been before or since, into a single body and breathed into it the breath of life' (*William Blake* 140).

Mitchell agrees that 'Blake's art is [not] representational, imitating a world of objective "nature"', but at the same time he contends, contra Hagstrum, that it is not 'allegorical, rendering an invisible, abstract, transcendent reality' (*Composite Art* 38). The separation of word and image (like the separation of soul and body, and time and space) is for Blake a result of the Fall. Rather than adding one to the other in order better to represent reality, Blake's 'poetry is designed to invalidate the idea of objective time, his painting to invalidate the idea of objective space' (*Composite Art* 34). Although Blake agrees with his pictorialist precursors that the sister arts should be united, this can occur only by turning to the human imagination, the source of them both. According to Mitchell, this effects a fundamental break with the tradition of *ut pictura poesis*. It shifts the locus of Blake's work from the re-presentation of subjective or objective reality to 'the parallel engagements of imagination and body with their respective mediums, and [. . .] their convergence in the more comprehensive idea of the "Human Form Divine"' (*Composite Art* 38).

Despite their vigorous independence, Mitchell judges the differences between word and image to be only apparent. '[I]f we are correct', he writes, 'the most disparate pictorial and verbal structures must conceal a subtle identity of significance'. First, 'the contrariety of poem and picture reflects the world of the reader as a place of apparent separation of temporal and spatial, mental and physical phenomena'. Second, the missing connections in work and world are supplied by the imagination, the source from which both emerge ('Composite Art' 62–3).

Oddly, these explanations reintroduce a relation of mimesis between world and work, bringing it into partial congruence with the tradition of *ut pictura poesis*. Perhaps for this reason, more recent Blake criticism often reworks these 'explanations' as stages in an experience of the romantic sublime (Otto, 'Sublime Allegory'). To take a representative example, in *Words of Eternity* V.A. De Luca argues that Blake's poetry effects 'a sharp division of the mind into two faculties', the Corporeal Understanding and the Intellectual Powers (22). From the point of view of the former, the text is experienced as 'a kind of wall, against which [the Corporeal Understanding] presses itself, groping along, trying in vain to peer through chinks in the hard, opaque surface' (32). The Intellectual Powers are, however, able to see what the Understanding cannot. The latter's failure to see through the text to 'some "supersensible" totality lying beyond' precipitates a moment of self-recognition in which 'the Intellect recognizes (reads) a glory that the same faculty has put (written) into [the text]' (34). In this moment, text and pictures (reading and recognition) converge, assuming the features of each other. They become hieroglyphs expressive of the '"I" of the poet's identity' (225).

One might complain that De Luca heals the division between word and image only to introduce it at a deeper level, in the division of the sensuous perceptions available to the corporeal understanding (sight and touch) from the images 'of intellect *embodied*' (226), in which the 'sensory surface offered by the text' is subordinated to the 'incorporeal (because verbal)' world of the mind. Yet this division is again only apparent, for the goal of Blake's illuminated poetry, De Luca contends, is 'a miraculous (or astonishing) compression of all contingent forms into one intellectual identity – the living Word of Eternity' (102). The vigorous independence of word and image is here lost in an order which subordinates the second to the first of these terms.

The argument developed by Mitchell and De Luca implies that it is in the work of creation that the 'glory' reflective of the reader's and the author's imagination can most clearly be seen. The difficulty is, of course, that as one turns to the work of creation this convergence retreats to a deeper level. Carr, for example, describes a 'radical variability [. . .] embedded in the material processes of producing illuminated prints', and which therefore 'always enters in the verbal-visual exchanges generated within each page' (182). This can be attributed to 'uncertainties in the marriage of paper and ink, to foul printing, blurring, and uneven or imperfect inking' (185); but it is also a product of

> the constitutive doubleness of each signifier on an illuminated page, of the double 'origin' of each sign both in time (at the etching of the plate and at the production of a page) and in its material inscription (as a printed character that is subsequently altered by illumination). (186)

The disjunction between these points of origin, like that between word and image, can be resolved only by turning to a deeper level of the creative process. The most important recent attempt to do so can be found in Joseph Viscomi's *Blake and the Idea of the Book*, which argues that 'The integrity of a page design, even one as complicated as *Europe*', results 'from the integrality of the acts of writing and drawing' in the creation of Blake's illuminated poetry (25). However, even here the opposition between word and image reappears. Unintentionally presenting the dilemma I am describing, Viscomi notes that drawing 'provides the place of origin, the place where idea and image are *found*' (40).

Mitchell, following Foucault's argument in *This is not a Pipe*, describes as characteristic of illustrated books a 'suturing of discourse and representation, the sayable and the seeable, across an unobtrusive, invisible frontier' (*Picture Theory* 69–70). All of the critics I have discussed explicitly or implicitly distinguish such books from Blake's illuminated poetry. They agree that the vigorous independence of word and image in the latter effects its emancipation from objective reality, and therefore from the order that governs the convergence in the former of the sayable and the seeable. Yet the same critics use a subjective reality, the imagination or a creative process, to achieve a similar end.

Despite these formal similarities, it would be foolish to understate the differences between these strategies for stitching the seeable and the sayable into a whole. According to Mitchell, this 'stitching' exemplifies

> the conditions that make it possible to say 'this is that' (designation), to assign proper names, to describe, to place in grids, strata, or genealogies. The dialectic of discourse and vision, in short, is a fundamental figure of knowledge as such. (*Picture Theory* 70)

The use of subjective realities, creative faculties or creative processes, rather than objective reality, to orchestrate relations between the seeable and the sayable, effects a dramatic change in what can be said and what constitutes knowledge. It completes the shift of attention, already evident in the work of late eighteenth-century proponents of *ut pictura poesis*, from the work of art to the beholder, while also bringing twentieth-century Blake criticism into dialogue with the dominant, neo-Hegelian currents of Romantic studies. Nevertheless, even in *There is No Natural Religion*, one of the earliest of Blake's experiments in illuminated printing, he lays the foundation for a more far-reaching break with the tradition of *ut pictura poesis*. In order to sketch this break, we will consider the last two plates of this work, along with their Swedenborgian rhetoric and iconography, in some detail.

3

On plate b10 of *There is No Natural Religion*, textual and graphic zones are defined, and at the same time divided from each other, by the trunk and limbs of a small tree standing in the bottom left-hand corner of the design (Figure 3.1). The tree's trunk and the lower of its two visible branches outline the top and left-hand side of a small, egg-shaped space. In the center of this space, a solitary bearded man rests on his knees, almost on all fours. He looks intently at, and the fingers of his left hand lightly touch, a triangle drawn on the ground. His right hand holds the divider he is using to determine the triangle's base. The tree's crown, outlined by its two limbs and by the upper and upper right-hand margins of the plate, provides a flat surface on which the following words are inscribed:

> Application
> He who sees the In-
> -finite in all things,
> sees God. He who
> sees the Ratio only
> sees himself only

The turn from image to text enacted in the previous paragraph shifts attention from the seeable to the sayable, from the 'visible properties of bodies' to the unfolding sequence of letters and words. As I begin to read the text on plate b10, the tree, the leaves implied by the letters of the text, and then the material body of the letters themselves, all recede as the meaning of the plate's text comes into view. In this moment, the signifier seems to become the transparent garment or external surface of the signified.

As if miming this transformation, the text (along with elements of the design) forms a calligram or hieroglyph that repeats this domination

Figure 3.1   Plate b10, *There is No Natural Religion*

of matter by meaning. First, the word 'God' stands at the center of the text (and of the tree's crown), the still point from which both word (signified and signifier) and image emanate. Second, 'The Ratio' and 'himself' are placed on different lines immediately beneath 'God', with the head and back of the 'solitary bearded man' located immediately beneath the lowest of these words: the flesh is evidently the most base form of existence. In this hierarchical world, one's sight can be directed only up to God or down to the disorder of the flesh. If the former, one sees the infinite in all things (God); if the latter, one sees only the finite world (the self).

The choice proposed by the text and the cosmic order implied by the calligram recalls the work of Swedenborg, in particular his *A Treatise concerning Heaven and Hell*. In the cosmic geography outlined in this work, although heaven is divided from hell, the two have a common boundary. Indeed, 'under every mountain, hill, rock, plain and valley [of Heaven], there [are] [. . .] arrangements of those infernal mansions' (para. 588). Despite this proximity, angels know nothing of the hell that lies beneath their feet because they attend only to God. Similarly, the devils are unaware of the heaven just beyond the horizon of their world, because they are preoccupied by hell. The latter is a chaotic world, riven by selfish passions. The former is organized according to the rational/ spiritual order that emanates from God.

Our psyches mirror this architecture, being divided between the internal (spirit) and the external (body). The first opens a conduit to heaven. The second provides channels of communication with hell. As in the calligram on plate b10, in Swedenborg's scheme of things, reason stands midway between these two realms, charged with the responsibility to choose whether we are formed by heaven or hell, God or the flesh. If we turn towards hell, our minds will be disordered by the passions. If we turn towards heaven, our bodies will gradually be made 'subordinant, and subservient' to God. The mechanics of this second process are most vividly described in Swedenborg's *The Delights of Wisdom concerning Conjugial Love*:

> the external conjugial principle [sexual passion] remains indeed, but it is continually purged and purified from its dregs by the internal; and this until the external principle becomes as it were the face of the internal, and derives its delight from the blessedness which is in the internal and at the same time its life, and the delights of its potency. (para. 148)

On plate b10, the eclipse of the image by the word, and of the signifier by the signified, effected when we read the text, mirrors this process; yet the same plate suggests that this subordination of bodies to a textual heaven is unstable. The ascent from earth to trunk, branch, leaf, letter and word implies that the higher levels depend on and secretly draw their strength from the lower. Some of the letters sprout vegetable growths, evoking the dynamics of a material world (a hell) in conflict with and irreducible to the Logos that it supports. The word 'sees' is repeated four times, but on each occasion it is enclosed by tendrils or ribbons, suggesting the material limits of the views canvassed by the text. Still more explicitly, 'Infinite' is printed 'In- / -finite', with the first and second parts of this word placed on different lines. This disruption of the relation between signifier and signified is an expression not of the Logos but of the material world (the length of the line, the size of the plate) on which the word rests. The design turns this perception of instability into an experience of vertigo.

4

Given Blake's concern in *There is No Natural Religion* with the limits of empiricism, it seems reasonable to suppose that the figure portrayed in the lower third of the plate is Locke's human understanding, shown inspecting the simple ideas impressed on the blank slate of the mind. This identification is complicated by at least three others. The man's posture closely resembles that of Nebuchadnezzar, as seen on page 44 of Blake's Notebook (Erdman, *Notebook*). His fixed gaze, the position in which he holds his upper body, and the activity in which he is engaged, anticipate the portrait of Newton in Blake's color print of the same name (1795). And his posture and use of dividers recall traditional images of God the creator, while also anticipating the 'Ancient of Days' as depicted in the frontispiece to *Europe* (1794).

The frontier between figure and discourse is here clearly visible, as a place of conjunction *and* contestation. At the same time, rather than designating a pre-existing meaning, the figure brings into relation four disparate semantic fields. In so doing, it violates late eighteenth-century codes of relevance or pertinence. What do these identifications have to do with each other or with the Swedenborgian allusions of the text, one may well ask. This literal incongruence, however, allows a metaphorical congruence to emerge.

The science of Newton and the philosophy of Locke converge with the theology of Swedenborg in the attempt to uncover an abstract, unchanging world behind the flux of experience. To the extent that this involves the imposition of 'eternal' form on the body, their work is similar to that of Nebuchadnezzar, ruler of Babylonia from 605 to 562 BCE and responsible for the destruction of Jerusalem and Judea, the ruin of the Temple of Solomon, and the Babylonian exile.

Nebuchadnezzar's tyranny made him for European cultures a symbol of 'the regal oppressor' (Carretta 162–6). Following George III's bout of mental illness in 1788–89, radicals commonly associated him with the Assyrian king, suggesting a link between despotism and madness. Blake's design implies that the same malady afflicts the god who, in the frontispiece to *Europe*, creates this world through the imposition of mathematical form. The allusions to Swedenborg, Locke, Newton, Nebuchadnezzar, the creator God and George III converge in the attempt to discover/impose the perfect structure and immutable laws underlying the visible universe.

In each case, the design implies that the search for an unchanging order, based on a congruence between mind and body, depends on (and itself effects) a radical transformation of the body. On plate b10, this is already well advanced: the kneeling body of the scientist/philosopher forms a grid, defined by the horizontal lines of his torso and lower left-leg, and by the vertical lines of his left arm and the upper-half of his left leg. The shapes formed by the figure's arms, by his legs, and by his torso and upper leg, all suggest triangles, doubles of the mathematical forms traced on the ground. The body is now almost completely subservient to heaven. This brings the body and mind to the point of collapse. Already a dark, chaotic mass has engulfed the lower half of his body. Rather than being contraries, order and chaos are negations, bringing us to 'the border of Blake's art that opens onto a void of meaninglessness' (Mitchell, 'Chaosthetics' 448).

It could, of course, be argued that the move from literal incongruence to metaphorical congruence becomes entangled with what this plate sets out to critique. Yet rather than leading to the subservience of image to word, and body to heaven, in Blake's design it is the first term in these pairs that provokes a disturbance in the 'heaven' of received meaning, causing readers to re-think its categories and discriminations. Moreover, the aim is not to introduce a 'truth' that would resolve the conflict between contraries but to propagate the view that equilibrium is always a contingent, temporary, ultimately unsuccessful resolution of a foundational conflict. The following plate takes this conflict as its subject-matter.

5

Whereas textual and graphic realms are on plate b10 joined by the trunk and limbs of a tree, suggesting relations of subordination and sublimation, on plate b12 they are divided by a thick, horizontal line, almost half the width of the plate (Figure 3.2). Rather than inspiring attempts to bring the temporal into accord with the eternal, difference here prompts an ongoing movement of the eternal towards the temporal, which opens the possibility of its contrary. The first recalls John's description of the Incarnation as an event in which 'the Word

Figure 3.2   Plate b12 *There is No Natural Religion*

became Flesh and dwelt amongst us' (John 1.14); the second implies the possibility of resurrection:

>Therefore
>God becomes as
>we are, that we
>may be as he
>is

The carefully organized hierarchy of the calligram found on the previous plate is here replaced by a vertical axis composed of the words 'be[comes]', 'are', 'be' and 'is'. The letter 'e' appears immediately above the first letter of 'be', and immediately above and below the first letter of 'becomes', repeating in each instance the word 'be'. This collocation of various forms of the verb 'to be' recalls the conventional definition of God as absolute or 'perfect existence' (Swedenborg, *Heaven and Hell* para. 303).

The uniformity and stasis implied by this axis places it in a relation of conflict with the text, with regard both to form (vertical versus horizontal axes) and content (the stasis of 'perfect existence' versus the twin movements of incarnation). This vertical axis also stands apart from the flamboyant vegetable growths that erupt from and between words, such as the plants that grow to the left and right of the word 'is', their tendrils reaching down, on both sides of the horizontal line, into the nether regions of the plate. If this is a calligram, it presents an aniconic God, unable or lacking the desire to master the exuberant vegetable-growths that erupt around him. In this instance, however, it is arguably the meeting within the plate's textual heaven of the divergent realms of word and image, the eternal and the temporal, that enacts part of the dynamic described in the text.

All accounts of the Incarnation must negotiate the paradox of a Divine that becomes one with, and yet remains distinct from, the Human. For Swedenborg, both terms of this paradox are important because Incarnation is a vehicle for the purification of the Human by the Divine, the process through which we become 'as he is'. The Incarnation (and the Word) therefore introduces into time a relation between the divine, the human, and the material, which precisely mirrors that between heaven, earth and hell.

In contradistinction to Swedenborg, plate b12 suggests that, rather than being formed through the gradual conformation of flesh to spirit, the Human form divine emerges in the exchanges between the disparate realms of flesh and spirit, the temporal and the divine. These contrary relations are suggested by the sketch in the right-hand margin of the plate, which takes the form of a question mark that, as one approaches its lower parts, is lost in the trailing strands of a vegetable growth. Between these incommensurate elements, as if forged by their interaction, one can see the head, outstretched legs, and upward reaching arms of an embryonic human form. The resurrection this implies is the subject of the remarkable image that occupies the lower half of the plate.

The claustrophobic space of the previous plate here becomes an open expanse. The reasoner, mesmerized by the eternal, his body almost congruent with mathematical form, is displaced by 'the Naked Human form divine' (E522) that emerges at the point of intersection between up and down, sky and earth, heaven and hell, now seen as contraries rather than negations. Rather than looking up to heaven or down to the body, the man's head looks out towards the reader, to a shared world. The rays of light that shine from his head, suggesting an aureole or sun, identify the man as Jesus, the incarnated Word.

One imagines that if Swedenborg were present at this scene, he would soon become impatient for the man to stand up, for the paradox of Incarnation to be resolved by the conformation of flesh to spirit. If he were joined by the Blake critics we have considered, it is probable that they would become equally impatient, albeit for the flesh to be made subservient to imagination. Yet a remarkable set of ambiguities defers both of these resolutions. It is uncertain, for example, whether the sun is rising or setting, the man lies on a small rock or in a vast landscape, this is the Incarnation or the Resurrection, and even whether he is about to rise up from or sink back into the earth.

To resolve these ambiguities would be to form a world by suturing, once again, 'discourse and representation, the sayable and the seeable, across an unobtrusive, invisible frontier'. In Blake's major prophecies, this is the work of Los, who tries variously to stitch together mind and body on the ground of Urizen (reason), Tharmas (the sensible world) and himself (the fallen imagination). Los's creative labors break and reforge the relations that bind word to image, and mind to body, demonstrating that whatever the form taken by these relations it is contingent, and that the limits imposed by each form can be exceeded. As the narrator explains in *Jerusalem*:

> Voltaire insinuates that these Limits are the cruel work of God
> Mocking the Remover of Limits & the Resurrection of the Dead
> Setting up Kings in wrath: in holiness of Natural Religion
> Which Los with his mighty Hammer demolishes time on time.
> (73:29–32, E228)

Yet in a paradox central to Blake's poetry and evident even in these lines, despite the importance of this work, Los is able, by himself, only to stitch word and image, mind and body, together once again, and so lay the foundations for another iteration of the fallen world.

The sequence of these iterations offers at best an indirect presentation of the ongoing struggle suggested by plate b12 (between heaven and hell, word and image, and mind and body), in which the incarnate Word, the Human form divine, perhaps even the Imagination itself can be seen.

This plate therefore turns from questions concerning the essence of a pre-existing world (the subject of the previous plate) to the relations *between* incommensurate realms or elements in which worlds are formed. The sovereign subject of Locke, Swedenborg and Newton finds itself bound to life, and therefore to its other (finitude, the passions, difference).

These transformations recall the discovery towards the end of the eighteenth century that the space of representations could not be divided from a life which exceeded it (Foucault, *Order of Things*). In Deleuze's assessment, these developments demand a radical mutation of thought, 'a thinking that no longer opposes itself as from the outside to the unthinkable or the unthought, but which would lodge the unthinkable, the unthought within itself as thought, and which would be in an essential relationship to it' ('Humans' 92). This kind of thinking 'would be traversed by a sort of fissure' which should not 'be filled in, because it is the highest object of thought' (92). Deleuze proposes ethnology, psychoanalysis, and linguistics as models for this thinking, because each exceeds the category of the Human, used in the nineteenth century to close this gap between life and thought.

Arguably, this use by reason of the concept of the Human reproduces, albeit in a new form, the dynamic we have analyzed in Swedenborg. In contrast, plate b12 suggests that for Blake the Human form divine is forged in the exchanges between life and thought, body and mind. What for Reason remains a fissure is, from the point of view of the whole man, the 'living form' of life, forged in the struggle between contraries. The fissure between thought and the unthinkable is here presented as the necessary condition for *and* the changing boundary which defines life itself. This 'bounding line' (stationary and moving, closed and open) is the form taken by a performance without script, in which mind and body (reason, imagination, and the passions) are actors. Where 'Mathematical Form is Eternal in the Reasoning Memory', 'Living Form is Eternal Existence' ('On Virgil', E270). Plate b12 therefore announces Blake's break with the tradition of *ut pictura poesis* not by reconciling word and image in a pre-existing faculty but by maintaining their difference.

6

The consequences of this break can be seen throughout Blake's *oeuvre*, in his prophetic psychology, 'doctrine' of contraries, and art of multiple interacting elements. It structures Blake's understanding both of prophecy (which details the relations in which particular realities are forged) and vision (which reveals that the relations constitutive of the fallen world can be changed). And of course, it inspires the remarkable variety of relations between 'vigorously independent modes of expression' that constitute Blake's composite art. In the interests of brevity, I won't catalogue here the permutations of this art; however, one can see some of the chief forms it takes, along with the drama that Blake's composite art is designed to interrupt, on plate 62 of *Jerusalem* (Figure 3.3).

On this plate, Jesus' claim to be 'the Resurrection & the Life', to be able to 'Die & pass the limits of possibility, as it appears / To individual perception' (lines 18–20, E213) is written, ironically, on the surface of a large rock, beneath which the body of a giant human figure has been entombed. Although his feet are still in flames, much of the rest of his body has already been consumed. Apart from its upper and upper right-hand edge, the stone has suffered a similar fate. Consequently, the text hovers in an eerie, empty space, as if no material reality remained behind it.

Grasping the top of the stone with both hands, the man's head appears above it, surrounded by large feathers, creating the impression that he is a rising sun. This sunrise differs from the one portrayed on the last plate of *There is No Natural Religion*. Here the man's head is attached to a textual rather than material body; and it has been circumscribed and compressed by the coils of a worm. Its aureole is composed only of feathers, each carrying an eye identical with those of the man. The relation between worm (emblem of the man's earthly existence) and head repeats that between word and body. The worm confines the head, while appearing also to shift the man's attention away from the body, up towards heaven. In so doing, the body's multiple organs and desires are reduced to the iterations of a single eye/I, reflections of the One. This sunrise is an illusion produced by flesh that has assumed forms consonant with the divine. It provides the material foundation of what Jerusalem mistakenly believes is the 'Spiritual Risen Body' (line 14, E213).

At the bottom of the design a naked man, usually identified as Los and/or the poet, stands between the burning feet of the entombed giant. He faces a scene which rehearses many of the relations between word and image with which Blake's composite art is concerned. First, within the plate's textual 'heaven', the frontier between word and image, mind and body, is almost invisible. The material world persists only as the signifier, the 'outward form' of what is signified. Even this remnant seems in danger, for flames have begun to consume the lower, right-hand side of the text. This second relation, or rather this absence of relation, between word and image portends the state described in the text as 'Death Eternal' (line 40, E213).

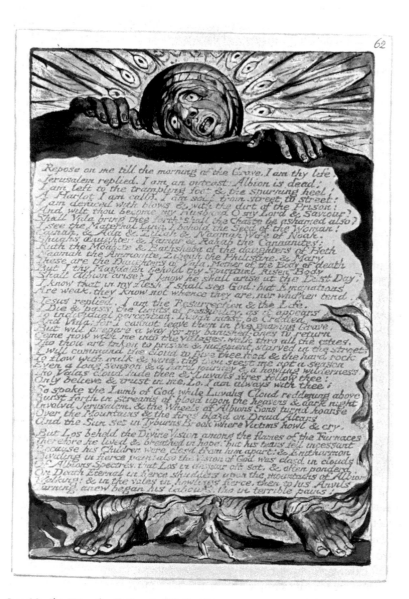

Figure 3.3   Plate 62 *Jerusalem: The Emanation of the Giant Albion*

Third, at the top of the plate, the frontier where the image is violently sutured to the word comes into view. As I have argued, this is the hidden foundation on which all textual heavens rest. Fourth, at the bottom of the plate, image and word are still disjunct, despite the flames that proceed apace to transform the former into the latter. Los seems transfixed by events in this part of the design. His hands, outstretched in a gesture of astonishment, point toward the burning feet and toward the gap that divides image from text. Los's attention has no doubt been caught by the fires purging the body, bringing it into congruence with the mind. At the same time, to the extent that word and image are still disjunct, Los glimpses the possibility that their relation could be reworked. This is why, immediately above him, the last two lines of the text announce that 'to his Anvils / Turning [Los] anew began his labours, tho in terrible pains!' (lines 41–2, E213). This plate is itself an instance of his prophetic work, which effects a powerful re-visioning of the fallen world.

The disjunction between word and image is for Los also the site of a fifth relation between word and image, described in the text as the 'Divine Vision among the flames of the Furnaces' (line 35, E213). Amidst the horrors of sublimation, and glimpsed in or between the successive iterations of Los's creative work, one sees the possibility of a contrary relation between word and image, relations in which the Human form divine could emerge. Los and his creative labors are, of course, not isomorphic with this vision. The line forming the top of Los's head touches the bottom of the design's textual heaven, placing him firmly within the relations that constitute Swedenborg's world (heaven and hell, word and image, mind and body).

In the following plates Los/the prophet must therefore continue his work, forging, breaking, and then forging again the bonds that tie image to word. This prophetic work is not contained by any single page. In a sixth interaction between word and image, the 'play' of elements established on any one page emerges in 'conversation' with the elements on adjacent pages. In perhaps the most striking feature of Blake's composite art, these 'conflicts' (within and between plates) generate a sense of time, space, and place that is both radically at odds with and an attempt to redescribe the world of late eighteenth- and early nineteenth-century science, politics, and culture.

On plate 63, for example, the spatial dynamics of the preceding design are reversed, with the image now placed in the center of the plate, bounded on both sides by large blocks of text. The tormented male giant, whose body stretches from the top to the bottom of the plate, is replaced by a woman whose body extends from the left- to the right-hand side of the plate. While the text covers and seems to weigh against the body of the former, it defines the limits of the space in which the latter is confined and displayed. The markings and color of the worm that coils around the giant's head reappear on the worm that twists itself around the body of the woman. In this second context, the worm also echoes the long, horizontal lines of text which unfold above and below her. Once again, the worm forces its victim's head up, towards the eternal.

While emerging in concert with the other faculties that compose the whole man, the prophet's attempts to forge a composite art also depend on the reader. Further complicating the visionary conversation we have been tracing, the next plate portrays readers who have no interest in this kind of art. At the top of the page, one of the readers lies asleep, slumped over a scroll. At the bottom of the page, the other lies on the ground, wide awake, with the pages of a book open before him. We can identify the first as Swedenborg's earthly reader, divorced from the mind, lost within the body of sleep. His scroll is an apt emblem of the undivided, bodily (figural) world that confines him. The second is Swedenborg's angelic reader. His book is an apt representation of the minutely ordered, textual heaven he inhabits. Demonstrating the fear of vertigo common to such readers, he uses the index finger of his right hand to keep his place in the book, and the outstretched palm of his left hand to shield his textual heaven from the influence of the earthly reader who is ironically above him.

Although divided by some thirty-eight lines of text, from the angelic reader's point of view the earthly reader is engaged in an improper activity. This is suggested by the two naked figures, a male and a female, who unroll the scroll beneath his sleeping head, drawing it out into the form of a gigantic phallus. There is, however, not much cause here for angelic concern. Far from being a sign of liberated desire, the unrolled scroll divides outside from inside, the man from the woman. The woman's legs are crossed, announcing her chastity. The phallus enacts its own, preliminary 'resurrection' of the flesh (Otto, 'Pompous High Priest'), anticipating the stone phallus erected on plate 69 and its description on the same plate as 'a pompous High Priest entering by a Secret Place' (line 44).

Given Los's ambivalent relation to the fallen world, the dependence of the Human form divine on all the faculties, and the reader's disinterest in composite art, it is hardly surprising that the following plates trace an ever more radical subjugation of image to word and of body to mind. On plates 65 and 66, the text expands almost to fill the page. In the former, all that is left of the image is a long chain that lies in the right-hand margin; in the latter, a cliff fills the same narrow margin. Its only inhabitants are a woman who stretches out her arm to stab the man on whose back she is perched. On plate 67 a man is contained by a long, narrow space at the bottom of the plate. With chains attached to his hands and feet, he has been stretched to such a degree that he resembles the lines of text stacked above him. On plate 68, the image has almost completely disappeared. A light blue wash applied unevenly to the upper half of the page suggests, first, that the body has finally dropped away, a victim of the warfare described on this plate, and second that with its imminent demise one can at last see beyond the text to an unearthly, immaterial heaven.

Blake describes his composite art as an attempt to pierce 'Apollyon with his own bow!' (*Jerusalem* 12:14, E155), to use the sense-making procedures of the fallen world to overturn that same world. Although remaining within the fallen world, the vigorous independence of its elements nevertheless effects a remarkable, prophetic redescription of that world. At the same time, one can glimpse in the conflict between the elements of Blake's composite art a more far-reaching transformation of the relations between word and image.

On the last plates of *Jerusalem*, the 'millenarian' art this conflict foreshadows is construed as continual Exodus,

> Circumscribing & Circumcising the excrementitious
> Husk & Covering into Vacuum, evaporating revealing the lineaments
>   of Man
> Driving outward the Body of Death in an Eternal Death & Resurrection
> Awaking it to Life. (98:18–21, E257)

For the eighteenth century, the paradigmatic form of 'the excrementitious / Husk' can be found in attempts by Swedenborg, Locke, Newton and Nebuchadnezzar, amongst others, to ensure the body's congruence with an atemporal ideal. The apparently contradictory movements of circumscription and circumcision emphasize that this husk is removed in the conflict between contraries, acting from within and without. To describe the living form that emerges, Blake resorts to an almost oxymoronic collocation of opposites. He writes, for example, of a 'rejoicing in Unity / In the Four Senses in the Outline the Circumference & Form' (98:21–2, E257).

This movement outwards is propelled by an interaction between faculties, described as conversation in 'Visionary forms dramatic which bright / Redounded from their Tongues' (98:28–9, E257). Released from (pre-existing) objective and subjective 'realities', word and image (speech and the movement of bodies) interact

> in thunderous majesty, in Visions
> In new Expanses, creating exemplars of Memory and of Intellect
> Creating Space, Creating Time according to the wonders Divine
> Of Human Imagination, throughout all the Three Regions immense
> Of Childhood, Manhood & Old Age. (98:29–33, E257–8)

Recalling plate b12 of *There is No Natural Religion*, the Human Imagination here enables, and the Human form divine takes the form of, a vigorous interaction between contraries. In yet another step away from the tradition of *ut pictura poesis and* a romantic poetics of expression, the human imagination becomes a power of opening the future, not as an expression of what we already are, but of what we cannot yet conceive (in part because it will be forged in relations with others). The elements of Blake's composite art attempt tirelessly to provoke this visionary conversation in which the future is forged and the 'lineaments of Man' are revealed. The independence of its elements gestures towards a future community, a Human form divine that, rather than representing a return to what we once were, must again and again be put on.

works cited and suggestions for further reading

Bindman, David, ed. *Blake's Illuminated Books*. 6 vols. Princeton: William Blake Trust, Princeton University Press, 1991–95.

Burke, Edmund [1756]. *A Philosophical Enquiry into the Origin of our Ideas of the Sublime and the Beautiful*. Ed. Adam Phillips. Oxford: Oxford University Press, 1990.

Carr, Stephen Leo. 'Illuminated Printing: Toward a Logic of Difference' in *Unnam'd Forms: Blake and Textuality*. Ed. Nelson Hilton and Thomas A. Vogler. Berkeley: University of California, 1986.

Carretta, Vincent. *George III and the Satirists from Hogarth to Byron*. Athens, GA: University of Georgia Press, 1990.

Deleuze, Gilles. *Foucault*. Trans. Sean Hand. London: Athlone, 1999.

——. 'Humans: A Dubious Existence' in *Desert Islands and other Texts: 1953–1974*. Trans. Michael Taormina and ed. David Lapoujade. Los Angeles, New York: Semiotext(e), 2004.

De Luca, V.A. *Words of Eternity: Blake and the Poetics of the Sublime*. Princeton: Princeton University Press, 1991.

Erdman, David V. ed. *The Notebook of William Blake: A Photographic and Typographic Facsimile*. Oxford: Clarendon Press, 1973.

Erdman, David V. and John E. Grant, eds. *Blake's Visionary Forms Dramatic*. Princeton: Princeton University Press, 1970.

Foucault, Michel. *The Order of Things: An Archaeology of the Human Sciences.* New York: Vintage Books, 1971.

——. *This is not a Pipe. With Illustrations and Letters by René Magritte.* Trans. James Harkness. Berkeley, London: University of California Press, 1983.

Hagstrum, Jean H. 'Blake and the Sister-Arts Tradition' in *Blake's Visionary Forms Dramatic.* Ed. David V. Erdman and John E. Grant. Princeton: Princeton University Press, 1970.

——. *The Sister Arts: The Tradition of Literary Pictorialism and English Poetry from Dryden to Gray.* Chicago: Chicago University Press, 1958.

——. *William Blake: Poet and Painter: An Introduction to the Illuminated Verse.* Chicago, London: University of Chicago Press, 1964.

Lee, Rensselaier W. *The Humanistic Theory of Painting.* New York: W.W Norton, 1967.

Lessing, Gotthold Ephraim [1766]. *Laocoön: An Essay on the Limits of Painting and Poetry.* Trans. Edward Allen McCormick. Baltimore, London: The Johns Hopkins University Press, 1984.

Mitchell, W.J.T. 'Blake's Composite Art' in *Blake's Visionary Forms Dramatic.* Ed. David V. Erdman and John E. Grant. Princeton: Princeton University Press, 1970.

——. *Blake's Composite Art: A Study of the Illuminated Poetry.* Princeton: Princeton University Press, 1978.

——. 'Chaosthetics: Blake's Sense of Form'. *Huntingdon Library Quarterly* 58 (3–4, 1996): 441–58.

——. *Picture Theory: Essays on Verbal and Visual Representation.* Chicago: University of Chicago Press, 1994.

Otto, Peter. '"A Pompous High Priest": Urizen's ancient phallic religion in *The Four Zoas.'. Blake: An Illustrated Quarterly* 35 (2001): 4–22.

——. 'A Sublime Allegory: Blake, Blake Studies and the Sublime.' *The Eighteenth Century: Theory and Interpretation* 21 (Winter 2002): 61–84.

Shaftesbury, Anthony Ashley, Earl. *Second Characters, or The Language of Forms.* Ed. Benjamin Rand. Cambridge: Cambridge University Press, 1914.

Swedenborg, Emanuel. *The Delights of Wisdom concerning Conjugial Love, after which follows The Pleasures of Insanity concerning Scortatory Love.* Trans. Revd. John Clowes. London: 1794.

——. *A Treatise concerning Heaven and Hell, and of the Wonderful Things therein, as Heard and Seen.* Trans. William Cookworthy and Thomas Hartley. 2nd ed. London: R. Hindmarsh, 1784.

Viscomi, Joseph. *Blake and the Idea of the Book.* Princeton: Princeton University Press, 1993.

4
blake and language

The last lines of Blake's last major poem, *Jerusalem*, have everything to do with the subject of language – its potential, its limitations, and its idiosyncrasies in Blake's work:

> All Human Forms identified even Tree Metal Earth & Stone. all
> Human Forms identified, living going forth & returning wearied
> Into the Planetary lives of Years Months Days & Hours reposing
> And then Awaking into his Bosom in the Life of Immortality.
> And I heard the Name of their Emanations they are named Jerusalem
> (J99.1–5, E258–9)

This is the culmination of an apocalyptic vision, which could be called an apocalypse of language itself. Beginning with 'The Four Living Creatures' who converse in 'Visionary forms dramatic' and thereby create Memory and Intellect, Space and Time (J98.24–31), it becomes a scene in which words themselves 'Humanize', taking the form of One Man, and appearing on golden chariots that proceed before the poet's eyes 'according to fitness & order' (J98.40–5). Blake imagines a state in which the Word merges with the thing, the action, and the supernatural speaker(s), all at once. Yet to evoke the vision he himself uses idiosyncratic and barely interpretable words. The present chapter will examine what leads Blake to this resonant act of naming at the culmination of *Jerusalem*, and how critics have tried to follow him there.

Blake's relationship to language is mainly a pragmatic, rather than a theoretical one. Although some of his contemporaries, like Coleridge, had a great deal to say about poetic language and linguistic philosophy, Blake himself did not articulate anything like a theory of language. Instead, he wrestled, experimented, and played with words. Blake did, however, take a clear stand on one kind of language: the traditional language of English poetry. In the Preface to chapter 1 of *Jerusalem*, he announces to the public his rejection of rhyme, calling it a 'bondage' on language and inspiration. 'Milton & Shakspeare & all writers of English Blank Verse' (pl. 3, E145) had also freed language from rhyme; but Blake goes further and rejects even their example. The 'Monotonous Cadence' of Miltonic or Shakespearean blank verse turns out to be 'not only awkward, but as much a bondage as rhyme itself' (E146). Instead of iambic pentameter, Blake, in his prophetic poems, will adopt 'a variety in every line, both of cadences & number of syllables'. Lest this irregularity be misunderstood as carelessness rather than the liberty proper to the inspired orator, Blake emphasizes his intention to suit the sounds and marks of language exactly to what they are meant to express:

> Every word and every letter is studied and put into its fit place: the terrific numbers are reserved for the terrific parts – the mild & gentle, for the mild & gentle parts, and the prosaic, for inferior parts: all are necessary to each other. (E146)

This principle of precision in poetic language corresponds to Blake's convictions about visual art: 'as Poetry admits not a Letter that is Insignificant so Painting admits not a Grain of Sand or a Blade of Grass <Insignificant>' (*A Vision of the Last Judgment*, E560).

Blake's declaration that every word and every letter is put into its fit place is part and parcel of his claim to write under inspiration – a fundamental aspect of his relationship to language. At the beginning of *Jerusalem*, he attributes his verse to Jesus the Saviour, who dictates to him every night as he sleeps, and guides his hand as he writes. Much more than a poetic convention, this claim reappears in Blake's prose and personal letters, where he also affirms that he has written his epic verse 'under inspiration' (E543), and that the spirit of his dead brother Robert dictates to him (E705).

Blake's poetic universe is full of inspired speakers: not only the poet himself, but the Bard in *Milton*, the character Milton, and Los and Albion in *Jerusalem*, among others. Accordingly, the words that fly between one character and another in Blake's prophetic poetry are 'permanent' (J13.60–1, E157–8) and 'all-powerful' (J24.1, E169). They are divine and human at once, two spheres that are nicely conflated at the climax of *Jerusalem*, where the protagonist Albion appears 'speaking the Words of Eternity in Human Forms' (J95.9, E255). For Blake, the power of language derives, crucially, from its participation in the eternal and divine as well as from the human form that any aspect of the divine must assume if it is to be meaningful to us. The ideal incarnation of the 'Words of Eternity in Human Forms', however, can only be achieved within an apocalyptic vision; elsewhere, Blake's writing is marked by an awareness that his human language is inadequate to express eternal vision. 'O how can I with my gross tongue that cleaveth to the dust', the narrator in *Milton* laments, 'Tell of the Four-fold Man, in starry numbers fitly orderd' (20.15–16, E114). Here, the need to 'order' words, and the 'numbers' of metrical verse, into their 'fit' place, is an anxiety-producing burden. An often-quoted line from *Jerusalem* identifies English as 'the rough basement' – a language with a 'stubborn structure' built by the mythic character Los (J36.58–9, E183). Human language is an unfinished and, at times, an unaccommodating habitation for the words of eternity, but it is the only one we have.

'Unfinished' and 'unaccommodating' may be how most readers perceive Blake's own language, especially in the prophetic poems. The reader of Blake faces what V.A. De Luca has aptly termed a 'wall of words': formidable, resistant language full of idiosyncrasies, neologisms, tantalizing but ambiguous allusions to other languages, lists of unknown and unpronounceable names. Along with these challenges, there is an unusual rhetorical insistence to Blake's language, as if he were constantly urging his audience, like the Bard in *Milton*, 'Mark well my words! they are of your eternal salvation' (2.25, E96 and elsewhere). Readers and critics of Blake have always had to confront his language head-on and, in seeking to interpret, try to account for the particular features of its strangeness. In the process, critics have explored his stylistic peculiarities as well as the place of language itself in his mythology. They have found that Blake's language resonates as much with ancient, biblical paradigms of the Word as with modern conceptions of the performative speech act.

Until the 1960s, few critics addressed the issue of Blake and language *per se*, but the most influential works of mid-twentieth-century Blake criticism conveyed implicit assumptions about how to read his language. Northrop Frye's ground-breaking *Fearful Symmetry* (1945), for example, reads the 'stubborn structure' of Blake's language within a context of biblical and archetypal symbolism that de-mystifies many of its allusions. As Frye admits in his Preface, in writing the book he 'felt all the resistance against grappling with a specific symbolic language' (n.p.) – but over the course of his commentary, this language is revealed to be, after all, the English of literature, myth, and philosophy, used to express Blake's radical vision. Another mid-twentieth-century attempt to come to terms with Blake's symbolic language ended by providing it with a proprietary lexicon. *A Blake Dictionary: The Ideas and Symbols of William Blake* (1965), a late project of S. Foster Damon, may be seen as a different way of presenting the overall interpretation of Blake that Damon had established in his 1924 book, *William Blake: His Philosophy and Symbols*. But the very enterprise of preparing a dictionary of the images, symbols, mythological figures, biblical characters, and place names that feature in Blake's writing signals a shift of focus toward Blake's language in the 1960s. From 'Abarim' (a mountain range east of the Dead Sea, mentioned in Blake's *Milton*) to the 'Zoas', Damon's *Blake Dictionary* provides biblical, mythological, historical, geographical, etymological, and psychological clues to the interpretation of Blake's idiosyncratic vocabulary. 'So novel was everything in this new world [of the psyche] that no vocabulary was prepared for him', writes Damon in the Introduction; 'But these psychic forces were so real that he *had* to name them. Thence arose his special mythology' (xxv).

At the time Damon's *Blake Dictionary* appeared, another founder of twentieth-century Blake studies, David V. Erdman, was overseeing the computer-aided preparation of a complete *Concordance to the Writings of William Blake*, which was published in 1967. Quantitative analysis of Blake's vocabulary contradicted the intuitive impressions of even experienced readers. For instance, Erdman was surprised to see that the words 'death' and 'night' appear so frequently in Blake's poetry, amidst the other terms one might expect to see among his favorites: 'man', 'love', 'eternal', 'earth' (Erdman vii).

The Concordance made possible a new level of detail in the stylistic analysis of Blake's language – a possibility taken advantage of especially by Josephine Miles. Before the Concordance appeared, Miles had included a chapter on Blake in her *Eras and Modes in English Poetry* (1957). There, she undertook a quantitative analysis of Blake's linguistic habits, analyzing key words in the first 200 lines of major poems from all stages of his career, noting the frequency of nouns, verbs, adjectives, and other parts of speech. Among other things, Miles found that Blake's poetry is unusually concerned with the relations between things and between characters, and that verb-forms, especially participles, predominate over nouns. Thus, while Blake shares with his eighteenth-century contemporaries a predilection for 'physical, descriptive, onomatopoetic, invocative, and declarative' language, his heavy use of verbs and participles creates a language that is dynamic rather than static, favoring 'the motion observed in process' (Miles, *Eras* 85). In 'Blake's Frame of Language' (1973), using the data made available by the Blake Concordance, Miles extends and deepens her analysis of Blake's style. Now it becomes apparent, for instance, that Blake's most-used word is 'eternal' – and this in itself sets him apart from most major poets in English, since it is rare to find three-syllable words in a poet's core vocabulary (Miles, 'Blake's Frame of Language' 86). Miles also finds that, compared with other English poets, Blake relies on an unusually high number of 'main adjectives' (87); that he uses frequent locational phrases, thus 'intensifying the spatial' (88); that the primary action performed in Blake's poetry is 'seeing' or 'beholding' (90); and that by far the most frequent 'referential term' is 'all' (90). Summarizing her findings, Miles translates her quantitative analysis into interpretative conclusions about Blake's mythology:

> He needs physical anatomy, an eye, an arm, a hand; he needs physical geography, rock, cloud, and mountain; he needs cosmology, heaven, time, eternity, divinity; he needs forms with names and feelings and monumental actions providing presence, he needs the earthly energy of bounding lines, in order to make his pictures. He needs wrath, forge, and fire to regenerate the generated and vegetable forms into their states beyond time, change, and progression. ('Blake's Frame of Language' 94)

One of the relatively few existing studies of Blake's poetic technique also appeared during the 1960s: in *Vision and Verse in William Blake* (1965), Alicia Ostriker analyzes Blake's use of rhythm, rhyme, alliteration, repetition, and other elements of poetic language, finding him 'an inveterate experimenter, contemptuous of his century, a continual seeker after liberated modes of verse' (6). Rather than metrical innovation, however, most of the studies of Blake's style published during the 1960s and 1970s focus on grammatical aspects: for instance, his unusually heavy use of adjectives and verbs, a feature that distinguishes his language from that of other poets. Robert Murray calls attention to Blake's idiosyncratic, but well-motivated, use of verbs and verbal forms in his later poetry. He agrees with Josephine Miles that Blake was seeking a correlation of style with meaning; more specifically, he argues that Blake sought to 'work out in practice a new ideal of poetic simplicity' (90), opposed to the eighteenth-century Augustan preference for verbal ornamentation. Murray demonstrates that Blake's ideal of stylistic simplicity is at work even in the long prophetic poems, which at first glance appear anything but simple. His use of nouns, verbs, and participles constitutes a 'sublime simplicity' (104) that allows him to evoke Eden, for instance, as a state in which 'everything is happening always and simultaneously' (102). One example of this eternal state, evoked through participles, is the apocalyptic scene in the final plates of *Jerusalem* already alluded to above:

> The Breath Divine went forth over the morning hills Albion rose
> In anger: the wrath of God *breaking* bright *flaming* on all sides around
> His awful limbs: into the Heavens he walked *clothed* in flames
> Loud *thundring*, with broad flashes of *flaming* lightning & pillars
> Of fire, *speaking* the Words of Eternity in Human Forms [. . .].
>   (*J*95.5–9, E255; emphasis added)

Another stylistic approach, Ronald Clayton Taylor's 'Semantic Structures and the Temporal Modes of Blake's Prophetic Verse' (1979), calls attention to Blake's heavy use of the 'processive' or 'ongoing' aspect of verbs. 'Blake's most prominent aspectual mode,' Taylor finds, 'consists of unending process. An incredible quantity of goings-on is sometimes amassed in the verse, without any feeling of resolution' (33). He cites an example from *Milton*:

> He *hoverd* over it *trembling* & *weeping. suspended* it shook
> The nether Abyss in t[r]*emblings.* he *wept* over it, he *cherish'd* it.
>   (3.31–2, E97; emphasis added)

Blake's unusually heavy use of 'ongoing' verbs creates a feeling of endless process, which may result in frustration for the reader who has the sense that no real action or change of state is ever achieved. Yet, ultimately, Taylor argues, Blake *is* a poet of action: his many processive verbs form the background against which moments of definite action stand out as unusually emphatic and dramatic. In fact, Taylor suggests that these definite actions take on a *performative* aspect: they seem not just to be described, but actually to occur, at the moment when Blake's language announces them. Thus, when the character Milton declares, 'I go to Eternal Death!' (*M*14.14, E108), the sudden, present-tense verb makes it seem that Milton goes even as he speaks.

During the 1960s and 1970s, then, as Blake's visual art was finally attracting serious attention from both art historians and literary scholars, and causing many critics to maintain that his poetry and illustration constitute a 'composite art' that needs to be considered as a whole (see Chapters 2 and 3 in this volume), the tools were also being developed for a more precise focus on Blake and language. Criticism began to pay attention to the different 'registers' of language in Blake's works and worlds: for instance, how language works differently within the world of

Innocence and that of Experience. Robert F. Gleckner, analyzing Blake's 'poetry of adjectives' ('Blake's Verbal Technique' 321), demonstrates that the main adjectives in *Songs of Innocence* (happy, cheerful, merry, pleasant, sweet, tender, soft, etc.) are all interconnected, and indissolubly unified with the nouns they modify. Indeed, these adjectives 'carry the weight of nouns and verbs' (323) in creating the web of relationships that constitute the state of Innocence. Experience, by contrast, is not only a state in which different adjectives prevail (starry, fallen, dewy, worn, drear, stony, cold, etc.), but one in which grammatical relationships are unsettled: adjectives are incompatible with their nouns and with one another, and they impose themselves on the perceptions of characters within that state. Harriet Kramer Linkin has also studied the differing languages of Innocence and Experience, focusing on the speakers within these poems. She shows how the 'idiolects' of innocent or experienced speakers in Blake's *Songs* reveal the limitations of their world-view, and the extent to which they have assimilated the vocabulary, the false logic, or the blind spots of their society with regard to such issues as racism and social institutions. In a similar vein, critics (including Hans Ostrom, and Gleckner in 'Most Holy Forms of Thoughts') analyze the differences between Blake's representation of 'fallen' language in such works as *Tiriel* or *The Book of Urizen*, and the possibility of an ideal language of Eternity or Eden – a state represented in Blake's longer prophecies as a perpetual, creative exchange of words.

To read the various idiolects or levels of language in Blake's poetry not only as elements of its form, but as integral elements of its meaning, is to recognize language itself as a primary subject within Blake's mythology. Hazard Adams describes Blake as a new kind of 'symbolist' who believed, as twentieth-century philosophers of language and mind would later claim, that humans must create symbolic or mythic worlds for themselves, and that these can only be created through language. This is, Adams argues, the conclusion to be drawn from such passages as plate 11 of *The Marriage of Heaven and Hell*, Blake's abbreviated history of the 'ancient Poets' whose naming of natural objects was superseded by the system of Priesthood. In 'Most Holy Forms of Thought: Some Observations on Blake and Language' (1974), Robert Gleckner argues that the fall and redemption of the Word is a (or even *the*) central aspect of Blake's myth, and examines Blake's paradoxical striving for a transcendent language even when he knows no poet can escape the inadequacies of 'a time-bound, space-bound syntax that passively mirrors the shattered mind and the excruciatingly finite limits of fallen sense perception' (93). To make the point that the role of language itself in Blake's myth has been neglected by readers and critics, Gleckner ventures an 'outrageously simplistic and sweeping' thesis: 'everything Blake says about Man, the Universe, society, imagination and the senses – in fact, everything that he says about anything – is translatable into a comment upon language, words, the poet's task, poetry' (100).

With the observation that everything in Blake is (about) language, Blake studies could be said to achieve its own 'linguistic turn'. This term has been applied to twentieth-century literary theory in order to describe the revolution triggered by Saussurean and Jakobsonian linguistics, bringing with it structuralist methodologies as well as intensely text-focused reactions to structuralism in the form of post-structuralism and deconstruction. At the same time that post-structuralist approaches paid new attention to the marks, margins, traces, and differences caught in the surface of the text, important developments in the philosophy of language caused scholars to pay new attention to voice, dialogue, and the performative qualities of language.

Inspired by post-structuralism, the study of Blake's language as a play of signifiers, etymological associations, anagrams, puns, and sound-patterns that complicate the semantic surface is best represented by the work of Nelson Hilton (see Chapter 5). Hilton's readings draw attention, for instance, to the patterns of sounds and marks that contribute to the 'onomastic vision' in the last line of *Jerusalem* ('And I heard the Name of their Emanations they are named Jerusalem') – specifically, the modulation of *Name* into *Emana*tions in an *Amen* that might also recall *lamen*tations ('Becoming Prolific Being Devoured' 420). Each of Blake's multidimensional words calls up a wealth of possible significations, while avoiding the direct path to a distinct referent. Blake's texts, according to Hilton, expand our perception of language to the point where the referent of his words is 'the entire vision of words in which each particular exists' (*Literal Imagination* 237). The work of the Santa Cruz Blake Study Group follows a similar trajectory. Its searching review of David Erdman's now-standard edition of Blake ('What Type of Blake?' [1986]) shows that any project of editing Blake's language raises profound questions about what constitutes a book, a line of poetry, a punctuation mark, or a mistake.

In the era of post-structuralism, critical approaches tended to highlight the strangeness of Blake's language, interpreting fragmentation and irregularity as an intrinsic part of what he has to say. Thus Peter Middleton writes about the 'revolutionary poetics' of Blake, wherein the stylistic challenges of Blake's texts form part of his revolutionary refusal of orthodoxy and finality. These irregularities include missing or odd punctuation, fragmentary sentences, non-standard uses of the verb 'to be', repetitions (but with discrepancies), and idiosyncratic names. Almost any passage from Blake's prophetic books would illustrate these features, but Middleton – like so many writers on Blake and language – focuses on the last lines of *Jerusalem* because there, if anywhere, we would expect a final revelation (see p. 63). The lack of full stops (periods) where we would normally expect them, and their presence where we would not, keeps the meaning of the lines off balance and shifting, so that the reader cannot be certain which subject goes with which verb or which object. Middleton stresses the ambiguities made possible by the 'lack of good grammar', and especially by the lack of grammatical subordination: 'The series of states is allowed to remain a series, without subordination or sublation into a final state or subject, because the subordination of conventional written syntax is not employed. The possible syntactic constructions form a dynamic set which is the actual grammar of the lines' ('Revolutionary Poetics, Part I' 36). If this is an apocalypse, it is a strangely open-ended one; according to Middleton, 'The failure of apocalypse as an absolute is the final sign of the unboundedness of language, and this unboundedness is shown to be a threat to any order that desires permanence' ('Revolutionary Poetics, Part II' 46).

Jerome McGann comes to similar conclusions about Blake's poetic practice, linking it to deconstruction and to modern poetry. Focusing more deliberately than Middleton on Blake's method of production, McGann calls attention to places where Blake gouged words out of his metal printing plates, leaving 'gaps' or 'ruptures' in the text. The 'finished' plates of the Illuminated Books appear strangely unfinished, demonstrating that poetry is a process of communicative action. Knowledge, for Blake, is a 'form of activity' (McGann 44), and even 'the truth' is something to be apprehended through experience, rather than as a unified whole. McGann and Middleton both provide detailed examples of how Blake's language frustrates the normal grammatical identifications of an agent with an action; instead, 'The acts that we witness appear as the simultaneous deeds of all the various figures in the text' (McGann 51). Both critics also suggest that Blake has a bold philosophical purpose: to collapse the distinction between signifier and signified (a distinction emphasized, in different ways, by both structuralist and post-structuralist criticism), so that words and signs become *things* that move or mark the reader, and reading becomes an experiential process.

According to the above interpretations, the strangeness of Blake's language is meaningful in itself: through his ruptured, fragmentary texts and idiosyncratic grammar, Blake is seen as countering the dominant political and aesthetic ideologies of his time. V.A. De Luca cautions, however, against too assiduous an attempt to explain Blake's idiosyncrasies:

> We do not serve Blake well when we treat the palpable strangeness of his poetic surfaces as something other than strangeness, as much criticism tends dangerously to do that seeks pragmatically to transmute the oddities of his verse into terms conforming to his thematic arguments. ('Proper Names' 6)

De Luca sets Blake's writing within the context of late-Enlightenment aesthetics and ideology, but in a way that emphasizes its strangeness. In his book *Words of Eternity*, De Luca develops a connection between Blake's language and the notion of the sublime expounded by his contemporaries Edmund Burke and Immanuel Kant. Unlike them, Blake is no theorist of the sublime, but De Luca contends that he is a practitioner of it. One of Blake's sublime modes, the 'bardic style', overwhelms the reader with rapid, staccato lines, a 'cascade of events' in which the bard himself is caught up, a 'profusion of tropes', and open-ended, bewildering 'mutations of forms' (De Luca, *Words of Eternity* 79). Blake also employs a different, 'iconic' style, consisting of language that stands still rather than racing onward, but that is no less overpowering to the reader. This is the resistant 'wall of words' that manifests itself as crowded and closely-written lines of script on the plates of Blake's prophetic books, or as impenetrable grammar, or as unfamiliar signifiers and invented names for which we have no referents. Blake's language tends toward the status of the icon by retreating from the referential function that we normally consider intrinsic to language; it proposes to become merely a graphic play of dark ink against white page. Images of stone tablets and stonehenge-like trilithons in Blake's illuminated plates intensify the sense that Blake's reader is left staring at a stony barrier that produces the same reactions of vertigo or blockage that Blake's contemporaries identified as the experience of the sublime.

Among the most resistant elements of Blake's language are his proper names, which often defeat the reader because they are either not limited to their usual signification (in the case of biblical or historical names, for instance), or else they are completely invented by Blake. As De Luca writes, names in general are 'intrinsically irreducible, hard givens, unavailable for paraphrase' ('Wall of Words' 235). The traditional way of interpreting Blake's names is to seek mythological identifications and etymological clues; this is the type of explanation pursued, for instance, by Frye, by Damon in his *Blake Dictionary*, and by Harold Bloom in his commentary in the Erdman edition of Blake's *Complete Poetry and Prose*. In 'Proper Names in the Structural Design of Blake's Myth-Making' (1978), De Luca counters these attempts by identifying alternative principles by which Blake generates proper names. He finds that: (1) Blake's invented names maintain their autonomy – resisting, rather than inviting, reference or allusion; (2) invented names generate further names, but through principles of phonetic resemblance rather than etymology (e.g., the sound-relationships among 'Enitharmon' and the names of her children Ethinthus, Manathu-Vorcyon, Antamon, Sotha, and Thiralatha); (3) Blake's names get associated into clusters that are related both through sound and through some other type of categorization (e.g., Urthona, Urizen, Luvah, Tharmas share phonetic resemblances in addition to being grouped together as the four Zoas).

Blake's use of proper names is an important sub-topic within the study of Blake and language. A strikingly original approach to the problem of naming is that of Aaron Fogel, who describes Blake's concepts, and even his characters, as 'pictures of speech'. A 'picture of speech', here, is a cluster of associations that may include sound-patterns, but that points primarily to a certain socio-historical context, identified with specific dialogical models. Thus, Blake's Leutha represents 'Protestant speech' – an association achieved partly through the pun on 'Luther', but mainly through her own verbal behaviour in Blake's prophetic poems, where she manifests 'Protestant' modes of speech such as public self-scrutiny, self-exaggeration, confession, and plain-spokenness. Similarly, London is represented in both the *Songs* and the prophetic poems as a 'field of cries' (Fogel 237). Fogel's rich but difficult analysis opens up new ways of reading Blake's proper names as dialogical, relational, and interactive: each name refers not to a single individual, but to a dialogic model or speech community. Sound-patterning is still an important element of Fogel's interpretation, as it was for De Luca, but the 'patterns' are more likely to be tension-filled juxtapositions that create an 'aesthetic of "nextness" – proximity of similar but crucially differentiated forms that "vibrate against" each other rather than sympathize euphoniously or merge' (Fogel 228).

Tracing the etymological allusions and sound-patterns in Blake's proper names, and his language in general, has often led critics to see connections with other modern and ancient languages. The extent to which Blake knew or studied any other languages is an unresolved question, and answers to it seem destined to rely on internal evidence from his own writings. In a letter of 30 January 1803 to his brother James, Blake sends a blithe report of his activities in the rural retreat of Felpham:

I go on Merrily with my Greek & Latin: am very sorry that I did not begin to learn languages early in life as I find it very Easy. am now learning my Hebrew: אבג I read Greek as fluently as an Oxford scholar & the Testament is my chief master. (E727)

Earlier, he had reported that his reading list included the Greek, Portuguese, Spanish, and Italian epic poets Homer, Camoens, Ercilla, and Ariosto (E714), although it is not clear in which languages he is reading them. The ambiguity and inexactness of Blake's allusions to other languages cause most critics to doubt that he read Greek or any other language 'as fluently as an Oxford scholar'. Recently, however, critics have pointed out that Blake's knowledge of other languages, and of language theory, needs to be considered in relation to the state of linguistic study during his own time. In her extensive investigations into the Hebraic background of Blake's language, Sheila A. Spector puts the topic into perspective by showing that almost all English writers *including* Oxford scholars read and used Hebrew in idiosyncratic and biased ways. 'We must [. . .] consider the possibility that Blake knew a different kind of Hebrew', she proposes (Spector 213) – namely, the Hebrew language as distorted by the prejudices of eighteenth-century Christian Hebraists. In Blake's time, the study of Hebrew was of increasing interest not only because of the newly-introduced Higher Criticism, which took a historical approach to the Bible and its various source-texts, but also because Enlightenment philologists were preoccupied with finding the origin, and the original forms, of all languages. Late eighteenth-century controversies over whether Hebrew was the language spoken by Adam in Paradise, and therefore the original language from which all others descended, seem to be reflected in Blake's assertion in the *Descriptive Catalogue*: 'All had originally one language' (E543). Although Blake sometimes uses correct Hebrew – and, in particular, seems to have been 'aware of the literal meanings of place names in the Bible' (Spector 205) – he more often uses faulty constructions. Spector argues, however, that his idiosyncratic and inconsistent usage needs to be re-evaluated given the biases of his age. In that context, she suggests, 'we have to explore the possibility that the Hebrew words [in Blake's work] interrelate with each other in associational clusters which might produce hidden levels of meaning' (Spector 209).

Eighteenth-century Hebraism, Hermeticism, and theories of the origin of language are also broached by V.A. De Luca in the last chapter of *Words of Eternity*. The antiquarians and mythographers who were Blake's contemporaries were intent on discovering the unified language of the age before Babel, 'when reality and sign formed a single being' (*Words of Eternity* 205). Exploring Blake's participation in these Hermetic and Kabbalistic speculations, De Luca arrives again at a fundamental paradox concerning Blake and language: in striving to return to a translucent language, Blake tends to create an impenetrable language that baffles and estranges his readers. Yet De Luca's reading, referring once again to the 'Words of Eternity in Human Forms' that we encounter at the end of *Jerusalem*, is ultimately redemptive: 'These words comfort', he writes, 'for they alone can display intellectual acts in a lasting, determinate, and autonomous form' (*Words of Eternity* 224). The final word of the poem – 'Jerusalem' – is a unifying and familiar 'name to destroy the power of the mystery of names, a name to bring us home' ('Proper Names' 22)

Daniel Stempel achieves a similarly optimistic reading of the end of *Jerusalem* when he examines Blake's name-giving in light of the classical *episteme*, or organization of knowledge, that prevailed in the eighteenth century. Blake inherits from the Enlightenment a commitment to naming as 'the interplay of imagination and resemblance' (Stempel 391): that is, a belief that the system of proper nouns is a compromise between human nature (one of whose properties is imagination) and external nature (one of whose effects is resemblance). Even though names are prone to corruption through the processes of linguistic change, Blake strives to recover an ideal of exact designation as the interaction of nature and imagination: 'Blake's names are natural in the sense that they attempt to restore each name to its proper place, but they are also arbitrary because they are deliberate coinages' (394). In the last lines of *Jerusalem*, this compromise is finally achieved: 'the relation between words and things is immediately visible as language and representation become one' (398). Given its engagement with naming and representation, Blake's art, according to Stempel, 'does not represent objects, it represents *discourse*, the language of the order of being' (405).

The past fifteen years have seen much more extensive scholarship on the various theories of language that prevailed during the Romantic period. The first major study of this kind, Robert N. Essick's *William Blake and the Language of Adam* (1989), looks at Blake's work in light of recent discoveries about his use of graphic media, but also in the context of linguistics and semiotics, as those disciplines existed during Blake's time. Like post-structuralist criticism (with which Essick still identifies), his book explores the nature of the linguistic sign, but adds a survey of the *historical* aspect of sign theory. He examines how the sign was understood in Blake's time, and how it was understood by Blake. According to Essick, Blake's poetic practice combines materiality, represented above all by his graphic art and his methods of book production, with the phenomenology of language – that is, a new emphasis on communication and community-building that was emerging in the early nineteenth century.

Essick surveys the history of theories of language in order to 'delineate the landscape of intellectual possibilities available in [Blake's] age' (27). From ancient Greek philosophy, through sixteenth- and seventeenth-century mysticism and attempts to invent ideal languages, to the eighteenth-century search for the origins of language, Essick traces the idea of the 'motivated' sign: that is, the idea that words are not arbitrary or conventional, but have an intrinsic connection with the thing they represent. In Blake's time, the philologist and radical politician John Horne Tooke made an influential attempt to prove that all words originate from nouns that denote concrete sensory experiences. But other philosophers around 1800 were investigating the intrinsic role of language in expressing individual, human identity, and in bringing speaker and listener into community through the medium of the word. Essick finds resonances between Blake and the nineteenth-century language theorist William von Humboldt (1767–1835), as well as the twentieth-century philosopher Heidegger: both of them describe the 'quasi-divine potency of the language of man' (12), a quality that Blake's writing and art suggest in practice. Since Humboldt and Blake both published erratically, and in different languages, there is no question of direct influence. On the contrary, Essick's survey of the history of linguistics tends to reinforce Blake's detachment from the development of linguistics, semiotics, or language theory as disciplines. The study of Blake's linguistic practices that Essick undertakes still has to rely on internal evidence within Blake's work to determine what constitutes a language of innocence or a language of experience, or how Blake conceived of the differences between orality and writing, or the significance of names. In considering Blake's later poetry, Essick finds Blake's language tending toward the ideals of articulation, conversation, and community: 'Rather than rigidly objectivist, grammatical, and spatial, this language is expansively subjectivist, instrumental, and temporal' (229). Like other writers on Blake and language, Essick ends his study with the final lines of *Jerusalem*. For him, these lines affirm Blake's hard-won belief in the generative power of language – that is, its ability to generate a meaningful environment for the human speaker. Thus, in the last lines of *Jerusalem*, Blake is identifying the 'Human Forms' of 'Tree Metal Earth & Stone' as their *names*, which are the ground of their being in the human world: 'The generative power of language, available to Blake and to us through our ability to create propositions never before heard, has become the generation of ontological out of verbal identities' (235).

Essick is one of several critics who, during the past decade, have begun to apply the term *performative* to Blake's language and to explore the concept of the *speech act* as a way of understanding his verbal practice. These terms derive from the philosopher J.L. Austin (1911–1960), who used the word 'performative' to refer to utterances that do what they say, such as 'I now pronounce you husband and wife', 'You're fired', or 'War is hereby declared'. These utterances – and ultimately, for Austin and most of his followers, *all* utterances – therefore count as actions rather than as descriptive or referential statements. The concepts of performative language and speech acts provide insight into the interaction that occurs among speakers, hearers, language, and the world. These concepts seem particularly applicable to Blake, whose works provide a multitude of evidence that he conceived of his own inspired utterances, and those of his characters, as verbal action – that is, as modes of speaking and writing that have immediate and demonstrable effects on the listener, the speaker, or the environment.

Gavin Edwards examines Blake's use of performative language in an essay focusing on Blake's 'London', a poem full of utterances that perform what they pronounce: 'ban', 'curse', 'charter', 'mark'. The concatenation of these explicit speech acts creates a poem that exposes what is done to people by the authoritative utterances of Church and State, as well as what the poetic 'I' does (to others) through language. As seen above, other critics writing in the late 1970s and 1980s, including Taylor and Middleton, also introduce the idea of the performative in trying to account for Blake's unusual use of verb tenses, or the way he depicts verbal interactions among his characters.

The most extensive study of Blake's work in terms of speech-act theory is my *Creating States: Studies in the Performative Language of John Milton and William Blake* (1994). This book identifies two broad categories of speech acts: *sociopolitical performatives*, which derive their force from the speaker's and hearer's positions within a societal institution (the Church, the law, the class system, etc.); and *phenomenological performatives*, which derive from the speaker's apparent ability to create a new reality through poetic or fictional utterance, independently of societal conventions but in accordance with literary conventions that ascribe creative, visionary, or prophetic authority to the speaking voice. The interaction, juxtaposition, and compromise between these two modes of performative language throughout Blake's work provide insight into both the constructive and destructive actions that words can achieve.

The *Songs of Innocence and of Experience*, for example, may be read in terms of the contrasting types of verbal action that dominate each state. Blake's

Innocence is a distinctive mode of language characterized by successful, creative, phenomenological performatives, while Experience is a mode of language characterized by failed speech acts and by the sociopolitical performatives that institutionalized power uses to impose its world-view on individual characters. Innocence is a world of answerable and answered questions, of symmetry between request and response, of stable identities that allow for meaningful verbal interaction between an 'I' and a 'you'. The 'Introduction' ('Piping down the valleys wild') inaugurates these forms of verbal behavior by presenting an exact correspondence of word and action in the reciprocal exchange between Piper and Child. Experience, by contrast, features unanswerable questions and inarticulate noises; speakers of uncertain identity, who fail to respond to one another; anonymous utterances; and destructive pronouncements backed by the power of Church and State. A disturbing example is the Priest in 'A Little Boy Lost', who declares from his 'altar high' that the little boy is a fiend who has set reason above 'holy Mystery'. In uttering these words, the Priest imposes his biased but authoritative definitions of the terms 'fiend', 'reason', and 'holy', and decrees the boy's destruction.

In the early *Songs*, contrasting modes of language serve to distinguish the contrary states of Innocence and Experience; but in Blake's later prophetic poems, especially *Jerusalem*, the relationship between sociopolitical and phenomenological performatives is much more complex. Within *Jerusalem*, there are many examples of verbal utterances that have an immediate effect on their hearers or on the environment. Blake's universe is one in which the words of Los, Urizen, Albion, the 'Divine Voice', and other speakers apparently have the force of actions due to the intrinsic, perhaps divine authority of the speaker. But can these authoritative voices – even that of the poet himself – be clearly distinguished from the voices that exercise sociopolitical authority to impose their vision of reality on others? *Jerusalem* obliges readers to contemplate the disturbing complicity of language and power. In Chapter 2, for instance, when the Law appears to condemn the protagonist Albion to death, his predicament is described by 'those in Great Eternity who contemplate on Death':

What seems to Be: Is: To those to whom
It seems to Be, & is productive of the most dreadful
Consequences to those to whom it seems to Be: even of
Torments, Despair, Eternal Death; but the Divine Mercy
Steps beyond and Redeems Man in the Body of Jesus Amen
And Length Bredth Highth again Obey the Divine Vision Hallelujah
(J32.50–6, E179)

The Eternal speakers acknowledge the performative power of the copula verb ('to be'), which is emphasized by being separated off visually and aurally in the line of poetry: 'Is:'. Both believing and saying that something 'is' appears to make it so. Yet the speakers also attempt to overcome Albion's delusion that Eternal Death 'Is' by uttering a contrary affirmation: 'but the Divine Mercy / Steps beyond and Redeems Man in the Body of Jesus Amen'. One vision of reality confronts another, because one affirmation confronts another.

What the Eternal speakers imply here about the performative power of 'is' is relevant to Blake's own use of the copula verb, and, accordingly, to the possibility of creating a new reality through language. When the poet claims that 'The Male *is* a Furnace of beryll; the Female *is* a golden Loom' (*J*5.34, E148; emphasis added), or 'Ulro *is* the space of the terrible starry wheels of Albions sons' (*J*12.51, E156; emphasis added), he defeats our usual assumptions about the way statements should be read, by conflating literal and figurative, abstract and concrete, and by using proper names for which we have no referents outside of his poetry. More blatantly than with other writers, Blake's grammar relies on affirmative statements, but invests such statements with performative force. 'There is a place where Contrarieties are equally True / This place is called Beulah', Blake writes at the beginning of Book the Second of *Milton* (30.1–2, E129). He follows this statement with an allusion to divine creation by the word:

As the breath of the Almighty. such are the words of man to man
In the great Wars of Eternity, in fury of Poetic Inspiration,
To build the Universe stupendous: Mental forms Creating.
(*M*30.18–20, E129)

It seems difficult to escape the implication that Blake's statements, too, create states (Beulah, Eternity) – and vice versa, that to create a state is always to make a statement. Blake's style underlines the performative force of affirmative statements; to put it differently, his poetry constantly demonstrates that all speech *acts*. By making a statement about the 'place where Contrarieties are equally True', Blake simultaneously creates the state of Beulah and gives it a name.

With the possibilities opened up by speech-act theory, in addition to the other approaches to Blake's language that have been outlined up until now, we may examine in more detail those 'Words of Eternity in Human Forms' that appear at the end of *Jerusalem*. Words that take on human form are as literal an image as one could imagine of speech that has the capacity for action, even independently of a speaker:

And they conversed together in Visionary forms dramatic which bright
Redounded from their Tongues in thunderous majesty, in Visions
In new Expanses, creating exemplars of Memory and of Intellect
Creating Space, Creating Time according to the wonders Divine
Of Human Imagination, throughout all the Three Regions immense
Of Childhood, Manhood & Old Age[;] & the all tremendous unfathomable
    Non Ens
Of Death was seen in regenerations terrific or complacent varying
According to the subject of discourse & every Word & Every Character
Was Human according to the Expansion or Contraction, the Translucence
    or
Opakeness of Nervous fibres. (*J*98.28–37, E257–8)

In a very literal sense, words on a page, particularly Blake's illuminated
page, 'create space'; they 'create time' when they are read aloud. Beyond
that, however, Blake's lines imply that words create the very world to
which they seem to refer. Words bring abstract thought into the here
and now, 'giving to airy nothing a name and a habitation / Delightful'
(*M*28.3–4, E125). They create types or 'exemplars' (a word Blake uses only
this one time) of memory and intellect; they open up new expanses of and
to vision; they make even infinite non-being available to contemplation
by naming it 'the all tremendous unfathomable Non Ens / Of Death'.

'Every Word & Every Character / Was Human' echoes Blake's prefatory
remark about his style, 'Every word and every letter is studied and put
into its fit place' (*J*3, E146); the echo is intensified by the allusion to
'regenerations terrific or complacent', which recalls Blake's distinction
between 'terrific', 'mild & gentle', and 'prosaic' parts of his text. No
longer elements to be put passively into place by the author, words are
now endowed with power and agency and released to assume their own
place in a human order.

The final lines of *Jerusalem*, crucial in this regard also, re-conceptualize
the act of naming, bringing together images of creation and images of
apocalypse (see p. 63). These lines look like the ultimate example of
a creative, liberating speech act, or a phenomenological performative.
Omitting almost all punctuation, and obliterating distinctions between
past and present, active and passive, subject and object, the first four lines
of plate 99 rely entirely on participles: 'identified', 'living going forth &
returning', 'reposing', 'Awaking'. Because they lack a main verb, nothing
is 'stated' or affirmed. Meaningfulness is achieved less by declaration
than by ordering and repetition: that is, by *spacing* and *timing*, or, as
Blake puts it, the creation of space and time. When 'All Human Forms

identified' is modified slightly to 'all / Human Forms identified', the emphasis on plurality gives way to an emphasis on unity through the line-end stress on 'all'. Without making any declarative statement, the parallelism between 'Tree Metal Earth & Stone' and 'Years Months Days & Hours' *implies* the identity between physical-spatial phenomena and temporal phenomena. Achieving meaningfulness by placing every word and every letter into its fit place, language appears to be liberated from the potential tyranny of the affirmative statement.

Only in the final line do a subject and a main verb re-appear, with the performative force that Blake's active verbs often receive against a background of participles: 'And *I heard* the Name of their Emanations they are named Jerusalem' (J99.5, E259; emphasis added). These words relate authoritative declaration to subjective perception, but the lack of punctuation between the two halves of the line makes it difficult to determine the extent to which one depends on the other. On the one hand, the first-person construction brings the genesis of the poem, and its apocalypse, back to the experience of the individual human subject. It is possible that the act of naming is effective *because* it has been experienced by the poet. 'And I heard the Name of their Emanations [therefore] they are named Jerusalem', we might read, as a confirmation of the visionary power contained in expanded sensory perception. Of course, this is also to identify the act of naming as one term in an infinitely regressive series of speech acts, an utterance that can be repeated here only because a similar utterance has been heard before. On the other hand, there is not necessarily a causal link between hearing the name and pronouncing it. The final line might be read as two separate phrases, wherein narrative ('And I heard the Name of their Emanations') gives way to arbitrary declaration ('they are named Jerusalem'). By virtue of his visionary experience, the poet assumes the right to make the kind of declaration – naming a state – that would normally be made by someone with political authority.

After dwelling on these last lines of Blake's last prophetic poem, it is worth noting that, in the most recent work on Blake's language, the poetic form of his less canonical early works has received new attention. Susan J. Wolfson highlights the 'intensely performative antiformalism' (Wolfson 65) of a poem like *The French Revolution* (1791), in which Blake's language enacts his ideal of liberation from oppressive forces, as well as the evidence of carefully crafted poetic form in his only conventionally printed work, *Poetical Sketches* (1783). Wolfson exposes delicate conjunctions of form and meaning, such as Blake's placement of the verb 'turn' at the end of an enjambed line in the lyric poem 'To Spring' (Wolfson 69). Sensitivity to these subtleties of poetic form allows us to perceive yet another way in which Blake's language functions as action. As Wolfson concludes, 'Language in poetic form is no static product for Blake; it is an action that compels awareness of the form of our readings – not only of a poet's book but also of the world that such books penetrate and engage' (81).

Most of the critical approaches outlined here have found Blake's language to be distinguished by *activity*, *process*, and *performance*. The stylistic features that account for this dynamism deserve further exploration. In particular, the study of Blake's language has yet to exploit the possibilities that have been opened up by the electronic publication of large portions of Blake's writings, as well as his art, in the William Blake Archive. The potential of stylistic and etymological study is expanded enormously by the searching and sorting techniques that the electronic Archive makes available. This resource should allow for new analyzes of the elements of Blake's language that Robert Gleckner listed over twenty years ago as things in Blake's work we don't yet know enough about: 'allegory, nonsense, imitation, rhetorical and verbal structures and strategies, allusion, language as a "stubborn structure"' ('Creed' 431).

More research also needs to be done on exactly how these linguistic features form part of Blake's ideology and philosophy of language. Both these investigations, the stylistic one and the linguistic-philosophical one, can only be carried out responsibly by learning more about Blake's historical context, about what elements of his language really are different, and how different they are, from the usages of his age and his milieu. Similarly, in order to evaluate the originality or the typicality of Blake's beliefs about language, we need to study the range of ideas about language that were discussed by his contemporaries. These include the linguistic practices that recent critics have identified as being of particular importance to Blake: Hebraism, prophecy, and the prevalent Romantic-period characterization of language as 'energy' or (as Wilhelm von Humboldt termed it) *energeia*.

Finally, the role of dialogue, in Blake's poetic universe and in his relationship with the reader, warrants special attention. Deen, Essick, Esterhammer, and others have discussed, in different ways, the special function of language in forming community in Blake's poems, but it is a central aspect of his work that generates many as yet unanswered questions. Blake's contemporaries, including Coleridge, Herder, and Humboldt, recognized the importance of dialogue for the formation of identity and subjectivity; even if Blake's interaction with Continental or even with British philosophy was limited, his strong emphasis on dialogue between characters should be brought into some relation with this relevant philosophical background. The more recent theories of Mikhail Bakhtin, Martin Buber, or Emmanuel Levinas may also help us develop a clearer idea of what Blake means by defining Eternity as a state of conversation or intellectual debate, and how this idealization of verbal interchange may affect the process of reading and responding to his work.

works cited and suggestions for further reading

Adams, Hazard. 'Blake and the Philosophy of Literary Symbolism'. *Essential Articles for the Study of William Blake, 1970–1984*. Ed. Nelson Hilton. Hamden, CT: Archon, 1986. 1–14.

Damon, S. Foster. *A Blake Dictionary: The Ideas and Symbols of William Blake*. 1965. Hanover: University Press of New England, 1988.

Deen, Leonard W. *Conversing in Paradise: Poetic Genius and Identity-as-Community in Blake's Los*. Columbia: University of Missouri Press, 1983.

De Luca, Vincent Arthur. 'Proper Names in the Structural Design of Blake's Myth-Making'. *Blake Studies* 8 (1978): 5–22.

——. 'A Wall of Words: The Sublime as Text'. *Unnam'd Forms: Blake and Textuality*. Berkeley: University of California Press, 1986. 218–41.

——. *Words of Eternity: Blake and the Poetics of the Sublime*. Princeton: Princeton University Press, 1991.

Edwards, Gavin. '"Mind-Forg'd Manacles": A Contribution to the Discussion of Blake's "London"'. *Literature and History* 5 (1979): 87–101.

Erdman, David V., ed. *A Concordance to the Writings of William Blake*. 2 vols. Ithaca: Cornell University Press, 1967.

Essick, Robert N. *William Blake and the Language of Adam*. Oxford: Clarendon Press, 1989.

Esterhammer, Angela. *Creating States: Studies in the Performative Language of John Milton and William Blake*. Toronto: University of Toronto Press, 1994.

Fogel, Aaron. 'Pictures of Speech: On Blake's Poetic'. *Studies in Romanticism* 21 (1982): 217–42.

Frye, Northrop. *Fearful Symmetry: A Study of William Blake*. Princeton: Princeton University Press, 1947.

Gleckner, Robert F. 'Blake's Verbal Technique'. *William Blake: Essays for S. Foster Damon*. Ed. Alvin H. Rosenfeld. Providence: Brown University Press, 1969. 321–32.

——. 'A Creed Not Outworn'. *Studies in Romanticism* 21 (1982): 431–5.

——. 'Most Holy Forms of Thoughts: Some Observations on Blake and Language'. *ELH* 41 (1974): 555–75. Rpt. *Essential Articles for the Study of William Blake, 1970–1984*. Ed. Nelson Hilton. Hamden, CT: Archon, 1986. 91–117.

Hilton, Nelson. 'Becoming Prolific Being Devoured'. *Studies in Romanticism* 21 (1982): 417–24.

——. *Literal Imagination: Blake's Vision of Words*. Berkeley: University of California Press, 1983.

Linkin, Harriet Kramer. 'The Language of Speakers in *Songs of Innocence and of Experience*'. *Romanticism Past and Present* 10.2 (1986): 5–23.

McGann, Jerome. 'William Blake Illuminates the Truth'. *Critical Studies* 1 (1989): 43–60.

Middleton, Peter. 'The Revolutionary Poetics of William Blake, Part I: The Critical Tradition'. *1789: Reading Writing Revolution*. Ed. Francis Barker et al. Colchester: University of Essex, 1982. 110–18.

——. 'The Revolutionary Poetics of William Blake: Part II – Silence, Syntax, and Spectres'. *Oxford Literary Review* 6 (1983): 35–51.

Miles, Josephine. 'Blake's Frame of Language'. *William Blake: Essays in Honour of Sir Geoffrey Keynes*. Ed. Morton D. Paley and Michael Phillips. Oxford: Clarendon Press, 1973. 86–95.

——. *Eras and Modes in English Poetry*. Berkeley: University of California Press, 1957.

Murray, Robert. 'Blake and the Ideal of Simplicity'. *Studies in Romanticism* 13 (1974): 89–104.

Ostriker, Alicia. *Vision and Verse in William Blake*. Madison: University of Wisconsin Press, 1965.

Ostrom, Hans. 'Blake's Tiriel and the Dramatization of Collapsed Language'. *Papers on Language and Literature* 19 (1983): 167–82.

Santa Cruz Blake Study Group. 'What Type of Blake?' *Essential Articles for the Study of William Blake, 1970–1984*. Ed. Nelson Hilton. Hamden, CT: Archon, 1986. 301–33.

Spector, Sheila A. 'Blake as an Eighteenth-Century Hebraist'. *Blake and His Bibles*. Ed. David V. Erdman. West Cornwall, CT: Locust Hill Press, 1990. 179–229.

Stempel, Daniel. 'Blake, Foucault, and the Classical Episteme'. *PMLA* 96 (1981): 388–407.

Taylor, Ronald Clayton. 'Semantic Structures and the Temporal Modes of Blake's Prophetic Verse'. *Language and Style* 12 (1979): 26–49.

Wolfson, Susan J. 'Blake's Language in Poetic Form'. *The Cambridge Companion to William Blake*. Ed. Morris Eaves. Cambridge: Cambridge University Press, 2003. 63–84.

5
–ᛯᛆᚼᛆ & the play of 'textuality'[1]
nelson hilton

The earliest citation of 'textuality' in the *Oxford English Dictionary* dates from 1836, nine years after Blake's death, when it appears as a synonym for 'textualism' or 'strict adherence to the text, esp. of the Scriptures'. This meaning of the word derives from Latin *textus*, used to denote a biblical passage, and embodies a quite different sense from that of more recent decades which celebrates 'textuality' as 'a weave of signifiers' (Barthes 159). Blake thus never uses and likely never encountered the word – even 'text' appears only once in his writing, and then in a quotation from Gray's *Elegy* ('Many a holy text around she strews') – so discussion of 'textuality' and Blake has an inescapably anachronistic aspect.

References to 'weaving' and its enabling technology of the 'loom', however, do occur with considerable frequency in Blake, usage whose significance comes in the etymological derivation of 'text' from Latin *texere*, 'to weave'.[2] The defining characteristic of 'text' may be seen as the criss-crossing, inter-woven 'warp' and 'woof' of the threads that make it up. Text, literally, holds together by the frictional resistance at each of its myriad intersections, and this latent energy or binding force one may take to be the chief concern of 'textuality'. It follows, then, that 'textuality' disappears when a text is unraveled or analyzed to some lower energy potential 'meaning' or 'point-of-view' or 'interpretation'. Textuality exists while we're in the midst of it.

The intersections of text we may also call 'nodes' or 'knots' – though each is 'tied' only by its own friction and that of the surrounding field. By this token, our subject might also be labeled 'Blake and the play of "nodality" or "knottedness"', terms whose neologistic awkwardness serves to refocus our attention toward the material instantiation of the nodes and knots as words, those 'bits of text' in which some critics find 'the text's irreducible textuality to lie' (Said 104). 'Words' entail the further consideration of the vastly larger text of language, in which a particular node – like the word 'textuality' – can carry different vectors. One can extrapolate the idea of node or knot to the classical Saussurian binary conception of the sign, with its immaterial signified and tangible signifier (S/s) – except that this sign itself immediately collapses, in the triadic model favored by Pierce, into a sign or representation whose meaning (for a necessarily present 'interpretant') we can never perceive (or 'read') in its entirety. For Pierce, the interpretant 'is nothing but another representation to which the torch of truth is handed along; and *as a representation* it has its interpretant again. Lo, another infinite series' (quoted in Sheriff 119). Textuality happens while we're making sense of it.

Consideration of 'Blake and textuality', then, turns on his manifold involvement with the many modes of the sign's operation, the ways of setting alight a signifier (the bright-burning 'Tyger', for instance), and the various ways readers have of making sense of that involvement. His play with words forms an obvious aspect for such consideration, as does his intentional involvement with – and unavoidable implication in – other bibliographic codes which convey significance and participate in the immediate and overall meaning of a text. Examples here include his alternative page arrangements of various copies of a work, his revising, covering up or even gouging out from the plate words or lines so that the text of a given page can vary, and his publishing of copies with widely different inking and coloring schemes.

Other words in our title solicit mention at the outset as well. A 'Blake' who reports that he 'has died Several times Since' his birth hints at the existence of multiple identities, and, in any event, is only 'actually existing in this world now in the various, recalcitrant, and material body of manufactured objects he had a role in producing' (Essick, 'Body' 217). On the back of a drawing for *Job*, he signs himself by the five characters that begin the title of this chapter, an 'auto-icon' that announces a finally unreadable or hieroglyphic or ideogrammic identity.[3] His 'surprisingly extensive experience with seeing plays' (Bentley, *Stranger* 385) might encourage us to view Blake's plates and pages as a theater of text where he staged his multimedia 'Visionary forms dramatic' (*J*98.28, E257). Even though the term was unknown to him, 'textuality' can be seen as the pervasive and enduring subject of his dramatic epic.

Perhaps the most obvious and pervasive aspect of Blake's textual involvement appears in the ongoing curiosity of his punctuation. This idiosyncracy appears full-blown in one of his earliest surviving manuscripts, pages for a prose 'poetical sketch' known by the first five words of its beginning: 'then She bore Pale desire father of Curiosity a Virgin ever young. And after. Leaden Sloth from whom came Ignorance. Who brought forth wonder' (E446). Very much can interest the reader here, not least the 'prose poem' format itself, used for the three concluding pieces in *Poetical Sketches* and evidently Blake's invention. But striking differences between that manuscript and the three published prose poems (which lack manuscript for comparison) appear in the latter's conventional punctuation ('Samson', for example: 'Pensive, alone she sat within the house, when busy day was fading, and calm evening, time for contemplation, rose from the forsaken east, and drew the curtains of the heaven' (E444)). One wonders whether the editorial wrestling by Blake's 'friends' with his punctuation prompts the volume's deprecatory advertisement to be '[c]onscious of the irregularities and defects to be found in almost every page' (E846) and whether such normalizing efforts led to Blake's apparent reluctance to distribute the volume that had been produced on his behalf. As his own printer he clearly didn't adopt any such improvements, and fifty years later the first editor of the *Songs* (1839) no doubt reflects the public impression when he writes that Blake's work suffered from 'inattention to the organizing rules of grammar' (Bentley, *Stranger* 132).

Blake's style of punctuation points up the act of punctuation. The material marks in his own etching can be difficult to determine, as periods turn into commas and exclamation marks buckle into interrogations. Even in the case of seemingly overt alterations, editors of typographic transcriptions – from Gilchrist through those of the Blake Archive – can refuse consistently to read what Blake puts before them, linking in every case, for instance, the exclamation mark in 'AH !SUN-FLOWER' (E25) to the word that precedes it, or eliminating the space that precedes the exclamation mark in:

Ah Sun-flower ! weary of time.

How to transcribe this? which is, how to make sense of this? And if in the usual fashion ('Ah!' [. . .] "Sun-flower!"), how to justify that choice?

'Textuality', as noted at the outset, meant originally 'strict adherence to the text', but if the text in question shows itself to be, on minute examination, undecidable, then the reader/critic is forced into some awareness of her or his participation in the act of interpretation. Just this concern was becoming culturally sensitive on the grandest scale through the project of 'higher criticism', brought to the attention of English readers in the early 1790s by Alexander Geddes. Building on the work of German biblical scholars, Geddes' 'fragment hypothesis' argued that the Bible 'comprised a heterogeneous collection of materials gathered together at different times by different redactors' (McGann 169). This radically new interpretation of the 'ultimate sacred text of the state' (Mee 170) entailed awareness of 'the very corporeality of the written word, tied as it is to the materiality of the book and limited to imperfect means of reproduction' (Green 3.2) and can be seen as authorizing a poetic practice 'predicated on a freedom from any notion of fidelity to the authority of a single, antecedent text' (Mee 164). Equally important, as Molly Anne Rothenberg points out, is Geddes' understanding 'that there can be no access to an original text' (38), given the indeterminancy involved in the evolution of the Masoretic punctuation or added diacritical 'pointing' of the Hebrew text. With the evidence of such 'interpretive mediations', Blake holds with Paine and others 'that what is held up as a disembodied "transcendental authority" [. . .] is actually a function of secular and institutional powers that disguise their own material processes and historical interests' (37) – a function Blake elsewhere lumps together as 'State trick' ('Annotations to Watson', E616). In Steven Goldsmith's characterization, 'Blake self-consciously developed an indeterminate text in response to the new scholarship that was demonstrating the historicized, heterogeneous, and ideological nature of the redacted Bible' (138). Textuality's power of inscription subsumes the Scriptures.

Texts arise in a system for their creation and publication – what Blake calls at one point 'the method in which knowledge is transmitted from generation to generation' (*MHH*, E40). This system, with its material and ideological components, involves a division of labor and accompanying standardization. In order to function, the system has built into it a certain amount of 'play', or space for the negotiation of difference as the text crosses from one level of organization or existence to another. A manuscript, for instance, might be block letters or script, single or double spaced, or punctuated unconventionally, but usually each step towards publication involves some regularization in the progression toward a printed artifact whose ideal is transparency – as if its material nature would finally fall away in the delivery of its purely ideational content. An artist with each material transformation to hand, like Blake, might however choose to maximize the degree of play at every juncture and end up with an artifact counter to the usual and expected and serving to put in focus such immaterial expectations.

As a true artist, Blake's defining preoccupation concerns the expressive potentials of his materials and the bounds on their utilization. Such potentials include, in the case of words, lettering, shape, sound, contemporary and historical usage, etymology, as well as associations capable of activation by letters and sound: homonyms, homophones, paronomasias, puns, rhymes, idiosyncratic associations. Not, of course, that all or most of these are or could be in play at any given instance. Consider for example this line from *The Book of Thel*, where the heroine has wandered 'in the land of clouds', 'listening to the voices of the ground': 'Till to her own grave plot she came, & there she sat down' (6.9, E6). First of all, we have the larger form of the line, of a piece with the poem's septenary meter that continually in the background evokes disconcerting associations to older English and translated epics. Then there is the echo of Psalm 137: 'By the waters of Babylon, *there we sat down*, yea, we wept, when we remembered Zion'. Finally, the 'grave plot', the arrival at which occasions the poem's denouement. The narrative anomaly of a young, vigorous female virgin in eighteenth-century England having a pre-assigned 'grave plot' highlights that collocation and may solicit ruminations on sudden narcissistic self-consciousness (the realization that one has become a victim of one's own machinations or 'plot') or on the existence of the work itself ('Thel') personified as an idea coming to view in Blake's brain as the 'ground' and plot of plate waiting to be etched, if not 'graved'.

Perhaps the earliest consideration of Blake and textuality (in the sense we now associate with the word) is Peggy Meyer Sherry's 1978 essay, 'The "Predicament" of the Autograph: "William Blake"', which appeared in the standard-bearer for American deconstruction, *Glyph*. Sherry's piece begins, in its first epigraph from Jacques Derrida, and concludes with reference to the talismanic term – textuality – and the riddle it represents as 'the place of crossing (topical as well as tropic) of the intrinsic and the extrinsic' (131). Sherry takes as her text the drawing and inscription known as 'Blake's Autograph' (E698). The quotation marks around the word 'predicament' point up that the precarious state of the self-inscription she glosses concerns its predication or assertion of an auto-grapher, 'Willam Blake'. Such an assertion is inherently at risk given awareness of the signature's sign nature (Sherry emphasizes 'Blake's sense of the signifying process' (143)), but triply so when Blake's writing itself highlights an image, doubts that 'an Artist can write an Autograph', and announces its 'Predicament' of being 'in some measure [a] work of Art & not of Nature or Chance' (that is, not the spontaneous gesture associated with an autograph). Sherry sees here Blake's 'suggesting that the system of difference in which his own nature inscribes itself is incapable of immediacy' (136).

The conjunction of word and image in the 'autograph' asserts the dynamic relation between the two which forms a particular characteristic of Blake's illuminated work. Blake's text includes graphic designs with its verbal signs. Interacting with their interaction – not just in a particular instance but often through alternative and analogous iterations – is a major requirement for Blake's reader.[4] Sometimes the interaction reflects a kind of supplemental gloss, like the tiny, profiled sweeper in the title of 'The Chimney Sweeper' in *Songs of Innocence* (E10), and sometimes almost decorative ornamentation,[5] as in that same poem's text where smoke streaming from the 'l' of 'little Tom Dacre' underscores his connection to our chimneys.

The version in *Songs of Experience* (E22–3) then recalls the earlier one not only by its title, but through the closer image of the sweeper, now in three-quarters view. Design can exert a major impact on our overall reading, however, if we carry over the chimney-smoke motif and here see the entire text as written on a smoke/thought bubble that emerges from a cozy cottage just down the lane from our window pane on the split scene.

The whole design thus becomes a kind of bi-stable image, like the title page of *Thel*,[6] in which, depending on our point-of-view, we attribute 'I' to the (exceptionally sophisticated) sweep or to some hypocritical liberal, writing from the comfort of his 'tent of prosperity' (see *FZ*35.11 ff.) and with whom we, in our glassed-in safety, are complicit.

'Textuality' arrived fully as a Blakean concern with a 1982 conference at University of California Santa Cruz, many of whose contributions were collected four years later in *Unnam'd Forms: Blake and Textuality*, and then with my *Literal Imagination: Blake's Vision of Words* (1983). The latter commemorates, in part, a most direct contact with Blakean textuality which occurred one grey London November afternoon in 1977 when, having struggled through forty-two inky-black lines of *Jerusalem*, copy A, plate 21, I stumbled in the midst of Albion's despair over the fate of his Children:

> I see them die beneath the whips of the Captains! they are taken
> In solemn pomp into Chaldea across the bredths of Europe
> Six months they lie embalmd in Silent death: warshipped
> Carried in Arks of Oak before the armies in the spring
> Bursting their Arks they rise again to life: they play before
> The Armies: I hear their loud cymbals & their deadly cries.
>
> (21.42–7, E167)

Realizing that 'warshipped' didn't appear elsewhere in Blake in any form, I soon confirmed its utter absence from the *OED* – the frequency of 'shipped' notwithstanding – yet there it lay, an emphatically undecidable *o/a* that powerfully sutures two highly disparate but meaningful frames of reference. The paradox of 'Blakean textuality' for me is that I never felt as close, as much 'in the presence of' the author as at that moment. In the phase-change of that pulsation of an artery, my sense of Blake started forth as a 'Revelation in the Litteral expression'. Nearly thirty years on, it seems a bit fantastical, and I am made uneasy by the experience of truly learned critics now seen as having been transported by their own projections. But when one reads, later in *Jerusalem*, of the thousands 'carried away [. . .] in ships closd up: / Chaind hand & foot, compelld to fight under the iron whips / Of our captains' (*J*65.33–6, E216–7), the neologism of 'warshipped' seems more than possible.

Other manifestations appeared. 'London' showed an acrostic in the initial letters of its third stanza which seemed to have hidden in plain sight for 180 years the self-enacting parable of a sense-enjambing written injunction to attend to the audible:

'I hear' – do you 'H. . ./E. . ./A. . ./R. . .'?[7] Such vertical organization was clearly pertinent to an author who took care to emphasize, by alignment, distinction between capitalization and lower-case: 'eternity :/ [. . .]Eternity ./' (*BU*20.1–2, E80). The implied author of *The Book of Urizen* hyphenates a reference to his metal plates to disclose his text as 'I in books formd of me-' (4.24, E72) while another orients a title-page by spatial arrangement and a flourish to suggest the scandalous possible of not one, but multiple marriages of Heaven and Hell (cf. Tolley):

'Los' becomes obviously Loss, our profit; Golgonooza, more complexly, remixes λογον ζωης ('logon zooas'), the 'living word' or 'animated' or 'energetic' that seems the life-blood of Al-bionic man.

Even before the Santa Cruz conference, from the mid-1960s through the 1970s, critics had noted Blake's 'flexible or multiple exploration of the word' (Rose 120), his 'varied verbal manipulations, which include puns or plays on words, continual yoking of two unlike words [. . .] and ultimately a vast, seemingly endless equation of nouns and adjectives' (Gleckner, *Verbal Techniquue* 330), an 'exploration of etymology [which] owes [. . .] much to his conviction that wisdom comes from penetrating to the inner workings of phenomena' (Kroeber 349); and that 'apart from Spenser and Shakespeare there have been few writers in our language more verbally inventive than Blake' (Nelson 175) given his 'almost Joycean awareness of the manipulability of words' (Damrosch 70). With the advent of deconstruction and its 'teasing out the warring forces of signification' (Johnson 5) and reveling in 'the galaxy of signifiers' (Barthes), Blake's words were ready for the road of excess. Indeed, arch-deconstructor Paul de Man was reportedly of the opinion that 'Blake's privileging of writing makes him less interesting to deconstruction, because it makes his work less resistant to its strategies' (Mitchell 91).

Blake's awareness of the arbitary nature of the signifier appears almost at the beginning of his career. Chapter 3 of ['An Island in the Moon'] (1784–85) revolves around an extended discussion of the question 'who was Phebus[?]' After one answer, which invokes ancient sacrifice and the rhetorical aside that 'you have read about that in the bible', the character 'Aradobo' agrees, 'I thought I had read of Phebus in the Bible'. 'Tilly Lally' laughs, 'Ha Ha Ha he means Pharoah', and 'Mrs. Sigtagatist', interjects, 'I am ashamed of you making use of the names in the Bible'. To which Tilly Lally responds with an 'ad nomine' attack, 'Ill tell you what Mrs Sinagain I don't think theres any harm in it'. The conclusion of the discussion seems voiced by 'the Pythagorean', who opines, 'Hang names [. . .] whats Pharaoh better than Phebus or Phebus than Pharaoh', only to be trumped by Blake's avatar, 'Quid the Cynic', 'hang them both' (E452).

Such play with names represents a fundamental aspect of Blake's textual awareness. 'Tilly Lally', for instance, seems to suggest the old English expression for nonsense 'tilly vally' (q.v. *OED*), and his epithet as 'the Siptippidist' might indicate a penchant to sip a tipple ('O ay', he says later when given a 'Rum & water'). One method of playing with names appears explicitly when 'Scopprell took up a book & read <the following passage.>': 'An Easy of [*Human*] <Huming> Understanding by John Lookye Gent John Locke said Obtuse Angle. O ay Lock. Said Scopprell' (E456). The choice of Locke's *Essay* (and the invocation of Hume's *Treatise concerning Human Nature*) here seems hardly fortuitous, given that philosopher's role in popularizing the notion of the 'arbitrary imposition' (3.2.8) that constitutes a word and its consequences for our understanding of words as 'the *Medium* by which we understand' (3.9.21). Some twenty-five years later, encountering the regret of Joshua Reynolds that 'our judgement upon an airy nothing [. . .] is called by the same name [that is, "taste"] which we give [. . .] to works which are only to be produced by the greatest efforts of the human understanding', but that 'we are obliged to take words as we find them' (quoted in Essick, *Language* 45), Blake, perhaps prompted by the reference to 'human understanding' writes, passionately but not much to the point: 'This is False the Fault is not in Words, but in Things Locke's Opinions of Words & their Fallaciousness are Artful Opinions & Fallacious also' (E659).

The aspect of textuality as physical, neural/mental inscription can lead us to ponder why Blake comes up here with the term 'fallaciousness', when Locke never uses that term in connection with words and, indeed, 'fallacious' only once in an oblique reference to them.[8] Considering also that, as Paul Yoder points out, 'Locke's understanding of language is finally not very different from Blake's', one begins to suspect that Blake, influenced perhaps by Milton's example, is caught up in alliterative play ('False [. . .] Fault [. . .] Fallacious'), diacope ('Opinions [. . .] Opinions'), and contorted allusion to *Julius Caesar* I.ii.140–1 (reading 'words' for 'our Stars') to enact Locke's opinion concerning the 'fault' of figurative language. Given Blake's related opinion that 'Mental Things are alone Real' and 'what is Calld Corporeal [. . .] is in Fallacy' (*VLJ*, E565), we might see him as moving to an idiosyncratic – 'mystical', some might say – notion of the sign to which he, as 'a Mental Prince', has particular access. Foremost, though, the annotation makes for wonderful textual theater as Blake sets out his vehemence in a marginal text which envelopes its occasion and suggests the possibility that the annotations function rhetorically rather than declaratively (see Rothenberg 87).

Unnam'd Forms: Blake and Textuality (1986), the first of two books that name 'textuality' as a concern with Blake, has a contributor denouncing the topic at the outset as one that has 'by now long since been installed in the Urizenic pantheon' and 'a dyscourse that has successfully put play to work supporting its own economy' (Mann 67). But the collection has been characterized even recently as presenting the 'significant resistance in Blake's textuality to any form of easy distillation' (Pierce, *Wond'rous Art* 12). The editors begin with the assertion that 'Blake literally took more care with the writing of his writing than any other author in our canons' and so appropriate for Blake Derrida's description of Hegel as 'the last poet of the Book and the first poet of writing' (4). Or, they suggest, 'let us call Blake the first epic poet of "print consciousness" – and hence "media consciousness"' or awareness of physical textuality which culminates 'the century of English satire against the economy and culture of print that begins with *A Tale of a Tub* and continues through *The Dunciad* and *Tristram Shandy*' (4). The title of the collection derives from the 'Printing House in Hell' episode in *The Marriage of Heaven and Hell*, where the next-to-last chamber presents 'Unnam'd forms, which cast the metals into the expanse' (E40). That 'these anonymous *forms* suggest, on one level, the printers' "bodies of type, secured in a chase, for printing" (*OED*)' makes them like 'unnamed signifiers' that 'exist only to cast what they have to tell "into the expanse"', where the transmission 'took the forms of books & were arranged in libraries' (4–5). While 'books' and 'libraries' may be identifiable entities, the editors would suggest, 'textuality' and 'Blake' are states more difficult to process.

Stephen Leo Carr's discussion of 'Illuminated Printing: Toward a Logic of Difference' emphasizes the material differences 'set into play by technical processes of writing, printing, and coloring whose effects are never perfectly determinable [and] continually open to new possibilities of meaning that are articulated as individual variants' (186–7). Highlighting the 'verbal-visual exchanges' that Blake creates, Carr cites variations in the appearance of the guiding figure in 'The Little Boy lost' as Christ-like or as 'distinctively feminine' (193) to suggest that now with access to the various versions, we face 'an ongoing, open-ended production of meanings rather than a representation of an original meaning' (190). Saree Makdisi, writing in 2003, finds that through such variations Blake 'literalizes' a principle of reading: that '[w]henever a text of whatever kind is cycled through – read in – different contexts, its meaning changes' (169).

Robert Essick's essay, 'How Blake's Body Means', develops the crucial caveat that 'the implied concept of "text"' – and hence, textuality – for most students of Blake bears little resemblance to that held by bibliophiles, editorial scholars, and print connoisseurs. 'Most people who write on Blake are English teachers', he notes, and not much interested in variations with 'low iconic yield' that cannot be interpreted as verbal text. But for Essick, the colors, textures, white-line hatchings, ink droplets, and brush strokes constitute the textual bed-rock which 'signifies its own material presence [. . .] physically inscribed with its history of production' (212, fn.) and so 'incarnates' Blake's body. Collecting the scattered portions of this body has become a major activity for Essick and his co-editors of the online Blake Archive. In *William Blake and the Language of Adam*, three years later (1989), Essick does not discuss textuality *per se*, but sets out most effectively 'to situate Blake within the history of language theory and to generate a hermeneutic on the basis of that history' (2).

Another enduring essay from *Unnam'd Forms* is V.A. De Luca's '"A Wall of Words": The Sublime as Text'. De Luca concentrates on 'those elements of Blake's text that tend to withdraw from referential function altogether' (218), passages where 'the text becomes iconic', or more to be seen than read easily. *Jerusalem*, pl. 16 offers an example:

And the Thirty-six Counties of Scotland, divided in the Gates
Of Reuben Kincard Haddntn Forfar, Simeon Ayr Argyll Banff
Levi Edinburh Roxbro Ross. Judah, Abrdeen Berwik Dumfries
Dan Bute Caitnes Clakmanan. Napthali Nairn Invernes Linlithgo
Gad Peebles Perth Renfru. Asher Sutherlan Sterling Wigtoun
Issachar Selkirk Dumbartn Glasgo. Zebulun Orkney Shetland Skye
Joseph Elgin Lanerk Kinros. Benjamin Kromarty Murra Kirkubriht
Governing all by the sweet delights of secret amorous glances
In Enitharmons Halls builded by Los & his mighty Children.

(52–60, E160–1)

though the typeface fails to do justice to Blake's cliff:

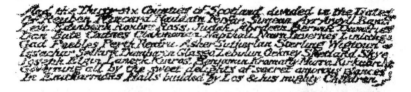

Such a 'wall of words', De Luca argues, offers a corollary to Romantic sublime natural objects, like steep and lofty cliffs, and the accompanying three-fold experience of encounter, then 'an episode of discontinuity (usually described as vertigo or blockage or bafflement)', and then a sudden break-through. Reminding us that 'the Sublime' begins as a rhetorical trope, he invokes Blake's celebrated description of his own work as a 'Sublime Allegory' and his further comment that such 'Allegory addressed to the Intellectual powers while it is altogether hidden from the Corporeal Understanding is My Definition of the Most Sublime Poetry' (E730). De Luca points to four specific devices in Blake's late works which effect the sublime experience and address 'the Intellectual powers': first, 'visual illustrations, often occupying a block of half a plate or larger'; second, a 'density of inscription to the point of visual strain'; third, a 'regular, periodic repetition of words and phrases'; and finally and most powerfully, 'the massive proliferation of proper names' (231–5, *passim*). Considering all these effects, De Luca concludes that '[a] critique of Blake's sublime and an exposition of textuality's role in his work come, then, to much the same thing' (240). He notes further that while the terminology of deconstruction, 'with its imagery of blocks, gaps, abysses, labyrinths, deferrals', is 'itself a sublime rhetoric', Blake would see this vocabulary as stuck in the second, 'intermediate or deprivative phase of the sublime moment without a promise of the fulfillment that makes the sublime worth its name'. 'For Blake', he concludes, 'Presence is available, and the transcendental subject exists; these are in fact the cornerstones of his faith' (240–1).

In an impressive book-length expansion of this essay five years later, *Words of Eternity: Blake and the Poetics of the Sublime*, De Luca recharacterizes Blake's goal in *Jerusalem* as the creation of a 'counter-sublime, the reification of a visionary textuality' (134). This textuality, as an ideal posited by and working to determine the poem's total form, 'refers to the sum of the resources of language available to make the operations of intellect visible and determinate [. . .] the sum of the conditions of ordering that make meaning possible' (134–5). Hence De Luca sees the longer poems as moving 'to culminations in which the poetic setting is ever more explicitly presented as virtually indistinguishable from a universe of textuality' (216).

Unnam'd Forms also previews Donald Ault's remarkable and monumental consideration of *The Four Zoas*, published the following year as *Narrative Unbound*. Blake's long manuscript poem offers a kind of delirium for textual editors in its many insertions, additions, erasures, overwriting, and revisions, not the least of which is the strike-through of the carefully calligraphed title, *Vala*, for the late scribbled addition. A sense of the torments or delights occasioned by 'Blake's elaborate, even obsessive, processes of composition and revision' (Ault, *Narrative* xii) appears in the much-revised opening lines, best consulted typographically in Bentley's edition:

[The Song of the Aged Mother] which shook the heavens with wrath   1 [[1]]
[*Hearing the march of long resounding strong heroic Verse*   2
[*Marshalld in order for the day of Intellectual Battle*]   3
                     [was]
The heavens *shall* quake. The earth *shall* move[d] & shudder[d]
                          & the mountains   6
With all their woods, the streams & valleys: wail[d] in dismal fear   7
[[[*Hearing*]]] [[[*march*]]]
[[*To hear the Sound of Long resounding strong heroic verse*   4 [[2]]
[[*Marshalld in order for the day of intellectual battle*]]   5 [[3]]

Four Mighty Ones are in Every Man: a Perfect Unity John XVII c. 21 & 22 & 23 v [[4]]
Cannot Exist. But from the Universal Brotherhood of Eden   John I c. 14 v
The Universal Man. To Whom be Glory Evermore Amen   και εσκηνωζεν εν ημιν

Apropos of the reference to the earthly non-availability of 'Unity', Ault comments that 'the very possibility of the poem's existing as a coherent, closed totality is a fundamental problem' that the poem addresses (xiii). Ault argues, counter-intuitively and much against then received opinion, that far from presenting an abortive or unfinished work,

the textuality of *The Four Zoas* challenges cherished assumptions concerning what in fact a text is. In its naked presentation of the traces of its struggle to be (re)composed, *The Four Zoas* pushes to the foreground the productive labor of its writing: it is a text that insists on its own radical heterogeneity, on its own struggle to be different from itself, indeed, ultimately on its process of eradicating a potentially unitary textual 'self' from which 'it' could 'differ'. (xiii)

Ault details, at remarkable length and with deft sensitivity to verbal repetitions, what he sees as 'the irreducible presence of multiple interfering and incommensurable structures that operate (1) to rule out a pre-existent underlying world that surface events (i.e., those narrated by the linear text) partially rearrange and partially distort, and (2) to generate a narrative field in which the past is not closed and complete but open – unfinished and revisable' ('Re-Visioning' 108–9). Regarding the notoriously difficult narrative, with its thirteen-some varying accounts of an originating Fall and also the inconsequential and various 'Last Judgments' (not to mention its complex inter-textual relationship with Blake's designs for Edward Young's tediously Christian *Night Thoughts*), Ault finds that

> Blake experiments with creating a text that cannot question its authentic existence independent of and prior to the narrative world in the process of being constituted through sequential acts of reading, thereby creating a reader whose perception is able to alter the very being of the text's supposedly fixed facts and devising a narrative world that, although it comes into existence temporally through the mutual interconstitution of reader and text, functions as the primary agent by which reader and text are able to transform one another mutually. (109)

Ault's approach is enhanced and applied further in Fred Dortort's 1998 'contrary reading' of *Jerusalem, The Dialectic of Vision*. The book's introduction offers a succinct presentation of a 'methodology' based on four 'covert narratological strategies' Ault discovered and which can function as 'organizing principles' (36–7). 'Perspective transformation', the first, 'requires a variance or conflict between two different but closely related events as experienced by the reader' (27); in this case the second appearance 'cancels the validity of the first', and so subverts the expected reading experience (for example, J6.1–2 and 17.55–7, which present conflicting accounts of the 'Sons of Albion' and their involvement with Los's division from his Spectre). Adept readers who grasp this effect will be able to attempt to discover 'narratological implications behind the discrepant versions' (28). A second process, 'aspectual interconnection, takes place when details migrate from inside a speech by a character into the narrative proper', so to reveal an interpenetration of narrator, characters, and landscape. Dortort instances J11.15, 'in the Cliffs of Albion', where we cannot determine 'whether the cliffs belong to Albion, or, in fact, are Albion' (29). A third process, 'nodal interference', occurs 'in sections of the text that may seem fundamentally organized at multiple cross-purposes', like the 'obsessively detailed descriptions' of Golgonooza in *Jerusalem*, pl. 13, which resist integration with the rest of the text. The fourth stratagem, 'termed by Ault Blake's most powerful method', is 'perspective analysis', whose effects come about only as readers become aware of its presence (32). It is perhaps 'most powerful' because available only to those experienced in the ways of the first three methods and so ready to contemplate the prospect of a *Jerusalem* not 'fundamentally indeterminate' (Rothenberg 70) but 'of intimidating intricacy' (33), an 'extraordinarily precise structure, organized to the most minute detail, and as such almost closed to scrutiny' (29). Such incommensurable conceptions of Blake's textuality tempt one to invoke Blake's comment that 'I am Mad or Else you are so both of us cannot be in our right senses Posterity will judge by our words' (E573).

Blake's iconizing of language was developed further in 1986 with W.J.T. Mitchell's 'Visible Language: Blake's Wond'rous Art of Writing', which focused on Blake's 'tendency to treat writing and printing as media capable of full presence, not as mere supplements to speech' (51). Furthermore, Mitchell contends that Blake's commitment to make language visible 'is also designed to undo certain oppositions within the world of textuality, most notably the gap between the pictorial and the linguistic use of graphic figures' (62). In the 'Questions and Answers' section appended to the essay Mitchell makes a key observation for the trajectory of this discussion in his observation that '"writing" is Derrida's name not just for inscription in the narrow sense, but for the possibility of semiosis' (87). Blake's works, then, 'exaggerate what Derrida argues are the traits and processes underlying all forms of writing, making them stand out more' (Makdisi 188).

A scant seven years after *Blake and Textuality*, the dedicated student could consider *Rethinking Blake's Textuality*. Somewhat like De Luca, Molly Anne Rothenberg sees, especially in *Jerusalem*, '[t]he value of textuality as an ideal' which has the 'potentially to disrupt *momentarily*' one 'signifying network' so that 'another can take its place' (132). While Rothenberg sees Blake's 'poststructuralist critics' posit 'textuality' as 'an ultimate value' or 'telos to be realized', she finds it rather 'an idealization with a double valence' (129), both aspects of which are finally illusory. 'The horizon of free play can never be realized as such', she summarizes, 'but can only appear as a function of the inevitably incomplete totalization of any system' (129). The attentive reader is returned to her own role in making sense of the text, finally to realize that in Blake's textual 'gymnasiums for the mind' (W.J.T. Mitchell's phrase) utterances 'function rhetorically rather than declaratively' (87). Having addressed successfully or teasingly the reader's 'intellectual powers', the text falls away, like a gantry when launch is imminent, only to reappear when, as always, the event misfires.

An important new note here is Rothenberg's sense of Blake as a willful rhetorician – a text technician – using and combining textual strategies, like a consummate deconstructionist, to reject the 'transcendent position from which meaning derives and truth can be guaranteed' (67). This rejection is epitomized in Milton's saying to Satan, with several allusions to *Paradise Lost*, that he knows his power 'thee to annihilate / And be a greater in thy place [. . .] / A covering for thee', but that since such victory would be only 'till one greater comes / And smites me as I smote thee & becomes my covering', he will not perpetuate the same dull round and instead 'come to Self Annihilation' (38[43]29 ff., E139). The perspectival irony here, which exemplifies Rothenberg's argument and reminds us of De Luca's third category of sublime effects, comes several plates on, as Milton unleashes full rhetorical firepower to enumerate all that 'in Self-annihilation & the grandeur of Inspiration' he comes 'To cast off [. . .]/ To cast off [. . .]/ To cast off [. . .]/ To take off [. . .]/ To cast aside [. . .]' (E142). That there is no zealot like the recently converted can't come as a surprise to all, and the poem's repeated punning evocation of (having a) 'Wild Thyme' and (going on a) 'Lark' emblematize how the text here again harkens back to the author's interest in 'making a fool of the reader' (E453) and our desire for absolute resolutions.

Rothenberg's greatest contribution comes with her situating of Blakean textuality in a context of political activity. For her, textual practice cannot be considered without reference to 'hegemony', the powerful ensemble of cultural relationships that produce – continuously, ubiquitously – 'mind forg'd manacles'. Blake's struggle to 'out' this power is expressed in his ongoing concern for 'the subversion of metaphysical presuppositions, the constitution of subjectivity, the ideological mediations that shape forms of consciousness, the nature of semiosis, and the relationship between systematicity and social tyranny' (1). For Rothenberg, Blake's affirmation 'that perception *could not take place* without the prior mediation of ideologically constituted interpretations – in effect, that all perception traces the lineaments of its constitutive ideological assumptions – provides the key to Blakean textuality' (37). To attend to the material signifiers entails an encountering of 'the act of perception in its double nature' (47): an 'experience of the already interpreted' – a smooth sense-making of what we read – and, 'on the other hand, and at the same time', an 'experience of the pressure-to-interpret provoked by the excess of potentiality of meaning' which arises with the other reading. Using her own experience as a model, she reports:

> When I read a Blakean text, I do not find counter truths that correct my erroneous thinking, but I do meet at every turn my own rage for determinacy, my own strategies for rigidifying what is inherently fluid, my own need to impose order and to dominate, my own desire for the very transcendent guarantees that legitimate tyrannies. Most importantly, however, I learn that I cannot read, cannot perceive, cannot conceive my own subjectivity *without* precisely those desires, those practices, those strategies. To be human, I must produce and devour the text, the world, myself, again and again. (45–6)

One recalls Edward Larrissy's comment that 'what you "enjoy" is inseparable from the activity of *reading the poem*' (156) – playing with Blake's textuality, working out in the mental gym. To partake of this textual joy, one must relish 'an ongoing reading [. . .] essentially incompatible with the straightforward linear sense of time, and indeed the very habits of reading, to which we have been generally conditioned' (Makdisi 164).

Two books published in 2003 offer the latest reports on 'Blake and Textuality'. John Pierce's *The Wond'rous Art: William Blake and Writing* studies Blake's 'self-conscious presentation of writing' as a thematic concern, as a formal category differentiated from speech, and as a theoretical construct, much inflected by Derridean criticism. Pierce offers a version of *Vala, or The Four Zoas* quite distinct from Ault's as he stresses the 'contingent nature' of a poem which generates 'a proliferation of critical interpretations as assorted layers are arranged to support, refute, or complicate an understanding of the textual site' (117, 129). His reference to 'site' connects to an 'archeological' approach which sees in Blake's *MIL/TON* (as some would represent the poem's fractured name[9]) its eponym 'rewritten not as a singular form with a singular site of intentions, but as a series of discursive fields' (150). Pierce situates Blake's writing 'within the revisionary tendencies of manuscript culture' and concludes that '[w]hat might appear as apparent flaws from the perspective of print culture enrich the overall textuality of Blake's writing' (157).

Saree Makdisi's *The Impossible History*, by contrast, sees Blake's work more as a mode of production which illuminates printing as the epitome of mass production 'at precisely the historical moment when manufacturers' were reorienting everything towards that end (201). So, '[t]he disruption of identity precisely through the process of repeatability may be exactly what is significant about the illuminated books as a mode of production' (199). Blake's textuality thus embodies his 'tinkering with and disrupting the core ideologies' (202) of an economy, in Blake's allusion to Adam Smith, 'No more / To be swayed by visible hand' (*The French Revolution*, 4–5, E286).

Discussion of 'textuality' could not be complete without mention of its subsequently formulated superset, 'intertextuality', which spans a gamut from the specific (or unconscious) references of allusion to wide-reaching transpositions in discourse like those seen by Makdisi. The presence of allusion in Blake offers a particularly complex field, as the scholarly consensus seems to be that Blake's cortex was inscribed so profoundly with certain core texts – the Bible, Milton, Shakespeare, Michelangelo, for starters – that it can be impossible to tell if an apparent verbal or visual echo carries an allusion that is 'significant', 'contextual', or entirely idiosyncratic (see Gleckner, *Blake's Prelude*). A revealing exercise can be to take an interesting phrase in Blake (for example, 'perilous path', 'Daughters of Albion') and search against it in a database of English literature. Consistently pursued, such practice will lead not only through the canon, but to curious byways of forgotten literature (translations not least). There is no easy way to begin searching out graphic allusions.

In 1986 the Santa Cruz Blake Study Group concluded its discussion of the limitations of reading Blake in a typographic edition with the vision of a future in which students would examine the illuminated books and manuscript materials on 'high-resolution screens, comparing variants in split-screen images, jumping instantly from plate to plate and copy to copy, having access to images of all the works without having to travel to the various collections' (330). The Blake Archive (www.blakearchive. org) today offers much of this capability for an impressive selection of works, various copies, and related materials. But even as the Archive's pages seem poised to realize the ultimate curatorial virtualization of a one-stop gallery, one can foresee Blake's textual energies 'Bursting their Arks they rise again to life: they play' (J21.46, E167). Students of the new digital age will be able to run the static copies into living forms of difference and to formulate database structures that help our visualization of his remarkable verbal and graphic associations. Textuality, with the study of semiotics which it borders, will probably merge into the growing domain of cognitive science and, like 'Reason or the ratio of all we have already known', show that it 'is not the same that it shall be when we know more' (E2).

notes

1. Alternatively: 'Blake and the Play of Textuality'.
2. On the pertinence of this metaphor to contemporary 'textuality's purveyor, see 'Deconstruction and Weaving' by Catherine Rooney. Peggy Sherry notes that 'the written text often figures in metaphors of warp and woof in both early and late Blake' (152).
3. The design is reproduced from Erdman's tracing of an inscription on design XIV of *Job* (Fitzwilliam Museum) in David V. Erdman, ed., *The Complete Poetry and Prose of William Blake*, E688.
4. This difficulty cannot be underestimated – though as Charles Bernstein asks recently, 'who among us has not secretly read our paperback, graphics-expurgated Blake with the glee of a schoolchild high on Cliff Notes, even after many professions of born-again faith in the only truth of his visualized hypermedia?' (182).
5. The best treatment of Blake's interlinear effects is Erdman et al., 'Reading the Illuminations of Blake's *Marriage of Heaven and Hell*'.
6. See Hilton, 'Blake's Early Works', 197.
7. 'Blake wants a writing that will make us see with our ears and hear with our eyes because he wants to transform us into revolutionary readers, to deliver us from the notion that history is a closed book to be taken in one "sense"' (Mitchell 86).
8. Locke criticizes 'subtlety' as 'consisting for the most part in nothing but the fallacious and illusory use of obscure or deceitful terms' (*Essay Concerning Human Understanding* 3.11.5).
9. See Thomas Vogler, 'Re: Naming *MIL/TON*'.

works cited and suggestions for further reading

Ault, Donald. *Narrative Unbound: Re-Visioning William Blake's The Four Zoas*. Barrytown: Station Hill Press, 1987.

——. 'Re-Visioning *The Four Zoas*' in *Unnam'd Forms: Blake and Textuality*. Ed. Nelson Hilton and Thomas A. Vogler. Berkeley: University of California Press, 1986. 105–40.

Barthes, Roland. *Image Music Text*. Trans. Stephen Heath. New York: Hill and Wang, 1977.

Bentley, G.E. Jr. *The Stranger from Paradise: A Biography of William Blake*. New Haven: Yale University Press, 2001.

——. *Vala; or, The four zoas. A facsimile of the manuscript, a transcript of the poem, and a study of its growth and significance*. Oxford: Clarendon, 1963.

Bernstein, Charles. 'Response: Every Which Way but Loose' in *Reimagining Textuality: Textual Studies in the Late Age of Print*. Ed. Elizabeth Bergmann Loizeaux and Neil Fraistat. Madison: University of Wisconsin Press, 2002. 178–85.

Carr, Stephen Leo. 'Illuminated Printing: Toward a Logic of Difference' in *Unnam'd Forms: Blake and Textuality*. Ed. Nelson Hilton and Thomas A. Vogler. Berkeley: University of California Press, 1986. 177–96.

Damrosch, Leopold, Jr. *Symbol and Truth in Blake's Myth*. Princeton: Princeton University Press, 1980.

104 palgrave advances in william blake studies

De Luca, Vincent Arthur. 'A Wall of Words: The Sublime as Text' in *Unnam'd Forms: Blake and Textuality*. Ed. Nelson Hilton and Thomas A. Vogler. Berkeley: University of California Press, 1986. 218–41.

——. *Words of Eternity: Blake and the Poetics of the Sublime*. Princeton: Princeton University Press, 1991.

Dortort, Fred. *The Dialectic of Vision: A Contrary Reading of Jerusalem*. Barrytown: Station Hill Arts, 1998.

Erdman, David V., with Tom Dargan and Marlene Deverell-Van Meter. 'Reading the Illuminations of Blake's *Marriage of Heaven and Hell*' in *William Blake: Essays in Honour of Sir Geoffrey Keynes*. Ed. Morton D. Paley and Michael Phillips. Oxford: Clarendon, 1973. 162–207.

Essick, Robert N. 'How Blake's Body Means' in *Unnam'd Forms: Blake and Textuality*. Ed. Nelson Hilton and Thomas A. Vogler. Berkeley: University of California Press, 1986. 197–217.

——. *William Blake and the Language of Adam*. Oxford: Clarendon Press, 1989.

Gleckner, Robert F. *Blake's Prelude: Poetical Sketches*. Baltimore: Johns Hopkins University Press, 1982.

——. 'Blake's Verbal Technique' in *William Blake: Essays for S. Foster Damon*. Ed. Alvin H. Rosenfeld. Providence: Brown University Press, 1969.

Goldsmith, Steven. *Unbuilding Jerusalem: Apocalypse and Romantic Representation*. Ithaca: Cornell University Press, 1993.

Green, Matthew. 'Visionary Materialism in Early Works of William Blake: The Intersection of Enthusiasm and Empiricism', unpublished m.s.

Hilton, Nelson. 'Blake's Early Works' in *The Cambridge Companion to Blake*. Ed. Morris Eaves. Cambridge, Cambridge University Press, 2002. 191–209.

——. *Essential Articles for the Study of William Blake, 1970–1984*. Hamden: Archon Books, 1986.

——. *Literal Imagination: Blake's Vision of Words*. Berkeley: University of California Press, 1983.

Johnson, Barbara. *The Critical Difference: Essays in the Contemporary Rhetoric of Reading*. Baltimore: Johns Hopkins University Press, 1980.

Kroeber, Karl. 'Delivering *Jerusalem*' in *Blake's Sublime Allegory: Essays on The Four Zoas, Milton, and Jerusalem*. Ed. Stuart Curran and J.A. Wittreich. Madison: University of Wisconsin Press, 1973.

Larrissy, Edward. *William Blake. Rereading Literature*. Oxford: Blackwell, 1985.

Lundeen, Kathleen. *Knight of the Living Dead: William Blake and the Problem of Ontology*. Selinsgrove: Susquehanna University Press, 2000.

Makdisi, Saree. *William Blake and the Impossible History of the 1790s*. Chicago: University of Chicago Press, 2003.

Mann, Paul. '*The Book of Urizen* and the Horizon of the Book' in *Unnam'd Forms: Blake and Textuality*. Ed. Nelson Hilton and Thomas A. Vogler. Berkeley: University of California Press, 1986. 49–68.

McGann, Jerome J. 'The Idea of an Indeterminate Text: Blake's Bible of Hell and Dr. Alexander Geddes'. *Studies in Romanticism* 25 (3) (Fall 1986): 303–24.

Mee, Jon. *Dangerous Enthusiasm: William Blake and the Culture of Radicalism in the 1790s*. Oxford: Clarendon Press, 1992.

Miller, Dan; Mark Bracher, and Donald Ault, eds. *Critical Paths: Blake and the Argument of Method*. Durham: Duke University Press, 1987.

Mitchell, W.J.T. 'Visible Language: Blake's Wond'rous Art of Writing' in *Romanticism and Contemporary Criticism*. Ed. Morris Eaves and Michael Fischer. Ithaca: Cornell University Press, 1986. 46–95.

Nelson, J. Walter. 'Blake's Diction – An Amendatory Note'. *Blake Studies* 7 (1975).

Otto, Peter. *Constructive Vision and Visionary Deconstruction: Los, Eternity, and the Productions of Time in the Late Poetry of William Blake*. Oxford: Clarendon Press, 1991.

Pierce, John. B. *Flexible Design: Revisionary Poetics in Blake's Vala or The Four Zoas*. Montreal: McGill-Queen's University Press, 1998.

——. *The Wond'rous Art: William Blake and Writing*. Madison: Fairleigh Dickinson University Press, 2003.

Rooney, Catherine. 'Deconstruction and Weaving' in *Deconstruction: A User's Guide*. Ed. Nocholas Royle. New York: Palgrave, 2000. 258–81.

Rose, Edward J. 'Visionary Forms Dramatic: Grammatical and Iconographical Movement in Blake's Verse and Designs'. *Criticism* 8 (1966).

Rothenberg, Molly Anne. *Rethinking Blake's Textuality*. Columbia: University of Missouri Press, 1993.

Said, Edward. 'The Problem of Textuality: Two Exemplary Positions' in *Aesthetics Today*. Ed. Morris Philipson and Paul J. Gudel. Revised Edition. New York: New American Library, 1980. 87–133.

Santa Cruz Blake Study Group. 'What Type of Blake?' in *Essential Articles for the Study of William Blake, 1970–1984*. Ed. Nelson Hilton. Hamden: Archon Books, 1986.

Sheriff, John K. *The Fate of Meaning: Charles Pierce, Structuralism, and Literature*. Princeton: Princeton University Press, 1989.

Sherry, Peggy Meyer. 'The "Predicament" of the Autograph: "William Blake"'. *Glyph: Textual Studies*. 4 (1978): 130–55.

Sławek, Tadeusz. *The Outlined Shadow: Phenomenology, Grammatology, Blake*. Katowice: Uniwersytet Śląski, 1985.

Tolley, Michael J. 'Marriages in Heaven and Hell: Blake's enigmatic Title-Page' in *Symposium on Romanticism*. Ed. Deirdre Coleman and Peter Otto. Adelaide: Centre for British Studies, 1990. 8–23.

Vogler, Thomas A. 'Re: Naming *MIL/TON*' in *Unnam'd Forms: Blake and Textuality*. Ed. Nelson Hilton and Thomas A. Vogler. Berkeley: University of California Press, 1986. 141–76.

Yoder, R. Paul. 'Unlocking Language: Self-Similarity in Blake's *Jerusalem*' in *Romanticism and Complexity, Romantic Circles Praxis Series*. <www.rc.umd.edu/praxis/complexity/yoder/yoder.html>. Consulted 24 February 2004.

part two
cultural approaches

6
blake and the bible

stephen prickett and christopher strathman

Blake's engagement with the Bible was as passionate as it was oblique. For him, as for so many of his contemporaries, it was not so much a book to be written about, as the quarry from which the foundations of his own work might be hewn, much as many eighteenth-century writers were quarrying ideas from that *other* great source of revelation – the Book of Nature. What was, of course, profoundly different from his contemporaries was that Blake disbelieved in the latter, and tried to construct from those basic building blocks of the former a new and complementary (or even rival) mythology of his own.

The metaphor of Blake as a builder or architectural creator has proved a potent one. For one thing Blake used it of himself – not merely in terms of 'building' Jerusalem in England's green and pleasant land, but more significantly in Los's famous assertion, 'I must Create a System, or be enslav'd by another Man's'./ I will not Reason & Compare: my business is to Create' (J10.20–1, E153). If, as most commentators seem to accept, Los in *Jerusalem* may be taken as representing Blake himself,[1] this opposition between 'Reason' and 'Creation' repeats a familiar antithesis between two forms of construction in his work. Reasoning and comparing is the activity of the Ancient of Days, famously measuring the universe with his dividers, or his human counterpart, Newton, similarly attempting to measure and parcel out the world. This is the sterile ratiocination that is described as constantly desiring more, but never capable of grasping the whole, in *There is No Natural Religion*. Creation, on the other hand, is the work of the true God – or his representative, the true artist.

Beyond the obvious biblical reference to God as Creator, lies a further complex of ideas no less biblically derived. At their heart lies a difference in ways of perceiving: 'He who sees the Infinite in all things, sees God. He who sees the Ratio only, sees himself only' (NNR, E3). For the modern reader, used to well-manufactured plate-glass, and equally well-made mirrors, St Paul's contrast between seeing 'through a glass, darkly' and 'face to face' has lost much of its force, but for an engraver, living in a century fascinated by optics and their metaphorical possibilities, the murkily reflective qualities of hand-made or otherwise semi-opaque glass were obvious enough.

Similarly, the notion that externally imposed systems constituted in themselves a form of slavery appears dimly to echo the enslavement of the Israelites in Egypt – condemned to make bricks without straw (Exodus 1–5). Though Exodus 1 tells us that the Hebrew slaves constructed the treasure cities of Pithom and Raamses, popular illustrators had little difficulty in associating their work with the best-known pieces of Egyptian architecture: the pyramids themselves. A rich vein of eighteenth-century mythology surrounding their construction produced a whole range of contemporary applications ranging, for instance, from mid-century Masonic rituals to illustrations of the mystical bases of both the British and American constitutions (most accessibly, of course, in the great seal of the US on the $1 bill which dates from at least 1770[2]). For Blake, who had used pyramids (and what looks like a bound slave) in the illustrations to *The Marriage of Heaven and Hell* (see Bindman plate 102b), and, with more obvious logic, in 'The Hiding of Moses' (Bindman plates 624a and b), the symbol of the pyramids as a metaphor of a mythopoeic system would have seemed both natural and irresistible.

Jon Mee, however, has argued that so far from being a master-mason, Blake was essentially what the French would call a *bricoleur*, an unskilled do-it-yourself worker whose artifacts constitute a *bricolage* – by implication a construction built of incongruous and ill-assorted materials. Bearing in mind that the term would also apply to Picasso's sculptures from familiar household objects, the word does not entail judgment as to the aesthetic quality of the objects so formed – only to their mode of construction. Without judging his system, therefore, Mee's metaphor constitutes a useful image for Blake's mode of working – not least in his discussions of the Bible.

It is typical of such *bricolage* that much of what we know of Blake's actual opinions of the Bible comes indirectly from references to other biblical interpreters. Thus *The Marriage of Heaven and Hell* (1790–93) is ostensibly a critique of two other deeply unorthodox biblical *bricoleurs*, Swedenborg and Milton. From 1757 onwards, Swedenborg, the Swedish scientist and mystic, had published a series of detailed 'eye-witness' descriptions of Heaven, Hell, the classes, habits and home-life of angels and so on, on the lines of scientific observations which had both inspired and irritated Blake – who, with his wife, had been founder members of the Swedenborgian New Jerusalem Church in London.³ As has often been pointed out, the structure of *The Marriage* is loosely Swedenborgian, though anyone who has read *Heaven and its Wonders and Hell: from Things Heard and Seen* (1758) is unlikely to be struck by any very close resemblances, and if it were not for the specific attacks on Swedenborg in plates 3, and 21–2, might miss them altogether.

The attack on *Paradise Lost*'s version of the Bible (plates 5–6) is much more pointed.

[T[he original Archangel, or possessor of the command of the heavenly host, is call'd the Devil or Satan, and his children are call'd Sin & Death.

But in the Book of Job, Milton's Messiah is call'd Satan.

For this history has been adopted by both parties.

It indeed appear'd to Reason as if Desire was cast out; but the Devil's account is, that the Messiah fell, & formed a heaven of what he stole from the Abyss.

This is shewn in the Gospel, where he prays to the Father to send the comforter, or Desire, that Reason may have Ideas to build on; the Jehovah of the Bible being no other than he who dwells in flaming fire.

Know that after Christ's death, he became Jehovah.

But in Milton, the Father is destiny, the Son a Ratio of the five senses, & the Holy-ghost Vacuum !

Note: The reason Milton wrote in fetters when he wrote of Angels and God, and at liberty when of Devils and Hell, is because be was a true Poet and of the Devil's party without knowing it. (E34–5)

This is not an easy passage, and it is small wonder that most commentators have preferred themselves to quarry it for nuggets in their turn (especially the final sentence), rather than try to disentangle an overall meaning. Though few English-speaking critics had begun to say so by the 1790s, German historical criticism had already begun to lay bare what was to become known as the documentary hypothesis, in which the Bible was itself seen as a tri-lingual palimpsest of overlapping self-referential texts spanning a period of anything up to 900 years – in short, a historical *bricolage*.⁴ Moreover, even if we treat Blake's later claim to be fluent in Greek and Hebrew with some scepticism,⁵ as a member of Joseph Johnson's circle, which included Godwin, Mary Wollstonecraft, Paine, Priestley, Holcroft, and Price, he was in touch with the Unitarians – virtually the only group in England to know of the new biblical scholarship, which had, as yet, made few inroads into a country still isolated, as ever, by a lack of widespread knowledge of any foreign language but French, and now also by war.

Milton was, in his own way, as much of a *bricoleur* as Blake, but the latter's quarrel with him is, as always, not so much over the detail but over the *system* – a matter of the total creation. What is unacceptable is not the parts, but the whole: specifically Milton's picture of a divinely-ordered hierarchical system of control that divides body from soul, reason from energy, piety from creativity. Ironically, in this respect at least Milton's universe is not unlike Swedenborg's deferential and class-ridden bourgeois life of angels. The difference is that whereas Swedenborg's heaven is (as one supposes it must be) completely static, and content to be so, Milton's more stormy and turbulent creation palpably self-destructs. Satan's revolt very nearly succeeds; Adam and Eve *do* fall; and despite what might seem the overwhelming advantages of omnipotence, omniscience, and foreknowledge, the rebels – Satan, Adam and Eve – enjoy at least a rhetorical and dramatic success. But, of course, it is the very dualism of Milton's system that is finally its failure. Blake's new system has to be neither static, like Swedenborg's, nor dualistic, like Milton's – it must rather be dynamic, inclusive, passionate, and, above all, in Blake's sense at least, *biblical*.

This is, of course, a controversial claim. For many critics, even if we discard the elaborately-named mythological figures of the prophetic books over which so much explicatory ink has been spilt – Beulah, Enitharmon, Los, Orc, Urizen, and so on – Blake's system of spiritual integration and liberation would seem so fundamentally *anti*-Christian and *anti*-biblical as to be better seen a reaction *against* the conventional religion of the day, than any form of re-construction of it. Even for those who would prefer to see eighteenth-century Anglicanism, with its leanings towards Deism and Natural Religion, as an aberration from the main stream of Christian thought, and Blake's thought as therefore more like a return to a longer-term orthodoxy, there is in him still too strong a whiff of universalism and antinomianism for comfort. A.D. Nuttall, for instance, sees Blake, like Milton, as an essentially Gnostic writer.

This is hardly a new position. Pioneering readers of Blake such as S. Foster Damon and J. Middleton Murry recognized in Blake's texts evidence of extraordinary and disturbing doctrines, while legendary mid-century critics like Northrop Frye and David Erdman tended to read Blake as (at least) a visionary – although whether primarily psycho-sexual or socio-political in orientation remains an open question. This initial view of Blake – as a heretic, an eccentric, or even a madman, or, more positively, a 'visionary' – has taken deep and lasting hold in the collective consciousness of students of Blake. In spite of a recent desire to insert him firmly back into the context of his time (or, put differently, to squeeze him back into the terms of a confession or a creed) it remains a touchstone for anyone seeking to embark upon the serious study of Blake.

In fact, according to Frye, in his classic *Fearful Symmetry*, Blake was a reclusive solitary beyond the pale of worldly affairs, for whom 'the spiritual world was a continuous source of energy', harnessing 'spiritual power as an engineer harnesses water power [. . .] to drive his inspiration: he was a spiritual utilitarian. He had the complete pragmatism of the artist, who, as artist, believes nothing but is looking only for what he can use' (8). For Frye, this artistic 'pragmatism' included Blake's reading of the Bible:

> If Blake can be consistently interpreted in terms of his own theory of poetry, however, the interpretation of Blake is only the beginning of a complete revolution in one's reading of all poetry. It is, for instance, quite impossible to understand Blake without understanding how he read the Bible, and to do this properly one must read the Bible oneself with Blake's eyes. (11)

Here one can certainly appreciate the importance for Blake of the Bible but, at the same time, one can begin to see that it is by no means clear that Blake read the Bible in the same way that many do today – or even that he read the same book. G.E. Bentley, Jr., for instance, observes that what Blake understood by the 'Bible' is by no means a foregone conclusion: 'the canon of the New [Jerusalem] Church Bible is so different from that of all other Protestants', Bentley argues, that it must be considered as a discrete text. 'The list of exclusions from the Swedenborgian Bible is formidable: Thirty-two books, about a fourth of the bulk of the Protestant canon, including Job, Proverbs, the Song of Solomon, Acts, and all the New Testament Epistles' (63).

Influenced by Frye's interpretation, Harold Bloom's engagement with Blake over the course of several decades led him to view the poet's wrestling with the necessary angel of biblical tradition as hardly religious at all but rather as part of a complex psycho-sexual conflict between poet and the past for the prize of creative autonomy. Of course, one immediately recognizes in this formulation Bloom's celebrated theory of 'the anxiety of influence' – the idea, that is, that modern poets must inevitably struggle with the residual presence of their precursors for control of their talent and their art. One unfortunate side effect of Bloom's theory, however, is a tendency to psychologize – and thus, despite its efforts to the contrary, to idealize – the interaction between individual and tradition so that the material context becomes easy to overlook. More recently, in *The Biblical Presence in Shakespeare, Milton, and Blake*, Harold Fisch has creatively revised Bloom by re-examining several of Blake's works, including the *Illustrations of the Book of Job*, within the context of his inheritance of biblical tradition via poets like Shakespeare and Milton. Stepping back from Bloom's angst-ridden Freudianism, Fisch re-negotiates the problem of influence by juxtaposing it with the Miltonic notion of effluence. Unlike influence, which moves in a single direction, from past to present, Fisch points out, '[e]ffluence works both ways. Blake is not only inspired by Milton; he incorporates and rewrites Milton's poems so as to render them into an instrument of the true spiritual revolution!' (viii).

Erdman's more historically circumspect and politically grounded reading in *Blake: Prophet Against Empire* has come to be equally as influential as, and in many ways more important than, Frye's. For Erdman,

> what most attracted Blake in the new psychology and the new religion [of his day] were their positive benevolism, their invitation to mine beneath codified meanings with which kings and pietists had restrained and perverted Life, and their promise that the infinite vital power of the genius in every man could be released through Love. (143)

For Blake, according to Erdman, 'what must not be negated by rod and rule is the divinity of the creative individual' (143). Among other things, this indicates that in spite of diametrically opposed views concerning the degree of Blake's involvement in the events of his time, both Frye and Erdman arrive at surprisingly similar conclusions regarding the autonomy of creative inspiration or, as Blake was inclined to call it, Poetic Genius. Apparently paraphrasing Robert Lowth's recently-translated *Lectures on the Sacred Poetry of the Hebrews*, Blake's 'Voice of one crying in the Wilderness' proclaims that 'The Religions of all Nations are derived from each Nation's different reception of the Poetic Genius, which is every where call'd the Spirit of Prophecy' (*ARO*, E1).

For Erdman, Blake's engagement with the Bible is a direct result of 'the continuity and development of [his] revolutionary sympathies' (22). Blake's appropriation of the Bible should be seen within the context of a prophetic biblical tradition that includes figures like Moses, Aaron, Ezekiel and Isaiah, rather than in terms of a superficial agreement between *doxa* and the 'codified meanings' handed down by 'kings and pietists [. . .]

in a culture that still discussed politics in moralistic and Biblical terms inherited from the English Civil War'. Blake thus 'viewed the American Revolution as a sort of mass resurrection or secular apocalypse that would overthrow poverty and cruelty and establish a new Eden in which the arts flourished and habitations were illuminated [. . .] not by destructive fires but by the joys of the noonday sun' (50). He assumes the role of a visionary giant of decidedly republican – even democratic – sympathies who is unable to fit his Poetic Genius beneath the beams of any of the established churches except for, briefly, the New Jerusalem Church.

Answering Erdman's call to place Blake's thought 'within the political and cultural context of his times', E.P. Thompson argues in *Witness Against the Beast* that it is 'Blake's unique notation of Christian belief – antinomianism – and not his "Jacobin" political sympathies, which still stands in need of examination' (xiii). For him, Blake is still prophetic, only now his vision stems from a counter-cultural reading of the Bible rather than from a political vision inspired by the American Revolution. Rejecting the view that Blake belongs primarily to a 'formal, classical intellectual culture [. . .] whose summits were attained at Oxford and Cambridge', Thompson contends that the poet found nourishment in 'alternative centres of intellectual culture [such as] the Dissenting Academies' and the 'obscure traditions of London Dissent' (xiv–xv). On this view, rather than being a product of mainstream institutions, Blake was a child of the autodidactic margins that emerged from out of the English Civil War and thrived between 1640 and 1790. Unlike Frye and Erdman, however, who see Blake as a solitary eccentric, *sui generis*, Thompson insists that Blake's poetry

> is writing that comes out of a tradition. It has a confidence, an assured reference, very different from the speculations of an eccentric or a solitary. It also assumes something like a radical constituency, an 'us' of 'the people' or of 'every man' as against the 'them' of the State, or of Bishops or the servitors of 'the Beast and the Whore' (62)

'Out of such an "education", of informal traditions and collisions, came many original minds: Franklin, Paine, Wollstonecraft, Bewick, Cobbett, Thomas Spence, Robert Owen. And it is in this kind of tradition', Thompson concludes, 'that we must place Blake' (xv).

More importantly, the strongest influence upon Blake 'comes from one major source – the Bible – *but* the Bible *read in a particular way*, influenced by Milton and by radical dissent' (33, emphasis added). In doctrinal terms, Blake was shaped by an antinomian tradition that saw grace and moral law as existing in diametrical opposition to one another. On this view, observes Thompson, 'the Ten Commandments and the Gospel of Jesus stand directly opposed to each other: the first is a code of repression and prohibition, the second a gospel of forgiveness and love' (14). However, and this is absolutely crucial, such 'particularity' governs Blake's hermeneutic outlook as well, *especially* with reference to the Bible:

> Blake had a different way of reading [. . .] He would look into a book with a directness which we might find to be naïve or unbearable, challenging each one of its arguments against his own experience and his own 'system'. This is at once apparent from his surviving annotations–to Lavater, Swedenborg, Berkeley, Bacon, Bishop Watson or Thornton. (xvi)

What makes this so intriguing is that, as Thompson notes, he

> took each author (even the Old Testament prophets) as his equal, or as something less. And he acknowledged as between them, no received judgments as to their worth, no hierarchy of accepted 'reputability'. For Blake, a neighbor, or a fellow-reader of a periodical, or his friend and patron, Thomas Butts, were quite as likely to hold opinions of central importance as was any man of learning. (xvi–xvii)

Discussing the marginal notes on the dispute between Paine and Watson, Thompson highlights the fact that Blake re-discovered in the Bible a profoundly shocking, and profoundly self-divided, book:

> Throughout these annotations – marginal notes written under the stress of direct responses and without thought of any audience – Blake oscillates between two uses of 'the Bible' which are directly opposed. He writes as one 'who loves the Bible': 'The Perversions of Christ's words & acts are attack'd by Paine & also the perversions of the Bible; Who dare defend either the Acts of Christ or the Bible unperverted?' At one point he cites the authority of 'the Bible' against Bishop Watson's apologetics; on the next page he is stung to fury by the Bishop's complacent endorsement of the Bible's authority for the divine justice of massacring the Canaanites [. . .] The 'Bible' is then divided between the Gospel and the 'Jewish Imposture [. . .] the Jewish Scriptures, which are only an Example of the wickedness & deceit of the Jews & were written as an Example of the possibility of Human

Beastliness in all its branches.' The opposition between these two is pressed to its furthest possible extent: 'Christ dies as an Unbeliever & if the Bishops had their will so would Paine.' (61)

Thompson's idea seems to be that Blake read the Bible as a book stretched over an immense abyss separating the 'gospel' and 'moral law' – and that in reading the Bible for the truth of 'love' and 'forgiveness' one is always somehow in danger of being drawn back over to the side of the 'law'. This complex attitude towards the Bible – accompanied by a profound ambivalence about the Jews – must be explored with caution, for Blake also seems periodically to challenge Greek and Roman tradition with the imaginative force of Hebrew tradition.[6] In the 'Preface' to *Milton*, for example, Blake insists that

[t]he Stolen and Perverted Writings of Homer & Ovid, of Plato & Cicero, which all Men ought to contemn, are set up by artifice against the Sublime of the Bible [. . .] We do not want either Greek or Roman Models, if we are just & true to our own Imaginations, those Worlds of Eternity in which we shall live for ever in Jesus our Lord. (E95)

What is perhaps most intriguing about Blake's understanding of the Bible is the resonance between this notion of it as an unfinished but infinite book and the fragmentary work the early German romantics identified as 'romantic poetry'.[7] Indeed, this is perhaps one of the most interesting areas of possible intersection between studies of Blake preoccupied with biblical tradition and studies preoccupied with romantic and contemporary criticism and theory.

Certainly Blake's marginal notes to Bishop Watson's refutation of Paine's *Age of Reason* are a crux in understanding his attitude to the Bible. Paine's book had caused immediate controversy when the first volume was published in 1793 – losing him almost all the popular good will that had been created by his earlier best-selling *Rights of Man*. True 'revelation' Paine claimed, resided not in the Bible, but in God's genuine creation, the Book of Nature (vol. 1, 22). Following this principle, the rest of the volume is devoted to natural religion, and to denigrating all forms of revealed religion. From the start Paine dismisses the 'three principal means that have been employed in all ages, and perhaps in all countries, to impose upon mankind'. These 'are Mystery, Miracle, and Prophecy. The two first are incompatible with true religion, and the third ought always to be suspected' (vol. 1, 45). Then follows a well-informed discussion of the meaning of 'prophecy' – its phraseology echoing Lowth's *Sacred*

Poetry of the Hebrews, which had been published in English shortly before, in 1787 – with the implication that attempts to find the fullfilment of biblical prophecy in contemporary events were futile:

> [I]t is owing to this change in the meaning of the words, that the flights and metaphors of the Jewish poets, and phrases and expressions now rendered obscure, by our not being acquainted with the local circumstances to which they applied at the time they were used, have been erected into prophecies, and made to bend to explanations, at the will and whimsical conceits of sectaries, expounders, and commentators. Everything unintelligible was prophetical, and everything insignificant was typical. (vol. 1, 50)

The second volume of *The Age of Reason*, however, is a very different kind of work. It was largely written in a French prison from December 1793 to November 1794, while Paine, who had been made a Deputy and a French citizen in 1792 during the first flush of revolutionary internationalist enthusiasm, was awaiting trial and almost certainly the guillotine during the Reign of Terror for his opposition to the execution of Louis XVI. As he explains in his introduction to the book in 1795, apologizing for the lack of the usual references, both he, and his book, had only survived because the American minister, James Monroe, had put pressure on the French government for his release. No doubt because of the circumstances of its composition, this volume shows nothing like the earlier range of reference, but consists simply of readings from the Bible with Paine's own comments. These are trenchant enough. On Numbers xii, v. 3, for instance, which describes what a Hebrew raiding-party had done with the inhabitants of one captured town, Paine comments that 'Among the detestable villains that in any period of the world that would have disgraced the name of man, it is impossible to find a greater than Moses, if this account be true. Here is an order to butcher the boys, to massacre the mothers, and debauch the daughters' (vol. 2, 12). After a review of similar atrocities, textual contradictions, and improbable events, Paine concludes:

> Of all the systems of religion that were ever invented, there is none more derogatory to the Almighty, more unedifying to man, more repugnant to reason, and more contradictory in itself than this thing called Christianity. Too absurd for belief, too impossible to convince, and too inconsistent for practice, it renders the heart torpid, or produces only atheists and fanatics. As an engine of power, it serves only the

purpose of despotism; as a means of wealth, the avarice of priests; but so far as it respects the good of man in general, it leads to nothing here or hereafter. (vol. 2, 86)

In the 1790s, under threat of French invasion, and in what amounted, under Pitt, to a police state, this was unlikely to go unchallenged, even though Paine himself, after his release from prison, had very sensibly fled to America. By chance or design, it fell to Bishop Watson to lead the charge.

Richard Watson would have been an unusual figure, to say the least, at any time – and certainly a most unusual Bishop. An able scientist, he had become Professor of Chemistry at Cambridge at the early age of twenty-seven, and was made a Fellow of the Royal Society only five years later. He had played an important part in the invention of the black-bulb thermometer and had made improvements in the manufacture of gunpowder which were estimated to have saved the British government more than £100,000 per year (many millions in today's terms) and so contributed later towards British victories in the Napoleonic Wars. With a flexibility perhaps only possible to an eighteenth-century polymath he resigned his Chair of Chemistry in 1771 to become Regius Professor of Divinity at Cambridge. In 1782 he left Cambridge to become Bishop of Llandaff, in Wales. At a period when the Anglican Church was commonly described as 'the Tory Party at prayer' Watson was a Whig, with strongly liberal sympathies. Alone among senior Anglican clergy he had showed some sympathy for the French Revolution in its early days, and as late as 1795 he had made a speech in the House of Lords opposing war with France, and predicting that

this abandonment of all religion in France will be followed in due time [. . .] by the establishment of a purer system of Christianity than has ever taken place in that country, or perhaps any country, since the age of the Apostles. Voltaire, Rousseau, Diderot, and the rest of the philosophers in France, and perhaps I may say, many in our own country, have mistaken the corruptions of Christianity for Christianity itself, and in spurning the yoke of superstition, have overthrown religion. They are in the condition of men described by Plutarch; they have fled from superstition; have leapt over religion, and sunk into Atheism. They will be followed by future Newtons and by future Lockes, who will rebuild [. . .] the altars which the others have polluted and thrown down; for they will found them on the pure and unadorned rock of Christian verity. (267)

Doubtless because of the unfulfilled hopes of the more radical writers and poets, when it became clear that at home he was as conservative as his fellow peers, Watson was subjected to unique abuse. In 1793 Wordsworth had written, but never sent, a sarcastic Letter to the Bishop of Llandaff, congratulating him, among other things, for his 'enthusiatic fondness for the judicial proceedings of this country' as well as for his belief that in England 'the science of civil government has received all the perfection of which it is capable' (43–4).

Watson's reply to Paine appeared in 1796 in the form of *An Apology for the Bible in a Series of Letters addressed to Thomas Paine*. On the back of the title-page in his copy Blake wrote:

> To defend the Bible in this year 1798 would cost a man his life.
> The Beast and the Whore rule without control.
> It is an easy matter for a Bishop to triumph over Paine's attack, but it is not so easy for one who loves the Bible.
> The Perversions of Christ's words & acts are attack'd by Paine & also the perversions of the Bible; Who dare defend either the Acts of Christ or the Bible Unperverted? (E611)

For Blake, Watson's 'defence' is simply 'perversion', his arguments mere casuistry: 'Paine has not attacked Christianity. Watson has defended Antichrist' (E612). Things rapidly come to a head with Watson's defence of Moses ordering the slaughter of innocents in Numbers xii. Here Watson turns for his reply to the very Book of Nature that Paine had seen as the source of true revelation in Part 1:

> You profess yourself to be a deist, and to believe that there is a God, who created the universe, and established the laws of nature, by which it is sustained in existence. You profess that from the contemplation of the works of God, you derive a knowledge of his attributes; and you reject the Bible, because it ascribes to God things inconsistent (as you suppose) with the attributes which you have discovered to belong to him; in particular, you think it repugnant to his moral justice, that he should doom to destruction the crying or smiling infants of the Canaanites. – Why do you not maintain it to be repugnant to his moral justice, that he should suffer crying or smiling infants to be swallowed up by an earthquake, drowned by an inundation, consumed by a fire, starved by famine or destroyed by a pestilence? The Word of God is in perfect harmony with his work; crying or smiling infants are subjected to death in both. (14–5)

Though as Watson says, there is nothing particularly new about this analogy with Nature to defend the atrocities of the Pentateuch – it had been used by Morgan, Tyndale, and Bolingbroke earlier in the century – it was, nevertheless, a shrewd blow against Paine's use of nature to disparage revelation. From a theological point of view, what is curious about this debate – traditionally one of the most difficult in all Christian apologetic – is that both Paine and Watson seem to accept the same naturalistic premise, that nature reveals its creator. Not for a moment does Watson suggest that the teachings of the New Testament cancel those of the Old, or raise the Pauline doctrine of the Fall – that all nature 'groans in travail' under the bondage of sin.

In this context, it is Blake, of all people, who emerges as a relative paragon of Christian orthodoxy:

> To me, who believe in the Bible & profess myself a Christian, a defence of the Wickedness of the Israelites in murdering so many thousands under a pretence of a command from God is altogether Abominable & Blasphemous. Why did Christ come? Was it not to abolish the Jewish Imposture? Was not Christ murderd because he taught that God loved all Men & was their father[?] (E614)

Before we conclude from 'Jewish Imposture' that Blake is as anti-semitic as he is anti-Episcopal, we should note that 'Jewish' here seems to be an alternative word for 'Old Testament' (a term which he rarely uses).[8] The contrast is, as ever with Blake, the Pauline one between the 'Spirit' and the 'Law'.

On the following page, Blake takes on the argument from Nature, and the justice of natural catastrophes, head on: 'The Bible says that God formed nature perfect, but that Man perverted the order of Nature, since which time the Elements are fill'd with the Prince of Evil who has the power of the air' (E614). To Watson's contention that it will be impossible to prove that the massacre of the Canaanites was 'a proceeding contrary to God's moral justice, to exterminate so wicked a people', Blake's answer is brief, and to the point:

> Horrible the Bishop is an Inquisitor. God never makes one man murder another, nor one nation
> There is a vast difference between an accident brought on by man's own carelessness & a destruction from the designs of another. The earthquakes at Lisbon etc. were the Natural result of Sin. but the destruction of the Canaanites by Joshua was the Unnatural design of

wicked men To Extirpate a nation by means of another is as wicked as
to destroy an individual by means of another individual, which God
considers (in the Bible) as Murder & commands that it shall not be
done. (E614–15)

Heretical or even Gnostic as Blake may be on some points, his rejection
of both Paine's Deism and Watson's naturalism is historically important.
Watson's argument is part of what Thomas McFarland has called the
'Spinozistic crescendo' of the late eighteenth century (53–106). From
Spinoza's pantheism – the argument that there is no personal God, but,
rather, all nature (including humanity) is part of divinity – springs the
rejection of the doctrine of the Fall, the closing of the gap between God
and his creation, and the deification of nature – implicit in all of which
(as Hegel saw) is the possibility of the perfectibility of man. Taken up by
Feuerbach and Marx, this doctrine, suitably secularized and politicized,
was to be one of the driving forces of twentieth-century communist
ideology. As Ernest Gellner once remarked, the Christian doctrine of the
Fall has, improbably, both kept the door open to idealism and provided
a vital strand of realism to European political theory.

The problem, of course, is that classical Hebrew, unlike classical Greek,
had no word for and no real concept of 'nature'. Every event, from the
rising of the sun each morning to Elijah's translation in a fiery chariot,
was construed as a direct act of God. Though there *are*, obviously, clear
doctrines of both Creation and the Fall running through Old and New
Testaments alike, there is no corresponding doctrine of Nature – which,
like that of the Trinity, is a largely post-biblical concept. Both owe much to
the infusion of Greek thought in the early Church, and are interlocking,
in that Father, Son, and Holy Spirit are alike 'persons' – separate and
distinct from the natural world, in which they intervene by revelation,
incarnation, or miracle.

Particularly interesting here is a growing discussion among scholars
concerning Blake's use of Hebrew tradition as a counterweight to what
he perceived to be the deleterious effects of predominantly Greek and
Roman influences. Paul Yoder, for example, has recently noted how Blake
distanced himself from the neo-classicism of Milton and Pope, taking
up instead the prophetic mode of Isaiah, Ezekiel, and even Balaam: 'Put
down thy *Illiad* and thy *Aeneid*, [Blake] seems to say, and pick up thy
Bible' (21). On this question, Blake seems to anticipate Derrida's dictum
(following Levinas) that we 'live in the difference between the Jew and
the Greek, which is perhaps the unity of what is called history' (53). That
is to say, among other things, that the Christian reading of the Bible has

been mediated too exclusively by Greek concepts and needs to recover for itself a greater sense of its origins as a profoundly *Hebrew* book written *by*, *about*, and *for*, Jews. Even Blake's relative disregard for, or indifference toward, nature echoes the profound anthropocentric tendency of the Hebrew scriptures.[9]

Though Blake's rejection of Watsonian (or spinozistic) naturalism suggests that he may have been more aware of these dangers than often supposed, casting doubt on the simple identification of him as antinomian – usually on the basis of some of the more violent 'Proverbs of Hell' in *The Marriage of Heaven and Hell*[10] – his concept of Nature needs further discussion. Once again, however, the best source material is oblique and from a source that needs to be treated with more than usual caution.

The Rev. Dr. John Trusler, an art critic, clergyman, and author of such books as *Hogarth Moralized*, *A Sure Way to Lengthen Life* and *The Way to be Rich and Respectable*, was not, to put it mildly, Blake's natural soul-mate. Having taken one look at the first of four watercolors ('Malevolence', 'Benevolence', 'Pride', and 'Humility') he had commissioned from Blake, he hastily canceled the contract.[11] In the course of his somewhat sarcastic reply to Trusler Blake offered what is perhaps his fullest direct account of what he saw as the relationship of art to Nature:

> This World Is a World of imagination and Vision. I see Every thing I paint In This World, but Every body does not see alike. To the Eyes of a Miser a Guinea is more beautiful than the Sun, & a bag worn with the use of Money has more beautiful proportions than a Vine filled with Grapes [. . .] Some See Nature all Ridicule & Deformity, & by these I shall not regulate my proportions; & Some Scarce see Nature at all. But to the Eyes of the Man of Imagination, Nature is Imagination itself. As a man is, So he Sees. As the Eye is formed, such are its Powers [. . .] To Me This World is all One continued Vision of Fancy or Imagination, & I feel Flatter'd when I am told so. What is it sets Homer, Virgil & Milton in so high a rank of Art? Why is the Bible more Entertaining & Instructive than any other book? Is it not because they are addressed to the Imagination, which is Spiritual Sensation, & but mediately to the Understanding or Reason[?] (E702)

The question here, as so often, is that of precise terminology. Such an insistence on the subjectivity of perception carries its own dangers. The dig at those who see Nature in terms of 'Ridicule & Deformity' is clearly aimed at the author of *Hogarth Moralized*, but, as A.D. Nuttall has argued, because the term 'imagination' concedes its own unreality, Blake has to add a parallel term, 'vision', a *cognitive* word, to clarify his point. 'Vision', unlike 'perception', already has religious connotations; it suggests a transcendent object: 'Blake's violent, polarizing intelligence found in the old Gnostic contempt for nature a protective colour for *his* response: the *gnosis* of eternity obliterates the frail, stunted products of perception by way of the five senses' (266–7). Nuttall concludes:

> it seems to me beyond doubt that Blake's Trinity is the adversarial Trinity of Gnosticism. The Son is preferred to the Father. The Holy Ghost [. . .] appears in Blake as a flawed presence. Protestant Grace is reconstrued as imagination and then, as the fictive implications of 'imagination' appear inexpugnable, reconstrued once more as vision. (270)

Though Nuttall is persuasive about the Gnostic Trinity, his argument is, strictly speaking, outside our subject of Blake and the Bible. Nuttall's second point, however, that Blake's 'imagination' (or 'vision') is related to the Protestant idea of 'grace' is more immediately germane. Luther's idea of grace was, in effect, a re-reading of the Pauline version, once the New Testament Epistles had been stripped of their medieval incrustation of typological readings and could be seen again as theological arguments. It runs much more powerfully through German theological traditions than English. There is nothing in Blake's tirade to Trusler that would not have been immediately familiar to the German Romantics – the Schlegels, Schleiermacher, or Novalis. There are obvious parallels with, say, the early Schleiermacher of the *Athenaeum Fragments*. Here, for instance, is fragment 350, published in 1799, the same year as Blake's letter to Dr. Trusler:

> No poetry, no reality. Just as there is, despite all the senses, no external world without imagination, so too there is no spiritual world without feeling, no matter how much sense there is. Whoever only has sense can perceive no human being, but only what is human: all things disclose themselves to the magic wand of feeling alone. It fixes people and seizes them; like the eye, it looks on without being conscious of its own mathematical operation. (Schlegel 71)

There is no room here to unpack the complex references to (among other things) Kant's *Critique of Judgment* (1790), Schiller's *The Aesthetic Education of Man* (1795) or Schleiermacher's own *Speeches on Religion* (1799).[12] Suffice it to say, though this use of 'imagination' was certainly less ambiguous and fictive than Nuttall suggests in German Romantic circles, for them, as for Blake, its ambiguous subjectivity was *always* part of the connotations of the word. Nature by itself is dead – without form and devoid of meaning. For Blake, as for his German contemporaries, only the transforming eye of grace/imagination allows the artist to give meaning to Nature. Such power is *never* automatic (that would be Catholicism) *nor* is it universal – though one day a cleansing of the doors of perception might allow all to see with the eyes of the artist.

Though not impossible, it is, to say the least, unlikely that Blake was aware of the ideas of his immediate German contemporaries. Links, however, exist through Swedenborg – who had corresponded with Kant, and even sent him copies of his visionary books. It might be an exaggeration to describe the *Critique of Judgment* in terms of Swedenborgian *bricolage*, but the relationship between Nature and art suggested there has been closely (and inconclusively) debated by critics ever since. Certainly, it would be a grave mistake to see in Blake the isolated and eccentric figure sometimes presented by earlier critics;[13] there is at least a case that underneath some of the wilder paradoxes was a deeply frustrated but essentially mainline philosopher and theologian.

In one of the most important single essays on Blake's hermeneutics to appear in recent years, 'The Idea of the Indeterminate Text: Blake's Bible of Hell and Dr. Alexander Geddes', Jerome McGann suggests an intermediary between Blake and the Germans, arguing that his understanding of the Bible was influenced not by any first-hand knowledge of the new German Higher Criticism (pioneered by such figures as Eichhorn, Lessing, Michaelis and Reimarus) as by the ideas of the Scottish Catholic priest, Alexander Geddes, whose *Critical Remarks upon the Hebrew Scriptures* (1800) had first introduced them to an English-speaking readership. Geddes, McGann points out, was

> one of Joseph Johnson's authors and a man who moved in the same circles with Blake in the early 1790s. Geddes was the chief conduit in England for the ideas which were being pursued and elaborated by the new German scholars of the Bible. In addition, Blake seems to have also been familiar with the numerous discussions of the new biblical criticism which appeared in the most important periodical associated with Johnson's circle, the *Analytical Review*. Indeed, in the years 1788–91 Geddes was Johnson's principal reviewer of this material, which included all of the leading works being produced in Germany by scholars like J. D. Michaelis and Eichhorn. (309–10)

McGann reconstructs a probable genealogy of influence, beginning with Geddes' attempt in the 1780s to incorporate the insights he discovered in German scholarship into a fresh translation of the Bible that would supersede both the Douai and Challoner Bibles for English Catholics. 'He first announced the method and goal of this work', McGann writes,

> in his *Prospectus of a New Translation of the Holy Bible* (1786). This work argued that the received biblical texts were corrupt because they all derived from unreliable base texts – indeed, the problems arose because of a failure to understand the historical character of the base texts. Geddes maintained that the foundational Hebrew text, the Masoretic Bible, was a heteroglot work and hence did not reflect some original and pure inspiration. The other early texts, the Greek Septuagint and the Latin Vulgate, were obviously secondary and equally in need of critical examination. A 'New Translation' could only be produced, then, by returning to the original Hebrew documents, which would have to be critically examined and purified. In Geddes' view this meant – so far as the Pentateuch was concerned – returning to the Samaritan Pentateuch as a far less questionable and far more authentic and reliable base text. (310–11)

When it appeared in 1786, the *Prospectus*'s challenge to the received ideas of a definite and authoritative biblical text came immediately under attack from both Catholics and Protestants. Geddes' three-volume translation of the Bible appeared between 1792 and 1800, together with five pamphlets between 1787 and 1794 defending his textual and editorial procedures. For conservatives it was seen as threatening the very foundations of revealed religion; but, argues McGann, tacitly supporting the case for Blake's 'mainline' theology, 'neither Geddes nor Blake saw their own work in this way – on the contrary, in fact. Both conceived that their work would set Christianity on a deeper and more firm footing' (311–12).

Indeed, as one of the present authors has argued elsewhere (Prickett, *Origins* xi), there is a sense that the changed hermeneutic assumptions engendered by the new biblical studies meant that the Bible became for the nineteenth century virtually a different book from that of a century before – and Blake may be seen as symptomatic of that hermeneutical shift. Though admittedly quite different in focus and in scope, this work reinforces many of the earlier insights of Fisch, McGann, and Thompson. The Romantic Bible, from this point of view, 'was at once a single narrative work, an on-going tradition of interpretation, and [. . .] a "metatype": a kind of all-embracing literary form that was invoked to encompass and give meaning to all other books' (1). As Frye suggests in the *Anatomy of Criticism*, romantic literary criticism itself rests on biblical foundations.

Here Blake's illustration of 'Jacob's Ladder' may serve as an emblem for the back-and-forth transmission of romantic period biblical influence.[14] Read in conjunction with early German romanticism, especially Schleiermacher, but also Schlegel, it suggests that behind romantic poetry's predisposition to infinite becoming lies the Bible as read in relation to its ongoing traditions of commentary, criticism, exegesis, and interpretation. As we have seen, Swedenborg and Kant's view of art's role as mediator between the realms of the sacred and the profane (the subject of Kant's *Critique of Judgment*) makes it easy to suggest that Blake's depiction of an angel holding a lyre on the stairway midway between heaven and earth may be read as his affirmation of art as a mediator between the noumenal and the phenomenal, the transcendent and the mundane, the extraordinary and the everyday, even, to speak hermeneutically, the past and the present. It is entirely in keeping with what we know of Blake and his intellectual context if we take this version of Jacob's Ladder as representing the visionary or imaginative bridge between the mundane and the transcendent that all the Romantics were seeking in their own ways. In such a reading, the eucharistic elements of religion would be purveyed by the ministering angels alongside the arts of music, literature, and science in the kind of intellectual synaesthesia also central to the literary absolute of so many forms of Romanticism. Such a spiral of arts and sacraments, leading from the sleeping earthbound shepherd to the divine radiance, would also be a very precise image of the new metatypical status of the Bible itself.[15]

Such an argument resonates with many insights in McGann's essay on Blake and Geddes, as well as supporting in historical detail territory pioneered some years ago in Philippe Lacoue-Labarthe and Jean-Luc Nancy's *The Literary Absolute*, especially in their chapter on 'The Idea: Religion within the Limits of Art'. In that chapter, on the *Ideas* from the *Athenaeum*, Lacoue-Labarthe and Nancy contend that the religious, even biblical, stakes of romanticism's fragmentary work have never been adequately examined. But this is, of course, an argument that can be stood on its head. What if the apotheosis of the romantic fragment is, after all, the Bible, whose criticism actually *anticipates* the question-begging (and criticism-inspiring) structure of the fragment?

More recently, a few readers have tried, with some success, to insert Blake into a more 'orthodox' template of biblical Christianity. Making use of the

ubiquitous trend among theologians toward 'Neo-Orthodoxy', Robert M.
Ryan in *The Romantic Reformation* manages to read Blake alongside Karl
Barth, the controversial twentieth-century Swiss theologian who took
liberal Protestantism to task for what he saw as its 'embourgeoisement'
of Christianity and its progressive abandonment of rigorous masculine
theology in favor of 'natural religion' (74). Nevertheless, this kind
of reading gives too little attention to the visionary power of Blake's
inimitable images and texts, their *artistry*, reducing their creative potency
to yet another form of orthodoxy. At the opposite end of the spectrum,
Martin Priestman follows Thompson to produce a reading of Blake in
Romantic Atheism that focuses primarily on the poet's flirtations with
'atheism', largely by way of a close study of the writings of the early 1790s
within the context of the historical development of religious fanaticism
and 'antinomianism'. Still, in spite of the potentially lurid contours of
such an inquiry, Priestman's argument is only partly convincing.

Navigating the Scylla and Charybdis of such views, Morton Paley's
Apocalypse and Millennium in English Romantic Poetry affirms once
more Blake's role as a poet-prophet, while Ian Balfour's *The Rhetoric of
Romantic Prophecy* extends this view by providing a fresh new account
of Blake's prophetic poetics. Reading *The Marriage of Heaven and Hell*,
America, *Europe*, and *Milton* against the background of the critic Walter
Benjamin's engagement with German romanticism and Hebrew prophetic
tradition, Balfour produces a stimulating reading that emphasizes Blake's
idiosyncratic sense of prophecy as extraordinary backward-and-forward
perception and vision (133). And, returning to the thought that Blake's
view of the Bible resonates with German romanticism's theory of literature,
Balfour notes that somewhat 'along the lines of Novalis's protest that
the Bible is not a "closed", that is to say, finished book, Blake argues for
the possibility of a permanent and generalized condition of prophecy'
(135). Coming full circle, then, Balfour affirms this mainline account of
Blake's prophetic vision, his Poetic Genius, examining not so much the
political content of prophecy as the literary and philosophical structure
of the prophetic mode. Here one might do well to re-visit Geoffrey
Hartman's essay 'The Poetics of Prophecy' which, although concerned
with Wordsworth rather than with Blake, nevertheless acknowledges a
chasm between biblical studies and literary criticism and asks, not entirely
in jest, 'how to get from there to here, or vice versa[?]' (34). Indeed, such
an essay as this one, on a poet such as Blake, only echoes this question
in deeper and more urgent tones.

notes

1. See S. Foster Damon, *A Blake Dictionary: The Ideas and Symbols of William Blake*, 251.
2. The reverse side of the $1 bill depicts a pyramid, a symbol of permanence and strength. The unfinished pyramid represents striving toward growth. The eye represents an all-seeing deity and places the spiritual above the material. On the pyramid's base, 1776 appears in roman numerals. The motto 'Annuit Coeptis' translates to 'He [God] Has Favored Our Undertakings'. 'Novus Ordo Seclorum' is translated as 'A New Order of the Ages' and signifies the beginning of the New American Era.
3. See Stephen Prickett, 'Swedenborg, Blake, Joachim and the Idea of a New Era'.
4. See Preface to *The Bible*, ed. Robert Carroll and Stephen Prickett, World's Classics, Oxford University Press, 1997.
5. 'I go on merrily with my Greek & Latin: am very sorry that I did not begin to learn languages early in life as I find it very Easy. am now learning my Hebrew [. . .] I read Greek as fluently as an Oxford scholar & the Testament is my chief master. astonishing indeed is the English Translation it is almost word for word & if the Hebrew Bible is as well translated which I do not doubt it is we need not doubt of its having been translated as well as written by the Holy Ghost' (Letter to James Blake, January 30, 1803, E727).
6. See R. Paul Yoder, 'Not From Troy, But Jerusalem: Blake's Canon Revision'. For an assessment of Blake's attitude towards Jews, see Sheila A. Spector, 'Blake as an Eighteenth-Century Hebraist'. 'While it may be tempting', Spector writes, 'to infer from this and other passages in the "Annotations", as well as in *The Marriage of Heaven and Hell*, that Blake was an anti-Semite, it seems more likely that the Jews qua Jews were irrelevant to Blake, other than as antagonists of his personal myth of the Christian dialectic' (219 n.16). See also Karen Shabetai, 'The Question of Blake's Hostility Toward the Jews'.
7. Friedrich Schlegel, *Philosophical Fragments* 31–2.
8. See Note 6 above. Blake also seems to have been interested in aspects of Judaism that extend well beyond Hebrew or the Hebrew Bible. See, for example, Sheila Spector, *Wonders Divine: The Development of Blake's Kabbalistic Myth* and *'Glorious Incomprehensible': The Development of Blake's Kabbalistic Language*.
9. To complicate matters further, Yoder notes that Blake's attack on neo-classicism turns not only on an assertion of Hebrew tradition, but also on the issue of English nationalism (18–19).
10. For example, 'Sooner murder an infant in its cradle than nurse unacted desires' (E38).
11. See Peter Ackroyd, *Blake* 209.
12. See Stephen Prickett, *Origins of Narrative: The Romantic Appropriation of the Bible* 184–92.
13. See T.S. Eliot, *The Sacred Wood: Essays on Poetry and Criticism* and W.W. Robson, *Critical Essays*.
14. See Stephen Prickett, 'Jacob's Dream: A Blakean Interpretation of the Bible'.
15. Prickett, *Origins of Narrative* 219.

works cited and suggestions for further reading

Ackroyd, Peter. *Blake*. London: Sinclair-Stevenson, 1995

Balfour, Ian. *The Rhetoric of Romantic Prophecy*. Stanford: Stanford University Press, 2002.

Bentley, G.E., Jr. 'A Swedenborgian Bible'. *Blake: An Illustrated Quarterly* (Fall 1990): 63–4.

Bindman, David. *The Complete Graphic Works of William Blake*. London: Thames and Hudson, 1978.

Bloom, Harold. *The Anxiety of Influence: A Theory of Poetry*. 2nd edition. Oxford: Oxford University Press, 1997.

——. *Blake's Apocalypse: A Study in Poetic Argument*. Ithaca: Cornell University Press, 1970.

——. *Ringers in the Tower: Studies in Romantic Tradition*. Chicago and London: University of Chicago Press, 1971.

——. *The Visionary Company: A Reading of English Romantic Poetry*. Revised and enlarged edition. Ithaca and London: Cornell University Press, 1971.

Damon, S. Foster. *A Blake Dictionary: The Ideas and Symbols of William Blake*. Providence: Brown University Press, 1965.

——. *William Blake: His Philosophy and Symbols*. Boston and New York: Houghton Mifflin Company, 1924.

Derrida, Jacques. *Writing and Difference*. Chicago: University of Chicago Press, 1978.

Eliot, T.S. *The Sacred Wood: Essays on Poetry and Criticism*. London: Methune, 1920.

Erdman, David V. *Blake: Prophet Against Empire*. 3rd edition. Garden City, New York: Anchor/Doubleday, 1991.

Fisch, Harold. *The Biblical Presence in Shakespeare, Milton, and Blake*. Oxford: Clarendon Press, 1999.

Frye, Northrop. *Fearful Symmetry: A Study of William Blake*. Princeton: Princeton University Press, 1947.

——. *Anatomy of Criticism: Four Essays*. Princeton: Princeton University Press, 1971 (1957).

Hartman, Geoffrey. 'The Poetics of Prophecy' in *High Romantic Argument: Essays for M.H. Abrams*. Ed. Lawrence Lipking. Ithaca and London: Cornell University Press, 1981.

Lacoue-Labarthe, Philippe and Jean-Luc Nancy. *The Literary Absolute: The Theory of Literature in German Romanticism*. Trans. Philip Barnard and Cheryl Lester. Albany, New York: State University of New York Press, 1988.

McFarland, Thomas. *Coleridge and the Pantheist Tradition*. Oxford: Oxford University Press, 1969.

McGann, Jerome J. 'The Idea of the Indeterminate Text: Blake's Bible of Hell and Dr. Alexander Geddes'. *Studies in Romanticism* 25 (Fall 1986): 303–24.

Mee, Jon. *Dangerous Enthusiasm: William Blake and the Culture of Radicalism in the 1790s*. Oxford: Clarendon Press, 1992.

Murry, J. Middleton. *William Blake*. London: Jonathan Cape, 1933.

Nuttall, A.D. *The Alternative Trinity: Gnostic Heresy in Marlowe, Milton and Blake*. Oxford: Clarendon Press, 1998.

Paine, Thomas. *The Age of Reason* in *The Theological Works of Thomas Paine*. London, 1827.

Paley, Morton D. *Apocalypse and Millennium in English Romantic Poetry*. Oxford: Clarendon Press, 1999.

Prickett, Stephen. 'Jacob's Dream: A Blakean Interpretation of the Bible' in *British Romantics as Readers: Intertextualities, Maps of Misreading, Reinterpretations*. Ed. Michael Gassenmeier, Petra Bridzun, Jens Martin Gurr and Frank Erik Pointer. Heidelberg, Germany: Universitatsverlag C. Winter, 1998.

——. *Origins of Narrative: The Romantic Appropriation of the Bible*. Cambridge: Cambridge University Press, 1996.

——. 'Swedenborg, Blake, Joachim and the Idea of a New Era' in *Emanuel Swedenborg: Herald of New Era*. Ed. Neville Jarvis. Sydney, Australia: The Swedenborg Lending Library and Equity Centre, 1991.

Priestman, Martin. *Romantic Atheism: Poetry and Freethought, 1780–1830*. Cambridge: Cambridge University Press, 1999.

Robson, W.W. *Critical Essays*. New York: Barnes and Noble, 1967.

Ryan, Robert M. *The Romantic Reformation: Religious Politics in English Literature, 1789–1824*. Cambridge: Cambridge University Press, 1997.

Schlegel, Friedrich. *Philosophical Fragments*. Trans. Peter Firchow. Minneapolis: University of Minnesota Press, 1991.

Shabetai, Karen. 'The Question of Blake's Hostility Toward the Jews'. *English Literary History* 63.1 (1996): 139–52.

Spector, Sheila A. 'Blake as an Eighteenth-Century Hebraist' in *Blake and His Bibles*. Ed. David V. Erdman. West Cornwall, CT: Locust Hill Press, 1990.

——. *'Glorious Incomprehensible': The Development of Blake's Kabbalistic Language*. Lewisburg, PA: Bucknell University Press, 2001.

——. *Wonders Divine: The Development of Blake's Kabbalistic Myth*. Lewisburg, PA: Bucknell University Press, 2001.

Swedenborg, Emmanuel. *Heaven and its Wonders and Hell: from Things Heard and Seen*. New York: Swedenborg Foundation, 1978.

Thompson, E.P. *Witness Against the Beast: William Blake and the Moral Law*. New York: The New Press, 1993.

Watson, Bishop Richard. *An Apology for the Bible in a Series of Letters addressed to Thomas Paine*. 8th edition. London: T. Evans, 1797.

——. Speech opposing war with France. *Parliamentary History* vol. 31: 267.

Wordsworth, William. 'Letter to the Bishop of Llandaff' in *Prose Works*, vol. 1. Ed. W.J.B. Owen and J.W. Smyser. Oxford: Oxford University Press, 1974.

Yoder, R. Paul. 'Not From Troy, But Jerusalem: Blake's Canon Revision'. *Blake: An Illustrated Quarterly* (Summer 1997): 17–21.

7
blake and gender studies

helen p. bruder

The Feminine & Masculine Shadows soft, mild & ever varying
In beauty: are Shadows now no more, but Rocks in Horeb.
(J68.69–70, E222)

Irene Tayler's 'The Woman Scaly' (1973) initiated feminist study of Blake by confronting head on Blake's troubling concept of 'female will', which had habitually been viewed as the essence of Blakean female psychology and either valued as insight or (more rarely) condemned as misogyny. The article broke new ground with the observation that 'female will' is not an aspect of essential sexual character but, rather, describes strategies used by the oppressed to gain covert power which are gendered female because women so often find themselves in this position: the 'jealousy, selfishness, and ruthless will to power that grows in the heart of the possessed object is "female" because in our culture it is especially females who have been treated as commodities' (79). Tayler's evidence is incontestable: 'the female will tyrannizes over women as well as men' (86). Feminism in the 1970s was characterized by anti-essentialist anger and the unmasking of stereotypes and Blake, Tayler implies, foresaw the importance of both rage and revelation. Her article, then, prepared the way for analysis of his extraordinary insights into the motivated social construction of gender identity and an account of feminist writing after Tayler shows how this crucial subject forced its way, albeit slowly, up the critical agenda.

Various theoretical approaches were adopted, but pioneering writers were united by a strong desire to formulate comprehensive explanatory theories. Susan Fox (1977) believed that a study of metaphor held the key, concluding that Blake's 'philosophical principle of mutuality is [. . .] undermined by stereotypical metaphors of femaleness' (507). Alicia Ostriker (1982/83) preferred to focus on 'internal inconsistencies'

132

and identified four distinct 'Blakean attitudes toward sexual experience and gender relations' (156). She found more to praise than blame and suggests readers shouldn't be 'surprised or dismayed to find in Blake both a richly developed anti-patriarchal and proto-feminist sensibility [. . .] and its opposite, a homocentric gynophobia' (164). The longer studies which began to appear in the 1980s borrowed their explanatory theories from psychoanalysis, with mixed results. Most scholarly is Diana Hume George's *Blake and Freud* (1980) which illuminatingly interleaves direct quotation from each thinker (29–72) and places the distinctions thus revealed at the heart of the thoughtful analysis which follows. George also identifies what is a crucial problem for students of Blake and gender, commenting on how his 'composite portrayal of females and the feminine has been the cause of continuous confusion' (195). Her attempt to clarify the relationship between these key terms (183–209) relies on biological determinism, but *Blake and Freud*, nonetheless, gave invaluable intellectual credibility to feminist Blake studies. It also steered well clear of the diagnostic enthusiasm which characterizes both Brenda Webster's *Blake's Prophectic Psychology* (1983) and Margaret Storch's *Sons and Adversaries* (1990). These writers are, respectively, wedded to Freud and Klein but the conclusions they reach are strikingly similar: whether struggling with an unresolved Oedipal conflict or baffled by the swing of Klein's good/bad breasts, their Blake is fueled by unconscious primal rage. Like George, they forced critical attention onto the abundant sexual imagery and stark familial violence so integral to Blake's vision but the unswerving misogyny identified by their pathologizing agendas – 'no male figure [. . .] is capable of the range and subtlety of cruelty that characterizes the women' (Storch 236–7) – tends to terminate inquiry.

Such ahistorical judgments about sexual power were not shared by writers who established the other main school of early gendered criticism. They draw upon materialist theories to illuminate what David Aers classically termed 'William Blake and the Dialectic of Sex' (1977). He (1981) found in Blake's work 'an original and profound understanding of the dialectics of sexual conflict and the internalization of repressive ideologies by their victims' (27) and through this lens brought into focus both the historical processes, and contemporary inflections, of sexual power. These writers also seek to demonstrate that contemporary patriarchal ideology, by necessity, circumscribed Blake's own thinking; however, although dominant ideologies deserve much attention their ability to infect his thought with masculinist prejudices is, perhaps, overdetermined. Certainly huge emphasis is laid upon their powerful influence by David Punter (1985), who stresses that Blake was 'himself a participant in the vicissitudes of the history and politics of patriarchy' and, further, insists that we ditch the unproblematically subversive Blake as we 'press toward a realization of historical trapping' (331). Punter's analysis of Blake's traumatic textual relationship with both willful and willing females (1984) found severe historical circumscription: it 'discloses a limit in the history of literary discourse about women' (475). By the end of the 1980s, then, firm foundations were laid and though feminism was not warmly welcomed by the Blake establishment (Bruder (1997) 1–37) much diverse scholarship followed. This chapter outlines its contours, but before plunging into minute particulars it's worth noting that opinion is at present acutely divided.

For over twenty years Anne Mellor (1982/83) has offered unwavering accounts of 'Blake's consistently sexist portrayal of women' (148). She is an original theoretician of feminine and masculine Romanticisms (1993) but in her view 'Blake shared his culture's denigration of the feminine gender' (22) and can, therefore, never achieve the desired goal of ideological cross-dressing. When Mellor turned to the question of enslavement and sexual bondage (1996), she reached distasteful conclusions: her Blake condones 'the continuation of female slavery under a benevolent master' (368). At heart, Mellor's (1998) conviction is that we're still in need of systems that construct '*difference* (rather than assimilation) as the highest social value' and since she identifies a 'Blakean temptation toward a dialectic in which one contrary finally takes precedence' (353), his gender system is irredeemable. Marc Kaplan is Mellor's heir, presenting a Blake (1995) whose 'mythic cosmos is not only gendered but hierarchal and masculinist' (151). Kaplan's work (1996/97) has significant implications since his view that gender hierarchy is not a trope or metaphor but rather an organizing principle or 'categorical imperative' legitimates the alarming contention that 'Blake has made gender-as-social construction identitical with gender-as-essence' (71). Indeed he goes further, arguing for the existence of 'a real and essential system of difference' (78), an 'absolute binarism' which the artist felt it a 'crucial error' to undo (154): 'Blake, as much as the patriarchy he condemns, fears the collapse of sexual difference' (78).

One suspects that Kaplan's heretically conservative assessments were deliberately provocative. The trangressions beloved by queer theorists certainly subvert such anxious sexual absolutes and Andrew Elfenbein (1999) has shown how Blake's own 'camp quotient skyrockets when he confronts sex/gender issues. For him nothing is as silly and as serious as gender relations in a heterosexist, patriarchal culture' (151). Christopher Hobson's *Blake and Homosexuality* (2000) complements this observation with a series of thoughtful analysis which both chart Blake's changing attitudes towards homosexuality and explain the historical significance of his acceptance of sexual perversity, ambiguity and same-sex coupling. After reading work from this critical perspective, the axiomatic importance of the unequal pair – central to compulsory heterosex and Kaplan's binary universe – looks questionable. Further doubts are raised by Claire Colebrook (2000), who employs Irigarayan theory to illuminate Blake's positive valuation of mulitiple difference and of dynamic relations of difference. For this valuation to serve its ethical function of acknowledging that which exceeds the self, namely the (female) other, definitions can never be fixed, hence Colebrook's crucial interest in Blake's 'refusal to decide the nature or boundary of sexual difference [. . .] [I]t is sexual difference that is most resistant to resolution in his work' (12).

Alternatives to the Mellor/Kaplan position are also offered by critics working in the tradition established by Aers and Punter, who like Jackie DiSalvo (1998) want 'to supersede general discussions by relating Blake to historical discourses concerning women' (xxx) and like Catherine M. McClenahan (1998) insist we value his insights into both 'the gender of power and the power of gender' (307). Because these writers believe 'Gender and politics are more then parallel terms [. . . and] a gendered struggle for priority and power [. . .] becomes the basic pattern for all social relations' (McClenahan 302), they cannot accept the claim that Blake's view of gender is essentialist. Rather, ideologies of sexual difference, though powerful, are as contested, temporal and arbitary as any other historically specific ideology and Blake is praised because, as McClenahan (1990) insists, he was acutely aware of this 'social construction of gender [and the] enforcement of gender stereotypes' (189, 205). My own work (1994/97) historicizes Blake within a range of specific sexual debates and finds that he contested so thoroughly the premises of oppressive dominant ideologies that he must be adjudged a radical and prescient sexual thinker. Central is his conviction that gendered aspects of identity (those 'Feminine & Masculine Shadows') must not be limited, fixed or imposed, for disastrous consequences ensue when beautiful possibilities harden into sexual imperatives. I will trace the history of gendered scholarship by outlining Blake's own battle with essentialist notions of sexual difference. Hopefully, this overview will show that a concern with the social construction of gender identity is not an anachronism foisted on him by feminist critics but is, rather, a profound preoccupation that we share with him.

songs of innocence and of experience

The cameos of family life and youthful activity which shine from the pages of Blake's *Songs* quickly attracted the attention of critics interested in gender. Since these poems are both for and about children, scrutiny initially fell upon the figures who loom largest in the child's world: his or her parents, and gendered parental substitutes. The first works – Micele Leiss Stepto (1978) and Norma A. Greco (1986) – raise doubts about the nature of *Innocence*, insisting that we lose ours and acknowledge early flashes of female will in the allegedly sinister actions of Blake's superficially ideal mothers. Mellor (1988) built upon this maternal skepticism and though she found warm breasts innocently offered, experience soon saw them denied. Mellor's Blake 'continued to perceive the female as inferior' (14) and *Innocence* and *Experience* offer mirrored inflections of this immutable sexism: passive women (whether good or bad) are only ever mothers or lovers, contained within the domestic sphere whilst active men (more good than bad) colonize the feminine emotions, execute both private and public roles, emblematize the artist, the rebel, the divine, and dominate both verbal and visual texts through images of idealized paternalism. Stepto had tempered her parental judgments with the observation that fathers were 'implicated in [. . .] victimization of their children' (361), but within Mellor's (and Greco's) gender hierarchy paternal crimes are venial, maternal mortal (quite literally, as they read 'To Tirzah').

This subject continued to exercise critics in the 1990s, though contextual analysis considerably slowed the rush to judgment. June Sturrock (1994) used an examination of pastoral tradition to illuminate the 'historically determined understanding of woman as protected protector' (98). In the *Songs* the 'mother is [. . .] preferred to the father as an image of safekeeping. Yet all this protection implies danger and fear' (100) and the question of what threatened mothers in the late eighteenth century is explored in Harriet Krammer Linkin's (1998) account of 'Blake's complex [. . .] representation of the dilemma of idealized maternity' (336). Linkin identifies a 'double bind' in contemporary 'domestic ideology' (335), which made impossible demands on the middle/upper class mothers who tried to obey its devotional imperative and which for their less wealthy counterparts was a sham, 'wish fulfillment' (329, 335), that mocked the realities of working class family life: high mortality rates, abandonment and prostitution. Blake's *Songs* invert the dominant 'maternity plot', enabling a 'recognition of a greater variety of maternal positions than contemporary cultural idealizations of the mother allow' (327).

In her *Songs*-based feminist revision of literary tradition, Elizabeth Langland (1987) shows how 'certain interpretations [. . .] have been canonized to support patriarchy' (232). The criticism summarized above undermines that distorting process and scholarship dealing with individual Songs also has a revisionary power which makes it noteworthy. The following list is partial but illustrative: Sturrock (1994/95) identifies an allusion to the 'sisters of Bethany' in the design of 'To Tirzah' (E30) whose presence undercuts the misogynistic rage against 'birth as death' (91) usually leeched from that poem; Eijun Senaha (1996) finds a 'carefully designed illustration of the female genitalia' (12) in 'The Sick Rose' (E23) and intriguingly suggests that the invisible worm is the finger of a masturbating girl; Katherine Trowbridge (1996) raises questions about the relationship of 'A Little Girl Lost' with patriarchy by highlighting the textual uncertainty over who utters the crucial lines, 'Ona! pale and weak! / To thy father speak' (E30); and Mark Lussier (2000) identifies ecofeminism as an interpretative context for the 'Introduction' to *Experience* and 'Earth's Answer', suggesting that 'Blake forges a link between capital exploitation of the planet and cultural exploitation of women' within the symbolic order of patriarchy (57–8).

These gendered readings of the *Songs* are invaluable innovations and interested readers also study Mary Lynn Johnson's (1989) invaluable overview, in which she notes that 'Blake takes special care to free "innocence" of its traditional associations with sexual immaturity' (61). He actually goes further, making sensual pleasures (stroking, playing, licking, kissing, touching) the defining characteristic of the state. In this context, sex is just another aspect of physical play, as the transitional 'The Little Girl Lost/Found' reveals. To the experienced eyes of Lyca's parents the 'beasts of prey' (32–3, E20) signal male predation, but in the sleeping Lyca's bisexual dream world, where 'the lioness, / Loos'd her slender dress' (49–50), they are harmless sexual playmates (39–42). Through reverse chronology the visual text retells this story of dreamy sensuality: the clothed girl's embrace of a naked youth leads, by the final plate, to a circling image of childish animal pleasure. Even when imagery becomes genital, as in 'The Blossom' (E10), a 'happy' (3, 9) mood reigns because sexual pleasures remain childish: the 'Merry, Merry Sparrow / Under leaves so green' (1–2) is surely penile but his 'swift as arrow' (4) penetration remains within the world of innocence because what he seeks is a 'cradle narrow' (5). 'The Gates of Paradise', it would seem, open more easily 'For Children' (E323) than 'For The Sexes' (E259–68).

Innocence, then, is not marked by an absence of sexual activity. Rather, it's the state evoked by Oothoon: 'Infancy, fearless, lustful, happy! nestling

for delight / In laps of pleasure' (*VDA*6.4–5, E49). But what are absent
are fixed and stereotypical gender roles. Moreover it is, as Johnson
observes, a 'manifestly uterocentric' (61) world and those interested in
gender will keenly note how the absence of authoritative patriarchs (63)
leads to freedom, for both sexes, from limiting gendered identities. Since
early childhood is the time when divisive gender oppositions are enforced
it is striking that Blake resists even mentioning the biological sex of his
children, much less conferring significance on it: the baby's sex in 'A
Cradle Song' (E11–12) is not given and even the female named 'Infant
Joy' remains an ungendered bundle of self-defining happiness. The same
is true of his older 'children': those heard, addressed and obeyed in the
'Nurse's Song' (E15) are sexually undifferentiated (1, 5) and the omnisexual
'joys' shared by generations of 'girls & boys' (17–18) on 'The Ecchoing
Green' (E8) remain emphatically mutual when the 'sports [. . .] end':
'sisters and brothers' flock 'Round the laps of their mothers' (24–6).

Johnson notes that Blake shared Mary Wollstonecraft's displeasure at
contemporary soldier boy/dolly girl divisions (61) and it is fascinating to
look at how far his own gendering departs from tough/soft stereotypes.
'The Chimney Sweeper' (E10) and 'The Little Boy lost/Found' (E11)
are profound poems (not least as portraits of paternal cruelty) and
unconventional gendering underpins their meaning. The horror of
Tom's fate is deepened when we note what moves this sensitive boy
to tears: not fear of flames but, rather, the shaving of his soft curly hair
(5–6). The illumination shows that chimney sweeps are emotional boys,
freely holding hands and hugging when released from deathly bondage.
Their lost/found brother is a kindred spirit, shamelessly admitting that
he cannot match his daddy's rapid stride, this boy uses the diminutive
'little' to name himself, openly cries when lost and is happy to be kissed
or led by the hand. Indeed, when we reach the illuminations we find a
world of complete gender fluidity: the lost boy's hair is so full and his
dress so fitted that he seems girlish, while the 'God' who appears 'like his
father' ('Found' 3–4) is even more feminized. The subtly androgynous
Christ from 'The Little Black Boy' (E9) is now a woman or so 'her' elegant
stride, flowing locks and gathered gown suggest. In this context it's hardly
surprising that adult males are as 'sweet' (1) and gentle as 'The Shepherd'
(E7), whose working life is defined by benign passivity. The 'ewes tender
reply' to her 'lambs innocent call' (5–6) is the caring ideal to which he
aspires and as a model of masculinity is both politically and historically
arresting, especially when viewed alongside the noisy, carefree girls who
sing ('Spring' E14–15) and giggle ('Laughing Song' E11) nearby. At the
spiritual heart of *Innocence* is a feminized, pastoral Christianity whose

greatest value is empathic love. Contemporary sensibility and radical incarnationalism combine in Blake's picture of the deliberately unsexed Christ child ('Cradle' 21–2, E11–12) and the gendering of a deity who expresses strength (adult/masculine) through weakness (infant/feminine) deepens this discussion considerably.

There is only one example of sexual segregation in *Innocence*, seen in the ranks of aproned girls and overcoated boys who march across the plate of 'Holy Thursday' (E13). By following aged patriarchs in to a city church they are unwittingly entering the realm of *Experience*, whose contrary status is established by its masculine gender. To characterize this state as one of malevolent matriarchy seems perverse since even cursory examination reveals a catalogue of explicitly patriarchal tyrannies: religious ('A Little Boy Lost' and 'The Garden of Love'), political-economic ('The Chimney Sweeper'), paternal ('Infant Sorrow'), sexual (numerous, including 'Earth's Answer' and 'A Little Girl Lost'). Moreover, whilst a handful of young girls and boys are united by suffering or admonishment ('Holy Thursday', 'Infant Sorrow', 'Nurse's Song'), few escape the divisive influence of harsh fatherly gendering. Patriarchal oppression provokes male protest, which hardens boys' sense of their developing masculinity and though the contentious complaints of the Schoolboy and Vagabond are innocuous, the cockier challenges of the 'heretic' and Sweeper contain seeds of the masculinist rage which fires Blake's rapist revolutionary Orc and fills the Epics with vicious father/son conflict. Girls, by contrast, passively accept a stifled yet emphatically sexualized existence under the rule of patriarchs and priests. The oppositional images – healthy blossom/sick rose, laughing mouth/'Harlots curse' ('London' 14, E26–7) emblematize female loss in the world of *Experience* where enforcement of the gendered Clod/Pebble dynamic is pervasive.

As we might expect, the heterosexual couple has a prominent role and disharmony is often generated by the pressure of sexual stereotypes. For example, the tainted gender dynamics active/passive, subject/object account for many of the sexual problems described in 'The Angel' and 'My Pretty Rose Tree'. Blake may wistfully hope that the defenseless Lilly 'shall in Love delight' (3, E25), but his own observation of how females are 'with bondage bound' by the 'Selfish father of men' ('Earth's Answer' 25, 11, E18–19) reveals that feminine passivity will not achieve that aim. Interestingly, there is one example of happy sexual 'play' in *Experience*, achieved by a 'youthful pair' who meet outside the realm of parental influence. Yet this lasts for but one day, since the 'pale and weak' Ona has been programmed to quail before her father's religious/sexual fears ('A Little Girl Lost' 16, 10, 30). It seems that until the gendered division between warm, pining, male 'Youth' and cold, shrouded, 'pale Virgin' has been undone sexual harmony will remain an aspiration ('Ah! Sunflower' 5–7, E25). Even the usually optimistic visual text reinforces this conclusion: females are wary of activity, they shun touch or make contact awkwardly ('Rose', 'Angel', 'Nurse', 'Sorrow', 'Fly'), with the loving caress of the generally excoriated 'To Tirzah' being the only exception.

The collection's theoretical poems suggest that an explicitly masculine philosophy (contrary to *Innocence*'s feminine theology) generates and justifies the horrors of *Experience*. Abstract masculine thinking is shown to pervert redemptive feminine qualities – 'Pity [. . .] Mercy' – into justifications for the abundant miseries which characterize this patriarchal state: poverty, unhappiness, selfishness and fear ('The Human Abstract' 1–6, E27). And it's noteworthy that the gender of this insidious ideology is established through the reversal of sexual stereotypes: all the devices used – 'Cruelty [. . .] holy fears [. . .] tears [. . .] Humility [. . .] Mystery [. . .] Deceit – to corrupt the 'Human Brain' (7, 9, 11, 14, 17, 24) are conventionally associated with the female or feminine, yet by deliberately masculinizing them Blake unmasks both the arbitrary nature of stereotypes and the gendering power of patriarchy. There is an illuminating parallel in 'A Poison Tree' (E28) where his borrowing from the masculine lexicon of war ('foe', 'wrath') tacitly reverses the gender of traditionally feminine 'fears', 'tears', 'smiles', 'soft deceitful wiles' (5–8) to illuminate the psychological genesis of murderous male conflict. The beautiful cruciform corpse who lies beneath the text recalls Blake's beloved Christ, whose efforts to reform masculinity and keep men from war underpin his entire epic project.

Finally, it's worth noting Johnson's observation that the *Songs* develop and elaborate a 'marginal genre' usually 'associated with women' (63). Two areas of future research flow from this. First, consideration should be given to Blake's unusual gendering of creativity/genius and of the artist/poet and, more importantly, the work of contemporary female poets must be seen as a primary interpretative context. *Songs*' critics have begun this revisionary task – Lauren Henry (1995) referencing Phylis Wheatley, Sarah Zimmerman (1997) Charlotte Smith, Thomas Kennedy (1998) Anna Barbauld – but we are still a very long way from an accurate perception of Blake's cultural context. As Keri Davies (1999) showed, one of the first people to read these poems was the lesbian bibliophile Rebekah Bliss, but do our literary histories have any place for her in their assumed audience? Shirley Dent and Jason Whittaker's (2002) account of how Blake has 'been a source of inspiration to women artists' (121) certainly suggests that we should feminize our theories of context and reception.

the book of thel **and** *visions of the daughters of albion*

Patriarchy's ability to enforce models of femininity is scrutinized by Thel and Oothoon, who query and defy essentialist prescriptions. The importance of their stories is evidenced by the mountain of criticism they've generated and I'll sketch the centrality of gender identity as a motivated social construction in these poems before examining some of this scholarship.

Thel's role is primarily interrogative. Visually, she stares; verbally, she questions (Otter 1991), and what Thel discovers is that the seemingly fluid feminine stereotypes she experiments with, which initially appear 'like shadows in the water [. . .] like music in the air' (1.9, 11, E3), are fixed by patriarchy into a hard ideology of submissive feminine nurture and deathly female sacrifice. The ultimate patriarch seduces his daughters with mild promises of nourishment (1.19–24) and his wives with lyrical promises of love (5.1–4) but these soft blessings hold a curse, since the price demanded for patriarchal benediction is a confession of female abjection: the Lilly defines herself through diminutive frailty ('I am a [. . .]weed, / And I am very small [. . .] lowly [. . .] weak' 1.16–18), the Clod, through debased stupidity ('Thou seest me the meanest thing, and so I am [. . .] I cannot know [. . .] I cannot ponder' 4.10, 5.5–6). Such subservient gendered mentalities serve the urge to make females 'natural' carers but, as Thel perceives, they also mask the destructiveness integral to patriarchal versions of feminine devotion, for the Lilly will not be 'fed with morning manna' (1.23). As a female she is the nurturer, not the nurtured, and minding a 'numerous charge among the verdant grass' (2.18) is just girlish preparation for what Thel apprehends: an adult life of pointless ('Giving to those that cannot crave' 2.4) female masochism ('the innocent lamb [. . .] crops thy flowers.while thou sittest smiling in his face' 2.5–6). The suicidal nature of the Clod's mother love is starker still: 'She bow'd over the weeping infant, and her life exhal'd / In milky fondness' (4.8–9).

Revealingly, the only nurturer not destroyed by parental duties in the realm of Har is the male Cloud, who not only has the power to compel a (tellingly reluctant) female consort to assist him (3.12–16), but who also knows that the emotional economy of patriarchy will repay male sacrifice with a life-enhancing abundance which is the absolute opposite of the females' reward for self giving: 'when I pass away / It is to tenfold life, to love, to peace, and raptures holy' (3.10–11). Thel tries out his stance of airy freedom (illumination plate 4), but when her view of an infant prompts fears that she will be consumed (3.23), the Cloud discloses why – in this essentialist world – Thel will never be able to share his male role: 'if thou art the food of worms [. . .] How great thy use. how great thy blessing' (3.25–6). The 'secret' of Har's 'grave plot' (1.2, 6.9) is that women are valued solely for their utility and the sacrifical doctrine (which still – Ferber (2002) – has male admirers) intoned by the Clod, 'we live not for ourselves' (4.10), is a gendered ideological delusion which seeks to naturalize the motivated valuations of sexual difference which demonstrably serve patriarchy but destroy women. The answer to the question, 'why should Thel complain?' (1.25) is, therefore, quite obvious. A tradition of sexist scholarship fiercely criticizes her flight from maternal embodiment but Blake's account of patriarchal deployments of 'the natural' in the service of the ideological suggests that his own judgment was rather different.

Visions' characterization of women's condition as one of enslavement (1.1, E45) by an imperial patriarchy which naturalizes its barbarities through ideologies of fixed sexual and racial difference certainly supports this contention. The slave/woman Oothoon is a threat precisely because her delight in the slippery multiplicity of female sexuality (1.3–10) impels her to fly in the face of the gendered active/passive binary which governs patriarchal heterosex (1.14–15). Bromion's controlling response is as revealing as it is violent (1.16–23): through rape (16) he attacks the site of her subversive pleasures, through perjorative redefinition – 'behold this harlot' (18) – he discredits them and, most important, he converts her into an enslaved sexual possession: 'mine [. . .] mine' (20). This enables the imprinting of notions of essential sexual and racial character. Those 'Stampt with' Bromion's 'signet' become what he desires: 'obedient, they resist not, they obey the scourge: / Their daughters worship terrors and obey the violent' (21–3). Sadistic males create the ideal of female masochism and in the process erect an ideology of starkly oppositonal sexual difference: 'Bound back to back [. . .] terror and meekness dwell' (2.5, see also Frontispiece).

Oothoon's ambiguous response to her bondage has attracted much interest and I'd like to highlight the two stances she adopts towards the gender system which enslaves her, namely assimilation through reflection (2.11–3.20) and defiance through rejection of its hierarchal binaries (5.3–8.10) in favor of politicized difference (as Julia Wright (1996) notes, Blake offers 'heterogeneity as a means by which hegemonic prescription can be undermined' (77)). Oothoon's attempt to persuade Theotormon to accept her rests upon the insistence that she is capable of reflecting his image (2.15–19). Purity is the key value here (2.28, 3.16) and she hopes to achieve assimilation through perfect mirroring. Such efforts prove to be 'in vain' (2.22) however, since she doesn't share his valuation of defilement (3.17–19) and no raped black woman will ever convince imperial patriarchy that (in Oothoon's words) 'I am white and pure' (3.20). The males' responses testify to their incomprehension: Theotormon asks a battery of questions which suggest he's lost the power of thought (3.21–4.10), while Bromion (4.13–25) – terrified at the 'Unknown [. . .] worlds' (16–17) opened before him – clings to the absolute certainties of patriarchal restriction, that 'one law for both the lion and the ox' (22). The speech which epitomizes Oothoon's second distinct strategy is perhaps the longest ever given, by the usually dialogic Blake, to a single character (102 uninterrupted lines) and opens with an assault on Urizenic masculinity's demonic construction of identity through likeness (5.3–6). In opposition, Oothoon exuberantly celebrates difference (5.7–17, 33–41/7.30–8.10), blasts the masculine abstractions which despoil *Experience* (5.19–20) and rages against patriarchal limitation with unparalleled ferocity (5.21–32). Crucial are the lines, 'Till she who burns with youth.and knows no fixed lot; is bound / In spells of law to one she loaths' (5.21–32), because Blake's description of the hateful sexual compulsions of legally enforced matrimony forges an unbreakable link with feminist discourse which criticism must illuminate further. Similarly important are his revelations about patriarchy's indoctrination of its 'accursed' values (7.12–13, 6.7–9); the unsettling of fixed systems of sexual difference through scrutinizing, reversing or re-gendering key stereotypes: virgin, whore, harlot, 'hypocrite modesty' (6.16, 6.4–21); and, of course, Oothoon's much vaunted eroticism. I've addressed the issue of sexual entrapment (7.23–9) elsewhere (1997, 55–89) and will discuss contradictions momentarily. Here I'll simply note what is incontestable: that it's through eroticism that Oothoon most powerfully assaults the binaries – viewer/viewed, holy/sinful, heterosexual/queer – which beat at the heart of the gender system which enslaves her. Indeed, her sexuality defies patriarchal definition, for though she wants to arouse Theotormon, Oothoon is equally stimulated by the feminine (6.21–7.2) and the female (7.25). Though problematic, the free love which she recommends (7.16–22) is unarguably screamed in defiance of greedy masculine assimilation and the pivotal question, 'Can that be Love, that drinks another as a sponge drinks water?' must be answered, no, it's just another example of husbandly 'self-love that envies all! a creeping skeleton / With lamplike eyes watching round the frozen marriage bed' (17/21–2). This is majestic feminist rhetoric, though dilemmas of course remain.

It took many years of feminist argument to establish that abused women don't usually believe that heterosex will liberate them, but discussions of this pivotal contradiction now abound. Steven Vine (1994) looks searchingly at the 'meaning of the body as both enslavement and enlightenment' (43); Fred Hoerner (1996) offers a post-structuralist twist in his argument that Oothoon 'exploits the resources of the discourse that enslaves her' (121), whilst Wes Chapman (1997) believes 'Oothoon's contradictory character' arises from Blake's anticipation of 'the crucial problems men have had in responding to feminism' (14). Looking more directly at those 'silken nets and traps' (7.23), Nicholas Williams (1998) depicts Oothoon as the 'subject of a utopian pornography' (95), whereas Hobson (2000) believes 'this opening to perversion' is a stepping stone towards acceptance of 'sexual gratification other than through heterosexual intercourse' (35). Robert Essick's critical edition (2002) of the poem summarizes new areas of debate but also queries celebrations of the 'transgressive implications of the text' (38).

What should never be forgotten is *Visions'* depiction of unaltered bondage – still 'Enslav'd, the Daughters of Albion weep' (1.1) – and accurate understanding of this situation will only come through a deepened sense of Blake's historical context. I sought to locate the poem within the webs of exploitative sexual discourse spun in the 1790s (1997, 59–73) and critics should push deeper into the history of pornography and erotica. They might also follow Blake's Luvah towards the East, for contemporary constructions of the sensual yet despotic 'Orient' are suggestive and surely inform the claim that 'Antamon call'd up Leutha from her valleys of delight / And to Mahomet a loose Bible gave' (*SL*3.28–9, E67 and 'Leutha's vale' in *VDA*1.1–15, E45–6). The neglect of this sexual geography is strange, since critics have illuminated Blake's sensitivity to the interdependence of national, cultural and sexual exploitation when looking at his treatment of slavery: Nancy Goslee (1990) shows how productive this 'master trope' is; Vine (1994) explores how the poem 'dramatizes [. . .] the violent logic of the slave-trade' (50); Anne Rubenstein and Camilla Townsend (1998) note that Blake refused 'to make slavery seem [. . .] natural' (294); Helen Thomas (2000) finds 'absolute egalitarianism' (123); whilst Debbie Lee (2002) believes he employed techniques of 'mock mimicry' to undercut contemporary racial stereotypes. Amongst the many virtues of this scholarship is the sustained attention it gives to Blake's role as an illustrator of other authors' books, in this case John Stedman's *Narrative of a Five Years' Expedition Against the Revolted Negroes of Surinam*. His work as a commercial illustrator has been neglected but it is often here that we find Blake most immersed in contemporary ideologies and for those wishing to historicize his visions of masculinity and femininity these designs are precious intertexts. It's also clear that a broader understanding of women's history and feminist discourse is needed. *Visions* routinely generates comment about Wollstonecraft's *Vindication of the Rights of Woman* and whilst much of this writing is valuable (Chapman, Vine and Clark (1994), for example) looking exclusively into the masculine genre of political polemic for expressions of feminism is unhelpfully ahistorical. Like Wollstonecraft herself, Blake's feminist contemporaries often favored fictional forms and a study of novelistic treatments (especially gothic) of paternal tyranny and the inequalities of patriarchal marriage would do much to illuminate the historicity of Blake's sexual radicalism and Oothoon's unending subjugation.

Thel may well be the most debated of Blake's poems. Its heroine has certainly attracted 'vicious, vituperative, debasing' (Gerda Norvig, 1995, 271) criticism. Both the quantity and quality of this work is revealing about sexual politics within Blake Studies (Bruder, 1997, 38–54), and current positions remain acutely divided. Hilda Hollis (1996/97) insists that we 'avoid the danger of falsely attributing a feminist agenda to Blake' and reanimates the tradition which denigrates Thel as a 'nay-saying virgin [. . .] a type of the female will [. . .] a metaphor for the limiting natural religion' (88, 89). Hisao Ishizuka (1997) goes further, making explicit the essentialism of his predecessors by locating the source of Thel's problems within her: because she's stifled her natural desire for heterosex Thel has contracted green sickness and through this diagnostic lens her flight is 'not a commendable resistence to ideology' but a 'literal and imbecile enactment' (262) of self-denial. The alternative tradition builds upon Kelvin Everest's (1987) insistence that Thel is caught in the throes of a genuine female dilemma, which accounts for her querulous and resistant character. Norvig offers a full elaboration in her account of the multi-valent position of feminized liminality occupied by Thel – an edgy borderline location 'from which specific, socially constructed definitions of gender are [. . .] called into question' (255). 'Thel's liminal identity' (256) entails the 'desire for a female subjectivity', which in turn involves criticism of that 'philosophy detrimental to the energies of real women even as it' serves 'the so-called feminine values of an empirical, deistical patriarchal order' (270–1). Norvig sees Thel as 'an icon of resistance to sexist indoctrination' (256) and all writers who lean in this direction stress, like Deborah McCollister (1996/97), how important it is that Blake 'does give her a choice' (94).

The debate, then, has been heated and though it has cooled in recent years contextual study will revive and clarify discussion. As I've shown (1997, 40–5), conduct literature is one rich source of intertextual illumination (see too Otter 1998), but other educational treatises would repay analysis, since they show how female 'excess leads' to anywhere but Blake's 'palace of wisdom' (*MHH*7.3, E35). Another interesting path is opened up by Kevin Hutchings (1997) whose demonstration of how 'anthropocentrism is not only related to, but *is*, precisely, *andro*centrism in Har's patriarchal economy' (174) reveals that all kinds of power are gendered through analysis of 'the violence of anthropomorphic colonization' (167) and offers a fresh view on Blake's attitude towards nature. Conventionally, critics identify a negative association of 'the female' with 'the natural' (Ferber 1985) but writers informed by environmental politics – who like James McKusick (2000) see Blake as 'the bard of ecotopia' (106) – offer highly suggestive revaluations of both terms. Hutchings' historicist elaboration of his argument (2002, 90–102) underscores this point and since botany and zoology were branches of science open to Blake's female contemporaries further contextual work could again interestingly overlap with innovative gender scholarship (see also Susanne Araas Vesely (1998) on Blake's response to women as 'popularizers of science' (24)).

the marriage of heaven and hell, america a prophecy, europe a prophecy

The static binaries unmasked in *Visions*, and the authoritarian philosophies/theologies which employ them, are targeted throughout *Marriage* (E33–45). Plate 3's dynamic contraries – so 'Necessary to Human existence' – dismiss all fixity. Plate 4's rejection of mind/body dualism is an axe to the root of Western patriarchy's conceptual structures and the rest of the text rejects, reverses or revalues countless conventional pairings: Heaven/Hell, angelic/infernal, good/evil and, striking for an understanding of Blake as a gender sensitive artist, fancy/genius (pl.6); wisdom/folly (Proverbs 3, 8, 12, 18, 32, 47, 52), sublime/beautiful (Proverbs 17, 61, 64). At the text's center (pl. 7–10) are 70 Proverbs of Hell whose irreducibly polyphonous quality translates Oothoon's politicized celebration of difference into an equally gendered, but now spiritual, celebration of infinity. Blake's most famous proposition – 'If the doors of perception were cleansed every thing would appear to man as it is: infinite' (pl.14) – lies at the heart of his sexual radicalism, because not only do women have the most to gain from the expunging of false notions about physical embodiment, they also direct the 'improvement of sensual enjoyment' which brings this liberation about and, as the fiery females burning across plates 3 and 14 testify, they share Blake's demystifying work: 'melting apparent surfaces away, and displaying the infinite which was hid'. The freedoms enjoyed by 'infernal' females are described by Dee Drake (2000) and it's worth noting that deliverance from religious limitation into bound(ary)less infinity can be instrumental in challenging patriarchy. On plates 12–13, for example, we hear how the prophet Ezekiel's desire to bring others 'into a perception of the infinite' led him away from 'subjection' to the traditions of patriarchal Judaism: his visionary methods are those which 'the North American tribes practise'.

What's most striking, however, is that none of these pregnant theoretical possibilities are brought to birth in the verbal text: despite that scarifying critique of patriarchal matrimony in *Visions*, 'Marriage' (pl.1) remains just a metaphor and none of the achingly suggestive contraries (reason/energy, love/hate, attraction/repulsion, restrainer/restrained) is explicitly gendered. Indeed the pair most plump with heterosexual suggestion (prolific and devouring) are explicitly described as 'two classes of men' (pl.16). The political context provides many answers, for this is generically Blake's manifesto, his contribution to the pamphlet war of the 1790s and the sexual exclusivity of the 'rights of man' is hugely relevant. In future, feminists must revisit the subtly nuanced political subcultures so meticulously reconstructed during the 1990s and attend to the place of women in the suggestive public spaces inhabited by Blake's radical contemporaries (we could, for example, follow David Worrall (2000) into the sexy political culture of Drury Lane). The female's relationship with political discourse is also central, since the 'firm perswasion' (pl.12–13) which characterized radical debating clubs and republican tavern culture may well have been a rhetorical stiffening only men were capable of. Critics must pay attention to the models of masculinity fostered by radical culture on both sides of the channel, for sexual identity played a key role in the formation of the new republican citizen and this has to be grasped if we want to understand the contemporary temptation to image the rebel as roaring (pl.2), pushy (pl.19), insulting (pl.21), 'heretical' (pl.22–3) (male) devil (*passim*). Though the visual text offers birth as a paradigm of energetic liberation (pl.3), *Marriage* firmly links phallic power and political rebellion, the consequences of which are apparent in *America*.

Male relationships are also privileged. In this work full of characters, none are female (except the anonymous 'woman taken in adultery' pl.23), which leads to the appearance of masculine priorities central in Blake's epic writing. The homoeroticism so integral to the 'Mental Fight' of 'Young Men' (pl.1) in *Milton* is strikingly foreshadowed during the metaphysical debate between Angel and Youth (pl.17–20), whose turning point comes when 'I by force suddenly caught him in my arms

[. . .] I flung myself with him directly into the body of the sun' (pl.19). Such abandon marks the moment when Los and Blake become 'One Man' (*M*22.12, E117) and calls to mind that much discussed image of sunny fellatio (*M* pl.21). Christianity is also given an outrageously masculinist inflection: 'The worship of God is [. . .] loving the greatest men best' (pl.22–3) and it's the impulsive Jesus conjured from this idea who has the (ironic/subversive) power to turn Angel to Devil (pl.24). The 'particular' friendship Blake enjoys with this convert seems to prefigure the ideal of redemptive brotherhood which predominates in *Jerusalem*, where fraternal equality threatens to occlude gender equity. More domestically, Blake seems to sense that male/female relationships founder upon the infernal ideal, 'Opposition is true Friendship' (pl.20). If so, we're returned to that emotional agenda I believe he shared with contemporary novelists, for who could deny that the contrary conflicts of courtship are an irresistible theme in women's Romantic fiction? Austen's proud and prejudiced lovers are only the most familiar of many abrasive couples.

Masculinity is also a major concern in *America* (E51–9), where gender is at work in two parallel, but by no means complementary, processes. On the one hand, Blake genders his mythological account of the American Revolution, which is a struggle of 'warlike men, who rise in silent night' (3.3). Narratives of revolution were often extravagantly sexualized and the gendered stories told by political caricature provide a particularly valuable interpretative framework since their literal embodiment of historical events resonates in innumerable (unexplored) ways with Blake's own 'Intense! naked!' (4.8) political bodies. In tandem with the telling of this masculinized historical narrative, there is an analysis of the violent variants of masculinity which emerge in times of war ('Then Mars thou wast our center' 5.4) and their problematic relationship with revolution's avowed aim to produce a peaceful polity. Carniverous, often sexual, predation is the key trope, as the 'Empire' of 'Lion & Wolf' (6.15) is, allegedly, terminated by a revolutionary force self-defined as 'an eagle screaming [. . .] a lion, / Stalking' (1.13–14). These ambiguities gather of course in Orc, whose 'fierce embrace' (1.10) of Urthona's daughter has attracted much gendered criticism. Aers (1987) was the first to stress how 'thoroughly macho' (251) this version of revolutionary force is and William Keach (1992) concludes that 'the whole scene is complicit with the worst kind of masculine fantasy' (33). Wright (1996) and McClenahan (1998) look, alternatively, at the female, focusing in particular on her 'powers of speech' (315). Wright's treatment of voice is particularly fine, since it establishes that Blake's females are 'more then the sum of their reproductive parts'; 'they speak, supplementing their uterine identities' (62–3).

However one responds to Orc's seizure of 'the panting struggling womb' (2.3), it is clear that his 'terrible' (2.6) male behavior is consonant with his devilish masculine identity as a 'Lover of wild rebellion. and transgressor of God's Law' (7.6). Orc is an archetypal fighter of the forces of imperial and religious oppression figured in Albion's Angel, and yet the seemingly perennial father/son struggle they enact raises questions about the liberty he desires. Aers (1987) believes there is 'omnious collusion' (251) between them and the stark mirror images (pl.8/10 illustrations) do suggest identification. As Peter Otto (1998) puts it, visually they appear 'strangely interdependent, perhaps even mutually constitutive' (235). Undoubtedly they share a masculinist mentality which sees women as sexual objects to be either repressed or ravished (or possibly both, as in 8.10–14) and in the Orcian scheme freedom from marital monogamy (15.19–26) is assumed to be the quintessence of female liberty. As ever, the visual text dissents, showing women burnt by Orc's flames (pl.15) or ravened by his talons (pl.13). William Richey (1998) thinks revolution only turns violent 'because of the unmerited and relentless attacks of its counter-revolutionary foes' (208) and though this is debatable it's surely significant that the text's revolutionary actors are motivated less by lustful rage than by philosophical indignation at dishonest and hypocritical religious perversion of humane (often feminine) values: 'Till pity is become a trade, and generosity a science, / That men get rich by' (11.10–11). *America* is not an easy poem to interpret and it leaves questions which only further study of historical masculinities will answer. It dreams of singing female captives, freed 'from the opressors scourge' (6.11), yet the phallus which enables liberation itself figures as 'the impure scourge' (*VDA*5.31) of patriarchal tyranny.

America, then, shows Blake's profound awareness that gender operates beyond the confines of individual psychology: a historical process, revolution, is shown to have sexual identity. *Europe* (E60–6) builds upon this insight, though the focus is on an institution, Christianity, and the gendering is feminine. Andrew Lincoln (1999) summarizes this progression toward 'the second, feminine, stage of imperial possession [. . .] conquest by conversion [. . .] in which gentle, "feminine" attributes are used to sweeten and justify reigns of terror and cruelty' (632, 639). Christianity is of course still the patriarchal religion of 'Urizen [. . .] And his brazen Book, / That Kings & Priests had copied on Earth' (11.2–4) and women are still subject to male dominion (visually to patriarch (pl. 8), Pope (pl. 10), warrior (pl. 5), revolutionary (pl.15)), but its work is done through feminine strategies: seduction, flattery, consolation and (especially) pity. Lincoln explores contemporary religions of the heart and it's worth noting how instrumental to patriarchal rule this soft and beguiling Christianity is, especially in Blake's later work. The genesis of the ensnaring triad – female/pity/net of religion – is traced in *The Book of Urizen* (18.13–19.9, 25.1–28.11 E78, 82–3) and its ideological function later revealed when Urizen instructs his daughters in hegemonic 'Moral Duty' in (*FZ*80.1–21, E355): 'Compell the poor to live on a Crust of bread by soft mild arts [. . .] Flatter his wife pity his children till we can / Reduce all to our will as spaniels are taught with art' (3, 9, 20–1).

The consequences for women are dire, since integral to patriarchal Christianity's gender system is the repressive notion that 'Womans love is Sin!' (5.5), which results in female lives governed by the resounding edict 'Thou shalt not' (12.28), itself ideologically justified through the delusive claim that prohibition equates to 'womans triumph' (12.25). This ambiguous situation, where the feminine reigns through imperatives which oppress females, is focused in the character of Enitharmon, herself the locus of much gendered criticism. Aers (1977) first showed that she isn't the willful bitch loathed by generations of critics, through his dialectical argument that 'forms of political and sexual domination are internalized to generate a "female will"' (508) and, building on this, Rajan (1995) explored how the poem 'inscribes gender as a site of excess unaccounted for by [. . .] vilification' (379). I (1997) found a historical explanation in the contradictory representations of female power thrown up during the French Revolution (133–78); Williams (1998) notes many ambiguities in Enitharmon's dream (79–84), whilst Lincoln's analysis of its exercise in the private sphere truly reveals the 'feminizing power of the dominant ideology' (635). *Europe* is a complex poem, but I have discussed this single aspect because it heralds Blake's great interest in the gender/ing of religious institutions, a concern which lies at the heart of his Epics. Indeed, the monumental edifice of *Jerusalem* is primarily structured by an exploration of patriarchy's disastrous feminine gendering of three of its major institutions: Judaism, Deism and Christianity.

Feminists have tended to avoid the religious/spiritual aspects of Blake's work and this must change. Not only because Christianity played a pivotal role in the history of British feminism, nor because religious movements granted women unprecedented public roles during Blake's lifetime but, more fundamentally, because of his profound belief in specifically spiritual liberation and his acute perception that Eve's sins always attracted more priestly censure than Adam's. Some subjects for research are obvious. Future treatments of biblical females could build on Sturrock (1992), who

writes about Blake's negative revaluations of Rahab, Tirzah and Mary; G.A.
Rosso (2002), who discusses Rahab's 'definitive and problematic' (288)
connection with the Book of Revelation or McClenahan (2002), who
foregrounds Dinah (Genesis 34). Feminist theology also has intriguing
resonances (G. Ingli James 1996). The tacit conservatism of much writing
on esoterica has tended to repel feminists, yet the visionary worlds of
the neoplatonists/alchemists/gnostics/kabbalists and of the Classical
and Vedic traditions pulsate with gender significance. Even the minimal
scholarship so far produced demonstrates this. See, for example, Peter
Sorensen (1996) on how the female presence in Gnosticism's godhead
revalues woman's role in narratives of fall and redemption and Drake
(2000), who identifies Blake's shift from early celebration of 'the divine
immanence of paganism's many Gods and Goddesses' to a 'privileging of
the transcendent God of Christianity' (13). Antinomianism's politicized
spirituality is even more suggestive, yet its sexual dimension has received
minimal analysis. Martin Priestman's (1999) discussion of gender in the
context of radical religion is a valuable exception; Whittaker's (1999)
writing on druids, deism and patriarchy (114–51) is also relevant whilst
Marsha Keith Schuchard's (2000) archival illumination of Blake's
'theosophy of desire' (47) is fascinating. The prophet Ezekiel told
Blake that Eastern philosophy 'taught the first principles of human
perception' (*MHH*12, E39) and Worrall (1995) shows that speculation
about comparative religion was rife (31, 131, 140, *passim*). Nonetheless,
critics have neglected non-Western spiritual traditions and feminists
could also face this lacuna, perhaps by considering the pertinence of
Hinduism's polytheistic pantheon when confronting Blake's perplexing
(male and female) Eternals. Or maybe Buddhism's dissolution of egoistic
illusions can help illuminate the annihilation of (masculine) selfhood
(*M*40.30–41.28, E142–3). For Blake, faith and art are indivisible and a
willingness to meditate upon the vast implications of his conviction that
'A Poet a Painter a Musician an Architect: the Man Or Woman who is not
one of these is not a Christian' (E274) would both clarify the questions
raised here and force feminists' attention towards Blake's visual art, which
we have, spectacularly, neglected.

the book of urizen, the book of ahania, the book of los

For essentialists, god-given scripts of absolute sexual difference are
inscribed in the book of nature as clearly as in books of religion and
law, but Blake's Urizenic trilogy turns round this tortuous teleology. Here,
female processes (gestation, labor, birthing, lactation) are relentlessly

troped to reveal not the essence of woman's natural fecundity but rather the primeval genesis of unproductive masculinity (and since critics have written pitifully little about this, Lussier's (2000) remarks on 'gestational symbolism' (174) and Tristanne Connolly's (2002) lengthy discussion of embodiment (73–154) are noteworthy).

As ever, the external world is an expression of the internal and in these poems the masculine landscape is one of chaotic elemental extremes, inhospitable to the nourishing of life. Unusually, the illuminations offer direct illustration and figures are seen struggling against nature in an 'unprolific!' (*BU*3.2, E70) environment, worlds away from Blake's usually teeming visual universe. There seems to be a crisis of masculine productivity, so that Urizen's 'Brooding [. . .] enormous labours' (3.22–5) generate nothing. Gestation is not a process of growth, but of 'battles dire / In unseen conflictions' (3.13–15) and the evidence of combative aggression at the embryonic stage of male creativity reveals the origins of this masculine crisis. The battle to subdue nature's abundance is pivotal in Urizen's first person account of the single item he can produce: books (4.6–40). An aggressive, clearly phallocentric, will to power is evident, as the vaunting egoism ('I alone, even I!') which mocks 'Natures wide womb' as a place 'Where nothing' is (16–18) proudly delivers its creative produce: 'alone I in books formd of metals / Have written the secrets of wisdom' (24–5). Colebrook (2000) notes that Blake 'clearly attacks romantic narcissism' (8), but more needs to be said about a male writer who represents literary males in this way. It's also noteworthy that the question Urizen addresses perplexed masculinist Romanticism too, that of mutability, of the changes time wreaks in human life. His solution is simple, change must be made impossible, joy must come 'without pain [. . .] solid without fluctuation' (10–11). This is only tenable in a world of singularity not of relationship, of identification not difference: 'each must chuse one habitation [. . .] One command, one joy, one desire [. . .] One King, one God, one Law' (36–40), a description of the narrowing 'logic' of phallocentrism which can hardly be bettered.

The irony is that Urizen is not alone. This isn't a monotheistic story and when the other Eternals – equally fired by masculine hubris – perceive his assumption of power, their response is marked by 'Rage, fury, intense indignation' (4.44). One of many bloody male conflicts ensues (5.1–37), as their wrathful flames beat down upon 'Urizen's self-begotten armies' (16). Blake's military lexicon deserves further study and the only respite from this particular battle comes through retreat to the female womb/ feminine heart (28–37). The most detailed masculine response to Urizen's predicament is that of the Eternal Prophet Los, who is nominated to watch over him. The passages which describe their relationship are complex (*BU*5.38–15.13; *BA*4.9–4.44; *BL*3.27–5.57) and I will stress only Los's confinement, his slow-healing birth wound and the work he does shaping his charge's body. Urizen's gestation is especially arresting in his own book, since Blake's anti-essentialism is sublimely ironic: the narrative of biological (female) creation provides metaphorical material for a critique of problematic (masculine) creativity. Even preliminary indicators of Los's formative abilities are not encouraging. He appears 'cursing his lot' (6.3), is terrified when body parts emerge and move around him (8.1–6) and his actions display a characteristically masculine urge to prove power and physical prowess. It's quite literally a case of 'hammer and tongs' as Los binds, beats, rivets, fires and solders the twisting, thrashing limbs (8.7–30). His work constitutes seven ages of 'dismal woe' for many reasons (this is a deliberately multivalent text), but one neglected cause of misery is surely Los's mechanical rather than organic mode of creativity. Its key metaphor here, birth, is seen as a process of industrial resurrection (akin to Frankenstein's furtive piece-work), where physicality's suggestive soft matter is subjected to procedures which fix and harden: 'bones of solidness, froze / Over all his nerves of joy' (10.40–1). Like the cowering foetal skeleton (pl.7 illustration), beings in this terrifying masculine environment are 'petrified' (11.23), scared both into, and out of, their lives. Worrall (1995) shows that 'Blake is [. . .] knowledgeable in 18th-century physiology' (136–8) and much light could be cast on the sexual politics of birthing and creativity if his unique ordering of fetal development (10.35–13.19) was placed in its contemporary context. Critical neglect of medical, especially anatomical, intertexts has been unhelpful and we need to build on the foundations laid by Connolly (2002, 25–72, 80–3), because significant viscera abound: for example, those 'muscles & glands [. . .] organs for craving and lust' which appear when Los 'beat on his anvils / Enrag'd' (*BA*4.32–3, 27–8).

The male's ambiguous relationship with bodies is further complicated by the Prophet's surprising response to the product of his labors. The 'seventh age' delivers a flailing, stamping infant (13.12–19), yet at this moment Los shrinks from his task: 'The bellows & hammer are silent now' (13.20–47). Practical fatherhood is discussed below but since maternal embodiment stereotypically entails mortal entrapment, we should note the 'ruinous fragments' of bodily life (*BU*5.9) generated by the masculine powers of conception. Horrified fear of appetite, intimacy and physicality combine with that will to power to produce a masculine version of embodiment which amounts to elemental bondage. This is the story told in Los's book (E90–4), a competing myth in which the bound Prophet watches the bound Urizen and, simultaneously, experiences incarnation in Urizen's world (*BL*3.27–5.9). Since manhood demands aggression, he fights to get free and the struggles are primeval: driven by fury, Los forces apart and divides fire, earth, air and water. The dust of Genesis has become in Urizen's masculine universe the primary matter he desired, that 'Solid / Without fluctation, hard as adamant [. . .] impenetrable' (*BA*4.4–6) and Los's hostility is especially fierce as 'Impatient, stifled, stiffend, hardned' the constricting rock is 'rent' by his urgent wish to achieve phallic mastery (4.14–16). Punter (1989) explores this conflict within patriarchy, as the 'doomed [. . .] dinosaur' Urizen is 'superseded [. . .] by a force whose "penetrative" power is in fact much greater' (90, 103) and Worrall (1995) shows how it 'historicises [. . .] the origins of patriarchy on which repressive political systems are founded' (199). True, but what's striking at the story's close is deadlock: Urizen is still 'a Form of impregnable strength' (5.20) confronted by Los, whose furnace/wombs take 'nine ages' to forge/birth yet another weapon (5.38–40). Moreover, the Prophet's binding of his enemy to this flaming orb wholly eclipses its/his power to illuminate: titanic male struggles merely result in 'Human Illusion' (5.56).

As Worrall (1995) reveals, the Urizenic trilogy was designed to challenge priestly imposition and this dissent is most apparent when Blake unmasks tales of sexual origin. The official theological script posits men as man: the singular, original, essential human form, of which women and children are derivative shadows. Blake questions this idealization of the primal man as 'That solitary one in Immensity' (*BU*3.43) by exploring his solipsistic masculine psychology: 'Self-closd, all-repelling [. . .] unknown, abstracted / brooding' (*BU*3.3–7). Intregral to this identity is horror at the existence, especially the physical presence, of others and, having explored man's ceaseless antagonism towards his peers, it's now important to note the violence which marks his intimate relationships. Urizen's family story is malign and infinitely revealing because his pathological terror of sensual otherness is extreme; moreover, the rules he fashions to control contact merely refigure the original problem, as sexuality leads to sin, sin leads to guilt, guilt leads to revenge, and revenge leads directly back to the other's warm body. This tale is told in two broad sweeps: *BU*20.30–28.34 (visual and verbal) is a picture of the moral and physical deformity of Urizen's children under his 'iron laws' which 'no flesh nor spirit could keep' (23.25–6); *BA*2.1–4.8 takes up this story, though the focus is narrowed onto Urizen's hateful relationship with his wife and eldest born. Fuzon is the 'Son of Urizen's silent burnings' (2.9), whose revolt forces his 'abstract non-entity' (2.11) of a father to face what he embodies: reproductive male sexuality. Unsurprisingly, Fuzon's weapon is sexual: Los's globe lengthens into a phallic beam (2.18–19) which pierces Urizen's defences to reveal his heterosexual shame. Hobson (2000) has shown (38–41) that Urizen pleasurably masturbates (*BU*10.11–23; *BA*4.11–16), but the poisonous revenge taken for Fuzon's exposure of his father's desire for Ahania illuminates Urizen's physical and moral abhorrence of the contaminating female other. She is hidden, a guilty secret, whilst his sublimated thoughts ejaculate thick mud from which hatches a horny serpent. Urizen fights and disembowels this phallic opponent, turning its infected entrails into an avenging weapon which is fired in homicidal torment through the heart of his (significantly feminized) son (3.41–2). Worrall (1995) shows that the poem parodies 'the doctrine of atonement' (153), yet the role of misdirected male sexuality in this archetypal story has received scanty attention. This must change, because gender is pivotal in all the debates (theological, political, psychological) the trilogy addresses. Indeed, it's the metasubject which illuminates interconnections, as Ahania's fate makes clear (*BA*2.29–43). The division of Urizen's self signaled by her appearance is appalling on many levels to the autoerotic, monotheistic, egoistical patriarch, whose response is to reincorporate Ahania into his interlocking systems of control: sexually, he seizes her; theologically, he 'called her Sin' (33); psychologically, she becomes his invisible unconscious, an aspect of being which cannot be: 'Unseen, unbodied, unknown' (42). Appropriately, her Book has few Illuminations, but the Frontispiece illustrates how (literally) central the domination of Ahania is to Urizen's multifaceted rule and when the tale of her expulsion is later expanded (*FZ*36.14–46.13, E325–31), sexual, theological and political tyranny are indivisible: 'Thou little diminutive portion that darst be a counterpart' (43.9), 'Am I not God said Urizen. Who is Equal to me' (42.19). Clearly, they are a symbolic couple drawn from the patriarchal narrative of sexual origins (in this context, see Angela Esterhammer on 'performative language' in creation stories (1999, 114) and Whittaker (1999, 37–41) on myths of origin).

Los and Enitharmon also have mythic status (*BU*13.48–20.45), though theirs is a more human story because the male partner lacks absolute potency. Like us mortals, Los is caught up in a process, forced to react in circumstances beyond his control. Most urgently, he has to respond to the Eternals' awestruck segregation of 'the first female form now separate' (18.15) and his initial gesture diametrically opposes theirs: they repel, Los embraces. Yet when thwarted by Enitharmon's independent will – 'she wept, she refus'd [. . .] She fled from his arms' (19.11–13) – Los retreats to that most ancient (Eternal?) masculine behavior: he chases and penetrates her, an action which leads directly back to Urizen's world where the female is eclipsed and heterosex becomes 'Man begetting his likeness / On his own divided image' (*BU*19.15–16). Plenty believe this is a Blakean ideal of sexual relations, but the inhuman shapes assumed by the embryo thus conceived (19.19–36) render this doubtful, as do the anguished paternal cruelties which ensue. That masculine tendency to see others as reflections of the originating male self is turned on baby Orc, who, quite literally the image of his father, is born a mature 'man Child' (19.40) and thereafter appears to Los as a rival for Enitharmon's attentions. The magnificent verbal (20.8–25) and visual (pl.19) images of protection and intimacy annihilated by masculine jealousy (a defining aspect (*BA*2.33–7) of Urizenic sexuality) are so arresting that they surely suggest censure. Kazuya Okada's (2000) analysis of 'the Urizenic family of restriction' identifies definite 'protest' (43) (see too Whittaker (1999, 122–5) and Connolly (2002, 127–30, 125–54) on jealousy and paternal violence).

A sterile circularity characterizes interactions in this masculine 'World of Loneliness' (*BA*4.64) which only its gendered contrary can relieve. This is seen, for example, when (feminine) pity and (female) life blood revive the vitiated relations of Los and Urizen (*BU*13.20–59). Readers also benefit, since the female characters' lucid speeches deliver us from the repetitive conflictual narratives and oblique syntax of masculine textuality. In particular, the 66 unbroken lines of Ahania's lament are an oasis of lexical and ontological clarity (4.52–5.47) which critics have long gravitated toward. Aers (1981), who condemns its 'conservative division of sexual roles' (36) and Patricia Cramer (1984), who finds an 'immortal impulse toward wholeness' (533), mapped out the interpretative polarities. Later critics are more equivocal: Worrall's (1995) historicism warns that it should not 'be trusted as verity: it is all derivation' (154) and scrutinizes both Ahania's 'recollection of paradisaical joy' and her 'spontaneous forgiveness of Urizen' (155). Priestman (1999) wonders whether the lament's 'hint of redemption' enables his readmission 'to the pantheon' whilst also noting that 'the female principle' proves 'treacherous to the stark oppositions from which the Urizen cycle set out' (121). Hobson (2000) celebrates the androgynous erotics, though cautions against taking images 'of harmony at face value' (42–5), while for Hatsuko Niimi (2000) Ahania's words come from an oral culture which anticipates a 'postmodern feminine ethics' of care, thereby revealing 'her commitment to a more amorphous and generous love relationship' (49). The lament undoubtedly provides refuge. Ahania's mode of address is intimate, her chamber the only domestic interior envisioned in these bleak poems. Moreover, the challenge she offers (though absolute) comes not through violent conflict but from persuasive contrast, most strikingly through oppositional visions of effortlessly abundant fertility (5.15–38). And it's crucial to note that sexual indeterminacy enables this fecundity: who gives and who takes is unclear, breasts are filled with both 'milk' and 'seed' (5.20–1) and the lament's enticing 'open bosom [. . .] lovely bosom' (5.12, 40) belongs not to mother Ahania but to the biggest daddy of them all, Urizen. Appropriately, sexual love brings her 'argument' to its climax, as self-giving feminine generosity finds expression in a female orgasm represented by the yielding fatness of 'My ripe figs & rich pomegranates' (5.24–34). It's a glorious challenge to Urizen, who can only regain/maintain ascendancy by attacking the physical site of this erotic economy, which he does by turning the female genitals into a 'spiders web, moist, cold, & dim' (BU25.10). This is the embryonic version of his 'Net of Religion' (BU25.1–28.24) and the illumination which shows the patriarch enthroned inside an ovoid vagina whose web-like labia trap a naked couple (BL pl.3) confirms the role genital degradation plays in patriarchal rule. Indeed, misogyny is integral to Blake's depiction of patriarchy and Urizen's denigration of Ahania's 'cavern shagg'd with horrid shades. dark cool & deadly' (FZ43.14, E329) demand serious consideration. Small wonder that Ahania complains that she is despised (BA4.62) or that her words are ignored, for though she employs many linguistic strategies – submission (4.65–71) (echoing the female bard Eno's indulgence of male vice (BL3.1–26)); protest (5.41–7) (recalling Experience's enchained female Earth); nostalgic/prophetic eroticism; pathetic appeals (4.45–64) on behalf of herself and her son – Ahania is entirely ineffectual. Why? Because despite multiple perspectives, the Urizenic trilogy does have one overarching theme: from various standpoints it condemns the barren cosmos created by patriarchal domination, 'Where bones from the birth are buried / Before they see the light' (BA4.45–6).

the prophetic epics

Gender is a monumental problem in Blake's epic poetry. The 'sexual' is relentlessly theorized and often figures as a covering (woven garment or vegetable sheath) which threatens to obscure the divine human beneath. Failure to comprehend its temporal mutability is a catastrophe which generates conflict, both between aggressively masculine characters who, like Tharmas, cling to the belief 'I am an identity' (FZ4.43, E302) and with such figures' feminized semblances, whose otherness manifests the gender difference which terrifies them. The sexual problems Blake describes are agonizing; the Divinity has to intervene, refuges outside of existence must be created for respite and only apocalypse can bring deliverance. As the exhausted Los eventually screams, 'Sexes must vanish & cease / To be' (J92.13–14, E252).

The deconstruction of gendered identities is an epic story; indeed, it's *the* Epics' story and gender studies on an appropriate scale are needed, for book-length treatments can illuminate the extent of the later Blake's sexual concerns and enable analysis of the Epics' perplexing structures, whose protean shape mediates so much of the sexual story. Given the turbulent nature of these works, it is surprising that one of the most pervasive myths about Blake's Epics is that they clearly depict a stereotypical heterosexual ideal expressed through the unequal relationship of ('male') zoa and subservient ('female') emanation. Just a glance at the first pages of *The Four Zoas* obliterates this commonplace, for the multiple 'Emanations' first appear as beings Los 'propagated' 'in the Auricular Nerves of Human life', thence becoming not wives but rather 'fairies of Albion afterwards Gods of the Heathen' (4.1–3, E301). The range of allusion is disorientating and while these lines certainly speak about gender, they do not depict a dutiful female partner. Immediately after this, Tharmas reveals another, most ironic, aspect of the term as he opines, 'Lost! Lost! Lost! are my Emanations' (4.7). This is a pointless lamentation, in fact, for an emanation will by definition emanate, become separate, and yet, orthodoxly, 'her' separate existence epitomizes the traumatic division 'she' is supposed 'naturally' to heal. Allegedly emblematic agents of harmony and communication achieved through female subordination, emanations rarely serve this function because they, of necessity, become separate beings (often outcasts).

Put briefly, emanations are more than females and females are much more than emanations, facts brought into focus by gender critics. For general theories see Punter (1989), who believes 'Emanations are a temporary accident' (93); Colebrook (2000), who thinks they sustain 'an essential recognition of alterity' (7); Hobson (2000), who finds that 'rigid gender identities' are attacked as 'Satanic' (171) in his analysis of emanations (especially the masculine Shiloh) and hermaphrodism (162–73) and Connolly (2002) on divisions and cominglings (155–91). Ololon has also attracted much comment, unsurprisingly since 'she' enters as a 'sweet River, of mild & liquid pearl' (M21.15, E115) and is simultaneously a multitude of 'mighty Hosts', 'a Virgin twelve years' old' (M36.16–17, E137) 'a Moony Ark [. . .] a Garment dipped in blood' (42.7, 12, E143). Despite this multiplicity, Kaplan (1995) suggests that the 'equation of actual women and emanations is Blake's intention' (174). Betsy Bolton (1997) is less sure, commenting on the poem's 'confused and confusing definition of "The Sexual" [. . .] which moves uneasily among biological sexes, gender roles and erotic attraction' (61), while Elfenbein disagrees completely (1999), believing Ololon 'stands not for the masculine, Blakean Sublime, but the omnigendered Blakean ridiculous' (176). From a camp viewpoint, M42.3–12 (E143) is a 'world in which gender roles have become irrelevant' (173). John Pierce (2000) perceives, at the very least, 'a dispersion of subject positions' (470).

Such varied criticism clearly shows that emanations exceed traditional interpretations of them as models of obedience. Other work is complementary as it demonstrates that female figures are more than emanations, magnetically drawn towards their domineering Zoas. Hobson (2000) offers an interesting perspective (150–62) as he explores female relationships in *Jerusalem*, suggesting that 'the disruption of the primal scene of lesbian harmony' (J19.40–7 and illustration pl.28) 'is a direct source of [. . .] evils' in the poem and 'generates much [. . .] later action' (157, 51). The contention that Blake did not share Albion's view of 'unnatural [. . .] friendships / Horrid to think of when enquired deeply into' (28.6–7, E174) is intriguing and deserves further discussion, as does the crucial issue of women's work. William's co-producer Catherine has been shamefully undervalued and few have explored the strenuous physical toil females undertake throughout the Epics. Los's Daughters 'expect no one to pity / For they labour for life and love, regardless' (J59.36–7, E209), but interest in sexual politics means this neglect cannot continue. One exception is Eugenie Freed-Isserow's (1998) account of Blake's sympathetic attitude towards female weavers (17–24), who despite exploitation 'are creating' (19). Critics have also revised assessments of 'negative' females. Hutchings' (2002) exploration of 'Vala, Patriarchy and the Politics of Nature' (172–88), for example, finds that she is 'very much a construct of the institutionalized discourses that name and define her significance' (175). One of the starkest examples of this is when Vala takes the hated form of 'Mystery' and readers are explicitly told, 'The Synagogue Created her from Fruit of Urizens tree' (FZ109.20, E378). Such discussions might be developed through analysis of the way violent females are often the byproduct of male conflict. J80.16–30 (E236) is especially interesting as it shows a confused Vala trying to explain what happened when her father/lover commanded her to 'murder Albion': 'Luvah framd the Knife & Luvah gave / The Knife into his daughters hand!' (16, 23–4, E236). The murderous Daughters of Albion are also fascinating in this context. Plate 68 (E221–2), for example, presents them as subjects in a militarized kingdom where they are 'Taught [. . .] to cut the flesh from the victim / To roast the flesh in the fire' (56–8). Essentialists have seen their ritualized violence as evidence of Blake's misogynistic fear of the sacrificial form religion takes when shaped by female hands, but this 'feminine' cruelty is utterly patriarchal: it 'delights the eyes of Kings.their hearts & the / Hearts of their Warriors glow hot' (16–17). Sturrock (1998) argues that the Daughters' behavior critiques the emergent bourgeois female who gained power through imperious chastity. Mary-Kelly Persyn (1999) demurs, pointing out that 'the sacrificial dynamic resulting from the law of chastity' (71) makes women victims as well as perpetrators of violence. Whittaker's (1999) discussion of the Daughters in the context of national myths (114–51, 164–7) opens up another important area of research, which McClenahan (2002) builds upon as she explains how Erin mediates the recent Irish rebellion and is 'the best embodiment of Jerusalem in Albion's land' (152). Stereotypical understandings of Epic womanhood have, then, been queried but there is of course no consensus. For Pierce (1998), Rahab (127–39) is still the 'ultimate form of female error' (135) and Kaplan (1996/97) believes England Brittannia 'the apotheosis of Blakean woman' (82), Jerusalem 'Blake's ideal female' (77). Los's devotional picture (J85.22–86.32, E244–5) certainly presents Jerusalem as 'the soft reflected Image of the Sleeping Man' (85.24), yet she also has 'Six Wings [. . .] three Universes of love & beauty' and within her 'Bosom' can be seen 'the Tribes of Israel [. . .] the River of life' (86.1, 3, 14, 17–18), which reveals much about spiritualized feminine ideals, but is in no way a depiction of a human female. Jerusalem is a dream, a city, a promise, her passion to show that 'Humanity is far above / Sexual organisation' (79.73–4, E236).

The characters through which Blake explores the equally complex relationship between maleness and masculinity are similarly fluid and diverse, though much less studied due to the lingering myth that man's sexual identity is coterminous with his humanity, is natural and unconstructed. Blake didn't think so, as his creation of that repository of masculinist hubris and misogynistic spite, the Spectre, testifies. From the outset this 'insane and most / Deformed' (FZ5.38, E303) creature tempts men toward an overdetermined sexual identity and is, interestingly, the only Blakean being who seems irredeemable. In Jerusalem, he is the gleeful 'author' of Los and Enitharmon's 'divisions' (88.35, E247) and must be 'cast [. . .] into the lake' (pl.37, E184), in Milton, 'a Selfhood, which must be put off & annihilated alway' (40.34–6, E142). The Zoas also need more gendered attention for they are far from being the neat quartet encountered in classic Blake Studies. Most obviously they cannot form a 'Perfect Unity' because each 'male' is riven by internal division. The fragmented form Urthona/Los (plus Spectres) most obviously disrupts the standard model, but the layerings of Luvah/Orc also undermine the idea that we are dealing with an equilibrium of just 'Four Mighty Ones' (*FZ*3.4, E300). If Blake has a clear story to tell about mens' growth toward male fullness as they integrate the four essential elements of their natural sexual identity, it's very well hidden in the Epics, even more so when we recall the ambiguous location of these dramas, outside/inside the mind/body of Albion/the Eternal Man. Navigating such choppy waters is a challenge for all Blake's interpreters, but a willingness to regard the multiple variants of Urthona, Tharmas, Urizen and Luvah as irresolute figurations of specifically masculine (not hu*man*) psychology and behavior could be a pole star for everyone.

Attending to men's relationships with each other is also important, and critics have begun to explore sexual connections. Kaplan (1995) thinks that homosexuality in *Milton* is just a 'trope [. . .] to assert [. . .] masculine superiority' (168), whilst Hobson (2000) shows how Blake denounced the cruel moral laws which persecuted homosexuals (113–43). The Epics were, of course, produced during years of relentless military conflict and the depiction of males who lay loving hands upon their enemies' bodies (for example, M19.1–14, E112) surely speaks to this context. Blake's ideal of brotherhood is also shaped by historical pressures, although Kaplan (1996/97) takes Gerda Lerner's developmental model of patriarchy as the basis for his argument that Blake's ideal community consists of a band of equal brothers who hold women sexually in common (70, 76–8, 82). Otto's (2001) discussion of ancient phallic religion provides a fresh perspective on such masculinism as it reveals how 'the phallus [. . .] erected by Urizen as a privileged image of the absolute' is also 'the ultimate source and guarantor of the law [. . .] unbending, singular, unequivocal' (5, 11). Connolly (2002) explores the more amorphous masculine shapes assumed by Reuben (65–105, 117–24).

Feminist work, then, has been extremely productive and its potential remains great, although this is a perilous moment because the ascendant rhetoric of post-feminism elides that distinction between sex and gender upon which such study is founded. We must contest this discursive delusion not only because it naturalizes inequality, but also because it is a perceptual error which Blake himself ceaselessly exposed. Indeed, delivering individuals from the gendered states they're forced to inhabit, 'Lest the Sexual Garments sweet / Should grow a devouring Winding sheet' (E268), is arguably Blake's most passionate ambition, which means that the analysis of gender must never be trivialized by any of his interpreters.

works cited and suggestions for further reading

Aers, David. 'William Blake and the Dialectic of Sex'. *English Literary History* 44 (1977): 137–44.

——. 'Blake: Sex, Society and Ideology' in *Romanticism and Ideology*. Ed. David Aers, et al. London: Routledge and Kegan Paul, 1981. 27–43.

——. 'Representations of Revolution' in *Critical Paths: Blake and the Argument of Method*. Ed. Dan Miller, Mark Bracher and Donald Ault. Durham and London: Duke University Press, 1987. 244–70.

Bolton, Betsy. '"A Garment dipped in blood": Ololon and Problems of Gender in Blake's *Milton*'. *Studies in Romanticism* 36 (Spring 1997): 61–101.

Bruder, Helen P. 'The Sins of the Fathers: Patriarchal Criticism and *The Book of Thel*' in *Historicizing Blake*. Ed. David Worrall and Steve Clark. Basingstoke: Macmillan, 1994. 147–58.

——. *William Blake and the Daughters of Albion*. Basingstoke: Macmillan, 1997.

Chapman, Wes. 'Blake, Wollstonecraft and the Inconsistency of Oothoon'. *Blake: An Illustrated Quarterly* 31.1 (Summer 1997): 4–17.

Clark, Steve. *Sordid Images: The Poetry of Masculine Desire*. London: Routledge, 1994.

Colebrook, Claire. 'Blake and Feminism: Romanticism and the Question of the Other'. *Blake: An Illustrated Quarterly* 34.1 (Summer 2000): 4–13.

Connolly, Tristanne J. *William Blake and the Body*. Basingstoke and New York: Palgrave, 2002.

Cramer, Patricia. 'The Role of Ahania's Lament in Blake's *Book of Ahania*'. *Journal of English and Germanic Philology* 83.4 (1984): 522–33.

Davies, Keri. 'Mrs Bliss: A Blake Collector of 1794' in *Blake in the Nineties*. Ed. Steve Clark and David Worrall. Basingstoke: Macmillan, 1999. 212–30.

Dent, Shirley and Jason Whittaker. *Radical Blake: Influence and Afterlife from 1827*. Basingstoke and New York: Palgrave Macmillan, 2002.

DiSalvo, Jackie. 'Introduction' in *Blake, Politics and History*. Ed. Jackie DiSalvo, G.A. Rosso and Christopher Hobson. New York and London: Garland Publishing, 1998. xiiv–xxxii.

Drake, Dee. *Searing Apparent Surfaces: Infernal Females in Four Early Works by William Blake*. Stockholm: Almquist and Wiksell, 2000.

Elfenbein, Andrew. *Romantic Genius: The Prehistory of a Homosexual Role*. New York: Columbia University Press, 1999.

Essick, Robert. *William Blake's Visions of the Daughters of Albion Edited, with a Commentary*. California: Huntingdon Library, 2002.

Esterhammer, Angela. 'Calling into Existence: *The Book of Urizen*' in *Blake in the Nineties*. Ed. Steve Clark and David Worrall. Basingstoke: Macmillan, 1999. 114–32.

Everest, Kelvin. 'Thel's Dilemma'. *Essays in Criticism* 37.3 (1987): 193–208.

Ferber, Michael. *The Social Vision of William Blake*. Princeton: Princeton University Press, 1985.

——. 'In Defense of Clods' in *Prophetic Character: Essays on William Blake in Honor of John E. Grant*. Ed. Alexander S. Gourlay. West Cornwall, CT: Locust Hill Press, 2002. 51–66.

Fox, Susan. 'The Female as Metaphor in the Poetry of William Blake'. *Critical Inquiry* 3 (Spring 1977): 507–19.

Freed-Isserow, Eugenie. '"Building the Stubborn Structure of Language": The Dynamic of Blake's Poetic Art'. *English Studies in Africa* 41.1 (1998): 11–28.

George, Diana Hume. *Blake and Freud*. Ithaca: Cornell University Press, 1980.

Goslee, Nancy Moore. 'Slavery and Sexual Character: Questioning the Master Trope in Blake's *Visions of the Daughters of Albion*'. *English Literary History* 57.1 (1990): 101–28.

Greco, Norma A. 'Mother Figures in Blake's *Songs of Innocence* and The Female Will'. *Romanticism Past and Present* 10.1 (Winter 1986): 1–15.

Henry, Lauren. 'Sunshine and Shady Groves: What Blake's "A Little Black Boy" Learned from African Writers'. *Blake: An Illustrated Quarterly* 29.1 (Summer 1995): 4–11.

Hobson, Christopher Z. *Blake and Homosexuality*. New York: Palgrave, 2000.

Hoerner, Fred. 'Prolific Reflections: Blake's Contortions of Surveillance in *Visions of the Daughters of Albion*'. *Studies in Romanticism* 35.1 (1996): 119–50.

Hollis, Hilda. 'Seeing Thel as Serpent'. *Blake: An Illustrated Quarterly* 30. 3 (Winter 1996/97): 87–90.

Hutchings, Kevin D. '"Every Thing that Lives" Anthropocentrism, Ecology, and *The Book of Thel*'. *Wordsworth Circle* 28.3 (Summer 1997): 166–77.

——. *Imagining Nature: Blake's Environmental Poetics*. Montreal and Kingston and London and Ithaca: McGill-Queens University Press, 2002.

Ishizuka, Hisao. 'Thel's "Complaint": A Medical Reading of Blake's *The Book of Thel*'. *The English Literary Society of Japan* 73 (1997): 245–63.

James, G. Ingli. 'William Blake and Feminist Theology: Some Observations on the Affinities'. *Feminist Theology* 11 (Jan 1996): 72–85.

Johnson, Mary Lynn. 'Feminist Approaches to Teaching Songs' in *Approaches to Teaching Blake's Songs*. Ed. Robert F. Gleckner. New York: Modern Language Association, 1989. 57–66.

Kaplan, Marc. 'Blake's *Milton*: The Metaphysics of Gender'. *Nineteenth Century Contexts* 19 (1995): 151–78.

——. '*Jerusalem* and the Origins of Patriarchy'. *Blake: An Illustrated Quarterly* 30.3 (Winter 1996/97): 151–78.

Keach, William. 'Blake, Violence and Visionary Politics' in *Representing the French Revolution*. Ed. James Hefferman. Boston: University Press of New England, 1992. 24–40.

Kennedy, Thomas C. 'From Anna Barbauld's *Hymns in Prose* to William Blake's *Songs of Innocence and of Experience*'. *Philological Quarterly* 77 (1998): 359–76.

Langland, Elizabeth. 'Blake's Feminist Revision of Literary Tradition in "The Sick Rose"' in *Critical Paths: Blake and the Argument of Method*. Ed. Dan Miller, Mark Bracher and Donald Ault. Durham and London: Duke University Press, 1987. 225–43.

Lee, Debbie. *Slavery and the Romantic Imagination*. Philadelphia: University of Pennsylvania Press, 2002.

Lincoln, Andrew. 'Alluring the Heart to Virtue: Blake's *Europe*'. *Studies in Romanticism* 38.4 (Winter 1999): 621–39.

Linkin, Harriet Krammer. 'Transfigured Maternity in Blake's *Songs of Innocence*: Inverting the "Maternity Plot" in "A Dream"' in *Blake, Politics and History*. Ed. Jackie DiSalvo, G.A. Rosso and Christopher Hobson. New York and London: Garland Publishing, 1998. 325–37.

Lussier, Mark S. *Romantic Dynamics: The Poetics of Physicality*. Basingstoke: Macmillan, 2000.

McClenahan, Catherine M. 'No Face Like the Human Divine?: Women and Gender in Blake's Pickering Manuscript' in *Spirits of Fire*. Ed. G.A. Rosso and Daniel Watkins. London and Toronto: Associated University Presses, 1990. 189–207.

——. 'Albion and the Sexual Machine: Blake, Gender and Politics, 1780–1795' in *Blake, Politics and History*. Ed. Jackie DiSalvo, G.A. Rosso and Christopher Hobson. New York and London: Garland Publishing, 1998. 301–24.

——. 'Blake's Erin, The United Irish, and "Sexual Machines"' in *Prophetic Character: Essays on William Blake in Honor of John E. Grant*. Ed. Alexander S. Gourlay. West Cornwall, CT; Locust Hill Press, 2002. 149–70.

McCollister, Deborah. 'The Seductions of Self-Abnegation in *The Book of Thel*'. *Blake: An Illustrated Quarterly* 30.3 (Winter 1996/97): 90–4.

McKusick, James C. *Green Writing: Romanticism and Ecology*. Basingstoke: Macmillan, 2000.

Mellor, Anne K. 'Blake's Portrayal of Women'. *Blake: An Illustrated Quarterly* 16.3 (1982/83): 148–55.

——. 'Blake's *Songs of Innocence and of Experience*: A Feminist Perspective'. *Nineteenth Century Studies* 2 (1988): 1–17.

——. *Romanticism and Gender*. New York and London: Routledge, 1993.

——. 'Sex, Violence and Slavery: Blake and Wollstonecraft'. *Huntingdon Library Quarterly* 58 (1996): 345–70.

——. 'Blake, Gender and Imperial Ideology: A Response' in *Blake, Politics and History*. Ed. Jackie DiSalvo, G.A. Rosso and Christopher Hobson. New York and London: Garland Publishing, 1998. 350–3.

Niimi, Hatsuko. '*The Book of Ahania*: A Metatext'. *Blake: An Illustrated Quarterly* 34.2 (Fall 2000): 46–54.

Norvig, Gerda S. 'Female Subjectivity and the Desire of Reading In (to) Blake's *The Book of Thel*'. *Studies in Romanticism* 34 (Summer 1995): 255–71.

Okada, Kazuya. 'Orc Under the Veil: Family Relationships and their Symbolism in *Europe* and *The Book of Urizen*'. *Blake: An Illustrated Quarterly* 34.2 (Fall 2000): 36–45.

Ostriker, Alicia. 'Desire Gratified and Ungratified: William Blake and Sexuality'. *Blake: An Illustrated Quarterly* 16.3 (Winter 1982–83): 156–65.

Otter, A.J. Den. 'The Question and *The Book of Thel*'. *Studies in Romanticism* 3.4 (Winter 1991): 633–55.

——. 'Displeasing Women: Blake's Furies and the Ladies of Moral Virtue'. *European Romantic Review* 9 (1998): 35–58.

Otto, Peter. 'Re-Framing the Moment of Creation: Blake's Revisions of the Frontispiece and Title Page to *Europe*' in *Blake, Politics and History*. Ed. Jackie DiSalvo, G.A. Rosso and Christopher Hobson. New York and London: Garland Publishing, 1998. 235–46.

——. '"A Pompous High Priest": Urizen's Ancient Phallic Religion in *The Four Zoas*'. *Blake: An Illustrated Quarterly* 35.1 (Summer 2001): 4–22.

Persyn, Mary-Kelly. '"No Human Form but Sexual": Sensibility, Chastity and Sacrifice in Blake's *Jerusalem*'. *European Romantic Review* 10.1 (Winter 1999): 53–84.

Pierce, John B. *Flexible Design: Revisionary Poetics in Blake's Vala or The Four Zoas.* Montreal and Kingston and London and Buffalo: McGill-Queens University Press, 1998.

——. 'Rewriting Milton: Orality and Writing in Blake's *Milton'*. *Studies in Romanticism* 39.3 (Fall 2000): 449–70.

Priestman, Martin. *Romantic Atheism: Poetry and Free Thought.* Cambridge: Cambridge University Press, 1999.

Punter, David. 'Blake, Trauma and the Female'. *New Literary History* 15.3 (1984): 475–90.

——. 'The Sign of Blake'. *Criticism* 26 (1985): 313–34.

——. *The Romantic Unconscious: A Study in Narcissism and Patriarchy.* Hemel Hempstead: Harvester Wheatsheaf, 1989.

Rajan, Tilottama. '(Dis) Figuring the System: Vision, History and Trauma in Blake's Lambeth Books'. *Huntingdon Library Quarterly* 58 (1995): 383–411.

Richey, William. '"The Lion and Wolf Shall Cease": Blake's *America* as a Critique of Counter-Revolutionary Violence' in *Blake, Politics and History.* Ed. Jackie DiSalvo, G.A. Rosso and Christopher Hobson. New York and London: Garland Publishing, 1998. 196–211.

Rosso, G.A. 'The Religion of Empire: Blake's Rahab in Its Biblical Contexts' in *Prophetic Character: Essays on William Blake in Honor of John E. Grant.* Ed. Alexander S. Gourlay. West Cornwall, CT: Locust Hill Press, 2002. 287–326.

Rubenstein, Anne and Camilla Townsend. 'Revolted Negroes and the Devilish Principle: William Blake and Conflicting Visions of Boni's Wars in Surinam' in *Blake, Politics and History.* Ed. Jackie DiSalvo, G.A. Rosso and Christopher Hobson. New York and London: Garland Publishing, 1998. 273–98.

Schuchard, Marsha Keith. 'Why Mrs Blake Cried: Swedenborg, Blake and the Sexual Basis of Spiritual Vision'. *Esoterica* 2 (2000): 45–93.

Senaha, Eijun. *Sex, Drugs and Madness.* Lampeter: Mellen Press, 1996.

Sorensen, Peter J. *William Blake's Recreation of Gnostic Myth: Resolving the Apparent Incongruities.* Lampeter: Mellen Press, 1996. 37–58.

Stepto, Micele Leiss. 'Mothers and Fathers in Blake's *Songs of Innocence'*. *Yale Review* 67 (1978): 357–70.

Storch, Margaret. 'Blake and Women: "Nature's Cruel Holiness"'. *American Imago* 38 (1981): 221–46.

——. *Sons and Adversaries: Women in William Blake and D.H. Lawrence.* Knoxville: The University of Tennessee Press, 1990.

Sturrock, June. 'Blake and the Women of the Bible'. *Journal of Literature and Theology* 6.1 (March 1992): 23–32.

——. 'Protective Pastoral: Innocence and Female Experience in William Blake's *Songs* and Christina Rossetti's *Goblin Market'*. *Colby Quarterly* 30 (1994): 98–108.

——. '"What have I to do with thee?"'. *Blake: An Illustrated Quarterly* 28.3 (Winter 1994/95): 89–91.

——. 'Maenads, Young Ladies, and the Lovely Daughters of Albion' in *Blake, Politics and History.* Ed. Jackie DiSalvo, G.A. Rosso and Christopher Hobson. New York and London: Garland Publishing, 1998. 339–47.

Tayler, Irene. 'The Woman Scaly'. *Midwestern Modern Languages Association Bulletin* 6 (1973): 74–87.

Thomas, Helen. *Romanticism and Slave Narratives*. Cambridge: Cambridge University Press, 2000.

Trowbridge, Katherine E. 'Blake's "A Little Girl Lost"'. *Explicator* 54.3 (Spring 1996): 139–42.

Vesely, Susanne Araas. 'The Daughters of Eighteenth Century Science: A Rationalist and Materialist Context for William Blake's Female Figures'. *Colby Quarterly* 34.1 (March 1998): 5–24.

Vine, Steven. '"THAT MILD BEAM": Enlightenment and Enslavement in William Blake's *Visions of the Daughters of Albion*' in *The Discourse of Slavery*. Ed. Carl Plasa and Betty J. Ring. London: Routledge, 1994. 40–63.

Webster, Brenda. *Blake's Prophetic Psychology*. London and Basingstoke: Macmillan, 1983.

——. 'Blake, Women and Sexuality' in *Critical Paths: Blake and the Argument of Method*. Ed. Dan Miller, Mark Bracher and Donald Ault. Durham and London: Duke University Press, 1987, 204–24.

Whittaker, Jason. *William Blake and the Myths of Albion*. Basingstoke: Macmillan, 1999.

Williams, Nick. *Ideology and Utopia in the Poetry of William Blake*. Cambridge: Cambridge University Press, 1998.

Worrall, David. *William Blake: The Urizen Books*. Edited with Introductions and Notes. London: The William Blake Trust/Tate Gallery, 1995.

——. 'Artisan Melodrama and the Plebian Sphere: The Political Culture of Drury Lane and its Environs, 1797–1830'. *Studies in Romanticism* 39.2 (Summer 2000): 213–27.

Wright, Julia M. '"And None Shall Gather the Leaves": Unbinding the Voice in Blake's *America* and *Europe*'. *European Romantic Review* 7.1 (Summer 1996): 61–84.

Zimmerman, Sarah H. 'Charlotte Smith's Lessons' in *Approaches to Teaching British Women Poets of the Romantic Period*. Ed. Stephen C. Behrendt and Harriet Krammer Linkin. New York: Modern Language Association, 1997. 121–8.

8

blake and psychology

david punter

Blake's work, visual and verbal, has been the locus of a 'psychological' debate for two centuries. Originally, of course, this debate was of a somewhat unsophisticated kind. Confronted by the complexities of the Prophetic Books, by the apparently esoteric nature of the symbolism, by Blake's own pronouncements about the 'visionary' sources of his art, and by his implacable resistance to ameliorating his message, even when that message apparently had very few potential or actual recipients – confronted by these peculiarities, as also by the curious legends that grew up around Blake's life, there were many commentators during the nineteenth century who came to the conclusion that Blake was mad.

Indeed, it could be argued that a substantial part of Blake criticism from the early twentieth century on has been devoted to exploring, substantiating or refuting this view. It also needs to be said, however, that 'psychological criticism' of Blake has inevitably followed the defiles of 'psychological criticism' in general. The move away from naïve intentionalism has left many critics at a loss. The crucial example here would be psychoanalysis. It is one thing to psychoanalyze a person; it is something quite different to apply psychoanalytic concepts to texts. Many of the 'psychological' debates about Blake have moved into areas claimed by other schools of criticism, perhaps most typically the debate about Blake's view of the 'Female Will', while the deconstructive turn, even though it relies massively on psychoanalytic insights, turns its face resolutely away from Blake the man and towards the complex textuality which is, after all, all we know of him.

To speak, then, of 'Blake and psychology' is to open up a difficult and convoluted field. One might think of the evidence of Freudian 'complexes' within the texts, or of gender attitudes and assumptions, or, following Harold Bloom, of the poet's attitudes towards his forebears,

167

or of the psychological significance of the various quasi-mythic figures that emerge especially in the later texts. But perhaps it is best to start with Blake's own view of psychology, insofar as we can reconstruct it from within the texts.

The first thing to be said here is that the realm of psychology as such in Blake can hardly be extracted from other fields of discourse. Particularly in the Prophetic Books, Blake develops a version of narrative in which he is constantly attempting to work at three levels at once: psychological, historical and cosmological. Thus, for example, the apocalypse at the end of *Jerusalem* is simultaneously a restoration of the whole human being, the end of human history, and a revelation of divine purpose. A large part of the difficulty of Blake's work lies in attempting to read these levels at the same time, seeing, for example, how minor details – 'minute particulars', as Blake would call them – of, for example, the American and French Revolutions can also figure as life-events for the individual and as evidence for the working out of a grand scheme of human redemption.

Here the critical terms are restoration and redemption. In psychological terms, one might say that Blake is working on the basis of a view of the human mind which was common in his time, and which is now most commonly referred to as 'faculty psychology'. In other words, his view is that the human mind – or perhaps 'soul' is a better word – is split into various parts or faculties. Most typically, we may see these as reflected in the four major figures of the later work: Urizen standing for reason, Orc for passion, Los for the imagination, and the somewhat more shadowy figure of Tharmas for the instincts. This is, of course, a simplification, but certainly the notion of a 'divided self' – to use a much later formulation – lies at the root of this mythic system, as it does at the root of the earlier and more accessible division between the realms of innocence and experience.

The normal condition of life for Blake, then, is a divided or fragmented one, but this division is given a specific inflection by his immersion in the Bible and Milton. For Milton too deals in a myth of a divided self, even though the theological dimension of this division is more evident than the psychological one. But in particular, Milton's myth of division is also a myth of usurpation, or at least of attempted usurpation, by Satan of a realm which is not properly his. Similarly, the origin of all the divisions in Blake's work lies in an act of usurpation, namely the arrogation of the power of creation by Urizen. It is this upsetting of what should be a harmonious order, where all the parts of the mind function together to produce and regenerate the whole man, which forms the origin – sometimes occluded though it is – of the master-narrative that lies behind much of his work, and it is the re-establishment of this harmony that forms the end-point towards which it strives.

In psychological terms, we should see this myth as reflecting what Blake clearly saw as an over-reliance on reason in his own times, and this can hardly be separated from sociological and ideological circumstances. When Blake refers to the 'infernal trinity' of Bacon, Newton and Locke, he means to refer to the contemporary cultural dominance of reason in the spheres of morality, science and philosophy; but he also means to refer to the effects this constellation has within the individual, a kind of closing of the doors of perception and, most particularly, an exiling of the imaginative power which it is the poet's task to reverse – as it is the task of Los to keep his creative furnaces alive despite the deathly cold of Urizenic domination.

This, then, would be a way of locating Blake against the background of his times – as it would also be, through the importance of the imagination, a way of locating his work in a more general context of romanticism. However, the critical history of Blake and psychology has tended less towards developing these connections than towards seeing his work in terms of the future: in other words, as prefiguring the insights of later psychologists. The clearest example is Freud. There has been a considerable amount of work on Blake and Freud, but perhaps the most wide-ranging study remains Diana Hume George's *Blake and Freud*, first published in 1980. One can get a basic idea of some of Hume George's directions from the list of chapters: 'Opposition Is True Friendship'; 'They Became What They Beheld'; 'Innocence and Experience'; 'Marriage: *Visions of the Daughters of Albion*'; 'Psychic Organisation and Sexual Dialectic in Blake's *Milton*'; 'Is She Also the Divine Image? Values for the Feminine in Blake'; and 'Freud and Feminine Psychology'. The emphases here are again on the divided self, on oppositions within the psyche. But there is also a different emphasis within Hume George's book, which she speaks about in her introduction: namely, a concern not so much with Freud's own texts (although plenty of them are cited) as with a specific kind of Freudian revisionism which characterized the 1970s and 1980s, a revisionism summarized in the names of Norman O. Brown, Herbert Marcuse and Wilhelm Reich.

Essentially, one might say that this strand in post-Freudian thinking seeks to engage the darker sides of Freud's thinking with a version of liberation. We all suffer, so the thinking goes, from various kinds of alienation, loosely linked to Marx's description of four types of alienation in the *Economic and Philosophical* Manuscripts; but rather than regarding this as the human lot, the task is to overcome these alienated states – through sexual liberation, through social progress, through revolutionary struggle, through the overthrow of capitalism, depending on the details of the point of view. Persuasive as these views seemed at the time, it could be said that they took no account of the major thrust of Freud's thinking, which was that any such struggle could only be permanent; an individual might be restored by psychotherapy in the sense that he or she might become able to resume what passes for 'normal life', but this is a very long way from the revolutionary possibilities envisaged by these thinkers.

Freud's 'system' – his view of the topographical arrangements of the psyche – changed a great deal during his life; but arguably the greatest single change came with his discovery, as he thought of it, of the death-wish. The opposition within the psyche ran deep, so deep, indeed, that every apparent attempt to restore harmony was opposed by a different drive that sought to pull things apart, to produce chaos, to return the human to the bestial, to the state of immobility or death. Hume George is at least in part aware of this, and she begins her book by juxtaposing two quotations. The first is from Blake's *Jerusalem*:

> O what is life & what is Man. O what is Death? Wherefore
> Are you my Children, natives in the Grave to where I go
> Or are you born to feed the hungry ravenings of Destruction
> To be the sport of Accident! to waste in Wrath & Love, a weary
> Life, in brooding cares & anxious labours, that prove but chaff.
> (J24.12–6, E169)

The second is from Freud's *Civilization and its Discontents*, one of the few of Freud's works that one might think of as 'social criticism':

> It is very far from my intention to express an opinion on the value of human civilization. I can at least listen without indignation to the critic who is of the opinion that when one surveys the aims of cultural endeavour and the means it employs, one is bound to come to the conclusion that the whole effort is not worth the trouble, and that the outcome of it can only be a state of affairs which the individual will be unable to tolerate. (144–5)

In one sense, Blake's reflections on the 'deathly desire' summarized in the phrase 'natives in the Grave' is very much of his time, echoing the work of graveyard poets like Thomas Parnell and Edward Young, whose melancholic *Night Thoughts* Blake illustrated; in another, however, critics have been right to point out that it is significant that, although in his early *Songs* Blake depicts the states of innocence and experience, he never devotes so much time to elaborating on the state of 'organiz'd innocence' (E697) which, he hints, would form a resolution between these two. The picture, however, that emerges of Blake under this kind of Freudian lens is necessarily mixed. On the one hand, there is certainly an awareness of self-destructive power at work within the individual and society; on the other, there is a search for resolution and redemption.

There are, however, also other connections between Blake and Freud.[1] Perhaps the most important is Blake's insistence on the significance of infancy and childhood. In this respect, again, he was certainly not alone in his time; one thinks also, and pre-eminently, of Wordsworth. But there is something quite specific in Blake's analysis of the formative power of early years, and especially of the influence exerted by parents (and not only parents – the figure of the nurse is also highly significant in Blake's poetry). In the poem 'The School Boy', for example, there is already a shadow looming large over the youngster as he undergoes a process that looks far more like an 'induction' into a hostile adult world than like an 'education' in the full sense of a 'leading out' – as we can see vividly in the final stanza:

> How shall the summer arise in joy.
> Or the summer fruits appear,
> Or how shall we gather what griefs destroy
> Or bless the mellowing year,
> When the blasts of winter appear. (26–30, E31)

Or, to translate speculatively into Freudian terms, how shall we continue to ascribe positive value to the world when we are in the grip of forces, internal and external, that conduce to an inevitable melancholia?

Another crucial aspect of Freudian theory is projection, the process whereby we shift inner states and conditions into the outer world; this may produce temporary psychological relief, but in the long run it is a process of distortion which removes any certainty from the relations between the inner and outer. The theme of 'they became what they beheld' could very easily be taken as a description of a process that finds its purest and most damaging form in the psychotic, where the boundaries between inner and outer threaten so catastrophic a breakdown that it is necessary to set up massive, even impenetrable, defence mechanisms in order to ensure basic survival. Similarly in Blake, it is important to bear in mind that Urizen, for example, is not only a 'character'; he is also a 'state', and when the world is in this 'Urizenic state', even Los cannot resist being reshaped by the prevailing psychic and ideological circumstances.

Jung, as is well known, took many of Freud's ideas and remolded them into the form of 'analytical psychology'. Perhaps his most significant, and certainly his best-known, elaboration of Freudian theory lies in the evolution of the concept of a 'collective unconscious', but he also differs hugely from Freud in the range and tone of his discourse. Freud's work is scientific, at least in intent, rigorously abbreviated, heavily reliant on case material, not at all inclined to the abstractions of metapsychology. Jung's, on the other hand, is often seen as 'artistic' or 'creative'; it relies hugely on myth and the interpretation of myth; it rarely comments on individual patients; and its scope is, in theory at least, enormous. Perhaps for these reasons, Jung was for quite a time considered by literary critics a more interesting source of psychological comparison than Freud, and Blake studies has been no exception. Again, I shall here pick just one book, Christine Gallant's *Blake and the Assimilation of Chaos*.

The key features of Jung's work that Gallant picks out for comparison with Blake begin with a notion of the self-contained, universal collective unconscious and with the way in which, according to Jung, it is this deeper level of the unconscious that generates archetypes. She then speaks of Jung's emphasis on 'individuation', which she refers to as 'man's psychological struggle to understand and accept his unconscious'; this broadening of the individual's psychic field can be clearly seen as analogous to Blake's emphasis on 'cleansing the doors of perception'. In this general area, one can also think again of the relations between order and chaos; Gallant likens Los's key task of the building of the city of Golgonooza to an attempt to bring order out of chaos. In these and other ways, the link between Blake and Jung – Blake's *prefiguration* of Jung – is persuasive. It is easy – all too easy, as Gallant very honestly says – to find archetypes and mandalas in Blake's work, and to map his 'faculties' onto the Jungian 'personality functions' of intuition, feeling, sensation and thinking. Where the Jungian analogy is, however, perhaps most vulnerable is in two areas: in the concept of the 'universal' and in the conceptualization of the self.

The problem with the universal is that, despite Jung's best intentions, it remains in analytical psychology a notion that borders on the abstract, on pure form and shape (as in the mandalas), and this runs directly opposite to Blake's thinking, in which it is the 'minute particulars', of history or of a person's life, that are, following from the biblical parable, the most 'sacred'. Furthermore, the more we read Blake the more we see that he is not looking for a general or abstract pattern; he is looking instead in the opposite direction, towards how to discern and invest meaning in the world around him. This is not, of course, to say that Jung was not doing that too, but in Blake the emphasis is differently placed. Jung's thinking in the end tends towards a massive 'overview', while Blake's search is always to look 'inside' the world, to perceive its minutest workings, to see 'infinity in a grain of sand'.

Similarly, we may reasonably suspect that Blake would have had a great deal to say about the notion of 'individuation'. Certainly one could say that Blake was highly conscious of what Gerard Manley Hopkins would later christen with the term 'inscape', the unique signature-effect by which each thing is in the process of continually becoming its own self. But on the other hand, one of Blake's major and most consistent objects of attack is what he terms the 'Selfhood', by which we may understand a sense of self that is guarded, protected, that tends towards the triumphalist and the separatist. If individuation is important in Blake, it is so only as one half of a dialectic, the other half being a sense of commonalty, a sense that 'achieving' the self is a matter of throwing oneself – one's 'self' – wide open, embracing the world and perhaps, in the end, dissolving, as in the wine-presses of Jerusalem.

There have been many 'post-Freudian' schools of thought. One of them, which has hardly been used in Blake criticism, stems from the thought of Melanie Klein and the object-relations school of psychology, and in many ways some of these insights seem peculiarly relevant to Blake. One way of looking at Klein's thought is to see it as originating in an analysis of infant fantasies. The infant, according to Klein, entertains various fantasies concerning his/her mother. Some of these fantasies, of course, and especially those centering around the 'good breast' (the present, nurturing breast) are positive and filled with gratitude and love; but others, concerned with the 'bad breast' (the withheld, absent breast) are deeply destructive. According to Klein, as the child develops he/she becomes increasingly ashamed and guilty about these 'bad' fantasies, and as a result of this introjected guilt becomes subject to angry attacks. Klein goes so far as to say that one result of this guilt is an unconscious need to make reparation, and that it is this instinct to make reparation, to set up a new 'whole object' in place of the damaged ones that the child fears he or she has caused, that results in the creation of works of art.

It should be said that this view of art has come under heavy attack, most effectively by Leo Bersani in his book *The Culture of Redemption*, where he shows us a litany of artists (Goya, Kafka, Beckett, for example) whose work seems to show rather little redemptive impulse. Nevertheless:

My mother groan'd! my father wept.
Into the dangerous world I leapt:
Helpless, naked, piping loud:
Like a fiend hid in a cloud.

Struggling in my father's hands,
Striving against my swaddling bands,
Bound and weary I thought best
To sulk upon my mother's breast. (E28)

Admittedly, this short poem 'Infant Sorrow' appears in the *Songs of Experience*, and we may therefore speculate as to quite what kind of voice is speaking to the reader, but on the other hand it appears to pre-echo Kleinian thinking in startling ways. There is, for example, a relativization of the notion of innocence: the infant depicted by Blake here is not the pure, sweet child whom the Victorians used to delight in finding in the *Songs of Innocence*. Instead, what we have is an infant who is born into a 'dangerous' world, a world of terror. The occasion of his birth is not one of joy, but one which is attended by groaning and weeping; the child may be an 'addition' to the family, but he is also a threat, and he immediately internalizes that sense of threat.

There may, again, be innocence present here on the surface, but this merely relates to how the child is sentimentally regarded; behind this façade (hidden within the cloud) there is quite a different, 'fiendish' being – which both prefigures what the child is 'bound' to become, and also signifies the emotional turmoil that may make up the infant's inner life. In the poem, the infant knows full well – at *some* level, which can presumably only be unconscious – that his power (his sense of omnipotence, as Klein would put it) is being restrained, and yet at the same time he understands his powerlessness, in a dreadful dynamic which can only have one outcome: a 'weary', disillusioned, resentful acceptance of the impossibility of the fulfillment of desire.

One may therefore read this poem as in tune with Klein's description of psychic life as an oscillation between two 'positions', the paranoid/schizoid position and the depressive position. Essentially, what she claims is that the infant's 'caught-ness' between power and powerlessness conduces to the paranoid/schizoid position, involving a strong sense of being oppressed by (adult) others which leads to fantasies of division, and will progress during maturation to a more realistic appreciation of what is and what is not possible in terms of the interaction between inner desire and outer constraint – the depressive position. Of course, if this maturation is thwarted, if the individual finds it impossible to come to terms with the 'swaddling bands' which represent, at one level, the armor of the self which has to be adopted in order to pass to social normalcy, then all kinds of mental illness occur; in particular, a different kind of armor may be adopted, one which may serve to prevent any real communication at all between inner and outer, the kind of armor that Blake refers to as the 'Selfhood'. One can see this process at work in, for example, 'The Angel':

> I Dreamt a Dream! what can it mean?
> And that I was a maiden Queen,
> Guarded by an Angel mild:
> Witless woe was ne'er beguil'd!
>
> And I wept both night and day,
> And he wip'd my tears away,
> And I wept both day and night,
> And hid from him my heart's delight.
>
> So he took his wings and fled;
> Then the morn blush'd rosy red;
> I dried my tears, & arm'd my fears
> With ten thousand shields and spears.
>
> Soon my Angel came again:
> I was arm'd, he came in vain;
> For the time of youth was fled,
> And grey hairs were on my head. (E24)

This extraordinary poem portrays – in some ways in a shortened version of arguments Blake puts forward in *The Book of Thel* – the way in which a young woman on the brink of puberty ('blush's rosy red' refers, it would appear, to the onset of menstruation) is solaced by a potential lover but regards this as a mere delusion ('Witless woe was ne'er beguil'd') and refuses to admit to her own matching desires. By the time he returns, all is too late: she has 'arm'd' her heart, and the fulfillment of desire has become an impossibility.

Of course, there are plenty of ambiguities in this poem: for example, the figure of the 'angel', which appears positive, or at least neutral, here often stands for a negative, controlling, superegoic influence in Blake; it is therefore possible that what Blake is depicting is more bleak, signifies the real impossibility of trust in a society in which the relations between the genders is built on social codes which deceive everybody. But on the whole, we might see here the destructive effects of the psychic myth of an inviolate self, where any intrusion of the 'other' is seen as potentially threatening and the individual is condemned to a world where the cynicism of 'experience' continually defeats the possibility of real, loving communication.

The mention of the notion of the 'other' moves us on naturally to the other major school of neo-Freudian thought—which figures, as do so many others, as a 'return' to Freud – namely, the French psychoanalytical school centered on the work of Jacques Lacan. Lacan's central achievement is to take further Freud's notion that the ego is always partial, always involved in 'patrolling' the more dangerous impulses emanating (it is no accident that Blake's female figures in the Prophetic Books are often referred to as 'emanations') from the unconscious, and to develop from that the idea that the self is always involved in the act of misrecognizing itself; indeed, that the very concept of the self enshrines an act of primal misrecognition (*méconnaissance*), which falsely places the conscious aspect of the psyche at the center of life.

In a subtle article called 'Rouzing the Faculties: Lacanian Psychoanalysis and the Marriage of Heaven and Hell in the Reader', Mark Bracher attempts a Lacanian reading of *The Marriage of Heaven and Hell*, concluding thus:

> [I]t is in such recognition of desire – such a marriage of heaven (the sacred code) and hell (desire) – that Lacanian psychoanalysis locates the efficacy of the psychoanalytic process. By evoking our repressed desires, by providing us with a new code that offers fuller recognition to our desire, and by interpellating us to a position where we must either accept such a code or construct it through interpretation, Blake's poem arouses our faculties to act in such a way as to enact a marriage that constitutes psychological transformation. This process constitutes a marriage of heaven and hell in another sense as well: by eliciting deep fantasies of phallic potency and castration within a metaphysical context, the poem allows our desire to assume more coherent, less conflicting forms, in which a (displaced and sublimated) fulfilment (heaven) is possible even in face of the inescapable reality of castration, or human finitude (hell). (203)

There is no space here to go into great detail about Bracher's argument, which hinges partly on the 'illustrations' of *The Marriage of Heaven and Hell*, but it is possible to sketch its main lines. He is claiming that Blake's work forms a conscious commentary on the vicissitudes of desire, on its inevitable lack of success, or deflation, when it encounters the 'real' world. According to Bracher, Blake's work provides the reader with a series of clues as to how to survive this encounter by coming to an accommodation between the illusion of fulfillment (heaven) and the inevitable and continuing dissatisfaction of desire (hell). Thus the displaced and dislocated ego may be able to negotiate a path (a Miltonic one, evidently) between heaven and hell, between hopes and fantasies on the one hand and the torturing reality of disillusionment on the other – and thus, indeed, the originary *méconnaissance* of the subject may be in some sense surpassed. *The Marriage of Heaven and Hell* therefore comes to appear as a kind of symbolic handbook for therapy; if the individual can suspend the illusory possibility of real fulfillment and can come to inhabit a space where there is a continuing tension between expectation and defeat, then that individual will have come to a point of stasis in psychic development, or at least to a point where the rival claims of order and chaos can be held in suspension. It may never be possible for the self to fully understand itself, but nonetheless it can find a space for itself from which to view its predicament and accept it, without joy, perhaps without love, but with a sense of being at home in a world from which the self is forever otherwise in exile.

And there is much to support this reading of Blake. To take the most obvious example, the 'giant' figure of Albion (representing, variously, the state of England, the integrated psyche and the possibility of bodily fulfillment) remains asleep for much of the trajectory of the Prophetic Books; Albion is, as it were, in exile from himself, 'unconscious' – in all senses of that term – of what is going on around him. The self, therefore, has no real purchase on the outer world; he is lost in dream, unable to make connections, betrayed and corrupted *ab initio*, and it is this which either causes or is the principal effect of the domination of Urizen. On this reading, then, Urizen would constitute the self's continuing misreading of its self: one is reminded of the way in which Urizen, while appearing from one angle to be or to claim to be all-powerful, is at the same time constantly depicted as in tears, as weeping over the failures of his efforts to bend the world to his will – or indeed to construct a world which he will recognize and which will do his bidding.

It could, however, be claimed that Bracher's reading of Blake is fundamentally 'recuperative'; it is as though somehow through a thorough reading of Blake the reader can transcend *méconnaissance* and can achieve imaginative and psychic clarity. And there are psychoanalytic thinkers who claim that, despite his apparent systemic radicalism, Lacan's thought in fact tends towards, or at least allows for, this possibility of recuperation. One such thinker is Jean Laplanche, who, in his *Essays on Otherness*, lays out a groundwork for misrecognition which goes considerably beyond Lacan's, and in some crucial ways opposes it.

Probably Lacan's most famous pronouncement was that the unconscious is structured like a language – and it is from this that spring his equally famous analyses of the forces of metaphor and metonymy, condensation and displacement, in psychic process. Laplanche's claim is that the unconscious is not structured like a language, because, in fact, it is not structured at all. That is why, or at least how, it is the unconscious at all. The unconscious is instead residue, enigma, and the repository of misunderstood messages. To fill in a little detail behind this: Laplanche claims that 'traditional psychoanalysis' has gone wrong because it has underestimated the extent of misrecognition or misunderstanding. The examples he gives center on the child's attempts to discover truths about the world around them, and in particular the accuracy of the various 'sexual theories' which the child entertains. The message the child sends to the adult outer world does not elicit truth, because the adult who responds is him- or herself sending back a message which is fatally vitiated by primal repression and which therefore will not 'make sense' in the way that the child's desire entertains. Thus communication is itself not, in any sense, 'structured like a language'; rather, it is a tissue or web of misunderstandings and evasions.

The position from which the adult delivers the 'return message' is, to put it another way, the residue of the adult's own lack of accommodation with the unconscious, and thus the 'enigma', in Laplanche's term, which lies at the heart of this web of messages remains intact and 'untranslated'. This is not to say, of course, that the *possibility* of an unraveling of the secret may not continue to haunt the texture of communication, but this possibility will always be deferred, always horizonal.

These issues of the secret and deferral are ones to which I shall return shortly, but for the moment, we might ask the question, which has not to date been asked by critics, of what a Laplanchean approach to Blake might look like. A text we might look at in this context is a short poem from the Pickering manuscript called 'The Smile':

> There is a Smile of Love
> And there is a Smile of Deceit
> And there is a Smile of Smiles
> In which these two Smiles meet

And there is a Frown of Hate
And there is a Frown of Disdain
And there is a Frown of Frowns
Which you strive to forget in vain

For it sticks in the Hearts deep Core
And it sticks in the deep Back bone
And no Smile that ever was smild,
But only one Smile alone

That betwixt the Cradle & Grave
It only once Smild can be
But, when it once is Smild
Theres an end to all Misery. (E482–3)

The most obvious reason for choosing this poem is, of course, that it is – if there can be such a thing – self-evidently 'enigmatic'. The poem is enigmatic, resistant to 'translation' (another key term for Laplanche), unyielding to the attempt to unlock its secrets. The smile too, we might fairly say, is enigmatic. We might want to ask what kind of smile it is, but here we are immediately thwarted. Is the 'smile of love' different from the 'smile of deceit' – or rather, how would we know? Is the apparent difference between them only the effect of the desire of the 'recipient of the smile', as it were, the reader of the expression, as s/he makes the attempt to interpret or translate what is essentially enigmatic into something recognizable, recuperated into an assumed repertoire of emotional transactions?

There has, of course, been much practical psychological work done on the infant's reception of the mother's expressions, which constitutes, after all, a 'language', or in Laplanchean terms a set of communications on which the infant is utterly dependent. What if these expressions were misleading from the start – not deliberately so, but because the chain of experience through which we learn expression, and indeed expressivity *per se*, were itself fractured from the beginning by the unassimilable intrusions of the unconscious into any attempt to provide accuracy or clarity? What if every smile were in fact not a revelation of an inner world of feeling but instead a defence mechanism conjured to prevent the self from being exposed to the outer world? The infant would then indeed be adrift, and would then have to have resort to the only remaining world, the world of fantasy: in which, indeed – but *only* in which – there could be a (fantasized) smile which would put an 'end to all Misery'.

Blake's poem would thus figure not as a statement about the 'state of things', but as a consolidation of the impossibility of interpretation, as a symbolic representation of the flight from the real, of the construction of the adult self as fundamentally based on a necessary misapprehension of the world around.

A further challenge for the psychological criticism of Blake would be represented in the revisionist psychoanalysis associated with the work of Nicolas Abraham and Maria Torok. Again, it would not be possible here to present a full account of their work, but some of the crucial arguments and terms are clearly relevant. Essentially, Abraham and Torok present a view of the psyche as 'haunted'. It is haunted by its own past, and the figures from that past which are variously incorporated and introjected as part of the psyche's efforts to sustain its development. Thus far, of course, we might fairly say that Abraham and Torok are adding little to Freud; but they go one step farther than him in identifying a layer of the psyche which lies, as it were, below what we conventionally mean by the 'unconscious', which they refer to as the 'crypt'. This crypt can be seen as an entity which is passed on through the 'family line'; in it are all the family secrets which have been repressed, undeclared, and which therefore figure to the individual only as a series of spectral shapes. It is not, Abraham and Torok say, possible fully to unlock this crypt; the keys have, as it were, been thrown away. Nevertheless, it continues to exert pressure on the present; it is felt, one might say, as a negative force, but it nonetheless shapes present thought and action. The task of the analyst is nevertheless to address this 'hidden' layer; hence the last word in the title of one of their books, *The Wolf Man's Magic Word: A Cryptonomy*.

What, we might ask, would it be like to apply a cryptonymic reading to Blake? The point from which one might start would be the omnipresence of the spectral in Blake. In chapter 2 of *Jerusalem*, we hear the voice of one of the 'Divine Family' lamenting these constant, and constantly unexpected, intrusions of the spectral:

> I feel my Spectre rising upon me! Albion! arouze thyself!
> Why dost thou thunder with frozen Spectrous wrath against us?
> The Spectre is, in Giant Man; insane and most deform'd.
> Thou wilt certainly provoke my Spectre against thine in fury!
> He has a Sepulcher hewn out of a Rock ready for thee:
> And a Death of Eight thousand years forg'd by thyself, upon
> The point of his Spear, if thou persistest to forbid with Laws
> Our Emanations, and to attack our secret supreme delights.
> (J33.2–9, E179)

There are many ways of interpreting the 'spectres' in Blake; indeed, it could be said that they constitute a significant point of instability in his symbolic system, so various are the meanings attributed to them. It sometimes appears as though the specter is the incarnation of cold reason, a kind of superegoic formation that violently criticizes and scorns all human action. But the imagery here seems to point instead to a deeper layer, to a normally hidden aspect of the self, the release of which will provoke a cataclysm. Behind the usual processes of human interaction, Blake here seems to be saying, there lies what we might call another narrative, another story, one which is not amenable to rational interpretation. In this 'other world', there are figures which are too terrible to be withstood if they are ever unleashed.

One might see here a kind of 'cryptic dynamics' of the psyche. The enormous pressure of repression (represented in one form by Albion's sleep) continually menaces us with the possibility that to attempt to reverse its effects would, in effect, be to disturb monsters of the deep. The opposite of repression would not be liberation but a violent upsurge of energy that would destroy all in its path. This, of course, is another way of looking at the entire Orc cycle in Blake's mythos, and from that we could move back to a consideration of the lessons Blake may have learned from the fate of the French Revolution where, as many historians then and now would agree, the violence of the *ancien régime* was not replaced by a new Jerusalem, but rather by a state of affairs that continued to replicate, in distorted form, the injustices of the past, continued to feel and manifest their pressure just as the individual psyche is shaped by its own hidden residues.

The crypt, we might hypothesize, is here the 'Sepulcher'; in it are buried, apparently without hope of retrieval, all our hopes for change – psychological or societal. There are moments when Abraham and Torok seem prepared to entertain the possibility that the crypt might indeed be unlocked – hence the force of the 'magic word' that they claim to discover, which will unlock the long-held secrets of Freud's case of the 'wolf-man'. But it would on the whole be fair to derive from their thinking a bleaker view than this, one in which splits in the psyche, the presence of crypts, locked rooms, haunted chambers, remain threatening and figure as unseen but sensed presences on – or below – the psychic terrain. Just so, denial in Blake breeds its own monsters. 'He who desires but acts not, breeds pestilence', runs one of the Proverbs of Hell in *The Marriage of Heaven and Hell*; the pressure of forcing things downwards in the psyche will cause a revolt against us in the form of a body that is 'insane and most deform'd', a figure of contamination and pestilence that will, in the end, grow in power over us and prevent our escape from the continual savage return of the past.

To turn to a recent and rather different reading: in an intriguing essay called 'The Preacher, the Poet, and the Psychoanalyst', the analyst Ronald Britton approaches Milton and Blake – and Blake on Milton – with a view to discriminating between the 'preacher' – the voice that seems to have a clear program, definable answers – from the 'poet', who in the elaboration of his images continuingly subverts the very message that appears on the surface of the work. From this starting point, Britton describes Milton's ostensible purpose in *Paradise Lost*, 'to justify the ways of God to men', as a pathological, defensive organization, designed to repress crucially disastrous personal, theological and political factors affecting Milton's own life. He further refers to this as 'destructive narcissism', and suggests that it is the fracturing of the self against which this formation is supposed to protect that Blake discerns when he speaks of Milton being 'of the Devil's party without knowing it'.

In the case of Blake's own work, Britton claims that when he reverses Miltonic formulations,

> he reproduces another recognisable defensive organisation, that of the True/False Self model described by Winnicott. As preachers, both Milton and Blake have given us verse form precursors of what, in twentieth-century psychoanalysis, were described as pathological organisations. Milton produces Satan to exonerate God, a bad self alongside an ideal self to protect him from believing in a cruel superego. Blake abolishes God the father, the superego, and substitutes the divine self, the idealised ego. (129–30)

D.W. Winnicott's 'True/False Self model' has to do with the notion that 'the psychic reality of the individual can be destroyed by any other reality opposed to it', a psychic state often referred to in clinical terms as 'borderline', or as a 'thin-skinned narcissism': 'in such patients the attempted integration of subjective being and objective thinking is believed to cause a psychic catastrophe' (Britton 126).

Here, then, we might be said to have come full circle and back to an attempt to discern Blake's own state of mind through his texts, but with a radical difference. Where earlier psychological critics may have been tempted to see in Blake an emancipatory seeking after (re)integration, what Britton's analysis suggests is that this very search constitutes, not a kind of psychological enlightenment, but rather the elaboration of a massive psychic defense system designed to prevent the self from being menaced by the 'difference' of the outside world. The monist trend in Blake's thinking ('He became what he beheld') thus signifies a fear of what might occur if this wish to merge were thwarted or rendered impossible.

For Britton, the hidden fear in Blake's work is of 'the void outside existence', a place where integration is impossible because the self has lost all measure. Britton also talks about the relevance of the state of Beulah, and although he does not quite say this, it would be reasonable to suppose that Beulah stands precisely for the place where the self can experience, if only in fantasy, the unity which it desperately craves. Of course, the state of Beulah is not the culmination of the story for Blake; but it may nonetheless signify a condition where the painful, even agonizing, divisions between self and world and within the psyche may be 'wished away', where an aesthetic and sensory plenitude may reassure us of the facticity of the self and offer a promise of integration.

We could build further on the kind of reading Britton offers. For example, the role of 'self-annihilation' might be reassessed as a counterpoint to the fear of annihilation; the notion that 'anything that can be believed is true' would mark an anxiety about reality-testing, a kind of 'psychic retreat' under the guise of expansion. It is of course interesting that the 'Blake' promulgated by generations of early critics dwelt so entirely within a world of 'innocence' when the most cursory reading of his longer works suggests a huge undertow of violence and rage.

Here, however, one must perhaps draw a line. Abraham and Torok chose to 'reopen a case', but inevitably the materials at their disposal are highly suspect; the wolf-man is long dead (although he continues to haunt psychoanalytic literature). To attempt to 'reopen the case' (or unlock the crypt) of Blake encounters similar difficulties; nevertheless, psychological, and particularly psychoanalytic, approaches to Blake's works have thrown up over the years a series of insights which are in no way the less valuable for the apparently contrasting nature of their conclusions. Perhaps the key to this lies in one of Blake's most famous proclamations:

> There is a Negation, & there is a Contrary
> The Negation must be destroyd to redeem the Contraries
> The Negation is the Spectre; the Reasoning Power in Man
> This is a false Body: an Incrustation over my Immortal
> Spirit; a Selfhood, which must be put off & annihilated alway.
>
> (M40.32–7, E142)

Here we have a statement about destruction and development, about true and false bodies and psyches, about 'incrustations', by which we might reasonably figure psychic defenses, about selfhood and annihilation; about, perhaps, the inevitability of contradictory readings of and within the self, such that no text can ever exhaust its possibilities, just as no psychological approach can ever eschew the possibility of its own defensiveness, its potential (critical) collusion with the 'dark materials' with which it has to deal.

note

1. Prominent among the connections between Blake and Freud is the former's seeming anticipation of the Oedipal family romance (see, for instance, the description of Los and Enitharmon's parenting of Orc in Chapter VII of *The Book of Urizen*, plate 20).

works cited and suggestions for further reading

Abraham, Nicolas and Maria Torok. *The Wolf Man's Magic Word: A Cryptonymy*. Trans. Nicholas Rand. Minneapolis: University of Minnesota Press, 1986.

Bersani, Leo. *The Culture of Redemption*. Cambridge and London: Harvard University Press, 1990.

Bracher, Mark. '"Rouzing the Faculties": Lacanian Psychoanalysis and the Marriage of Heaven and Hell in the Reader' in *Critical Paths: Blake and the Argument of Method*. Ed. Dan Miller, Mark Bracher and Donald Ault. Durham, NC: Duke University Press, 1987.

Britton, Ronald. 'The Preacher, the Poet, and the Psychoanalyst' in *Acquainted with the Night: Psychoanalysis and the Poetic Imagination*. Ed. Hamis Canham and Carole Satyamurti. London and New York: Karnac Books, 2003.

Brown, Norman. *Life Against Death: The Psychoanalytical Meaning of History*. Middletown, CT: Wesleyan University Press, 1985.

Freud, Sigmund. *Civilization and its Discontents* in Standard Edition of the Complete Psychological Works of Sigmund Freud. Ed. James Strachey. Vol. 21. London: Hogarth Press, 1953–74.

Gallant, Christine. *Blake and the Assimilation of Chaos*. Princeton: Princeton University Press, 1978.

George, Diana Hume. *Blake and Freud*. Ithaca: Cornell University Press, 1980.

Jung, Carl Gustav. *Aion: Researches into the Phenomenology of the Self*. Vol 9, pt. 2 of *Collected Works*. Ed. Herbert Read, Michael Fordham, Gerhard Adler and William McGuire. Trans. R.F.C. Hull. Princeton: Princeton University Press, 1968.

——. *Archetypes and the Collective Unconscious*. Vol. 9, pt. 1 of *Collected Works*. Ed. Herbert Read, Michael Fordham, Gerhard Adler and William McGuire. Trans. R.F.C. Hull. Princeton: Princeton University Press, 1968.

Klein, Melanie. *Envy and Gratitude (1946–1963)*. New York: Free Press, 2002.

Lacan, Jacques. *Écrits: A Selection*. Trans. Alan Sheridan. New York and London: W.W. Norton and Company, 1977.

Laplanche, Jean. *Essays on Otherness*. London: Routledge, 1998.

Marcuse, Herbert. *Eros and Civilization: A Philosophical Inquiry into Freud*. London: Routledge and Kegan Paul, 1956.

Winnicott, D.W. 'Ego Distortion in Terms of True and False Self' in *The Maturational Processes and the Facilitating Environment*. London: Hogarth Press, 1965.

9

blake and science studies

mark lussier

SCIENCE is the Tree of DEATH (E274)
The dark Religions are departed & sweet Science reigns (E407)

preludium

The epigrams above, drawn respectively from 'The Laocoön' engraving
and the final page of *The Four Zoas*, capably capture the complexity of
William Blake's attitudes toward science and aptly provide the poles
for this exploration of how Blake viewed science, how Blake scholars
have analyzed its presence and, more importantly for our own age,
how contemporary science has found new relevance for Blake. When
Blake describes 'science' as a 'tree of death', he articulates a deep-
seated suspicion of the mechanical applications of instrumental reason
shared with his contemporary William Wordsworth, who knew well
that 'meddling intellect' was capable of 'murdering to dissect' (131).
However, Blake primarily critiques instrumental reason and its ideological
pretensions, a symbolic exploration traced in the mythic figure of Urizen
and derived from his forefathers 'Bacon & Newton & Locke' (J98.9,
E257), and as the last words of *The Four Zoas* suggestively assert, the
attack on the emergence of science as an ideology in its own right does
not negate but actually unveils a 'sweet science' defined by the dynamic
interactivity of mind and matter in space-time (what Donald Ault termed
a 'visionary physics' (xii)).[1]

Of course, Blake certainly provided ample evidence to fuel the
initial critical view of his opposition to science, with one of the most
quoted letters in his corpus often functioning as the most damning
evidence:

Now I a fourfold vision see
And a fourfold vision is given to me
Tis fourfold in my supreme delight
And three fold in soft Beulahs night
And twofold Always. May God us keep
From Single vision & Newtons sleep. (E722)

The visual critique of the unitary vision Blake associated with Newtonian materialism appeared seven years earlier in the painting *Newton* (Figure 9.1), where the Lucasian Professor of Mathematics, head and eyes turned downward, rests on a rock in the depths of the Blakean 'Sea of Time and Space', mapping with his compass the course of a cosmos governed by clockwork mechanics. Blake certainly recognized, even feared, the imaginative attraction offered by Newtonianism in his time, since, as Robert Markley rightly asserts, 'the intellectual prominence of Newton's work [. . .] would be difficult to overestimate' (184) across the eighteenth century and since 'Newtonian ideology existed chiefly at a popular level' (Hankins 9).

Figure 9.1   *Newton*

In his response to the interlocking epistemologies of Newtonianism and Enlightenment, Blake rejects a monological universe defined by absolute certainties and forced unities and articulates a heterological multiverse defined by complementarities, complexities, and relativities.[2] This description of Blake's anti-system helps gloss one of the more curious aspects of Blake's work, one best engaged through the opening quatrain to 'Auguries of Innocence' (and to a slightly lesser extent by 'The Tyger'):

> To see a World in a Grain of Sand
> And a Heaven in a Wild Flower
> Hold Infinity in the palm of your hand
> And Eternity in an hour. (E490)

This provocative passage has been heavily appropriated by those who might be considered the poet's intellectual enemies, the contemporary inheritors of Newton who write the 'new physics' of relativity, quantum, and chaos. Yet the elasticity of perception at work within discrete acts of observation evoked by Blake's lines has been used to explain relativistic effects in space-time, the role of the observer in determining physical events, the drive for symmetry in contemporary physical theory, and the complexity surrounding contemporary views of complementarity (I will return to this play of Blake in contemporary physics later in the chapter). The preliminary view of Blake as utterly opposed to science has been somewhat reconfigured relative to the current view of the poet's relevance in discussions of complex physical theory, and this chapter will initially focus on Blake's direct engagements with science, move toward the analysis of this presence within Blake studies, and conclude with an assessment of the visionary poet's presence in discussion of the contemporary physics of our own day.

blake and science

In Michael Ferber's reading, Blake's view of science was closer 'to Christian Science than to the bourgeois science of the Birmingham Lunar Society' (38), a stance certainly not surprising given the latter's involvement in the ongoing integration of science and technology at the foundation of the industrial revolution. This confluence, addressed early and often by Blake, synthesized scientific experimentation and industrial innovation, a tell-tale trace of how the mechanical philosophy slowly insinuated itself in culture at the level of daily practice. New technologies pressed into the service of the burgeoning industrial revolution, often imaged by Blake as 'a mill with complicated wheels' (E2), began to displace subjects from labor, helped to alienate them from nature, and sought to shape those subjects in its own image, giving rise to the 'Satanic mills' (E95) that despoil England's 'green and pleasant land' while transmuting England's populace, in the process, into 'sexual machines'.[3] To borrow Saree Makdisi's broad description of the problem, 'the dark satanic mill here is a figure not just of the organization of production in early industrial society; it is a figure of the social, political, and religious constitution of the individual psychobiological subject, determined – produced – by social and political circumstances, rather than being given by the laws of nature and nature's god' (131).

The representation of science in Blake's work appears quite early in the tractates *There is No Natural Religion* (A and B) (1788) and remains a steady state of concern across the illuminated prophecies and *The Four Zoas* (1797–1807). However, tracing Blake's response to science in his art is often like chasing a specter, since the term itself was not in wide use during the period and has shifted radically to arrive at our own usage of the term. 'For Blake', as Mark Greenberg explains, 'science is fundamentally a logocentric activity which implies and causes the conditions it represents' (116),[4] and as S. Foster Damon suggests in his influential *Blake Dictionary* (the initial critical location for most students of Blake), the difficulty students and scholars alike have in discerning the meaning and function of 'Science' for Blake derives from those 'two contrary meanings' of the term evoked by the epigrams above (359). The critique of science inaugurated in the tractates grapples not with the disciplines of natural history, natural philosophy, and mixed mathematics *per se* (the relevant descriptors in use during the late eighteenth century), but with the type of view (single vision) that conditions the practice of those disciplines. Thus, Blake critiques the animating spirit of science, which motivates its practices, and he especially rebels against a singular view of scientific striving shorn of its creative and imaginative elements, for, as the 'Conclusion' to *There is No Natural Religion* (B) suggests, 'If it were not for the Poetic or Prophetic character the Philosophic & Experimental would soon be at a ratio of all things & stand still, unable to do other than repeat the same dull round over again' (E3).

Blake's position at the beginning of his literary career, then, is in remarkable accord with that expressed much later by Albert Einstein during the revolution in physics in the opening decades of the twentieth century, who proposed that 'physical concepts are free creations of the human mind, and are not, however it may seem, uniquely determined by the external world' (76). Indeed, Blake's primary objection to the evolution in physical theory with which he was confronted (which included advances in cosmology, chemistry, geology, mathematics, and neurology) concerned the dominance accorded the rational faculty at the expense of other aspects of the self – a point argued by Ault at length (24–56) – and its implication for individual identity.[5] Blake saw 'reason' as the animating spirit and feared its application within every arena of human life, a process already well established by the 1780s.

The problem represented by rationalism and empiricism resided not simply in their deification of reason as the one measure of the world but the degree to which, as Jacob Bronowski suggested, the epistemology of Enlightenment, as represented by Bacon, Newton, Descartes, Locke, and Hume, crystallized into a 'rigid' and 'abstract' system (137). Four years following the tractates (1792), Blake inaugurates a frontal assault on such limitations in his critique of 'the restrainer or reason' (E34) in *The Marriage of Heaven and Hell*. While this quirky and energetic explosion of creativity resists easy categorization (critics have interpreted the work as parody, philosophic primer, prophecy, and satire to name only a few), given the wide range of its concerns, the composite text clearly undertakes as a crucial element of its 'unlearning' the deconstruction of reason, which through its epistemic dominance in Blake's age functioned, for the poet/prophet, as 'the bound or outward circumference of energy' (E34). To render the rigidity of rationality – with its desire for control, order and utility – dynamic rather than static, Blake counters with his theory of contraries, proposing that 'Without contraries is no progression. Attraction and Repulsion, Reason and Energy, Love and Hate, are necessary to Human existence' (E34). Blake's proposed epistemic shift asserts a mode of thinking based on complementarity, where elements syzygistically interact, and thereby maintain individual integrity while operating holistically, a position opposed to the implied teleology of Hegelian dialectical thinking yet conversant with the theory of complementarity articulated in the twentieth century by Niels Bohr.[6] 'Blake's notion of contrariety', as Arkady Plotnitsky notes, 'is close to complementarity insofar as the latter entails the necessity of operating with conflicting modes of description – "contraries", as Blake calls them – without synthesis' (28–9).

Six years after the tractates (1788) and two years after *The Marriage*, the critique of 'Reason or the ratio of all we have already known' (E2) embedded therein focused in the character of Urizen, and *The Book of Urizen* (1794) seeks to account for its genesis while providing the first extended exploration of the limitations resulting from the historical dominance achieved by empirically driven rationalism, with the work becoming the Genesis of the 'Bible of Hell' promised in the closing pages of *The Marriage of Heaven and Hell*. *The Book of Urizen* has functioned as the primary prophetic work wherein to read Blake's stance against reason and science as divisive forces, where disciplinary knowledge fragments, moving toward ever greater specialization. The 'divisions' of Urizen's book into nine chapters provide one specific instance where Blake was not wholly hostile to scientific knowledge, since he draws this structural element from the nine-month gestational cycle of human formation in the womb, and this symbolism, employed inversely, also structures Urizen's individual emergence from the collective known at this point in the canon as 'the Eternals'. Even as Blake parodies the pieties of Genesis, his symbolism insists on the biological as a crucial aspect of his emerging mythological effort to establish connections between cosmos and consciousness, a point made in different ways by Kay and Roger Easson and Paul Mann.[7]

The gestational cycle through which Urizen emerges into physicality is inaugurated by an act of division, as Urizen separates from other elements of thought (later to become the zoas) in pursuit of a sovereign self, as the rational faculty strives for dominance:

> Let each chuse one habitation
> His ancient infinite mansion
> One command, one joy, one desire
> One curse, one weight, one measure,
> One King, one God, one Law. (E72)

With the symmetry of eternity thus shattered, Urizen moves to establish ideological control through the rational configuring of consciousness, and the monological insistence discussed previously as operating at the core of scientific striving re-emerges here as the solitary plumb line by which one must read the world of generation, a world now founded in difference. Here Blake's thinking intersects with that offered by other Romantic thinkers; Percy Shelley, in his *Defence of Poetry*, begins with a distinction between reason and imagination: 'Reason is the enumeration of quantities already known; Imagination the perception of the value of those quantities both separately and as a whole. Reason respects the differences, and the Imagination the similitude of things' (510). Reason, for Shelley, quantifies through difference, while the imagination forges connection, a position clearly conversant with Blake's own view.

The type of critique broached in the tractates and extended in *The Marriage* achieves greater specificity in this work, for the fallen world created by Urizen's act of division occasions a response by the other elements of thought which, in turn, also fall, with each element assuming a type of Urizenic aspect that only promulgates widening division. Having experienced the division in their ranks, the Eternals send Los (the figure associated with the imagination and often Blake himself) to create a body for the error now known as 'Urizen', a strategy of containment doomed to fail, since the act of limitation foisted upon the imagination forces it to function like reason itself. Los, in acting Urizenic, also falls further from shattered symmetry through 'becoming what he beholds' (a common formulation in the prophetic epics). After continuously reshaping the framing body for Urizen across the gestational cycle, a process that begins with the development of the physical brain and spine in the 'first Age' and extends to the final formation of limbs in the 'seventh Age', Los himself divides into male and female aspects. The Eternals, horrified at the emergence of discrete genders, seek to cloak this troubling development by weaving 'strong curtains of darkness' which they call 'Science'.

Few would deny the power of *The Book of Urizen*, and the work, through the intervention of Los, clearly establishes what Blake will later call 'the limit of contraction' as faculties fall from primordial unity, arriving at a space wherein to inaugurate a countermovement from materiality back to eternity. However, the work also tends to operate mythologically, with Blake fashioning the initial elements of mind (reason and imagination) as representative contraries operating within consciousness. Yet Blake's prophetic commitments also extended to history, and the poems bracketing *Urizen* – *The Song of Los*, *America: A Prophecy*, and *Europe: A Prophecy* – trace historically the progress of intellect undergirding the ultimate success of scientific paradigms, the debilitating effects of reason's dominion, and the rebellion such dominion creates in its wake. At this stage of his developing psycho-historical mythology, Blake has operated critically, seeking to unveil the operations of contemporary 'science' and its ur-source, reason, as a corrective to the divisive excesses of his age. He had yet to articulate, except in occasional passages, the model of mind and matter with which he would oppose the mechanical operations of consciousness conceived by Locke and the error of dualism implicit in the Cartesian *cogito*.[8] Blake, across the next ten years, strives to consolidate his system in *The Four Zoas*, *Milton*, and *Jerusalem*, and what emerges is a cosmology and psychology clearly at the vanguard of resistance to mechanical models codified from Newton and Locke and just as clearly prophesying the participatory 'multiverse' of space-time currently defining the physics of cosmos and consciousness in our own day.

As the original title to *The Four Zoas* – *Vala* – suggests, Blake, having articulated in the early illuminated works a critique of pure reason divided from other psychic elements, turned his attention to the nature of matter. Near the opening of *Jerusalem*, Blake identifies Vala as 'the Goddess Virgin-Mother! [. . .] Nature!' (18.29–30, E163), and Blake's identification of nature with mother and the feminine (matter/*mater*) continues a long, problematic tradition of association shared with, for example, Bacon, Newton and Locke. While I would argue that, ultimately, Blake swerves in his representation in an attempt to construct an 'organic' cosmos founded in 'panvitalism and hylozoism' (Hutchings 62), arriving at a more dynamic, interactive and interdependent model, nonetheless this association has served as the location for strong feminist counter readings of Blake's theory of emanations and its implied misogyny.[9] Ironically, while Blake sought to resist almost every dimension of Enlightenment epistemology as it emerged as a controlling ideology, his interrelation of the feminine with the material actually continues a problematic association embedded deeply within the very thing he resists. In fact, numerous works published in the last generation – especially the work of Ludmilla J. Jordanova, Londa Schiebinger, Ann B. Shteir, and Linda Jean Shepherd – have powerfully analyzed such problematic associations both within the Romantic period itself, as well as in the history of science.

Generations of scholars have warned wary readers that this apparent one-to-one identification is precarious at best, since Blake asserted that perception was a veil draped over nature (remember the 'tent of science' erected by the Eternals in *Urizen*). 'This illusory veil', to quote Nelson Hilton, 'serves as the magical boundary of separation and division between the introjected "within" and the projected "without"' (*Literal Imagination* 132). Functioning as the primary cause of Albion's fall in this heavily revised and finally unpublished epic, Vala enmeshes the Eternal Man in 'dreams of soft deluding slumber', with the consequence that 'those sweet fields of bliss / Where liberty was justice & eternal science was mercy' (39.16, 10–11, E327) grow fallow. The science that emerges from this situation, for Blake, can only be 'self delusion' (40.5, E327), 'a tree of death', since the perceiving subject now worships an abstract nature disconnected from perceptual dynamics ('Man fell upon his face prostrate before the watry shadow' (40.7, E327)).

The solution to this development, not surprisingly, requires healing the fissure between subject and object, consciousness and cosmos, by re/cognizing that 'the vast form of Nature' (42.17, E328) cloaks and deludes, thereby walling off eternity until ripped asunder. Until this act of perception, the cosmos is a literal 'universe' (a monological description created from received knowledge) 'Shrunk into fixed space' (57.12, E339) yet a universe with both 'the Limit of Opacity [Satan]' and 'the Limit of Contraction [Adam]' (54.19, 21, E338) now established. In such a universe, 'the Sciences were fixed' (73.21, E350), with visionary free play replaced by 'intricate wheels invented Wheel without wheel' (92.26, E364). Blake's understanding of the results of this 'unfortunate fall' – severe contraction – is stunning and couched in language directed against Enlightenment *praxis*; once deluded, Urizenic ideology itself dictates that 'In ignorance [we] view a small portion & think that All / And call it Demonstration blind to all the simple rules of life / Now now the Battle [mental war] rages round thy tender limbs, O Vala' (92.32–4, E364–5). At the approximate center of *The Four Zoas*, Vala actually begins to operate against Urizen's creation of a fixed system, not surprising given her aspect as 'natural change', and finally 'destroys the stability of [Urizen's] system' (Ault 111). As 'The Eternal Man' rises from his slumberous dreams of materialism and empiricism, the 'Wide Universe' (134.30, E403) begins an alarming and welcome transmutation as it moves increasingly away from 'the bitter words / Of Stern Philosophy' (138.14–15, E406) and towards the interactive model elaborated across *Milton* and *Jerusalem*.

While *Vala, or The Four Zoas* begins a reconstruction of the cosmos along visionary lines, the most detailed direct engagement with the debilitating elements of Enlightenment epistemology is pursued in *Milton*, which also offers the most detailed representation of the contours of Blake's visionary multiverse. A constricted reading of the work might certainly support the view voiced by Paul Gross that Blake 'rejected all forms of inquiry upon which modern science was built' (1), but this view collapses in the face of Blake's theory of the vortex, the marriage of time and space, the annihilation of dynamic contraries, and the complex complementarities presented in the work. Indeed, as I have argued elsewhere ('Blake's Vortex'), the physical dynamics described in this work are actually much easier to understand by accessing concepts resident in the 'new physics' of relativity and quantum (e.g. wormholes, space-time continuum, and particle annihilation).

Like *Vala, or The Four Zoas*, Blake's *Milton* defies simplistic summation, but the basic plot concerns the explosive departure of the dead poet John Milton from his abode in eternity as he descends into materiality to redeem his emanation Ololon. Milton's descent brings him to the garden at Felpham cottage and into Blake himself as he composes the poem at hand. Blake organizes the work through bilateral symmetry (as two books), but such symmetries are broken within the work's tripartite narrative structure. However, for the dedicated purpose of this chapter, the focus will be on the degree to which Blake succeeds in imaginatively overcoming the mechanical operations of Newtonian cosmology and Cartesian/Lockean psychology. Almost immediately, the poem denigrates 'Mathematical Proportion' and embraces 'Living Proportion' (4.27, E99), and following the Bard's Song, the work plunges readers into the wake of Milton's passage from eternity to materiality through the agency of the 'vortex'. The moment of descent, which is equally the moment of entering the vortex, is captured on the stunning title page to the work, which visually trans-shifts a discursive moment not experienced by readers until plate 15 (Figure 9.2) and thereby establishes at the textual level a bridge between two separate moments of reception.

The physical concept that facilitates Milton's passage from eternity to generation, the vortex, provides, within Blake's psycho-historical myth, two-way transportation, becoming the vehicle by which matters eternal descend to the limit of contraction and matters generational ascend to the eternal realms of thought. The image of the vortex had a long literary tradition prior to Blake's deployment of it, as Charles D. Minahen has charted, and often functioned as a vehicle for the 'synthesis of complex and even contradictory properties' (48). Setting aside its classical manifestations in the Pre-Socratics, Plato, Epicurus, Lucretius and Dante, the vortex played a crucial role in the mechanical world-view with which Blake grappled (for example, Descartes wrongly proposed the concept 'to account for planetary motion' (Minahen 71)), and Blake highlights this negative function of the vortex in *Vala, or The Four Zoas*, when Urizen's passage into the material universe creates 'many a Vortex fixing many a Science in the deep' (72.13, E349). However, in *Milton*, as Stuart Peterfreund convincingly argues, Blake inaugurates 'a pilgrimage through the vortex of the material and into the realm of spirit [and] energy' (*Newtonian World* 54), with the concept operating as a vehicle to express 'the unity of matter and spirit in space and time' (Charon 31–7).

Given the crucial operation of the elaborate vortex passage, which Ault proposes as 'one of the most compelling and complex in all literature' (154), it must be quoted at length:

> The nature of infinity is this: That every thing has its
> Own Vortex; and when once a traveler thro Eternity.
> Has passed that Vortex, he perceives it roll backward behind
> His path, into a globe itself infolding; like a sun:
> Or like a moon, or like a universe of starry majesty,
> While he keeps onwards in his wondrous journey on the earth
> Or like a human form, a friend with whom he livd benevolent.

Figure 9.2   Frontispiece, *Milton a Poem*

As the eye of man views both the east & west encompassing
Its vortex; and the north & south, with all their starry host;
Also the rising sun & setting moon he views surrounding
His corn-fields and his valleys of five hundred acres square.

Thus is the earth one infinite plane, and not as apparent
To the weak traveler confin'd beneath the moony shade.
Thus is the heaven a vortex passd already, and the earth
A vortex not yet pass'd by the traveler thro' Eternity.

(15.21–35, E109)

This description becomes a crucial element for Blake's evolving participatory cosmos, a physical and psychological boundary condition framing spatial and temporal configurations of existence. In its widest context, the vortex images the fusion of time and space, identity and universality, annihilation and apocalypse, even becoming the primary symbolism for the last judgment that concludes *Vala, or The Four Zoas*. Thus, the operations of the vortex as expressed in *Milton* oppose those of the circle, the same dull round addressed in the tractates and associated with Newtonian celestial mechanics.

When Milton enters the vortex, he falls 'Precipitant loud thundering into the Sea of Time and Space' (15.46, E110) and must avoid falling into a void of 'Opacity' at the limit of contraction named 'Satan', a term indicative of one possible state of eternal consciousness in the space-time of generation. The Bard already articulated the nature of this state in his song, where Satan, echoing Urizen's earlier assertion, declares that 'I am God alone / There is no other! Let all obey my principles of moral individuality' (9.25–6, E103). Singularity banishes alterity ('There is no other!') in preference for an illusory objectivity of self ('individuality'), and this state, in many ways, functions as a conceptual black hole, where an individual enters, in Stephen Hawking's phrase, 'a region of space-time from which it is not possible to escape' (89). The parallel narrative universe of *Jerusalem* elaborates on this complex, as voiced by Albion's specter at the opening of the second chapter, for Satanic essence enters 'a white Dot calld a Center from which branches out / A Circle in continuing gyrations' (29.19–20, E175). The circle, with selfhood functioning as center, implies wheels within wheels and leads to the same dull round of existence (an echo of the concerns voiced in the early tractates), where the endorsement of 'Rational Power' (29.5, E175) leads to gravitational collapse into 'a white Dot [of] Opacity'.

Blake's construction here holds implications for his emerging 'sweet Science', since the perceptual selection of boundary conditions determines the state of the cosmos as individually experienced. Indeed, quantum cosmology has arrived at a similar position, for as Fred Alan Wolf argues, 'no clear dividing line exists between ourselves and the reality we observe. Instead, reality depends upon our choices of what and how we choose to observe' (*Quantum Leap* 128). While Milton's track leads into generation and limitation, the vortical movement flows from cosmos to consciousness, a dynamic movement emanating exotic imagery connecting two flat sheets of space-time (eternity and materiality) representing the spartio-temporal locations of Milton and Blake, respectively. Interestingly, quantum cosmology can and does posit a parallel description; as Paul Davies and John Gribben observe, 'Such a connection between different parts of the same space-time is officially known to relativists as a wormhole' (275). Wormholes tunnel through 'the contorted space-time geometry of black holes', forging connections 'to other universes' and emerging 'into our own universe at some other time and place' (Sullivan 197), and little effort is needed to find great accord between this description and the physical processes Blake describes. Obviously, normative classical models like Newton's disallow literal convergence between past and present persons and events, but as Ronald Grimes suggested long ago, Blake's poem proposes that 'a figure from the past, a poetic character, and a man of the present are not sealed off from one another in visionary perception' (61).

The space traversed by Milton, again as Ault has noted, forges connections between the Newtonian and Cartesian views, synthesizing 'different aspects of the void, absolute space, Newtonian attraction, and its imaginative consistency' and displaying, in the process, 'his extraordinary grasp of the intuitive nature of physical concepts' (Ault 156). As Milton enters the 'Sea of Time and Space', Blake offers a stunning further synthesis that anticipates contemporary physical theory in his wedding of space and time: 'Los is by mortals nam'd Time Enitharmon is nam'd space' (24.68, E121). Los and Enitharmon (zoa and emanation), introduced in *The Book of Urizen*, are husband and wife, existing in parallel with Milton and Ololon – and William and Catherine Blake. Blake's marriage of time and space, which reconnects what was separated by Newtonian mechanics, becomes a prominent feature of his theory of everything. In more specific language offered by the 'new physics', 'time is imaginary and is indistinguishable from directions in space' (Hawking 135), which indicates that 'time [is] married to space, and space to time [. . .] as spacetime' (Zee 70). With the marriage of time and space achieved, Blake turns to their renovation by endorsing a type of experiential model which eschews 'Mathematical Proportion' in preference for 'Living Proportion', the tension presented early in the work.

The Sons of Los (progeny of time and space) create structures of experience, building 'Moments & Minutes & Hours / And Days & Months

& Years & Ages & Periods' (28.44–5, E126), yet immediately Blake ties
the production of time to the body in relativistic fashion:

> Every Time less than a pulsation of the artery
> Is equal in its period & value to Six Thousand Years.
> For in this period the Poets work is Done: and all the Great
> Events of Time start forth & are concievd in such a Period
> Within a Moment: a Pulsation of the Artery. (28.62–29.3, E127)

The smallest, unmeasured increment of time equals 6,000 years, quite
likely a typical Blakean reading of the clock-time calculations supporting
Christian cosmology, yet Blake here establishes the relativistic experience
of time. Having now expanded 'a Pulsation of the Artery' into 'six
Thousand Years', Blake turns to renovate space in similar ways.

When Blake addresses space, the language of the text shifts more
directly to (en)counter the technological elements of science that mediate
or veil our view of the operations of nature (the 'veil' of Vala discussed
above), evincing in the process his thorough understanding that the very
instruments of sensation create faulty structures of knowledge:

> Such are the Spaces calld Earth & such its dimension:
> As to that false appearance which appears to the reasoner
> As of a Globe rolling thro Voidness, it is a delusion of Ulro
> The Microscope knows not of this nor the Telescope. they alter
> The ratio of the Spectators Organ but leave Objects untouched
> For every Space larger than a red Globule of Mans blood. opens
> Into Eternity of which this vegetable Earth is but a shadow:
> The red Globule is the unwearied Sun by Los created
> To measure Time and Space to mortal Men. (29.14–24, E127)

Blake's move deconstructs the Newtonian theory of the 'Void', a procedure
leading directly to his attack on the instrumental mediation of perception,
and continues to unveil his own cosmological model articulated beyond
classical mechanics.

The degree to which Blake conceptually anticipates the 'new physics'
can be discerned in a description offered by the physicist Michael
Murphy directed to precisely the same mediational process: 'In this
sense, a particular state of consciousness is like a particular scientific
instrument – e.g. a telescope or microscope – because it gives us access
to things beyond the range of our ordinary senses' (quoted in Herbert
223). Blake's critique of Newtonian mechanics connects the macroscopic

and microscopic, where 'every Space' at the macroscopic level pulsates with visionary potential and where 'every Space' at the microscopic level 'opens / Into Eternity'. For Blake, the consummation of time and space occurs in the corpuscular, where the body expresses this consummation rhythmically through its own biological processes. Thus, the individual body, rather than inert machinery, provides the best measure of time and space, of eternity and infinity, since instruments only alter the organs of perception whereas, for Blake, mind's movement animates and structures the universe. In the process of resisting Newton, Blake also provides a visionary physics capable of healing the fissure between object and subject, between cosmos and consciousness. Again drawing upon a pithy phrase from the physicist Fred Alan Wolf, 'Thus it is that mind and matter cannot be truly separated . . . The universe is to be created. Mind is the creator' (*Star* 66). This is Blake's participatory model, as he makes very clear later in the work through his assertion that the perceiving subject proceeds 'in fury of Poetic Inspiration / To build the Universe stupendous: Mental forms Creating' (30.19–20, E129).

With the renovation of time and space complete, Blake returns attention to Milton's passage into materiality, which now completes his destruction of classical models based on dualism, taking the form of an annihilation of the privileged position of observation implicit in Newton's *Principia*, and rejecting the premises supporting Enlightenment epistemology:

> I come in Self-annihilation & the grandeur of Inspiration
> To cast off Rational Demonstration by Faith in the Saviour
> To cast off the rotten rags of Memory by Inspiration
> To cast off Bacon, Locke & Newton from Albions covering
> To take off his filthy garments, & clothe him with Imagination
> To cast aside from Poetry, all that is not Inspiration. (41.2–7, E142)

Blake makes no clearer statement of his stance against the empirical tradition of 'Bacon, Locke & Newton', with self-annihilation and inspiration opposed to rational demonstration and its dependence on memory, thereby liberating perceptual dynamics from the fixed-point perspective from which Newton makes his pronouncements, and thus denies the integral role played by the observer's energies in the determination of reality in preference for an illusory objectivity.

Through *Milton*, one can begin to discern the contours of Blake's participatory multiverse, foregrounding a theory of cosmogenesis oscillating between the complementary poles of mind and matter – an expanding and contracting universe quite familiar in our own intellectual milieu. However, the most particular description of the nature of this relativistic, quantized multiverse occurs near the conclusion to *Jerusalem*, at the virtual end-point of Blake's poetic career:

the all tremendous unfathomable Non Ens
Of Death was seen in regenerations terrific or complacent varying
According to the subject of discourse & every Word & Every Character
Was Human according to the Expansion or Contraction, the Translucence or
Opakeness of Nervous fibres such was the variation of Time & Space
Which vary according as the Organs of Perception vary & they walked
To & fro in eternity as One Man reflecting each in each & clearly seen
And seeing: according to fitness and order. (98.33–40, E258)

The language of *Jerusalem* clearly builds upon the physical dynamics described in *Milton*, with its emphasis on 'Expansion or Contraction', 'Translucence or Opakeness', 'variation of Time & Space', and 'the Organs of Perception'. As well, both of the final epics place heavy emphasis on the poetic functions of the imagination, which connects the closing analysis of cosmogenesis with the early tractates, articulating a view of physical theory in the opening decades of the nineteenth century not endorsed scientifically until the end of the twentieth century. As Roger Jones confesses in *Physics as Metaphor*, contemporary physics has arrived at very Blakean conclusions: 'I had come to suspect, and now felt compelled to acknowledge, that science and the physical world were products of human imagining – that we were not the cool observers of that world, but its passionate creators. We were all poets and the world was our metaphor' (3).

blake studies and science

Of the poets classified as 'Romantic', Blake has quite often functioned as the primary example of the period's seeming hostility to science, although such a characterization would certainly collapse in the face of Wordsworth's meditation in *The Prelude* on the statue of Newton at Cambridge, Coleridge's musings in late chapters of *Biographia Literaria* or Shelley's use of physical theory in works like *Prometheus Unbound* (not to mention the interdisciplinary scientific work in natural history and optics pursued by Goethe).[10] As D.M. Knight indicates, even historians of science studying the Romantic period, often focusing on comments like Keats's drunken 'damnation of Newton', generally ignored the degree to which these writers were deeply engaged with the revolution in physical description unfolding around them (54–5). Thanks to critics such as W.J. Bate, in Edward Profitt's estimation, Romanticism became associated 'with everything at odds with science', leading to the assumption that 'the romantic spirit and the scientific are deemed to be alien' (55).

Of course, with the collapse of the New Criticism and the rise of historicism and post-structuralism, this view began to shift, although the emphasis usually remained on Romanticism's attempted 'replacement of the "mechanical philosophy" by an organic view of the cosmos', where Romantic thought was seen as pursuing 'a desperate rearguard action against the spirit and the implications of modern science' (Eichner 8). In response to the mechanical world-view, Wordsworth and other writers proposed, in H.W. Piper's apt phrase, an active 'universe [that] was a living entity which could be known through the imagination' (3).[11] Of course, Blake's response to Wordsworth's 1815 *Poems*, which characterizes the future poet laureate as 'the Natural Man rising up against the Spiritual Man' (E665), make clear his distance from this view and his general alignment with the philosophy of Bishop Berkeley as expressed in *Siris* (E663–4).

In general, Blake studies initially endorsed the view of Blake's hostility to science, with writers such as William Michael and Dante Gabriel Rossetti, Algernon Charles Swinburne and William Butler Yeats preferring to read his work as mysticism, yet Blake's response to science was always more nuanced than rigid denial. Even in an early work like the massively influential *Fearful Symmetry*, Northrop Frye argues that Blake's 'unfavorable comments on science always relate to certain metaphysical assumptions underlying science', rendering his position 'much closer to the inductive scientist than to the "reasoner"' (28). As Ault suggests, the impetus to read Blake's response to science more favorably began within the work of Jacob Bronowski, initially in *Science and Human Values* and his extremely personal *William Blake and the Age of Revolution* and continuing across numerous other works.[12] In the dialogue that concludes the first work, Bronowski asserts that 'No lyrical account of science is now complete without a quotation from William Blake' (*Values* 106), and this position continues to attract the contemporary physicists addressed in the conclusion to this chapter.

In spite of Bronowski's efforts, the exploration of science by Blake scholars was slow to emerge, at times focused on Swedenborg's conversion from scientist to mystic, the track of his dissatisfaction with 'the doctrine of a scientific materialism' (Gaunt 36–43), and at other times focused on Blake's attempt 'to picture a universe that transcended modern mechanistic views' (Schorer 50). However, these occasional views, usually embedded in larger discussions of Blake's work, continued to reify the poet's 'contempt for science', although as Erdman indicates, 'that contempt is complex' (106). This 'complexity' began to receive greater scrutiny in the 1970s, with critics beginning to pursue the implications of Blake's 'sweet Science' (for example, Johnson and Wilkie), with increased emphasis placed on the structure of time and space in the prophetic works (Grimes 59–81). For example, in 1970, William S. Doxey proposed 'a new level of interpretation' relative to 'The Tyger', one 'based on science [. . .] especially astronomy' (5), but the real breakthrough was achieved by Donald Ault in *Visionary Physics*, which probed at book-length Blake's response to Newton and which, as my own citations to this work indicate, exerted a shaping influence for all subsequent science studies applied to Blake work.

Once Ault's work broke the ground, Blake scholars began to apply physical theory to read Blake's works, establish historical connections and tease out theoretical implications. For example, later in the decade Nelson Hilton collides Newton and Swedenborg in the enriched atmosphere of *The Four Zoas*, mapping a distinction between 'science' and 'sweet Science' in that work ('Science' 84), and at the close of the decade, Stuart Peterfreund, one of the most intense scholars pursuing the science connection through Blake, explored space, time, and artistic response in the emergent interdisciplinary journal *STTH: Science/Technology & the Humanities*. Peterfreund also opened the 1980s (a particularly rich decade for science studies of Blake) with a rhetorical analysis of Blake and Newton, suggesting that works like *Milton* clearly anticipated 'the insights set forth by relativistic physics concerning the space-time continuum' (*Blake* 22). Mark Greenberg's work also appeared early in the decade and provided a historical and linguistic context for Blake's use of the term 'science', which pushed the limit of the term's usage, and both Greenberg and Peterfreund continued their efforts across the decade, even editing significant interdisciplinary collections at the opening of the 1990s focused on the rapidly developing field of 'Literature and Science'.

As the 1980s drew to a close, the emphasis on literature and science grew in intensity, fueled in part by similar critical developments located in the wider sphere of the 'long eighteenth century', which impacted nineteenth-century studies, with two collections, edited by Ludmilla Jordanova and George Levine respectively, setting the stage of the explosion of science studies across the 1990s. In the opening year of the decade, the study of science and literature in Romanticism received firm historical contextualization in the important collection *Romanticism and the Sciences* (ed. Cunningham and Jardine), whose essays span the spectrum of scientific concerns in a broader European context. As well, one year later Jonathan Bate published the highly influential *Romantic Ecology: Wordsworth and the Environmental Tradition*, a work that inspired my own re-assessment of Blake's relationship to nature ('Blake's Deep Ecology'), and by the middle of the decade several journals focused on Romantic studies offered special issues addressing matters ecological (for instance, *Studies in Romanticism* 35, ed. Bate). At approximately the same time, Peterfreund gathered his various essays on Blake, science and literature in the important *William Blake in a Newtonian World*, and by the end of the decade, the examination of Blake's work through the critical lens of science studies had achieved critical mass, with criticism probing historical, political and social contexts (which in turn provided a solid foundation from which to explore the theoretical implications of Blake's stance).

blake and contemporary physics

In the face of the interdisciplinary work discussed above, Blake's supposed hostility to science began to be reconfigured, being replaced by a more nuanced and complex view of his attitudes. Yet most critical valuations of Blake's relationship to science remained somewhat mono-directional, moving from discrete works to the historical and cultural fields within which they were situated. As a result, most Blake scholars failed to note that, across the same period of development (extending from Bronowski's work to the present), the visionary poet became a constant presence within works seeking to elaborate the new physics. While the following discussion is not intended to be exhaustive, since such a study would extend well beyond the scope of the present effort, it should provide a sense of the degree to which Blake's thought anticipates the revolution in physics across the twentieth century. Although this development should not necessarily be surprising, given Bronowski's sense, alluded to above, that no lyrical description of contemporary science would be complete without an allusion to Blake's work, the breadth and depth of appropriation has gone somewhat unnoticed nonetheless.

For the remainder of this chapter, then, I wish to chart some of the uses contemporary science makes of Blake's work, and one obvious appropriation, conditioned by Bronowski, is the use of the frontispiece to *Europe: A Prophecy* ('The Ancient of Days') as book cover art, a predicable choice since the image shows a hoary-headed 'Nobodaddy' associated with Urizen inscribing with a compass a mathematical order onto a chaotic universe. Bronowski's affection for the image is everywhere apparent, with the image functioning as the frontispiece to *Science and Human Values* (which also reproduces Blake's 'Glad Day, or The Dance of Albion' to open the first chapter) and redeployed in *The Ascent of Man*. The image also appears on the cover of more contemporary physics books, like Ian Stewart and Martin Golubitsky's *Fearful Symmetry* and Michael Redhead's *From Physics to Metaphysics*, but as Stewart and Golubitsky's comments make clear, they have misread the image by ignoring its minute particulars.[13]

Bronowski appropriated other Blakean images as well, selecting one of Blake's designs for *The Gates of Paradise* ('I want! I want') as cover art for *The Origins of Knowledge and Imagination*, and in *The Visionary Eye* the visionary scientist analyzes an image drawn from Blake's *Milton* (plate 29), which shows Milton as a star falling into Blake's foot, and 'The Tyger', an appropriation that has rippled through other books of physical theory ever since. Such uses of Blakean images have exerted a predictable impact, given the lectures Bronowski delivered in almost every major location wherein scientific experiment on relativistic physics and quantum dynamics was conducted (from Cambridge to MIT); the influence of this intrepid scientist on subsequent generations of physicists would be hard to over-estimate. Of course, Bronowski also explored the relevance of Blake's poetry for discussions of the murkier aspects of science, whether drawing upon a randomly selected couplet from 'Auguries of Innocence' ('A Robin Red breast in a Cage / Puts all Heaven in a Rage' (*Origins of Knowledge* 45)), challenging 'the belief of philosophers that the brain receives a neutral picture of the world' (*Identity of Man* 33), or charting the implications of Blake's 'symbolism of wheels turning on wheels' (*Common Sense of Science* 55).

Bronowski disseminated Blake to subsequent generations of scientists, and I am no longer surprised by the poet's presence in almost any discussion of physical theory, although this presence is often solely epigrammatic. Blake's justly famous lament of 'Newton's blindness' (imaged as 'single vision' and discussed at some length previously), serves to contextualize the cracks and fissures in the Newtonian world-view emerging during the late eighteenth century, when Thomas Young challenged the corpuscular view of light and when John Michell provided the first mathematical postulation of black holes.[14] Thus, Blake's presence in a work like *Science Deified & Science Denied* does not surprise, for Richard Olsen discusses at some length the degree to which Blake feared 'calculative reason' (361), and in similar fashion John D. Barrow offers Blake as a counter to the 'Newtonian interpretation of Nature' (76). However, just as clearly when chasing Blake citations, the poet functions as the forerunner of a multi-vectored science shorn of its mechanical dictates, with such citations operating across the disciplines of science, whether in discussions of neuroscience like that offered by William H. Calvin, in Tyler Volk's attempts to articulate a physiology of the earth, or in Arthur Zajonc's and Amit Goswani's analyses of the crucial role of perception in constructing reality. This citational register could be extended *ad nauseam*, but I shall close with a brief consideration of two particular poems by Blake, 'The Tyger' and 'Auguries of Innocence', that have proved protean for the construction of contemporary physics.[15]

When Roger S. Jones, seeking to understand the gauge symmetries at play in experimental outcomes from high-energy physics, asks 'who is it that recognizes and apprehends the numbers and symmetries, and who created them', he turns immediately to William Blake's own meditation on this problem from *Songs of Innocence and of Experience*, 'The Tyger': 'What immortal hand or eye / Could frame thy fearful symmetry?' (146). Blake's poem has relevance for such questioning, since as Michio Kaku notes (before citing the same poem), one of 'the most interesting features of the Standard Model is that it is based on symmetry' (124), and the physicist most acutely aware of the degree to which Blake's poem speaks to this issue, A. Zee, also positions 'The Tyger' as the portal of entry for his provocative work *Fearful Symmetry: The Search for Beauty in Modern Physics* (vii). Unlike the majority of physics texts included here, Zee's engagement with Blake is continuous, intense and extending, and he even appropriates and transmutes two well-known Blake images (the 1795 painting 'Elohim Creating Adam' and 'The Ancient of Days') to address, respectively, gauge symmetries emerging in quantum cosmology and Einstein's well-known resistance to the emergence of the uncertainties inherent in quantum dynamics ('The Good Lord does not play dice' with the universe (Zee 137)). Of course, 'The Tyger' also serves, for Peterfreund, as a vehicle for the play of power and energy, a dynamic which he reads as an '*enacted* critique of Newtonian metonymic logic and natural theology' (*William Blake* 129–30) and which he connects to Blake's larger enterprise.

As a way of closing this brief discussion of Blake's play within contemporary physical theory, the best poetic location remains the oft-cited opening quatrain to 'Auguries of Innocence' (1–4, E490, quoted above p. 188), which is used to explain for lay audiences some of the more exotic concepts emerging from the new physics. As scientists began to confront the seeming mystical aspects of the new physics of quantum, they sought within Blake's quatrain poetic language capable of imaging for lay person and scientist alike the quirkiness resident in relativity and quantum, and this quatrain seemed a 'natural' fit, since the passage asserts the role that discrete acts of perception play in the construction of reality. The play of this passage is wide indeed. Fritjof Capra, in his influential and widely read *The Tao of Physics*, evokes it to clarify 'interpenetration' and the notion that every particle contains within it 'all the others' (288), and shortly thereafter, in another well-known popularization of the new physics, Gary Zukav offers the passage to gloss the elusiveness of contemporary notions of time and space (170). In their effort to describe the holism at work in David Bohm's implicate theory of quantum dynamics, John P. Briggs and F. David Peat also turn to Blake's quatrain as emblematic 'of an encoding pattern of matter and energy spreading ceaselessly throughout the universe' (111–12).

The 1980s also saw the emergence and codification of complexity and chaos theory, and James Gleick, in one of the inaugural works, offers Blake's passage to describe 'the notion of self-similarity' (115), and Timothy Ferris uses the passage to connect Eastern mysticism to Niels Bohr's theory of complementarity (92). Jennifer Trusted, arguing the shared drives of physics and metaphysics, draws upon Blake's quatrain to offer a counter to empirical natural philosophy, wherein 'the role of imagination was underestimated' (125), while Leonard Shlain sees the passage as defining the difference between Blake's relativistic and quantized view of time and space and the views of Newton and Kant, who 'saw space as Euclidean and time as sequential' (95). When scientists began, late in the 1990s, to speak openly of the restoration of spirit in the scientific endeavor and returned their efforts to the physics of consciousness, Blake's protean passage was used to argue that 'the infinite always accompanies the finite' (Mansfield 193) and to shatter 'our commonsense understanding of the world' (Walker 7). Clearly, the scientific appropriation of Blake's 'Auguries of Innocence', which extends from Bronowski to the present day, suggests that Blake continues to function as a strange attractor for those engaged in articulating the entire spectrum of contemporary physical theory – from quantum consciousness to quantum cosmology – and equally suggests that Blake's resistance to Newtonianism and Enlightenment epistemology actually articulated a 'sweet Science' very much in accord with our own view of physical and psychological complexity.

notes

1. My characterization of 'science as ideology' generally follows from Louis Althusser's introductory course for scientists (*Philosophy and the Spontaneous Philosophy of the Scientists*), flows through Stanley Aronowitz's arguments

in *Science as Power* and intersects Nicholas Williams' sense of the 'double perspective' defining Blake's ideology (5). I would suggest that the best linguistic way to represent this concern would be '(I/Eye)deology'.

2. As most historians acknowledge, defining the Enlightenment is an elusive task, and as Lester G. Crocker argues, the concept is perhaps best viewed as a mode of thinking, since earlier historical eras like the Renaissance could equally well qualify as ages of reason: 'The way of thinking set in place in Western culture a new dominant mode that would persist into the future: the free play of critical and constructive reason, employing available knowledge, in the humanistic search for a better society, better behavior, greater happiness on earth, better understanding of what men are capable of, and what can and should be done with them' (1).

3. Blake's formulation here bears uncanny resemblance to the 'desiring machines' discussed by Giles Deleuze and Felix Guattari, one possible outcome of an individual's response to the processes of subject formation in capitalism (331–3).

4. As Greenberg further argues, Blake objected to the division of science and art, which resulted 'from changes in [science's] definition that occurred during Blake's years and which he experienced' (117).

5. The spectrum of the revolution in physical theory occurring during the Romantic period is readily apparent in the essays appearing in *Romanticism and the Sciences*, ed. Andrew Cunningham and Nicholas Jardine.

6. Although I arrive at different conclusions, my discussion is illuminated by David Punter, *Blake, Hegel and Dialectic* (72, 122, 252–5). For analogies between Blake's contraries and Bohr's complementarity, R.V. Jones provides ample connections in 'Complementarity as a Way of Life'. Interestingly, Bohr actually created the concept from his intense reception of the psychology of William James.

7. As Roger and Kay Parkhurst Easson suggest, 'Blake seems [in *The Book of Urizen*] to anticipate the theory that ontogeny, the individual's life history, recapitulates phylogeny, the history of the species' (72). The emphasis on the body in this work, in Paul Mann's estimation, creates a type of 'biobibliography', where the representational intermingling of book and body seems to say that 'to take on the body, Urizen must first be a book' (50–1).

8. Antonio Damasio argues that this split between subject and object became one of Descartes' fundamental errors (248).

9. See, for example, Brenda Webster, *Blake's Prophetic Psychology*, 203–49.

10. I discuss the knowledge of physical theory cultivated by Coleridge and Shelley in separate chapters of *Romantic Dynamics: The Poetry of Physicality*, as well as in separate essays appearing in *The Wordsworth Circle* ('The *Rime* of Physics' and 'Shelley's Poetics, Wave Dynamics, and the Telling Rhythm of Complementarity') and *Romanticism on the Net* ('Wave Dynamics as Primary Ecology in Shelley's *Prometheus Unbound*').

11. Through this analytic doorway, I would argue, critics such as Jonathan Bate and Karl Kroeber passed in order to elaborate our contemporary view of Romantic ecology. See *Romantic Ecology: Wordsworth and the Environmental Tradition* and *Ecological Literary Criticism: Romantic Imagining and the Biology of Mind*, respectively.

12. See also Bronowski's *The Identity of Man*, *The Ascent of Man*, *The Common Sense of Science*, *The Origins of Knowledge and Imagination* and *The Visionary Eye: Essays in the Arts, Literature and Science*. All these works engage Blake to a greater or lesser degree, but all establish Blake's crucial role for understanding the response to science offered during the Romantic age and further suggest Blake's anticipation of concepts emerging within the revolution in physics occurring during the twentieth century.

13. The misreading occurs when Stewart and Golubitsky rightly assert that Blake's design 'anticipates [. . .] bilateral symmetry' (4), but fail to note the element of critique embedded in the image, which shows the 'creator' leaning out of another eye.

14. A representative sampling of works evoking Blake's letter would include Fritjof Capra, *The Web of Life: A New Scientific Understanding of Living Systems;* Ian Marshall and Danah Zohar, *Who's Afraid of Schrödinger's Cat?;* Ilya Prigogine and Isabelle Stengers, *Order Out of Chaos;* and Arthur M. Young, *The Reflexive Universe*.

15. For those interested in other evocations and appropriations not included, see Jeremy Campbell, *Grammatical Man: Information, Entropy, Language, and Life;* Freeman Dyson, *From Eros to Gaia* and *Infinite in All Directions;* Stanley L. Jaki, *The Road of Science and the Ways to God;* Dennis Overbye, *Lonely Hearts of the Cosmos;* F. David Peat, *The Philosopher's Stone: Chaos, Synchronicity, and the Hidden Order of the World;* and Fred Alan Wolf, *The Dreaming Universe: A Mind-Expanding Journey into the Realm Where Psyche and Physics Meet*.

works cited and suggestions for further reading

Althusser, Louis. *Philosophy and the Spontaneous Philosophy of the Scientists.* London: Norton, 1990.

Aronowitz, Stanley. *Science as Power.* Minneapolis: University of Minnesota Press, 1988.

Ault, Donald. *Visionary Physics: Blake's Response to Newton.* Chicago: University of Chicago Press, 1974.

Baine, Rodney. *The Scattered Portions: William Blake's Biological Symbolism.* Athens: University of Georgia Press, 1986.

Barrow, John D. *The World within the World.* Oxford: Oxford University Press, 1990.

Bate, Jonathan. *Romantic Ecology: Wordsworth and the Environmental Tradition.* London: Routledge, 1991.

Briggs, John P. and F. David Peat. *Looking Glass Universe: The Emerging Science of Wholeness.* New York: Simon and Schuster, 1984.

Bronowski, Jacob. *The Ascent of Man.* Boston: Little, Brown, 1972.

——. *The Common Sense of Science.* Cambridge: Harvard University Press, 1978.

——. *The Identity of Man.* Garden City: Anchor, 1965.

——. *The Origins of Knowledge and Imagination.* New Haven: Yale University Press, 1978.

——. *Science and Human Values.* New York: Peter Smith, 1956.

——. *The Visionary Eye: Essays in the Arts, Literature and Science.* Cambridge: MIT Press, 1985.

——. *William Blake and the Age of Revolution*. New York: HarperCollins, 1965.

Calvin, William H. *The Throwing Madonna: Essays on the Brain*. New York: McGraw-Hill, 1983.

Campbell, Jeremy. *Grammatical Man: Information, Entropy, Language, and Life*. New York: Simon and Schuster, 1982.

Capra, Fritjof. *The Web of Life: A New Scientific Understanding of Living Systems*. Garden City: Anchor, 1996.

——. *The Tao of Physics: An Exploration of the Parallels between Modern Physics and Eastern Mysticism*. 4th edition. Boston, MA: Shambhala Press, 2000.

Charon, Jean. *The Unknown Spirit: The Unity of Matter in Space and Time*. London: Sigo Press, 1983.

Crocker, Lester G. *The Blackwell Companion to the Enlightenment*. Oxford: Blackwell, 1991.

Cunningham, Andrew and Nicholas Jardine, eds. *Romanticism and the Sciences*. Cambridge: Cambridge University Press, 1990.

Damasio, Antonio. *Descartes' Error: Emotion, Reason, and the Human Brain*. New York: Quill, 1994.

Damon, S. Foster. *A Blake Dictionary: The Ideas and Symbols of William Blake*. Boulder: Shambhala Press, 1979.

Davies, Paul and John Gribben. *The Matter Myth: Dramatic Discoveries that Challenge Our Understanding of Physical Reality*. New York: Simon and Schuster, 1992.

Deleuze, Gilles and Felix Guattari. *Anti-Oedipus: Capitalism and Schizophrenia*. Trans. Brian Massumi. Minneapolis: University of Minnesota Press, 1983.

Doxey, William S. 'William Blake and William Herschel: The Astronomer and "The Tyger"'. *Blake Studies* 2.2 (1970): 5–13.

Dyson, Freeman. *From Eros to Gaia*. New York: Random House, 1992.

——. *Infinite in All Directions*. New York: HarperCollins, 1988.

Easson, Roger and Kay Parkhurst Easson, eds. *The Book of Urizen*. Boulder: Shambhala Press, 1978.

Eichner, Hans. 'The Rise of Modern Science and the Genesis of Romanticism'. *PMLA* 97.1 (1982): 8–30.

Einstein, Albert. In *Einstein and Buddha: The Parallel Sayings*. Ed. Thomas J. McFarlane. Berkeley: Ulysses Press, 2002.

Erdman, David V. *Blake: Prophet Against Empire*. Princeton: Princeton University Press, 1954.

Ferber, Michael. *The Social Vision of William Blake*. Princeton: Princeton University Press, 1985.

Ferris, Timothy. *The Mind's Sky: Human Intelligence in a Cosmic Context*. New York: Bantam, 1992.

Frye, Northrop. *Fearful Symmetry: A Study of William Blake*. Princeton: Princeton University Press, 1947.

Gaunt, William. *Arrows of Desire: A Study of William Blake and His Romantic World*. London: Folcroft Library Editions, 1956.

Gleick, James. *Chaos: Making a New Science*. New York: Penguin, 1987.

Goswani, Amit. *The Self-Aware Universe: How Consciousness Creates the Material World*. New York: Putnam, 1993.

Greenberg, Mark. 'Blake's "Science"'. *Studies in Eighteenth-Century Culture* 12 (1983): 115–30.

Greenberg, Mark and Lance Schachterle, eds. *Literature and Technology*. Bethlehem and London: Lehigh University Press, 1992.

Grimes, Ronald L. 'Time and Space in Blake's Major Prophecies' in *Blake's Sublime Allegory*. Ed. Stuart Curran and Joseph Wittreich. Madison: University of Wisconsin Press, 1970.

Gross, Paul, Norman Levitt and Martin W. Lewis. *The Flight from Science and Reason*. New York and Baltimore: New York Academy of Sciences, 1996.

Hankins, Thomas L. *Science and the Enlightenment*. Cambridge: Cambridge University Press, 1958.

Hawking, Stephen. *A Brief History of Time: From the Big Bang to Black Holes*. New York: Bantam, 1993.

Herbert, Nick. *Elemental Mind: Human Consciousness and the New Physics*. New York: Penguin, 1993.

Hilton, Nelson. *Literal Imagination: Blake's Vision of Words*. Berkeley: University of California Press, 1983.

——. 'The Sweet Science of Atmospheres in *The Four Zoas*'. *Blake: An Illustrated Quarterly* 12 (Summer 1978): 80–6.

Hutchings, Kevin. *Imagining Nature: Blake's Environmental Poetics*. Montreal and Kingston and London and Ithaca: McGill-Queens University Press, 2002.

Jaki. Stanley L. *The Road of Science and the Ways to God*. Chicago: University of Chicago Press, 1978.

Johnson, Mary Lynn and Brian Wilkie. 'On Reading *The Four Zoas*' in *Blake's Sublime Allegory*. Ed. Stuart Curran and Joseph Wittreich. Madison: University of Wisconsin Press, 1970.

Jones, R.V. 'Complementarity as a Way of Life' in *Niels Bohr: A Centenary Volume*. Ed. A.P. French and P.J. Kennedy. Cambridge: Harvard University Press, 1985.

Jones, Roger. *Physics as Metaphor*. Minneapolis: University of Minnesota Press, 1982.

Jordanova, Ludmilla, ed. *Languages of Nature: Critical Essays on Science and Literature*. New Brunswick: Rutgers University Press, 1986.

——. *Sexual Visions: Images of Gender in Science and Medicine between the Eighteenth and Twentieth Centuries*. New York: Harvester Wheatsheaf, 1989.

Kaku, Michio. *Hyperspace: A Scientific Odyssey through Parallel Universes, Time Warps, and the 10th Dimension*. Oxford: Oxford University Press, 1994.

Knight, D.M. 'The Physical Sciences and the Romantic Movement'. *History of Science* 9.1 (1970): 54–5.

Kroeber, Karl. *Ecological Literary Criticism: Romantic Imagining and the Biology of Mind*. New York: Columbia University Press, 1994.

Levine, George, ed. *One Culture: Essays in Science and Literature*. Madison: University of Wisconsin Press, 1987.

Lussier, Mark. 'Blake's Deep Ecology'. *Studies in Romanticism* 35.3 (1996): 393–408.

——. 'Blake's Vortex: The Quantum Tunnel in *Milton*'. *Nineteenth-Century Contexts* 18.3 (1994): 263–91.

——. 'The *Rime* of Physics'. *Wordsworth Circle* 29.1 (Winter 1998): 84–8.

——. *Romantic Dynamics: The Poetics of Physicality*. Basingstoke: Macmillan, 2000.

——. 'Shelley's Poetics, Wave Dynamics, and the Telling Rhythm of Complementarity'. *Wordsworth Circle* 34.2 (Spring 2003): 91–5.

——. 'Wave Dynamics as Primary Ecology in Shelley's *Prometheus Unbound*'. *Romanticism on the Net* 16 (Nov. 1999).

Makdisi, Saree. *William Blake and the Impossible History of the 1790s*. Chicago: University of Chicago Press, 2003.

Mann, Paul. '*The Book of Urizen* and the Horizon of the Book' in *Unnam'd Forms: Blake and Textuality*. Ed. Nelson Hilton and Thomas A. Vogler. Berkeley: University of California Press, 1986.

Mansfield, Victor. *Synchronicity, Science, and Soul-Making*. Chicago: Open Court Publishing, 1995.

Markley, Robert. *Fallen Languages: Crises of Representation in Newtonian England, 1660–1740*. Ithaca: Cornell University Press, 1993.

Marshall, Ian and Danah Zohar. *Who's Afraid of Schrödinger's Cat?* New York: Perennial, 1997.

Minahen, Charles D. *Vortex/T: The Poetics of Turbulence*. University Park: Pennsylvania State University Press, 1992.

Olsen, Richard. *Science Deified and Science Defied: The Historical Significance of Science in Western Culture*. Vol. 2. Berkeley: University of California Press, 1990.

Overbye, Dennis. *Lonely Hearts of the Cosmos*. New York: HarperCollins, 1991.

Pagels, Heinz R. *The Cosmic Code: Quantum Physics as the Language of Nature*. New York: Bantam, 1982.

Peat, F. David. *The Philosopher's Stone: Chaos, Synchronicity, and the Hidden Order of the World*. New York: Bantam, 1991.

Peterfreund, Stuart. 'Blake on Space, Time, and the Role of the Artist'. *STTH: Science/Technology & the Humanities* 2 (1979): 246.

——. ed. *Literature and Science: Theory and Practice*. Boston: Diane Publishing, 1990.

——. *William Blake in a Newtonian World*. Norman: University of Oklahoma Press, 1998.

Piper, H.W. *Active Universe: Pantheism and the Concept of Imagination in the English Romantic Poets*. London: Athlone Press, 1962.

Plotnitsky, Arkady. *Complementarity: Anti-Epistemology after Bohr and Derrida*. Durham: Duke University Press, 1994.

Prigogine, Ilya and Isabelle Stengers. *Order Out of Chaos*. New York: Bantam, 1984.

Profitt, Edward. 'Science and Romanticism'. *Georgia Review* 34.1 (1980): 55.

Punter, David. *Blake, Hegel and Dialectic*. Amsterdam: Rodopi, 1982.

Redhead, Michael. *From Physics to Metaphysics*. Cambridge: Cambridge University Press, 1995.

Schiebinger, Londa. *Nature's Body: Gender and the Making of Modern Science*. Boston: Beacon Press, 1993.

Schorer, Mark. *William Blake: The Politics of Vision*. New York: Peter Smith, 1959.

Shelley, Percy. *Shelley's Poetry and Prose*. Ed. Donald H. Reiman and Neil Fraistat. New York: Norton, 2002.

Shepherd, Linda Jean. *Lifting the Veil: The Feminine Face of Science*. Boston: Shambala Press, 1993.

Shlain, Leonard. *Art and Physics: Parallel Visions in Space, Time and Light*. New York: HarperCollins, 1991.

Shteir, Ann B. *Cultivating Women, Cultivating Science: Flora's Daughters and Botany in England, 1760 to 1860.* Baltimore, Maryland: The Johns Hopkins University Press, 1999.

Stewart, Ian and Martin Golubitsky. *Fearful Symmetry: Is God a Geometer?* London: Blackwell, 1992.

Sullivan, Walter. *Black Holes: The Edge of Space, The End of Time.* Garden City: Warner, 1979.

Trusted, Jennifer. *Physics and Metaphysics.* New York: Routledge, 1991.

Volk, Tyler. *Gaia's Body: Toward a Physiology of the Earth.* New York: Copernicus Books, 1998.

Walker, Evan Harris. *The Physics of Consciousness: The Quantum Minds and the Meaning of Life.* Cambridge: Perseus Publishing, 2000.

Webster, Brenda. *Blake's Prophetic Psychology.* Athens: University of Georgia Press, 1983.

Williams, Nicholas M. *Ideology and Utopia in the Poetry of William Blake.* Cambridge: Cambridge University Press, 1998.

Wolf, Fred Alan. *The Dreaming Universe: A Mind-Expanding Journey into the Realm Where Psyche and Physics Meet.* New York: Touchstone, 1994.

——. *Star Wave: Mind, Consciousness, and Quantum Physics.* New York: Simon and Schuster, 1984.

——. *Taking the Quantum Leap: The New Physics for Non-Scientists.* New York: Perennial, 1989.

Wordsworth, William. *William Wordsworth: The Oxford Authors.* Ed. Stephen Gill. Oxford: Oxford University Press, 1984.

Young, Arthur M. *The Reflexive Universe.* Mill Valley: Anodos Foundation, 1976.

Zajonc, Arthur. *Catching the Light: The Entwined History of Light and Mind.* Oxford: Oxford University Press, 1993.

Zee, A. *Fearful Symmetry: The Search for Beauty in Modern Physics.* New York: Macmillan, 1986.

Zukov, Gary. *The Dancing Wu Li Masters: An Overview of the New Physics.* New York: Bantam, 1979.

10

blake and the history of radicalism

andrew lincoln

For at least sixty years now Blake scholars have been exploring Blake's place in the history of radicalism. In the work of these scholars Blake loses his image as an intellectually isolated, otherworldly figure, and is identified as part of a social class or group, a group that is seen as radicalized by its ongoing struggle against dominant social forces and specifically by the political crisis induced by the French Revolution. Blake is repeatedly rescued from his bad angel – that scholar who works to cut him off from his society and its historical crises, to depoliticize him by presenting his poetry as concerned with a purely 'mental' conflict, or as an enclosed system informed primarily by obscure mystical traditions, a system that transcends the moment of its production.

The tradition of scholarship that seeks to historicize and politicize Blake in this way has its deepest roots in Marxist theories of literature, although by no means all of those engaged in this work would consider themselves as Marxists, and not all see the need to explain their methodology. One critic who does both, Stewart Crehan, sets out in simple terms some of the assumptions that may govern this kind of scholarship. Crehan insists that Blake's work as an artist is not to be seen simply as the expression of an individual style – such a notion rests on the 'bourgeois-Romantic belief in the individual as creative center of his own work' (183). Instead we have to think in terms of larger social forces, or what Crehan terms 'class forces' that operate in a particular environment at a particular historical moment and generate aesthetic ideologies. The interpretive goal is to grasp the 'deeper' political content so often obscured by other kinds of criticism, but the 'search for *overt* social or political meanings is unnecessary' (1), since 'no artistic form or style is ever politically or ideologically neutral'. Blake's work, for all its idiosyncrasies, should be seen as in some sense representative of concerns shared with others (2–3). One of the key aims in Crehan's work – and the work of other Blake scholars – has been to identify those others and their common concerns. Crehan aligns Blake with 'English Jacobinism [...] a movement of politically conscious artisans and small tradesmen who were opposed to the monarchy, aristocracy, the tax system and all distinctions of rank' (18).[1] Most scholars would probably agree with at least part of this description, but the room for qualification, elaboration and confusion has proved large enough to accommodate a considerable number of alternative explanations.

The first significant attempt to define Blake's place in the larger history of radicalism was Jacob Bronowski's pioneering study, *William Blake: A Man Without a Mask*. Bronowski's Marxist approach locates Blake within a history of relations:

> There is nothing odd in what happened to Blake; for it was happening to many thousand others. The fine London watchmakers were becoming hands in sweatshops. The learned societies of the Spitalfields weavers were rioting for bread. The small owners were losing their place, and their skilled workers were losing their livelihood [...] [I]t is not the poet's story, nor the painter's. It is the story of Blake the engraver. (2)

For Bronowski, the engraver is the essential Blake because the work of engraving determined Blake's relationship to the wider economy (whereas painting was subsidiary and less reliable as a source of income, while poetry was insignificant). The material conditions of Blake's working life (rather than the products of his engraving) are what really interest Bronowski, as these provide not only a focus for Blake's political anger but a way of approaching the question of his intellectual allegiances. As an engraver Blake was sometimes employed by the bookseller Joseph Johnson, whose circle included some prominent dissenting radicals (such as Thomas Paine, Mary Wollstonecraft, William Godwin) who shared a belief in reason and universal principles of justice. Bronowski was aware that in some obvious respects Blake did not share these beliefs, and that he had an interest in mystical writers such as Emmanuel Swedenborg. And so he placed Blake somewhat uncomfortably between the otherworldly mysticism of Swedenborg and the rational dissenters' this-worldly vision of social change. It is clear which of these two poles Bronowski himself favors. He reveals that much of his book was written in 1942, when he was working daily 'at the tasks of destruction which war sets for a scientist' (16). As a scientist, Bronowski saw himself as a part of the Enlightenment tradition that Blake tended to attack – and he was keen ultimately to stress Blake's own cultural relation to that tradition. Indeed, he tends to align Blake rather uncomfortably with those who 'made the Industrial Revolution' (103), a revolution that Bronowski is inclined to celebrate.

This alignment is consistent with his attempt to keep Blake in touch with a 'living tradition', and to rescue him from the world of the dusty 'source books' (17). But in view of this it should come as no surprise that Bronowski is distinctly uncomfortable with Blake's 'prophetic manner'. He classifies the more obscure parts of Blake's prophetic works 'not as poetry, but as rhetoric' (9), and he argues that even as rhetoric the prophetic works often fail because '[t]he rhetoric clogs and mumbles with unheard names, Oothoon, Orc, Enitharmon; and we are suddenly aware that Blake has wandered off into those mazes of their family troubles which henceforth fill his prophetic books. This is not mysticism, but mystery, and mystification' (44). What Blake has wandered off from, apparently, is that common world of everyday struggle that he shared with a generation of skilled craftsmen. The phrase 'family troubles' implies a retreat from the world at large to more private issues, as if the private is in some sense less historical and less political than the public, and must lose its social definition. Blake's enigmatic manner is rooted in a failure of confidence, a failure to be 'foolhardy' in the face of government legislation designed to suppress radical protest (52).

If Bronowski recoils from the difficulties of Blake's prophecies, his vivid politicizing of Blake's work represents a significant breakthrough in Blake studies. By seeking out the economic and social factors at issue in the writing he consistently sheds new light on familiar themes. John Locke, for example, who is often considered primarily in philosophical terms in Blake criticism, appears in Bronowski's account as an active part of an economic system: 'William III put John Locke into the Board of Trade to lay down the ends of Whig society [...] Blake saw truly when he came to use Locke's name as a byword for a selfwilled society of poverty' (23–4). In such observations Bronowski brought a new dimension to Blake scholarship.

Three years after Bronowski, Mark Schorer published a study based on quite different assumptions. Whereas Bronowski sets Blake among groups of workers linked by the material threat to their work, Schorer conceives of politics much more as an exchange of ideas formulated by individual writers in particular texts. Like Bronowski, he links Blake's radicalism to the rational dissenters associated with Joseph Johnson and he even assumes that Blake includes William Godwin and Thomas Holcroft among his friends. When Schorer uses the term 'Revolutionary theory' (164) it seems to stretch little further than the ideas of the Johnson group.

However, since Blake doesn't share their faith in 'men as reasonable creatures capable of building a system on abstract principles' (165), Schorer argues that they provide 'an atmosphere of opinion in which he found a direction rather than a set of fixed ideas' (115).

While making this link, Schorer announces his intention to ignore the 'archaic systems of thought and symbolism from which Blake drew' and declares himself 'eager to dissociate Blake from the dubious company of the mystics' (ix, 47). But in spite of these avowed aims, Schorer finds himself exploring in some detail Blake's debt to Swedenborg and Boehme, mentions a Moravian influence (which he attributes to Blake's father), notes a passing resemblance to the popular prophet Richard Brothers, and observes that Blake's antinomianism has 'many connections with earlier Protestantism' (135), specifically with those seventeenth-century groups like the Seekers or the Familists. With hindsight we can see that although Schorer has read widely in the history of ideas, he struggles to relate these influences and affinities to his understanding of Blake's politics because he lacks a cultural map that might link them meaningfully together; they seem either 'accidental' (122) or mere idiosyncrasies, rather than characteristics that can be discussed in socio-political terms. Like Bronowski, he regards the prophetic language of Blake's work as symptomatic of an unfortunate, if necessary, retreat from political danger. And since Schorer judges from a norm of reasonableness and proportion that Blake consistently flouts, it is hardly surprising that he turns with impatience from 'the rigmarole of events' in the prophecies, and assumes that in some respects Blake's sensibilities were 'deranged' (270, 49).

Some of the problems that emerged in these pioneering studies were addressed powerfully in David Erdman's Marxist study *Blake: Prophet Against Empire*, a great work of scholarship that has advanced our understanding of Blake's relation to radical history more than any other book. Erdman was not satisfied with indicating the 'general context' of Blake's writing. His study is organized around particular moments and periods – the American war, the peaceful eighties, the French Revolution, the 'Pitt Terror', the war years (with some movement back and forth), and it attempts to show how each shapes a particular response from Blake and other radicals. Erdman attempts 'to get close to the eye-level at which Blake witnessed the drama of his own times' (xii). In doing so he widened the scope of his enquiry beyond that of earlier critics, to include newspaper reports, prints and paintings, political debates and pamphlets. He assumes that Blake was among 'politically sympathetic friends' when he wrote his revolutionary prophecies of the 1790s, but unlike Bronowski and Schorer, he does not count members of the Johnson coterie among these friends: 'we do not know whether any of the English Jacobins was aware of Blake except as a minor engraver occasionally employed by Johnson' (154). Nevertheless he notes Blake's familiarity with the ideas of the Paine set, and finds in Blake 'a stronger affinity for the artisan radicalism of the Constitutional and Corresponding Societies than for the more Whiggish radicalism of such younger men as Wordsworth and Coleridge' (162). Whereas Bronowski gave a generalized account of the struggles that linked Blake the engraver with weavers and watchmakers, Erdman begins to explore more closely the socio-political environment that Blake entered as engraver. In a chapter on 'Republican Art' for example, he reviews the activities of The London Society of Antiquaries (previously seen as a dry and conservative institution), finds within it a 'democratically biased interest in the relics of British history' (31) and begins to investigate the preoccupations of individual members and associates, building up a profile of their activities. He notes, for example, that Blake's fellow engraver William Sharp was a leading member of the reforming London Society for Constitutional Information, that he joined the Society of London Swedenborgians – and later turned to the popular prophets Joanna Southcott and Richard Brothers. Here Erdman begins to outline a kind of study that others would follow in more detail. It derives its political understanding not simply from a general appreciation of economic and social problems, and not simply from a set of arguments circulating between groups of publishing radicals, but also from the interests and affiliations of (sometimes obscure) individuals in a particular social environment. He begins, that is, to delineate systematically a cultural map within which Blake can be securely located. When Schorer notes Blake's interest in Swedenborg, and compares him with Richard Brothers, these things seem connected primarily by Blake's idiosyncracy. When Erdman outlines William Sharp's interests, these things begin to seem more typical of a particular social location. In this respect Erdman's book represented a major advance in Blake's studies. Its influence is still, some fifty years after its publication, inspiring innovative work along the lines it opened up.

Erdman was not content to write off the prophetic books as simply an unfortunate retreat into mysticism; he attempted to show, through detailed commentary, how specific aspects of these works might be related to the contemporary political situation. In doing so he follows a method adumbrated (but not pursued) by Bronowski, who suggested that since Blake dared not name contemporary figures such as Pitt and George III, he may have called them Rintrah and Palamabron instead (52). In

Erdman's hands this assumption opens up the prophetic works to detailed political interpretation:

> Although he often veiled his opinion or elaborated it into a complex symbolic fabric having little to do with public matters on many of its levels of meaning, it has been possible to trace through nearly all of his work a more or less clearly discernable thread of historical reference. (xiv–xv)

Erdman, like Bronowski, tends to think of politics in terms of 'public matters', and of Blake's prophecies as 'visualizations of current history' (202). He finds models for such visualization in graphic as well as verbal sources in contemporary journalism, including political cartoons. The link with cartoons, supported with a convincing comparison with a Gillray print, counteracts the impression of Blakean obscurity, since the cartoon can build complex political statements from relatively simple elements, and is an art form that depends on identifiable figures and easily understood narratives. In practice, Erdman could find in the most complex prophetic narrative a relatively simple political allegory. In *Europe*, for example, what had appeared to be a celestial battle involving mysterious godlike forces becomes instead a highly specific political allegory, translatable into a dated sequence of specific events: 'Rintrah, furious king' becomes William Pitt, the three unsuccessful attempts to blow the trump of doom 'may be taken as the three crises contrived by Pitt in the half decade before war with France finally came', while the 'Guardian of the secret codes' driven from his ancient mansion allegorizes the downfall of Chancellor Thurlow on June 15, 1792 (212–214). The attraction of this kind of interpretation, as well as its weakness, is its unambiguous specificity. Not all of Blake's symbolic characters are given political equivalents, but they do tend to acquire an allegorical rigidity. Orc, for example, is always a symbol of revolutionary energy. He is always potentially liberating, so that in the Preludium of *America* his rape of the Shadowy female has to be glossed in approving terms as an 'embrace'. For all its interpretive shortcomings, however, his study remains immensely illuminating.

Since Erdman's book first appeared scholars have worked to broaden and deepen our view of contemporary radicalism. In particular, the politics of the skilled workers and small tradesmen of Blake's London has been subject to intensive investigation, and his affinities with 'plebeian' culture have been emphasized. Among the most notable developments has been the realization that the antinomian aspects of Blake's thought (that reminded Schorer of seventeenth-century radical sects such as the Ranters) might be seen as part of a continuous radical tradition still operative in Blake's London. This idea was formulated in an influential book by A.L. Morton, who acknowledged that it wasn't possible to prove that Blake had read any of the seventeenth-century writers he cites, but appealed to the evidence of their surviving influence in his social environment:

> What can be shown is that he and they shared a common body of ideas and expressed those ideas in a common language. We can show, too, that many of the sects of the seventeenth century, Quakers, Muggletonians and Traskites, for example, did survive in London till Blake's time. And it is certain that they persisted most strongly, as they had sprung up originally, among the artisans and petty tradesmen of the thickly-peopled working-class quarters. These were exactly the social circles and the geographical areas in which Blake was born and in which his whole life was passed. (135)

For Morton, this tradition is central to an understanding of Blake: 'I was able to trace the essentials of all Blake's main ideas in these seventeenth-century writers, though Blake often deepened and enriched them' (11). In identifying Blake's 'main ideas' he adopts a strategy that others have followed, of isolating statements of doctrine and apposite symbols from selected works and letters. His comparison of Blake and the Ranters, for example, draws on sentences and proverbs from *The Marriage of Heaven and Hell*, selected lines from *Songs of Experience* and 'The Everlasting Gospel'. The strategy can be justified on two grounds. First, for many readers the parts of Blake that mean most in terms of doctrine probably *are* representable in selected, relatively accessible extracts. And second, the ideas Morton identifies clearly are common to antinomian tradition and to Blake – such as the identification of god and man, the assertion that the law is no longer binding, the idea of an everlasting gospel, and the symbolism of Babylon and Jerusalem. However, the relationship between these ideas and the bizarre narrative procedures that sometimes accompany them in Blake's work is far from clear. Morton finds no way to engage with the more 'grotesque and obscure' (33) aspects of Blake's language, which therefore seem extraneous to the tradition he identifies.

    If Morton's book showed that there was more to learn about the politics of 'artisans and petty tradesmen' than Erdman had seen, our understanding of such matters was transformed by E.P. Thompson's monumental study *The Making of the English Working Class*, which attempted to rescue the lost causes of plebeian politics 'from the enormous condescension of posterity', and helped to place the role of a host of little-known figures, including the popular prophet Richard Brothers and the ultra-radical Thomas Spence, in relation to the better-known political activism of the period (13). Subsequently the work of Michael Ferber, Iain McCalman, Jon Mee, David Worrall and others has furthered our understanding of the diversity of plebeian politics, its methods and organizations, and the government machinery of surveillance that attempted to control and suppress it. Among Thompson's own further contributions is a study of Blake, in which he vigorously pursues the antinomian connection. Here, referring to Robert Redfield's notion of a 'great' (or polite) and 'little' (or popular) culture, Thompson argues that Blake 'inhabited both at will', but suggests that Blake's 'mind and sensibility were formed within a different, and particular tradition' (xviii). Thompson appears to think of tradition as a formative origin that fixes the identity, in relation to which other cultural influences will tend to remain supplementary, non-essential. The tradition Thompson identifies could hardly be more particular, as he attempts to establish 'a Muggletonian derivation for Blake's vocabulary' (94), firstly by comparing specific symbols and doctrines (as Morton does), and secondly by endowing Blake with a Muggletonian mother (having massaged the archival evidence, as Keri Davies has shown). But Thompson is aware that the pursuit of tradition can entail a narrowing of perspective. His sense of Blake's inheritance is actually very much broader and more complex than the Muggletonian origin he identifies, as it includes both Swedenborgianism and the 'confluence of antinomian and of Jacobinical and deist influences' (xix). Nevertheless Thompson's attempt to isolate an essential identity for Blake, to 'show us who he was' (xx), leads him to distance Blake from a range of polite and 'academic' (199) influences. He suggests, for example, that when Blake wrestled with Deism he 'was less influenced by acknowledged thinkers of the enlightenment than by Volney's *Ruins of Empire*, which the cognoscenti of the London Corresponding society – master craftsmen, shopkeepers, engravers, hosiers, printers – carried around with them in their pockets' (vii). This suggestion, like Thompson's vivid model of Blake's reading, is perfectly consistent with the social profile he develops – although since Blake makes explicit references to (and claims to have read) 'acknowledged' Enlightenment thinkers, but nowhere mentions Volney, we might suspect that Thompson's model is beginning to simplify Blake.

The identification of a common tradition inevitably entails a search for shared doctrines and symbols; but Blake's linguistic affinities with other radical groups can be defined in other terms. Heather Glen's study of Blake and Wordsworth, taking language rather than tradition as its starting point, argues that what Blake shares with the London artisans and tradesmen among whom he spent much of his working life is a 'questioning' of the 'controlling definitions of polite "common sense"' (26). Indeed, this questioning of the authority of hegemonic language links Blake with a wide spectrum of writers and groups, including the popular prophets Richard Brothers and Joanna Southcott, antinomian sects, Swedenborg, Paine and his followers, William Hone and William Cobbett (167). But following his disenchantment with the Swedenborgian New Church, Blake aligns himself with the 'swinish multitude' of newly articulate plebeian radicals who challenged political definitions in pamplets and other publications (89). Glen notes that much of the radical writing addressed to plebeian audiences in the 1790s is informed, like Paine's, by a new confidence in the liberating power of the vernacular, and a newly ironic sense of the way language had been used to mystify and control. She makes highly effective comparisons between some of Blake's ironical usages in the *Songs* and the definitions in works such as Daniel Eaton's *Pigott's Political Dictionary*, while insisting that such similarities are a matter not of 'influence' but 'ambience' (169). And while she demonstrates Blake's 'apparent detachment from the polite literary culture of his day' (28), she also explores his critical engagement with that culture, since she sees the *Songs* as taking part in a debate with hymn writers such as Isaac Watts and Mrs Barbauld (15). The study offers a series of brilliant readings of the *Songs*, contrasting them with the language of Wordsworth's more 'polite' *Lyrical Ballads*.

Could Blake, then, have had a 'plebeian' readership in mind when producing his (relatively expensive) works in illuminated printing? David Bindman, considering the visual designs in the illuminated books, concludes that Blake did have 'hopes of reaching an audience beyond those with the cultural background to understand the Elevated Style' of his paintings (712). Blake's first works in illuminated printing 'would probably have been taken by Blake's contemporaries to belong to the world of popular publishing' (712). Plate 11 of *Europe*, for example, which 'associates the state tyranny of his own time with the spiritual tyranny of the Papacy' (712–713) shows the influence of a tradition of polemical anti-Catholic Protestant imagery, a tradition that stretches back to the seventeenth century, still alive in Blake's day. Other designs in Blake's work are influenced by the popular tradition of 'Hieroglyphic' prints, an influence Blake shares with the radical visionary engraver Garnet Terry. 'Blake, therefore, had good reason to suppose that his designs could have more meaning to the "Great Majority of Fellow Mortals" than to the artistically educated' (717). David Worrall, while conceding that Blake did not in fact achieve an extensive contemporary readership, considers his work in relation to a potential audience. He points to an emergent 'artisan public sphere' with its own public spaces (the street, the working-class tavern), a sphere that emerged as a 'collective reaction to restraints on the spoken word and print media, allied to the necessity for self reinvention within a linguistic space perceived to be distant from Burke's literary high ground' ('Blake' 202). This separate sphere becomes the ground in which the radical concern with the demystification of language (noted by Glen) could be expressed, and the ground of a 'common vocabulary' ('Blake' 208) that Blake shared with figures such as Thomas Spence and Nathanial Citizen Lee (a vocabulary that indicates some shared interests but by no means identical purposes). Blake's expensively produced prophetic works might look remote from such a sphere, but Worrall suggests that 'Before he turned to the more elaborate, less precisely controlled and probably more expensive books in colour-printing for 1794 and 1795, Blake worked with a degree of political provisionality reflected in the topicality of his works' ('Blake' 194). The evidence to support this is the uncolored printings of *America* and *For Children: The Gates of Paradise* and the 'unique copy L of *A Song of Liberty* printed as an uncolored, independent pamphlet on laid paper' ('Blake' 195). Worrall argues that 'The prose pattern of *A Song of Liberty* and its "Chorus" with its crucial opening verb ("Let the Priests [. . .]") repeats the format of early 1790s radical songs and toasts' that would have been heard in working-class taverns of the period ('Blake' 207). He notes that political songs played a prominent part in the conflict between the increasingly polarized ideologies of the 1790s, and that 'Church and ale house were sites for competing gestures of approbation' ('Blake' 204). And he invites us to place Blake's *Songs of Innocence and of Experience* against the 'groundswell of political contrariety in which songs, pamphlets, anonymous letters and other ephemera competed for ideological supremacy in a society undergoing rapid political polarization' ('Blake' 205).

The movement that Worrall identifies, from relatively inexpensive publications towards the production of illuminated books in more expensive forms, can be explained in the light of the machinery of surveillance, harassment, prosecution and punishment by which the state sought to control and suppress radical opinion, a machinery that Worrall and others have investigated (for example, in Worrall's *Radical Culture*). Michael Phillips sees Blake's development of the expensive, labor-intensive process of color-printing as a protective measure in the face of the very real threat of arrest. He points out that Blake 'substantially wrote the *Songs of Experience*' in the spring and summer of 1792, at the beginning of Pitt's Terror, shortly before the establishment of the Association for the Preservation of Liberty and Property against Republicans and Levellers, that members of the Lambeth Association lived close to his home at 13 Hercules Buildings, and that the Association invited all Lambeth housekeepers to sign a declaration of loyalty. If we put the arguments of Glen, Worrall, and Phillips together, we find a movement towards 'plebeian' or 'vulgar' forms in the language of Blake's illuminated books, accompanied by, or rapidly followed by, a movement towards a more exclusive form of visual presentation – a paradoxical movement explicable in terms of contemporary political pressures, but one that calls for further investigation.

Such studies have provided a much fuller understanding of plebeian radicalism – of its traditions and modes of operation, of the constraints it faced, of Blake's relationship with it – than Bronowski or Erdman could draw upon. But Blake's relationship with the aims of Painite radicalism has sometimes remained a source of difficulty. Thompson claims, for example, that when Blake wrote 'London' in *Songs of Experience* he 'had come to share much of Paine's political outlook' even though 'he did not share his faith in the beneficence of commerce' (*Witness* 179). Saree Makdisi's wide-ranging study of Blake and the 1790s should help to dispel confusion in this area. Thompson recognized that the term 'artisan' needed to be qualified when applied to Blake. Makdisi clarifies this point, arguing that Blake dissociated himself from that version of artisan activism that 'tended towards an imagined inclusion in an emergent bourgeois class' (54). Makdisi draws a fundamental distinction between 'hegemonic liberal-radical writers' (including Paine, Thelwall, Price, Priestly, Godwin, Wollstonecraft) and figures like Thomas Spence and Richard Lee (who were at odds with them). By characterizing the former group as 'hegemonic' in relation to other, less respectable radicals, he foregrounds their complicity with the economic systems that Blake protests against; and by characterizing them as 'liberal' he keeps in mind their inheritance of the Locke tradition Blake opposed. He points out that these writers evoked 'a sense of industrious and *productive* virtue and sober work discipline, in which desire could be subject to control', and that they would have been shocked by 'Blake's orgasmic excess', which they would have associated with 'the degeneracy and voluptuousness of European palaces and Oriental seraglios' (44). Moreover, since they mostly assumed that 'the worker, like the citizen, has an independent existence and hence certain "inalienable rights"', they had little interest in 'the sort of detailed psychosocial investigations of workers being produced by conservative writers' (such as Patrick Colquhoun and the Bentham brothers), an interest that Blake shares, since he is engaged 'oppositionally in the discourse of carceral and disciplinary institutions used for organizing productive labor' (101, 103). This acknowledgement that Blake's radicalism might in some respects associate him with writers whose views he opposes reminds us that political and intellectual alignments may take complex and seemingly paradoxical forms.

In contrast to studies that tend to emphasize Blake's detachment or separation from bourgeois culture, we might consider Edward Larrissy's characterization of Blake's cultural position. Larrissy acknowledges that Blake belongs to the 'underground' tradition of antinomian radical Protestantism that survived since the civil war, and that this probably accounts for both the radical and the arcane elements in his work ('a fact which renders futile the urge of critics to pick one and play down the other') (36). But he argues that this model of Blake can be made 'more subtle' by thinking about the cultural significance of Blake's position as engraver. In explaining this significance he uses terms rather different from those developed by Bronowski and Erdman:

> His occupation as a commercial engraver moves him towards the middle class. He comes into contact with fashionable literary theories, styles and movements. Hence his use of the Sublime and his imitations of the fashionable *Ossian*. Blake's Milton is not only the Protestant prophet of Christian Liberty, but also the most favoured candidate for 'sublimity' in the modish cult of the Sublime. Blake, then, combines both old artisanal and new middle-class political and artistic ideologies: Bunyan meets both Paine and Romantic sensibility and sublimity. (36)

Like Maksidi, Larrissy sharply distinguishes Blake's conception of liberty from 'the individualistic, bourgeois conception of his poetic contemporaries', but sees that this does not preclude Blake from sharing in and transforming some of their cultural interests. This way of thinking about Blake accounts for the convergence in his work of a wide range of interests and rhetorical characteristics drawn from polite and popular culture, from rational and enthusiastic forms of radical dissent and from much more conservative writings. It implies that political identity is not – as so many scholars appear to assume – only developed through beliefs or doctrines that are shared with like-minded groups and individuals. And that, as Crehan argues, we do not have to look for '*overt* social or political meanings' in order to consider the political significance of writing. A remarkable essay by David Punter offers a key example of what this might mean for an analysis of Blake. Writing on the assumption that 'questions of poetic form are inseparable from wider questions of ideology and of social and economic organization', Punter relates Blake's use of ballad form to a radical tradition of street literature, and finds the influence of that tradition in the irregularity of Blake's longer, Ossianic poetic lines, defining 'an ideological connection between septenary form and political feeling' (186, 188). He interprets Blake's movement from a politically resonant ballad form to 'what now looks to us like a more obscurantist and reactionary form' (194) not simply as a reaction to censorship, but in ideological terms. In the ancient 'heroic Gothic' world of Macpherson's Ossian (which Punter distinguishes from the reactionary 'Chivalric gothic') Blake found 'intimations of a social order free from commercialism, and of the political and religious struggle close to his own heart, and it is this ideological content which underlies his formal choice' (200). We might note that, politically, Blake would seem to have little in common with James Macpherson, who had been employed by North's ministry to defend their American policy. But he can find in Macpherson elements that can be adapted to his own radical purposes. Like Larrissy's, Punter's sense of the relationship between aspects of style and political and social positions would allow a more complex reading of Blake's radicalism than that provided by those who look simply for overt political affinities.

Jon Mee's important study *Dangerous Enthusiasm: Blake and the Radical Culture of the 1790s* combines Glen's interest in radicalism's relationship to hegemonic language with Punter's interest in the ideology of poetic form. Showing the influence of new historicist methodologies, Mee approaches the language of Blake's poetry as a rhetoric constructed from the interactions between discourses that operate across a wide range of texts, emphasizing the plurality of meanings in his work. Earlier critics had focused on the multiple allusions of Blake's poetry (outlining, for example, alternative sources for the Tree of Mystery). In Mee this multiplicity is conceptualized rather differently: Blake's technique 'produces forms, plots, and figures which stand at significant confluences between discourses' (7). Thus in *The Book of Ahania* the Tree of Mystery is placed in a context that links druidism with Christian priestcraft while it also 'takes up' Edmund Burke's conservative symbol of the British state as English oak (7, 8). This means that 'Aspects traceable to the issues and language of one discourse can also be made sense of in other discursive contexts so that simplistic notions of sources and influences have to be abandoned' (8). The critic must show a keen sensitivity to the 'political resonances' of Blake's rhetoric (6). The scope of Mee's study is restricted to the 1790s in order to focus on the specific conditions of the revolution debate and its immediate consequences.

Mee's book offers a wide variety of contexts, analogues and possible sources for both the rhetorical features and thematic concerns of Blake's prophetic works. It argues that, in some respects, Blake's work can be related to what Iain McCalman has identified as 'a long tradition of convergence between millenarian religious ideas and popular forms of scepticism and materialism', a convergence that 'surfaces repeatedly in the 1790s', and can be seen in the writings of radicals such as Daniel Isaac Eaton, Thomas Paine and Thomas Spence (5). It argues that, in other respects, the writings and designs Blake produced in the 1790s can be compared with the ballad collections published by the republican antiquarian Joseph Ritson in their use of 'primitive' or 'vulgar' formal devices and traditions (116). It considers Blake's prophetic rhetoric in relation to a wide range of practices: the Bible, Robert Lowth's discussion of biblical rhetoric, polite primitivist writing (including Macpherson's Ossianic poems, Gray's 'The Bard', the works of Welsh antiquarians), the visionary writings of Swedenborg, as well as popular prophecy of figures like Richard Brothers. It shows that, depending on which features one chooses to emphasize, Blake's rhetoric has something in common with all of these, and that attempts to link Blake exclusively to one particular source or influence tend to simplify the effect of his language.

Mee's study engages more widely and more persuasively with Blake's language than any other scholarly account of Blake's relation to radical tradition. His book presents a compelling view of Blake as an enthusiast whose opposition to hegemonic authority is signaled in part by his use of stylistic features of the kind found in 'vulgar' writers, including vulgar prophets. In view of the diversity of the material surveyed, it is perhaps not surprising that when Mee tries to locate a specific 'basis' for Blake's language he runs into difficulties. In the first chapter he argues that while Blake's prophetic radicalism has features in common with a whole range of texts produced from the broader culture of enthusiasm, 'the basis' of his rhetoric 'lies in the culture of vulgar enthusiasm' as represented by such figures as Richard Brothers, George Riebau and Garnet Terry (20). But in practice the argument moves uncertainly between these enthusiasts (who are acknowledged to be more pious than Blake, and to look to a transcendent divinity of the kind Blake tends to satirize) and writers like Paine and Spence who combine skepticism with millenarian ideas. The slippage arises from the urge to establish Blake's typicality in relation to an identifiable group, and the difficulty of identifying a group that adequately represents the broad range of rhetorical features Mee actually identifies. The introduction attempts to establish a more inclusive model, by describing Blake as a 'bricoleur', alluding to the model provided by the anthropologist Claude Lévi-Strauss. Lévi-Strauss applies the term 'bricoleur' to the 'primitive' mythmaker, whose mythical discourse constructed from 'a collection of oddments left over from human endeavour' is contrasted with the 'transparent', scientific discourse of the engineer (16–27). Established in these terms, the distinction is deeply problematic, as Derrida showed when he mischievously suggested that the engineer was a myth invented by the bricoleur (285). Lévi-Strauss also contrasts the bricoleur with the craftsman, but Mee makes these 'comparable' in order to suggest an analogy between primitive bricoleur and Blake the autodidact engraver.[2] This dehistoricizing suggestion seems irresistible (since Mee needs to make a connection between bricolage and what Thompson would call 'anti-hegemony') although it is at odds with the historical methodology of the book as a whole. Mee goes on to develop a revised definition of bricolage: 'An approach which unapologetically recombines elements from across discourse boundaries such that the antecedent discourses are fundamentally altered in the resultant structures' (3). But this definition is also problematic, since one might claim that such combination is a feature of many different kinds of writing.[3] Establishing a specific typicality for Blake's rhetoric seems inherently more difficult than illustrating its relationships with a range of other practices.

In Glen, Mee and others, Blake appears to find his radical voice most clearly after his disillusionment with Swedenborg in the early 1790s. But in the ongoing work of Marsha Keith Schuchard the Swedenborgians have emerged as a heterogeneous group riven by political differences, part of a complex international network that linked them with radical Illuminists and Freemasons (and which may have influenced the symbolism and visual designs of his radical narratives). There is clearly much more to learn about the radical networks of Blake's London, by piecing together the fragmentary evidence not only of those who lived and worked in the city, but also of foreign organizations and contacts.

conclusions and problems

One might reasonably claim that the work of Blake scholars has done more than any other body of work to illuminate the social and cultural history of the 1790s, reaching so far beyond the oeuvre of Blake himself that the poet sometimes begins to appear a mere pretext. What conclusions can be drawn from this body of work?

One tendency of this line of enquiry is to separate the prophet, whose language and illuminations are in touch with vulgar idioms, from the artist who paints in what Bindman terms the 'Elevated Manner'. Some important work has been done on the political implications of Blake's comments on art and artists, notably John Barrell's discussion of key terms and Morris Eaves's wide-ranging study of Blake's critique of 'English-school discourse', but as yet it has proved difficult to integrate this kind of investigation with the study of plebeian radicalism, and Blake the painter is often marginalized in studies of Blake the radical prophet.

Among the more general features of the historicizing and politicizing of Blake is the tendency to present Blake as writing to the moment, responding to immediately topical issues and debates, debates usually arising during a few years of the 1790s, while taking for granted, or ignoring, the relevance of this Blake to our own age. Can Blake speak to us in any way except through the historical researches of scholars? Larrissy argues that to define Blake's allegiances 'only provides the conditions of existence of Blake's work [. . .] essential to explanation and description, but tending to reductionism unless filled out by more minute formal description which allows for the autonomy of artistic tradition' (36). But the idea of an autonomous artistic tradition is in conflict with the conviction, shared by Marxist and New Historicist critics, that (as Crehan puts it) 'no artistic form or style is ever politically or ideologically neutral' (2–3). Crehan himself reproduces this conflict when, thinking about Blake's appeal to modern readers, he claims that 'Blake's art has *transcended* the historical conditions within which it was produced' (239). For this idea of transcendence threatens to dehistoricize the work, and Crehan must head off the threat by arguing that 'the particularized, the sensuous and the "universal-in-the-local" are at one level the way a work of art carries within itself the implied reproduction of certain social relations or a struggle to transform those relations' (240). Art, that is, can be understood at more than one 'level'; the historically generated particulars of the work can have a 'universal' significance, and so speak to twenty-first-century readers who are far beyond the historical moment of the work. But this appears to readmit the concept of the 'semi-autonomy' of art that Crehan had explicitly condemned at the outset as tending to 'justify and uphold the *autonomy* of art and ideas [...] while appearing to give ground to economic, social and political determinants' (4). Crehan's sense that Blake *may* in some way speak directly to modern readers, then, appears to violate one of the assumptions that govern his methodology. Most scholars in the field, from Marxist to New Historicist, avoid addressing the issue that Crehan runs into, and show little interest in considering the supposed 'autonomy' or 'universality' of Blake's art.

This doesn't mean that Blake has been represented as of only historical interest. But those critics like Bronowski, Erdman and Makdisi, who relate Blake to the larger struggles against modernization, including (in the case of Erdman and Makdisi) the struggle against empire, are inevitably more successful at suggesting Blake's significance for our own times than those who focus more narrowly on the finer points of millenarian thought or on competing antiquarian theories. Others, like Larrissy and Nicholas Williams, have shaped their investigations not only in relation to Blake's contempõraries, but also in relation to the theoretical models and/or political arguments of modern writers. Williams, for example, investigates Blake's own understanding of what would now be termed ideology, by drawing on the works of Ricoeur, Althusser, Habermas and other recent writers. He considers the libertarian claims of Blake's work in relation to the 'Mannheim paradox' (the position of the critic of ideology, whose own critique is itself subject to the charge of ideology), comparing Blake's ideas with those of Rousseau, Wollstonecraft, Paine, Burke and Robert Owen. Thus Blake is connected to radical (and conservative) tradition, both eighteenth-century and modern, by analogy. To those interested in uncovering the material conditions in which Blake's ideas were produced, this may seem like a methodological regression. But it allows Williams to make unfamiliar comparisons – for example considering the Blake of *Jerusalem* in relation to Robert Owen (since they share a concern with the conditions of the working poor, and imagine new communities to be realized in the actual world) and in relation to Habermas (since both have an interest in defining a public created through the exchange of differing and freely expressed views). And it refuses to concede that discussion of Blake's radicalism must concern itself not with what he means today, but only with what Blake may once have meant.

Another general problem is the place – or absence – of gender issues in the study of Blake's radicalism. Helen Bruder, in *William Blake and the Daughters of Albion*, looks at the failure of the '"new radicalism" of Blake's age to include anywhere on its agenda demands for, or even a concern for, the rights of women' (91). Indeed, she notes that 'It is quite possible that women's opportunities for engagement in political activity actually decreased in these years' (92). At the same time she argues that modern scholars 'have made very few efforts to redeem the gender-blindness, if not outright sexism' of the politicians of Blake's time (91). She attempts to redress this situation with a brief review of male radicals

Godwin, Paine and (especially) Spence, who attempted to incorporate some kind of concern with gender into their general political theories, but who usually retreated to politically safer ground. And she then reviews some contemporary female radicals: Catherine Macaulay Graham (who 'studiously avoided any discussion of gender issues' in much of her writing, 103), Mary Hays and Mary Wollstonecraft (who without a female audience for the kind of activist message their logic requires fall back on an appeal to 'reasonable' men to behave more 'philosophically' in relation to women, 104–13). These brief surveys certainly make visible what is often excluded in Blake studies, while tending to confirm the difficulties of overcoming the prevailing masculinist culture (rather than redeeming the radicals from its influence). Given such negative conclusions it is perhaps not surprising that Bruder's challenging reading of the prophecies – whose difficulties she does not shy away from – draws rather sparingly on this specific context, and engages more productively with the ideology of conduct literature, and with the British perceptions of women in pre-revolutionary and revolutionary France. Bruder's Blake emerges as a 'proto-feminist' influenced by an awareness of Wollstonecraft's observations on the oppression of women – a view anticipated by some other writers. But the wider issues raised in Bruder's study have yet to be addressed satisfactorily by Blake scholars.[4]

Finally, it has to be said that in spite of the best efforts to make Blake's prophetic works genuinely representative of an identifiable contemporary community or popular tradition, in some respects they remain stubbornly idiosyncratic and apart. While we often read that Blake shares a 'vocabulary' with other radicals, terms like 'Enitharmon' or 'Palamabron' apparently form no part of that vocabulary. Nobody else seems to have used this mythical idiom, which remains unassimilably unique. In consequence, there has been a tendency (with some notable exceptions) to write about Blake's language in ways that simply evade many of the difficulties posed by his mythical narratives. In general scholars of Blake's radicalism have moved from dismissing the obscurities in his narratives as signs of failure or deranged sensibilities, to describing them as residual elements of the discursive practices from which Blake is trying to liberate his readers. Mee, for example, finds in *Europe* a 'determination to frustrate any attempt to allegorize the poem against contemporary history' since the narrative 'obscures any simple historical referent' (*Dangerous* 26). He sees this process taken further in poems like *The Book of Urizen* and *The Book of Los* in which 'disorientating conjunctions and confusing internal repetitions' make the narratives 'difficult to reduce to any kind of straightforward story', which seems to imply that their plots have become virtually unreadable (26). The idea that obscurity frustrates allegory is questionable, while the view that Blake's critique of narrative authority implies an undermining of narrative itself seems unhelpful in relation to a poet who thinks of the prophet as a teller of poetic tales, and who accordingly produces many different kinds of narrative. Makdisi tends to avoid interpretive approaches 'based on narrative, or allegory, or symbolism' since Blake's 'obscurity' and 'general tendency towards inscrutability' make these difficult (188). In the middle of his admirably erudite discussion Makdisi suggests a 'new' approach to reading Blake that 'would involve unlearning whatever it is that makes us learned' (162). Oddly enough this new method of reading may seem familiar to anyone who has spent any time reading Blake, except that it stops short of following up any curiosity aroused by what is not too explicit. Instead, Makdisi enacts a Thel-like recoil from a text that tries 'to seduce the reader into its hidden confines' (162), leaving his readers in the hermeneutic equivalent of the Vales of Har. To evade the narrative challenges in this way, I would argue, is to disarm the thrust of Blake's radical critique of his own civilization, which depends on a sustained analysis of the relations between causes and effects ('If you go on So / the result is So' E617). While scholars of Blake's radicalism repeatedly proclaim the need to rescue Blake from de-politicizing critics, the effect of this kind of evasion is to leave the investigation of the internal relations of Blake's narratives in the hands of critics like Northrop Frye, whose view of the struggle for political liberty seems remote from the world of riots, meetings, pamphlets, government agents that characterized the struggle actually waged in Blake's London, but who is able to treat Blake's mythology as profoundly meaningful. One of the major challenges still facing students of Blake's radicalism, then, is to find ways of coming to terms with Blake the myth maker, whose (sometimes allegorical) narratives are means by which he participated in the radical thought of his own age.

notes

1. Crehan is aware that the term 'class' is used anachronistically in this context, since at this time these social groups 'lacked the collective consciousness and deep class solidarity that was to weld together the working-class reform societies, trade union and cooperative movements of the industrial north' (8).
2. The phrasing in the translation of Lévi-Strauss (as in the original) is weak: 'The bricoleur uses devious means compared to a craftsman' (16–17). But the context makes clear the contrast between the improvising bricoleur (whose tools and materials 'bear no relationship to the current project' 17) and the craftsman (whose training, tools and materials are specifically appropriate to

his project). In quoting the above translation, Mee substitutes 'comparable' for 'compared'.

3. When Alexander Pope, for example, combines elements derived from classical epic with descriptions of modern 'Dulness' in *The Dunciad*, he may intend to defend rather than undermine hegemonic values, but nevertheless the discourse of heroism is (I would argue) fundamentally altered in the resulting structure of the poem. Mee may need a more specific terminology to distinguish Blake's subversion of hegemonic authority from such transformative 'recombining' of discourses, which is a common feature of many kinds of writing.

4. After a brief review of the male preoccupation with apocalypse in the romantic period, Anne K. Mellor asks, 'why was the female imagination on the whole *not* inspired by millenarian, apocalyptic thinking?' See 'Blake, the Apocalypse and Romantic Women Writers'.

works cited and suggestions for further reading

Barrell, John. *The Political Theory of Painting from Reynolds to Hazlitt*. New Haven: Yale University Press, 1986.

Bindman, David. 'William Blake and Popular Religious Imagery'. *The Burlington Magazine* 128 (1986): 712–18.

Bronowski, Jacob. *William Blake: A Man Without a Mask*. London: Secker and Warburg, 1943.

Bruder, Helen. *William Blake and the Daughters of Albion*. Houndmills: Macmillan, 1997.

Crehan, Stewart. *Blake in Context*. Atlantic Highlands, NJ: Humanities Press, 1984.

Davies, Keri. 'William Blake's Mother: A New Identification'. *Blake: An Illustrated Quarterly* 33:2 (1999): 36–50.

Derrida, Jacques. *Writing and Difference*. Trans. Alan Bass. London: Routledge and Kegan Paul, 1978.

Eaves, Morris. *The Counter-Arts Conspiracy: Art and Industry in the Age of Blake*. Ithaca and London: Cornell University Press, 1992.

Erdman, David V. *Blake: Prophet Against Empire*. 3rd ed. Princeton: Princeton University Press, 1977.

Ferber, Michael. *The Social Vision of William Blake*. Princeton: Princeton University Press, 1985.

Glen, Heather. *Vision and Disenchantment: Blake's 'Songs' and Wordsworth's 'Lyrical Ballads'*. Cambridge: Cambridge University Press, 1983.

Larrissy, Edward. *William Blake*. Oxford: Blackwell, 1985.

Lévi-Strauss, Claude. *The Savage Mind*. London: Weidenfeld and Nicolson, 1966.

Makdisi, Saree. *William Blake and the Impossible History of the 1790s*. Chicago: University of Chicago Press, 2003.

McCalman, Iain. *Radical Underworld: Prophets, Revolutionaries and Pornographers in London, 1795–1840*. Cambridge: Cambridge University Press, 1988.

Mee, Jon. *Dangerous Enthusiasm: Blake and the Radical Culture of the 1790s*. Oxford: Oxford University Press, 1994.

——. '"The Doom of Tyrants": William Blake, Richard "Citizen" Lee, and the Millenarian Public Sphere' in *Blake, Politics, and History*. Ed. Jackie DiSalvo,

G.A. Rosso and Christopher Z. Hobson. New York and London: Garland, 1998. 97–114.

Mellor, Anne. 'Blake, the Apocalypse and Romantic Women Writers' in *Romanticism and Millenarianism*. Ed. Tim Fulford. New York, Houndmills: Palgrave, 2002. 139–52.

Morton, A.L. *The Everlasting Gospel: A Study in the Sources of William Blake*. London: Lawrence and Wishart, 1958.

Punter, David. 'Blake: Social Relations of Poetic Form'. *Literature and History* 8 (1982): 182–205.

Schorer, Mark. *William Blake, The Politics of Vision*. New York: Vintage Books, 1946.

Schuchard, Marsha Keith. 'Blake and Grand Masters: Architects of Repression or Revolution?' in *Blake in the Nineties*. Ed. Steve Clark and David Worrall. Houndmills: Macmillan, 1999. 173–93.

——. 'Blake's Tiriel and the Regency Crisis: Lifting the Veil on a Royal Masonic Scandal' in *Blake, Politics, and History*. Ed. Jackie DiSalvo, G.A. Rosso and Christopher Z. Hobson. New York and London: Garland, 1998. 115–35.

——. 'The Secret Masonic History of Blake's Swedenborg Society'. *Blake: An Illustrated Quarterly* 22 (1992): 51–71.

Thompson, E.P. *The Making of the English Working Class*. Harmondsworth: Penguin, 1979.

——. *Witness Against the Beast: William Blake and the Moral Law*. Cambridge: Cambridge University Press, 1993.

Williams, Nicholas. *Ideology and Utopia in the Poetry of William Blake*. Cambridge: Cambridge University Press, 1998.

Worrall, David. 'Blake and the 1790s Plebeian Radical Culture' in *Blake in the Nineties*. Ed. Steve Clark and David Worrall. Houndmills: Macmillan, 1999. 194–211.

——. *Radical Culture: Discourse, Resistance and Surveillance 1790–1820*. Hemel Hempstead: Harvester Wheatsheaf, 1992.

——. 'Robert Hawes and the Millenarian Press: A Political Microculture of Late Eighteenth-Century Spitalfields' in *Romanticism and Millenarianism*. New York and Houndmills: Palgrave, 2002. 167–81.

11
blake and the communist tradition

> When shall Jerusalem return & overspread all the Nations
> Return: return to Lambeths Vale O building of human souls
> Thence stony Druid Temples overspread the Island white
> And thence from Jerusalems ruins.. from her walls of salvation
> And praise: thro the whole Earth were reard from Ireland
> To Mexico & Peru west, & east to China & Japan.
>
> William Blake, *M*6.18–23, E100

> The earth will be laid out to form, over its whole extent, one City, to be composed of separate townships with their required appliances; and each will be a paradise of a township, connected with all other such townships over the globe, until they form the earth gradually into this one great city, which may be called the New Jerusalem, or united earthly paradise.
>
> Robert Owen

'Every social movement, every real advance in England on behalf of the workers links itself on to the name of Robert Owen', writes Friedrich Engels. 'As long as he was simply a philanthropist, he was rewarded with nothing but wealth, applause, honour, and glory', Engels observes,

> but when he came out with his communist theories that was quite another thing. Three great obstacles seemed to him especially to block the path to social reform: private property, religion, the present form of marriage. He knew what confronted him if he attacked these – outlawry, excommunication from official society, the loss of his whole social position. But nothing of this prevented him from attacking them without fear of consequences, and what he had foreseen happened. (693)

Indeed, thanks in no small part to the work of Engels himself, Owen has long been thought of both as the father of English communism and – often taken to be much the same thing – as a thoroughgoing secularist. But while he was quite consistent in his hostility to the 'errors' and 'divisions' propagated by all the institutionalized religions 'which have hitherto been forced on the minds of men' (quoted in Morton, *Life of Owen* 155), Owen was also quite willing and able to draw on a long line of radical millenarian thought that ran back from his own time to the great explosion of religious and political experimentation in England in the mid seventeenth century, a line of thought whose centrality in the communist tradition has not yet – even with the great work of E.P. Thompson, Christopher Hill and A.L. Morton already behind us – received the recognition that it deserves.

For, after all, the vision of the 'united earthly paradise' of collectively owned parishes as it is described by Owen was a direct outgrowth of that earlier tradition, which made its way to Owen via Thomas Spence and his followers in the 1810s and 1820s (some of whom regarded Owen's scheme as Spenceanism 'doubly dipped'[1]), although to Spence's agrarian concern with land Owen would add a layer of industrial-age theories of cooperation. We can also trace continuities between Owen's vision of a millennial Jerusalem and earlier millenarian enthusiasm, including Spence's, which itself had roots in seventeenth-century English articulations of an earthly communism as the fulfillment of biblical prophecy: a state in which, as Gerrard Winstanley saw it, just as 'one spirit of righteousness is common to all, so the earth and the blessings of the earth shall become common to all; for now all is but the Lord, and the Lord is the all in all' (27). It is, for example, but a small step from Spence's calls for a millennial jubilee to the tune of 'God Save the King' ('Hark how the Trumpets Sound, / Proclaims the Land around, / The Jubilee; / Tells all the Poor oppressed / No more shall they be cess'd, / Nor landlords more molest / Their Property') to Owen's admittedly somewhat more prosaic vision of the New Jerusalem as a global paradise of collectively owned townships. And if in turn Owen's vision of the New Jerusalem of an earthly paradise also looks remarkably like William Blake's – whose own similarities to Winstanley were noted as long ago as the 1950s by A.L. Morton and reiterated by Michael Ferber in the 1980s, before receiving renewed attention in more recent scholarship – that is because Blake too was drawing on the same line of thought, and because Blake's work too must be situated as one of the outgrowths of a communist tradition that was all along far more diverse, colorful and heterogeneous than some of those who laid claim to that tradition in the twentieth century would ever have liked to imagine.

In short, it was because Blake too was a communist. He was not, of course, an adherent of an internally consistent or self-regulating party or school of thought – for he was (thankfully) far too undisciplined and anarchical to ever be imagined to conform to such regulation; and in any case, not only was the word 'communism' never even used in his lifetime (it entered the language only in mid century), but there was no such party in his own time. If, however, one conceives of communism as a significantly more discontinuous and unevenly heterogeneous set of arguments, thoughts, provocations, and desires running right through modernity – for which only the nineteenth century would invent a name and a more or less coherent set of ideals (e.g., 'from each according to his abilities, to each according to his needs', or 'the free development of each is the condition for the free development of all') – then there is no doubt that Blake was an active participant in communist thought, and that certain principles of central importance to the communist tradition running from, say, Spinoza onwards (via, in England, the Ranters and antinomians in the seventeenth century and Spence and Owen in the nineteenth) also play a vitally important role in Blake, during whose lifetime this discontinuous tradition experienced enormous transformations, out of which would emerge the strand of communist thinking that links itself to the name of Karl Marx.

In fact, while much of Marx's early work prepared the way for the *Grundrisse* and *Capital*, it also served to link his later more fully elaborated critique of capital – and what we might think of as the mature, fully theorized communism of the later nineteenth century – with the very same older tradition of communist thought to which Spence, Owen and Blake were also indebted, or really to mediate between that older tradition and its industrial and post-industrial successors. This older tradition was principally concerned with questions of being and ontology, and in seeking to ground not just religion but politics (as well as economics and indeed aesthetics) in ontology it differed markedly from a parallel and to a certain extent competitive movement in political thought – democratic liberalism – which ran in England from the time of the Levellers and John Locke in the seventeenth century, through the time of Tom Paine and the London Corresponding Society in the 1790s, to that of Chartism and Victorian liberalism more generally. 'The *forming* of the five senses', Marx would write in *1844*, 'is a labour of the entire history of the world down to the present' (*1844* 141). In so linking the development of the human sensorium – and human subjectivity both in particular and in general – to the history of political struggle, as its foundation, Marx was in fact reasserting a connection between *being* and *struggle* (as well as aesthetics) that the tradition of liberalism, for its part, had sundered in its insistence on a notion of individual subjectivity as something standing prior to and outside of social and historical development, as, in short, a transhistorical given.

Blake, too, was working at a moment when it seemed essential to preserve a sense of the connection between history and ontology, and to maintain a way of thinking of history itself *as* ontological struggle – surely, along with the five senses, one of the central concerns of the illuminated books. This set Blake apart from the many radicals who during his lifetime were willing to forgo ontology and the question of being in their rush to embrace what Blake saw as the consensus that 'Englishmen are all Intermeasurable One by Another, certainly a happy state of Agreement to which', as he wrote in the last year of his life, 'I for One do not Agree' (E783). In order to appreciate the significance of Blake's position, however, and its relationship to Marx's early ontological elaborations of the critique of capital – and the broader communist tradition in general – it is necessary to step back a little and to retrace some of the historical ground that these struggles transfigured, as well as to take stock of the extent to which modern criticism has taken this ground and these struggles into account in the historical and political contextualization of William Blake.

For much of the twentieth century, the consensus among those scholars interested in Blake's political context and the historical significance of his work took more or less for granted an understanding of Blake that was derived from David Erdman's elaboration of the extraordinary connections between Blake and the political and historical events of his own time (which proposed a quite different Blake, and a different line of scholarly enquiry from the one inaugurated by Northrop Frye in *Fearful Symmetry*, which seemed, at least, to emphasize the symbolic life of Blake's texts over and against their political nature). While Erdman's great book *Blake: Prophet Against Empire* pioneered the attempt to ground Blake in historical realities, the Blake depicted in that book was a sturdy, frugal artisan, steeped in Enlightenment rationalism, and seeking, like the better known radicals of his day (Tom Paine, John Thelwall, Mary Wollstonecraft), to overthrow tyranny in the name of an apparently rather uncomplicated concept of Liberty, whose primary source of inspiration was taken to be the American struggle for independence – that is, life, liberty, and the pursuit of (individual) happiness.

This understanding of Blake owed a great deal to his Victorian biographer, Alexander Gilchrist, according to whom Blake was 'an ardent member of the New School, a vehement republican and sympathizer with the Revolution, hater and contemner of kings and king-craft. [. . .] To him, as to ardent minds everywhere, the French Revolution was the herald of the Millennium, of a new age of light and reason' (109–13). This understanding of Blake as a kind of proto-Paineite bourgeois persisted through a long line of criticism and scholarship, and it led to the consolidation of the dominant academic consensus that, insofar as he had a political edge at all – in other words, insofar as he stood for something more than merely the expression of the dizzying circuits of mythic and symbolic referentiality that seemed to emerge from Frye's reading of the illuminated books – Blake and his politics could be understood by direct reference to the work of Paine and the American War of Independence, the French Revolution, and the English 'revolution controversy' of the 1790s. *America: A Prophecy* – which seemed to readers working in the tradition established by Erdman to celebrate the conventional understanding of the freedom of the property-owning individual, the bourgeois self – was thus taken to be Blake's most 'political' work, the clearest statement of his political principles as someone for whom 'liberty' was what the American rebels and Tom Paine had understood it to be.

Running in parallel to the political and historical framing of Blake as defined by Erdman, there was, however, another, strangely (but not inexplicably) much less influential line of scholarship that sought to ground Blake in a different political genealogy from the one elaborated by Erdman. This line of enquiry emerged from the resurgent interest in the cultural politics of the mid seventeenth century – an age when, as the title of Christopher Hill's influential book reminds us, the *World Turned Upside Down* – among a group of British historians in the middle of the twentieth century. Hill and other historians, including A.L. Morton, recovered from the dustbin of history a number of colorful plebeian figures, individuals and groups whose presence in the drama of the English Revolution and Civil War vastly complicated the received understanding of that turbulent moment in Britain's cultural formation as essentially a contest between Cromwell and the Parliament on the one hand and the King and the royalists on the other: a reading of history 'from below' that would be extended to the late eighteenth and early nineteenth centuries in E.P. Thompson's groundbreaking work *The Making of the English Working Class.* Chief among these figures (besides the Levellers) were a number of people – Ranters, Diggers, antinomians – who elaborated a heady combination of religious and political enthusiasm proposing such heretical concepts as the immanent human constitution of god, the common inheritance and sharing of the earth and its resources, and a notion of being-in-common that emphasized the essential unity – even divinity – of all humankind, and indeed of all life.

A.L. Morton was among the first to notice that certain concepts that proved foundational to the seventeenth-century antinomians – such as the notion of an Everlasting Gospel, and other expressions of what Morton identified as 'political ideas in a religious form' – would turn up and play a significant role in Blake's work over a hundred years later. Even during the Commonwealth, Morton argued, plebeian heretics 'were often persecuted, and after the restoration of the Monarchy in 1660 they were driven underground, preserving their faith in little, obscure conventicles, treasuring subversive pamphlets in old cupboards, holding the ideas of the revolution, as it were, in suspension, until, towards the end of the eighteenth century, the world seemed ready for them again' (*Gospel* 36). In his 1985 book *The Social Vision of William Blake*, Michael Ferber retraced more of the connections between Blake and the seventeenth century, pointing out, for example, that Blake seemed to share a great deal in common with Winstanley and others from that earlier revolutionary context, much more so, in fact – at least epistemologically – than with the radicals of his own time. E.P. Thompson's book *Witness Against the Beast* revised the assessment of Blake in his earlier classic work and produced an image of the author of *Jerusalem* not merely as a sturdy Paineite advocate of the Rights of Man, but also as someone steeped in a rich mystical heritage as well. Thompson's point is that this heritage offered Blake a basis from which to question and to resist certain aspects of the Enlightenment epistemology 'represented by the blunt, humane ultra-radicalism of Paine and [Constantin] Volney', which could be seen to have 'collided with an older antinomian tradition, [which] co-existed in Blake's heart and argued matters out inside his head' (*Witness* 128).

Taken together, these views vastly complicated the understanding of Blake's politics which had been developed in the historically inclined strand of criticism stemming from Erdman. For one thing, the link between politics and mysticism which was essential both to the seventeenth-century heretics and to Blake himself seemed to demand a much more complicated understanding of Blake's relationship to history than was allowed for by most of the then existing historicist scholarship on Blake (which tended to see his representation of politics as one concerned strictly with contemporary events such as the revolution in France, and hence tended to read Blake allegorically, rather than allowing for a more complicated understanding of his political commitments and engagements with history). At the same time, the work of Morton, Ferber and Thompson suggested a deficiency on the part of the Blake scholarship that followed in the more hermeneutically introspective (and at times markedly apolitical) trajectory of North American Romanticism, for much of which mystical, religious or imaginative language seemed to suggest a departure from politics and even from reality itself. What the return to the seventeenth-century heretics revealed is that imaginatively mystical or religious language could serve immediately political purposes, not merely at the level of narrative, but also in enabling the exploration of politically charged relationships among language, subjectivity and power – an exploration in which hermeneutics turns out to be the very *basis* of history rather than marking a departure from it, and the point of departure for political intervention.

The problem with this approach, however, was that it paradoxically ran the risk of losing sight of the very historical continuities that it also brought to the fore. The language of revolution, according to Morton, changed dramatically in the passage from the seventeenth century to the eighteenth, 'and the old ideas were barely intelligible to the men who listened to Paine and Thelwall, and mere crazy nonsense to the more sophisticated followers of Bentham'. Nevertheless, he adds, 'they did provide a means of communication for a great poet: Blake's tragedy was that he was speaking a language which was already becoming obsolete'; Morton continues, 'he was the greatest English antinomian, but he was also the last' (*Gospel* 36). Even Thompson's work seemed to situate Blake as more or less the last in a long line of antinomians, all alone in a modern world from which such heresies had apparently been banished. Thanks to the work of a new wave of literary and historical scholars (including Iain McCalman, Peter Linebaugh, Marcus Rediker, David Worrall and Jon Mee, among others), we now know that Blake was not quite as alone as we might otherwise have thought. This new scholarship has revealed that, quite in addition to the world of radical intellectuals from Godwin to Paine, which has long been more familiar and accessible to modern scholarship, a thriving, colorfully heterogeneous and much less 'respectable' radical plebeian subculture – to which Blake would have had many points of access – persisted in London through his lifetime. This plebeian subculture can be traced not merely through the contemporary reprinting of such seventeenth-century antinomian classics as John Saltmarsh's *Free Grace; Or the Flowing of Christ's Blood Freely to Sinners*, but also by a proliferation of new versions of the old heritage as well as a general boom in prophets, prophecies and varieties of millenarian or antinomian enthusiasm of varying forms and degrees of intensity, from Richard Brothers and Joanna Southcott to Thomas Spence, Garnet Terry, Richard Lee, Robert Wedderburn, Thomas Evans, and of course William Blake himself.[2] This was a subculture in which antinomian and millenarian as well as identifiably communist thought flourished, sometimes alongside, sometimes in dialogue with, and sometimes in outright contention with more 'rational' and ultimately more quantitative forms of radicalism, which would be nourished in the wake of Paine by the work of Jeremy Bentham, Thomas Malthus, Richard Carlile and Francis Place.[3]

This subculture, out of which Owen's work emerged (and indeed Owen's thought brought Malthus and Ricardo into dialogue with Spenceanism in a remarkable way) only began showing signs of fading away in the 1830s and 1840s, as new forms of radical thinking began to emerge from it which, although they were to a certain degree indebted conceptually and epistemologically to the older traditions which they would eventually supplant, were also more adequately armed for the analysis and critique of modern capitalism as well as of bourgeois liberalism itself, and hence were ultimately quite different in their political aims and modes of critique. This is partly because the forms of radical and communist thought that would emerge after the first third of the nineteenth century – particularly after the first Reform bill – were engaged not primarily with the residues of the old regime (which preoccupied radicalism in, say, the 1790s), but above all with capitalism itself, which had also through this time developed and matured into the recognizably modern form which persisted at least up through the leap into its fully globalized postmodern or 'late' form toward the end of the twentieth century. However, although nineteenth-century communism would require a more theoretically formidable set of concepts and tools – which Marx would provide in the *Grundrisse* and *Capital* – it would be historically misleading to detach it from the earlier tradition, out of which it was born, and from which it would carry various concepts that derive from the heritage going as far back as Spinoza.[4]

Bearing in mind some sense of the various trajectories and lines of thought and struggle that would run from the seventeenth and eighteenth centuries into the nineteenth, even a cursory evaluation of Blake's work reveals the extent to which it was saturated with certain concepts that would prove as indispensable to future forms of radical thought (like Marx's) as they had been to previous generations of communists. Consider, for example, some of the broad consequences of the elaboration of the alienation of labor, which would prove foundational for Marx's critique of capital – and which we can relate back to Blake and indeed to the communist tradition going back to the seventeenth century. At one point, according to Marx, it had seemed possible to think of nature as what he calls 'man's *inorganic* body', such that humans, their labor, those materials on which that labor was exercised and the very products of that labor, all seemed to constitute a 'universal' physical, imaginative and even spiritual continuum: a universality held in common that could have been thought of as constitutively and collectively human, and that came to define what Marx calls our *species being*. 'The universality of man is in practice manifested precisely in the universality which makes all nature his *inorganic* body – both inasmuch as nature is (1) his direct means of life, and (2) the material, the object, and the instrument of his life-activity. Nature is man's *inorganic* body – nature, that is, in so far as it is not itself the human body', Marx argues. To say that 'Man *lives* on nature', he continues, 'means that nature is his *body*, with which he must remain in continuous intercourse if he is not to die' (*1844* 112). Alienated labor, then, not only splits the worker from the object of his labor (which is no longer his, but belongs to another who appropriates it); it also splits man from nature and indeed man from himself, from 'his own active functions, his life-activity', and hence it turns the (collective) life of the species – in which the distinction between individual and social is quite literally meaningless – into a means of merely individual life: 'it makes individual life in its abstract form the purpose of the life of the species' (*1844* 112–13). Once this form of labor (that is, the form of labor that would prove essential to capitalism) has come to dominate humankind, what had once seemed constitutively human powers (of spirituality, of production) now seem to become alien to human beings:

> The alienation of the worker in his product means not only that his labour becomes an object, an external existence, but that it exists outside him, independently, as something alien to him, and that it becomes a power of its own confronting him; it means that the life which he has conferred on the object confronts him as something hostile and alien. (*1844* 108)

And the more productive human labor becomes, the more that is produced, and the greater the power that seems to be embodied in the products of labor, the more impoverished the (alienated) laborer, the more powerful the alien object world that seems to dominate him.

'Let us now see, further', Marx suggests, 'how in real life the concept of estranged, alienated labour must express and present itself':

If the product of labour is alien to me, if it confronts me as an alien power, to whom, then, does it belong?

If my own activity does not belong to me, if it is an alien, a coerced activity, to whom, then, does it belong?

To a being other than me.

Who is this being?

The gods? To be sure, in the earliest times the principal production (for example, the building of temples, etc., in Egypt, India and Mexico) appears to be in the service of the gods, and the product belongs to the gods. However, the gods on their own were never the lords of labour. No more was nature. [. . .]

The alien being, to whom labour and the produce of labour belongs, in whose service labour is done and for whose benefit the produce of the labour is provided, can only be man himself.

If the product of labour does not belong to the worker, if it confronts him as an alien power, this can only be because it belongs to some other man than the worker. If the worker's activity is a torment to him, to another it must be delight and his life's joy. Not the gods, not nature, but only man himself can be this alien power over man. (*1844* 115)

What is most interesting for our purposes in working through these passages in Marx is that they generate at once an economic, a political, an aesthetic and a religious (or at any rate a spiritual) argument, in fact, an argument that is simultaneously and inextricably political, economic, aesthetic and religious (or spiritual). For one thing, the process of alienation that estranges the products of human labor from human beings themselves has according to Marx an exact correlate in religion. Just as 'the worker puts his life into the object' only then to see that 'his life no longer belongs to him but to the object', Marx argues, 'the more man puts into God the less he retains in himself' (*1844* 108). And the alienation of labor leads to the dissolution of the earliest (and according to Marx universal) aesthetic principles, for whereas animals (ants, bees, and so on) build and produce only in the most mindlessly material sense – in that they execute their works without imagination – human beings are capable of producing (and in unalienated conditions *do* produce) according to a universal standard of beauty in a way that unifies mental and manual labor, that fuses together conception and execution, ideal and real, imagination and materiality, and is able to express human freedom precisely by such universal production. 'A spider conducts operations which resemble those of the weaver, and a bee would put many a human architect to shame by the construction of its honeycomb cells', Marx would later point out in *Capital*, 'but what distinguishes the worst architect from the best of bees is that the architect builds the cell in his mind before he constructs it in wax. At the end of every labor process, a result emerges which had already been conceived by the [unalienated] worker at the beginning, hence already existed ideally' (284). Indeed, the art created through unalienated labor – genuine art – is for Marx the proof and foundation of our species being. Far from being the expression of individual consciousness, individual genius (in the Romantic sense of that term), such art for Marx reveals the true extent to which consciousness itself 'is from the very beginning a social product, and remains so as long as men exist at all' (*German Ideology* 158). And hence such art – like unalienated labor in general – reveals a bridge between imagination and the material world, between material and immaterial, between the particular and the general, the individual and the social or universal: it is the basis of life itself, or, as he puts it, our 'active species life' (*1844* 114).

In capitalism, all these continuities are split apart, so that not only is the worker alienated from the product of his labor, he is alienated from the object world surrounding him, which seems to gain more and more power over him the more alienated – and the more stripped of his imaginative, conceptual potential – he becomes, or in other words the more he himself becomes reduced to the level of an object, in an object world that seems to have assumed the very powers of subjectivity, and even in certain cases of divinity, of which he has been deprived. But if, of course, capitalist society is founded on the basis of alienated labor, what communism offers, according to Marx, is not merely freedom from the capitalist exploitation of labor but also a reunification of all those principles and practices – spiritual, material, economic, aesthetic and political – that the world of estranged or alienated labor had split apart, or in other words what he calls 'the consummated oneness in substance of man and nature' (*1844* 137). Communism therefore offers 'the re-integration or return of man to himself', Marx argues; it must be understood 'as the real appropriation of the human essence by and for man' and

as the complete return of man to himself as a social (i.e., human) being – a return become conscious, and accomplished within the entire wealth of previous human development. This communism is the genuine resolution of the conflict between man and man – the true resolution of the strife between existence and essence, between objectification and self-confirmation, between freedom and necessity, between the individual and the species. Communism is the riddle of history solved, and it knows itself to be this solution. (*1844* 135)

This is, however, a 'solution' in the form of practice and struggle rather than of illusory ideals toward which we should supposedly strive. 'Communism is for us not a state of affairs which is to be established, an *ideal* to which reality [will] have to adjust itself', Marx argues. Rather, he says, 'we call communism the *real* movement which abolishes the present state of things' (*German Ideology* 162). Communism hence exists not in ideal form but rather in the set of relations, affects and practices through which it is immanently constituted. Communism is in this sense not an abstraction toward which we should aspire, much less a bundle of abstract rights that we should demand from this or that power; rather, it is an ontological process that we should live in reconstituting a present free from alienation and exploitation. In short, communism is – or it ought to be – life itself.

Like Marx, Blake resisted both conceptually and in his own practice the alienation of labor which was the foundation of modern capitalism. And as with Marx, there is a very powerfully articulated ontological ground in Blake's understanding of work, of art, and of life itself. It would in fact be difficult to overstate the extent of Blake's concern with alienation. It appears in terms of his treatment of organized religion, as, for example, in those lines in *The Marriage of Heaven & Hell* where Blake reminds us 'that All deities reside in the human breast' (E38), and thus in effect anticipates Marx's point that human beings themselves endowed the object world around them with a sense of divinity, in the process seeming to forget that ultimately only human beings – not God or the gods – have power over other human beings. It also appears in his treatment of the modern industrial mode of production, which he experienced first-hand in his contact with the commercial world and tried to resist in his own labor on the illuminated books, in which he unified all the facets of production that the commercial publishing industry would ordinarily have broken down and distributed among a variety of trades. His resistance to alienation is even manifested in the form and design of the illuminated books themselves, which each exist in an array of heterogeneous 'copies' with no prior original or prototype, with often considerable variations among and between them, and with a significant degree of inter-referentiality – or really inter-dependence – among not only each copy of the 'same' book, but also the various copies of different books (among which certain lines of text and images were often recirculated), thereby totally undermining and subverting not only the logic of uniform replication which would allow contemporary observers (such as Charles Babbage) to see in the engraving process the prototype of all industrial factory production, but also the idea of the commodity as a unique and self-contained object.[5]

In thinking of the process of alienation in terms of what he called the separation of conception and execution (the kind of split that separates the commercial engraver from the 'original' artist who had already conceived the image that the engraver was merely supposed to replicate), Blake was able to link together economic, political, religious and aesthetic principles. For Blake saw that the distinction between conception and execution runs through and hence ties together a number of crucial social oppositions: the split between the *idea* of an art-work and its actual *composition* (a division that Blake profoundly resisted in his own work); the cleavage between the industrial worker, reduced in one of those dark satanic mills to merely muscular or physical motive power, and the intellectual faculty who directs and organizes the work in the factory, assigning each his place 'In sevens & tens & fifties, hundreds, thousands, numberd all / According to their various powers' (*FZ*33.19–20, E322); the division between the people and a thoroughly unrepresentative government; and, finally, the gap between a human being and the sense of divinity abstracted and alienated from him and projected onto a sense of God somehow outside of him (God the Father, God the Patriarch, God the Nobodaddy), which could allow him to forget not only that 'All deities reside in the human breast', but, moreover, that 'God is Man & exists in us & we in him' (E664). But if all these splittings apart seemed to Blake to be part of the same continuous process – manifested now in aesthetics, now in politics, now in religion – the point was that they could (and should) all be subjected to the same forms of resistance and subversion.

'Some will say, Is not God alone the Prolific?' Blake asks in *The Marriage of Heaven and Hell*; 'I answer, God only acts & Is, in existing beings or Men' (E40). Far more than simply resisting the separation or division of the human and the divine, Blake insists also that by reunifying what had otherwise been split apart, we can recognize the awesome creative and ontological power of the imagination, which for Blake was not a power to be distinguished as conception from execution or ideal from real, but was on the contrary a human capacity to reunify what had once been split apart. For if '[t]he Eternal Body of Man is THE IMAGINATION. that is God himself', the 'Divine Body' of which 'we are his Members' (E273), our collective life ought to be a life of endless, prolific creativity and indeed creation in the most profound ontological sense. Blake's concept of the imagination thus unifies body and mind, thought and action, the material and immaterial worlds; it defines an absolute unity of mental and bodily activity, or in other words the unity of the principles that by Blake's time had been split apart – thereby providing the very foundation of alienated labor – as conception from execution. The freedom to imagine in Blake's sense is thus the power to create the world, and in Blake that power is human rather than divine (or rather such divine power ought to be recognized as inherently human: 'God is Man & exists in us & we in him'). As a result, the ultimate political and economic – as well as religious and aesthetic – power (of creation, of making, of *poesis*) rests with humanity rather than with abstracted and alienated gods and rules, systems of nature, unquestionable structural principles which we are all routinely asked to obey precisely as though they had been naturally or divinely ordained in a way that would seem to place them safely beyond human intervention. For to affirm that 'the imagination' is God is to say that it is a principle of pure creativity, and to affirm that 'Man is all Imagination God is Man & exists in us & we in him' is to say that the power of the imagination is a collective human power, that humanity in the collective sense, not God in the abstract and alien sense (as in God & his Priest & King), possesses and defines creative power. Thus, in effect, what communism is for Marx, the imagination is for Blake: an immanent, collective, unifying, constituent power.

This may seem a bit of a leap, but it should come as less of a surprise when we consider that, in articulating this sense of the imagination, Blake was drawing on older, seventeenth-century understandings of the imagination (or fancy), such as James Harrington's or Spinoza's, for whom, as Antonio Negri has argued, 'fancy and imagination do not simply mediate between the concrete and the abstract – they are not epistemological functions; on the contrary, they are ontological and constitutive functions' (120–1), and hence they are functions that assume an immediately political character. For this reason, among others, this older conception of the imagination does not belong in a (private) realm separate and cut off from the public, the political, the social or the collective (or what Marx would later call the species being). This perhaps above all is why, with his insistence on the power of the imagination, it would be a terrible mistake to read, understand and think of Blake as an idealist (as has often been done). In order to appreciate his stance, however, we must take seriously the proposition that, as he says in the *Marriage*, 'a firm perswasion that a thing is so, make[s] it so' (E38), or in other words that 'perswasion', fancy, and imagination possess ontological, creative power, albeit as a collective rather than simply an individual function – which is why Blake invokes them as the prerogative not of one man but rather of that 'divine body' of which we are all 'members'. What Blake is interested in, then, is the imagination as a collective power, a power that constitutes life itself, and that in the process ties all human beings into that 'divine body' in which we all exist and which indeed we all constitute immanently, from within, from below. This sense of a humanly and immanently constituted creative, and really fully *human* God – essential to any full understanding of Blake – is surely one of the clearest points of contact between Blake's work in the eighteenth and nineteenth centuries and that older communist tradition running back into the seventeenth, certain strands of which would reappear in Marx himself.

As I suggested in the opening of this chapter, it is possible to locate just such a sense of God in various radical and communist experiments in mid-seventeenth-century England. Arguing against the narrowly defined appeal for political rights emanating from the so-called Levellers, an appeal which was firmly grounded in the logic of private property and self-propriety – where, via the more thoroughly elaborated theories of John Locke, it would remain through the eighteenth century and on into Blake's time and our own – Gerrard Winstanley, for example, called for the abolition of private property and the division of labor and for sharing of the earth and its fruits among all human beings, so that 'none shall lay claim to any creature and say, This is mine, and that is yours, This is my work, and that is yours. But every one shall put their hands to till the earth and bring up cattle, and the blessing of the earth shall be common to all' (27). For Winstanley, of course, such sharing in the material world was only the logical and appropriate correlate for the spiritual sharing and being in common that he identified with the 'universal spreading of the divine power, which is Christ in mankind', or in other words the immanent human constitution of the divine, the sense that 'mankind, thus drawn up to live and act in the law of love, equity and oneness, is but the great house wherein the Lord himself dwells, and every particular one a several mansion. And as one spirit of righteousness is common to all, so the earth and the blessings of the earth shall become common to all; for now all is but the Lord, and the Lord is the all in all' (20). Winstanley can be seen here to deploy a radical reading of the New Testament to ground his communist beliefs in the notion that humans can share 'one power in all' in order to constitute themselves as the all in all. Christ or God must in this sense be thought of not as transcendent, external, supervisory powers – alien to human beings – but rather as the immediate expressions of an immanent human power. For here not only does God exist in all creatures: God has no existence apart from the creatures (or, as Blake would phrase precisely this point a century later, 'God only acts & Is, in existing beings or Men'). Such a notion of God, and of human ontological and creative power, flourished in seventeenth-century England. In *The Light and Dark Sides of God*, for example, the antinomian Jacob Bauthumley would argue not only that God 'is the subsistence [that is, the substance] and Being of all Creatures and things, and fills Heaven and Earth and all other places', but also that God 'hath his Being no where else out of the Creatures'. Thus, Bauthumley could conclude, all creatures in the world 'are not so many distinct Beings, but they are one intire Being, though they be distinguished in respect of their formes; yet their Being is but one and the same Being, made out in so many formes of flesh, as Men and Beast, Fish and Fowle, Trees and Herbes' (232–3). Blake would sum up this standpoint in that memorable line from *The Marriage* (which would be reiterated in his other works), 'every thing that lives is Holy' (E45).

Nor was Blake alone in reiterating such antinomian and communist heresies in his own time. I mentioned earlier that there was a resurgence of interest in these arguments and points of view in Blake's lifetime, not only as expressions of religious belief in some mystical or otherworldly sense, but also as expressions of a clear political and economic stance against private property and that narrowly rights-based discourse of liberty which was in turn founded on the logic of private property and the division of labor. Richard Lee, for example, was one of the most outspoken of the anti-government radicals of the 1790s, and was as happy to proclaim his interest in 'King Killing' – the title of a leaflet that got him into some considerable trouble with the state – as he was to celebrate the coming of the eagerly anticipated new day when we shall all 'reap NATURE'S BLESSINGS unpaid for and free', when 'all the wide World sweet FREEDOM shall share', when 'The Earth, and the Sea, and the Stream shall resign, / To ALL undistinguish'd, whate'er they contain; / The Light of the Day on our Dwellings shall shine; / As freely as Heav'n first gave it to Men' (9–10). And Thomas Spence himself – most famous for his stubborn refusal to abandon his call for agrarian communism in the face of the bourgeois argument in favor of private political rights (as articulated most famously by Tom Paine) – also anticipated a happy future state, unmistakably Winstanleyan in tone and language, 'when there shall be neither lord nor landlords, but God and man will be all in all' (38). In fact Spence's communist enthusiasm ran through his work at least from as far back as 1782, when he wrote his 'SONG, to be sung at the end of oppression', which I just quoted, to his work in the early nineteenth century, when he would continue to condemn the 'specious, but partial Rights of Man' celebrated by Paine and his followers, and to anticipate instead the coming day of genuine freedom, the New Jerusalem indeed, when the whole earth shall

> be at rest and in quiet, and shall break forth into singing, and they shall say, 'Now we are free indeed! Our lands which God gave us to dwell upon are now our own: Our governments now free from aristocracy are easily supported with a small proportion of our rents; and the remainder being our own, we spend in parochial business and divide among ourselves. Amen' (38)

By the time Blake announced his own dissatisfaction with the 'happy consensus' with which he himself could not agree – on the rights-based 'intermeasurability' of Englishmen – the communist tradition was already undergoing the momentous set of transformations that would indeed enable it more adequately to contest the bourgeois logic of individual rights and monadic 'intermeasurability' while also articulating a more rigorous critique of capitalism. In the course of this transition, the communist tradition would lose (or abandon) the explicitly religious language which had propelled it from at least the seventeenth century on (and whose traces we can detect as late as Blake, Spence, Wedderburn, and Owen himself). It would, however, retain the underlying philosophical (we might even call them, in the strictest materialist sense as articulated by a Spinoza or a Blake, spiritual) basis of that language, namely, the emphasis on common unity and collective self-determination, the very sense of *species being* that would allow Marx and Engels to later develop the *Communist Manifesto*'s call for a society in which the free development of each is inseparable from the free development of all, or in other words, a society in which the one and the many – each and all – exist in a single, immanently constituted continuum, an 'all in all'. That the *Manifesto*'s call turns out to be a secular version of the older, religiously articulated, antinomian version of the same principle, ought not to trick us into thinking that they are not in fact part of the same long tradition, however discontinuous, uneven and heterogeneous it may turn out to be, a tradition in which Blake's work must be situated in order for it to make any sense at all.

For after all, in warning against the baleful prospect of a world in which 'art' or 'the arts' are alienated from the broader ensemble of material and imaginative practices that constitute life, Blake was also warning us away from a dead world, a world of objects, a world in which people and commodities alike are reduced to the level of 'intermeasurability' which in a way provides the social fuel necessary for the logic of capitalism. But if, on the other hand, 'the whole Business of Man Is The Arts', a new form of art presupposes a new way of understanding and making the world, a new way of living and of practice and struggle; and if, as Blake used to insist, 'the whole Business of Man Is The Arts & *All Things Common'* (E273, emphasis added), a new form of unalienated art presupposes a new way of sharing, of living, of being in common.

notes

1. See Iain McCalman, *Radical Underworld* 200; see also 181–203 in general. Also see Olive Rudkin, *Thomas Spence and his Connections* 180–203.
2. See Jon Mee, *Dangerous Enthusiasm: William Blake and the Culture of Radicalism in the 1790s* and *Romanticism, Enthusiasm and Regulation.*
3. See Saree Makdisi, *William Blake and the Impossible History of the 1790s.*
4. Hence the longstanding interest among twentieth-century Marxists and communists in the work of Spinoza. I am thinking here of Gilles Deleuze among others.
5. I discuss all these issues at much greater length in chapters 3 and 4 of *Impossible History.*

works cited and suggestions for further reading

Bauthumley, Jacob. *The Light and Dark Sides of God* in *A Collection of Ranter Writings from the Seventeenth Century.* Ed. Nigel Smith. London: Junction Books, 1983.
Deleuze, Gilles. *Spinoza: Practical Philosophy.* Trans. Robert Hurley. San Francisco: City Lights, 1988.
Engels, Friedrich. 'Socialism: Utopian and Scientific' in *The Marx–Engels Reader.* Ed. Robert Tucker. New York: Norton, 1978.
Erdman, David V. *Blake: Prophet Against Empire.* Princeton: Princeton University Press, 1977.
Ferber, Michael. *The Social Vision of William Blake.* Princeton: Princeton University Press, 1985.
Gilchrist, Alexander. *The Life of William Blake.* Reprint. Mineola, NY: Dover, 1998.
Hardt, Michael and Antonio Negri. *Empire.* Cambridge: Harvard University Press, 2001.
Hill, Christopher. *The World Turned Upside Down: Radical Ideas during the English Revolution.* Harmondsworth: Penguin, 1991.
Lee, Richard. 'Let us Hope to See Better Times' in *Songs from the Rock.* London: 1795.
Linebaugh, Peter and Marcus Rediker. *The Many-Headed Hydra: Sailors, Slaves, Commoners, and the Hidden History of the Revolutionary Atlantic.* Boston: Beacon Press, 2000.
Makdisi, Saree. *William Blake and the Impossible History of the 1790s.* Chicago: University of Chicago Press, 2003.

Marx, Karl. *Capital*. Vol. 1. Trans. Ben Fowkes. New York: Vintage, 1977.

———. *The Economic and Philosophic Manuscripts of 1844*. Trans. Martin Milligan. New York: International Publishers, 1964.

———. *The German Ideology* in *The Marx–Engels Reader*. Ed. Robert Tucker. New York: Norton, 1978.

McCalman, Iain. *Radical Underworld*. Cambridge: Cambridge University Press, 1988.

Mee, Jon. *Dangerous Enthusiasm: William Blake and the Culture of Radicalism in the 1790s*. Oxford: Oxford University Press, 1994.

———. *Romanticism, Enthusiasm and Regulation*. Oxford: Oxford University Press, 2003.

Morton, A.L. *The Everlasting Gospel: A Study in the Sources of William Blake*. London: Lawrence and Wishart, 1958.

———. *The Life and Ideas of Robert Owen*. New York: Monthly Review Press, 1963.

Negri, Antonio. *Insurgencies: Constituent Power and the Modern State*. Minneapolis: University of Minnesota Press, 1999.

Owen, Robert. *A New View of Society and Other Writings*. Ed. Gregory Claeys. Harmondsworth: Penguin, 1991.

Rudkin, Olive. *Thomas Spence and his Connections*. New York: Augustus Kelly, 1966.

Spence, Thomas. *The Political Works of Thomas Spence*. Ed. H.T. Dickinson. Newcastle: Avero, 1982.

Thompson, E.P. *The Making of the English Working Class*. New York: Vintage, 1966.

———. *Witness Against the Beast: William Blake and the Moral Law*. New York: New Press, 1993.

Winstanley, Gerrard. *Gerrard Winstanley: Selections from his Works*. Ed. Leonard Hamilton. London: Crescent Press, 1944.

Worrall, David. *Radical Culture: Discourse, Resistance, and Surveillance, 1790–1820*. New York: Harvester Wheatsheaf, 1993.

12
blake and postmodernism

edward larrissy

romanticism and postmodernism

The question of Blake and postmodernism may usefully be considered as part of the broader question of Romanticism and postmodernism, which is beginning to become a subject of intellectual debate. A traditional model of the relationship between past and present might be used to support the claim that, just as modernism was indebted to Romanticism, so postmodernism is indebted to such features as Romantic irony, the cult of the rootlessly self-fashioning hero, and possibly a certain valuing of the incomplete and fragmentary. There are also some more particular questions: the continuing fascination of the Gothic, and the theory of Lyotard that both modernism and postmodernism are inheritors of the concept of the sublime (specifically the Kantian sublime), an idea with strong romantic connections.[1] All of these possibilities are addressed in my edited volume, *Romanticism and Postmodernism* (1999), which includes essays touching on Wordsworth, Coleridge and Gothic fiction. It also includes a theoretical essay by Paul Hamilton which traces the ancestry of postmodernist 'indeterminacy' back to the concept of the sublime: associating the poetics of the sublime with the fashion for pantheism, Hamilton notes that 'the monism resulting from pantheism, in which, since you cannot find God "outside" you must find him everywhere, has all sorts of other implications. Fundamentally, it makes all critique immanent. It leads to the equality of particulars' (27).

Lyotard's thesis includes the influential notion that the postmodern 'would be that which, in the modern, puts forward the unpresentable in presentation itself; that which denies itself the solace of good forms' (81). The idea of the 'unpresentable' is developed out of his discussion of the sublime, which, according to Lyotard, 'takes place [...] when

254

the imagination fails to present an object which might, if only in principle, come to match a concept' (78). The idea of the unpresentable clearly has the potential for flexible adaptation to all kinds of artistic experiment, though Lyotard makes the important qualification that modern and postmodern aesthetics take different approaches to it: modern aesthetics, unlike postmodern, remain 'nostalgic', longing for what is 'missing' (81). What is missing is some totalizing framework which traditionally would have been conceived in terms of what Lyotard calls a 'grand narrative'. For our purposes it is interesting to note that William H. Galperin, in *The Return of the Visible in British Romanticism* (1993), asserts the 'postmodernism' of Byron's *Childe Harold* in a manner which is indebted to Lyotard. Specifically, he finds Cantos I and II to be characterized by postmodernism because they show the visible world without assimilating it to an overarching narrative, even as they gesture towards narratives of various kinds. In Canto IV, the narrator is seen as renouncing his appropriation of the visible at points where he is represented as feminized, and this too is seen by Galperin in terms of the category of postmodernism (257–70).

Some (though not all) of these topics are of obvious potential relevance to Blake. For instance, it could be said that Blake's irony is far more destabilizing than would be allowed by an interpretation that showed it as undermining false prospectuses of one kind or another. Thus, one may concede that there is undoubtedly a strategy in *Songs of Innocence and of Experience* which leads us towards mutual ironizing as constitutive of the relationship between the two 'contrary states': the reader perceives the limitations of each state, and is led to ask how the qualities of each might be enhanced, and the limitations overcome, by their integration. But it is possible to suggest that this strategy is itself undermined by a combination of factors. The subtlety and far-reachingness of the irony, combined with the absence of a clear way out of the impasse of innocence and experience, and the way in which each contrary term actually contains hints of its supposed opposite, could be claimed to demonstrate that this binary was in fact a way of representing an unstable politics of power in the self and in society: one that was too unstable, indeed, to be explained in terms of a political ideology. As we shall see, precisely this kind of point is made by Nicholas Williams, in his *Ideology and Utopia in the Poetry of William Blake* (1998), though he uses the example of *The Marriage of Heaven and Hell* (209–19). It is worth noting that he also links the ideological indeterminacy of *The Marriage* to Lyotard's concept of the 'unpresentable' (212).

But to return to Romanticism in general, it must always be remembered that we ourselves are to a significant degree constructing the Romanticism to which we are supposedly to some degree indebted. This is a process which has been going on since the word 'Romanticism' was adapted in the 1840s to define a supposed movement, after most of those we now think of as the canonical Romantic poets were dead. In the so-called 'Romantic period' it was Walter Scott, Samuel Rogers and Thomas Moore who dominated the poetic scene, as Byron recorded in his journals (3: 220). These writers were gradually replaced over the course of the nineteenth century by the canon we have come to know in the twentieth, a process involving, among other things, the further promotion of Wordsworth and Coleridge and the addition of Blake. When one analyzes this in more detail, it appears that the canonization of this group is in fact part of a wider tendency towards Modernism. Indeed, their canonization is only part of the story, for there is also selection within their works, in such a way that the lyrical and the intense is valued over the discursive. Thus Frank Kermode, in his classic work *Romantic Image* (1957), can isolate a tradition of concentration on the image, of allowing its radiance or eloquence to do the work of the discursive, a process which clearly leads up to Modernism. Arguably, however, the thesis, though valid, is made to look more straightforward than it really is by an unwillingness to confront the complexity of the literary history of the large period it surveys. In this connection it seems worth noting that, in the contemporary era, Blake has become one of the most approved artists from the past, and this too is something the postmodern appears to share with the modern. Blake was admired by Wilde, Yeats, Shaw, Auden and Huxley. He went on to be admired also by Dylan Thomas, Ginsberg, Ted Hughes, Geoffrey Hill and Angela Carter. One of the interesting questions about Blake and the canon is why he appears to be important to the process by which the modernists defined themselves and why, in the postmodern, he continues to be important, becoming one of the few sages to be largely immune from postmodernist habits of cynicism and debunking.

The postmodern also brings to the past a self-consciousness about reading and interpretation, about the inescapability of sign and convention, and about the inaccessibility of any truth beyond such signs, for which arguably there is no strong precedent in the Romantic period. However, the point about the inaccessibility of truth is that it bears on questions of historical truth, and this complicates the idea of constructing the past. For some postmodern thinkers, there is no truth or historical reality to construct, for the fact that one cannot get beyond the interpretative sign means that one cancels out the idea of objective truth in the equation: it simply has no function. A radical expression of this view is to be found in Ira Livingston's *Arrow of Chaos: Romanticism and Postmodernity* (1997), in which he characterizes changes in historical views and historiography in relation to the image of a snake which represents the whole of history. In such changes, 'history *really* moves across its whole length at once or doesn't move at all', and he goes on, correctly, to point out that, 'This is very different from weaker assertions that our perspective on the past and future change, or that we "reinterpret" events as we will come to be reinterpreted. These assertions are simply damage-control maneuvers to preserve the notion of an objective reality' (14). Livingston's book is a significant contribution to the question of Romanticism and Postmodernity, but it has added relevance for our discussion since he attempts, as we shall see, to promote his thesis with some interesting discussions of Blake. As far as the general question about Romanticism and postmodernism is concerned, not surprisingly we find the whole snake (or perhaps just the snake from the Romantic period onwards) moving in a very postmodern kind of way. The canceling out of objective reality is important, but even more significant is the accompanying assumption that chaos theory furnishes the postmodern with its chief intellectual paradigm. Fractal patterns iterate all the way down the snake of history. For that matter, the word 'pattern' is too univocal: we should think of 'patterns, tricks, episteme engines, ideologemes, programs, protocols, genes, dynamos, mantras, paradigms, metaphors, metonyms, symbols', and so on, and they are to be understood as shallow rather than 'deep' structures (2). These 'tricks' or 'patterns' are structured around similarity and difference: 'things are always falling apart and together in the drift of the Arrow of Chaos' (xi). This, then, is the process that iterates all the way up and down history, and from the smallest to the largest cultural phenomena.

blake and the postmodern: an early theory

An early attempt to relate Blake and 'the postmodern' was that of Hazard Adams in 1969, in Alvin H. Rosenfeld's collection, *Essays for S. Foster Damon*. He notes, though without offering many examples, that 'postmodernism' in literary theory encourages a dialectical criticism 'of a Blakean sort', but is also influenced by Husserl's phenomenology and by existentialism (7). The reference to dialectic evokes the period of the rise of the New Left and the revival of Marxist criticism in the English-speaking world. Adams also reminds his readers that languages 'build actuality' in Blake, who is inimical to the idea of 'unmediated experience' (17). This was an emphasis promoted at roughly the same time by another respected Blakean (to whom Adams refers) – Northrop Frye, in his collection of essays, *The Stubborn Structure* (1970). Frye's insistence on the inseparability of literature, education and knowledge from structures, forms and conventions was congenial in a period when structuralism had joined Marxism as a fashionable intellectual current.[2] This insistence, as is well known, had grown out of his study of Blake in *Fearful Symmetry* (1947), which pre-dated and prepared the ground for his great theoretical work, *The Anatomy of Criticism* (1957).

There is yet more to be learned from Adams's essay: references on the one hand to phenomenology and on the other to the linguistically constructed world again make it very much of its time, a period when English-speaking readers are aware of the phenomenologist Merleau-Ponty's essays in *Signs* (1960, trans. 1964) as well as of the early work of Barthes. Merleau-Ponty's essays mark the point at which a Husserlian concern with intentionality, perception and living experience enters into negotiation with structuralism, including structural linguistics.[3] It is worth remembering that this is the area of negotiation in which Derrida began to evolve his characteristic concepts, even though his conclusions are not sympathetic to Merleau-Ponty's. The key concept of *différance* was developed, in *Speech and Phenomena* (1967, trans. 1973), as a central part of the critique of Husserl's notion of self-present signification. Arguably, there is thus a broad connection between the ideas discussed in Adams's essay and later postmodernist developments. This is also suggested by his characterization of postmodernism as involving plurality and difference in the construction of reality: he notes with approbation that Ernst Cassirer 'refused to limit ways of knowing to the understanding and proposed the existence of additional ways of "constituting" reality' (9).

It would be unfortunate, though, if one were merely to see the importance of Adams's essay through the lens of our own fashionable perspective. Contemporary readers may have something to learn, and to apply to Blake, by re-examining the phenomenological idea of the bodily situatedness of the subject. But the still noticeable distance of Adams's essay from the dominant theoretical trends of today may also serve to remind us that in the late 1960s 'postmodernism' was a term used without its current implication of a profoundly ironic, and possibly alienated, world-view. In those days, it seemed to refer either to further developments of modernism or simply to the world after modernism without any confident sense of what that world was like. For this reason, I prefer to use the word 'postmodernity' or 'the postmodern' as a term to cover the whole period from the mid-twentieth century onwards, and 'postmodernism' for the radically ironic tendencies in some art from the 1980s onwards. In what follows, 'postmodernism' is subsumed into a discussion of Blake in postmodernity.

blake in postmodernity

It is something of a truism of literary history that the 1940s, under the pressure of war and social crisis, see a reassertion of the Romantic tradition in a manner which is congenial to the idea of the artist's privileged and therapeutic vision of ancient and possibly sacred truths. Perhaps one of the most Blakean literary works in English literature is Joyce Cary's *The Horse's Mouth* (1944), whose artist narrator's every perception is buttressed by a quotation from the master. Gulley Jimson is known to be based on the painter Stanley Spencer, who was indeed influenced by Blake. The novel's date offers a plausible point of entry into the postmodern. Set in London just before the outbreak of the Second World War, it nevertheless seems a characteristic work of Forties Britain in its valuing of the visionary and forthrightly anti-bourgeois artistic genius, selflessly dedicated to his work in a world of unpredictable chaos. Its outrageously bohemian ambience of drunken pub-going painters and self-taught intellectuals also seems very much of its time. Blake's works, which are quoted with genuine knowledge and understanding, are enlisted in the service of the idea of artistic genius, and Jimson also pays Blake the tribute of putting a high valuation on the ideal in art. Thus he labors for many pages over a painting of 'The Fall'. Nevertheless, one of the delights of this appropriately energetic and witty book resides in its memorable, if painterly, evocations of the sensuous and concrete: indeed, the painterliness is really as significant as the sensuousness, for it implies that Jimson is far more indebted to impressionism, in the broadest sense of the term, than his Blakean utterances would suggest. Indeed, as Annette S. Levitt points out, Jimson's thoughts about his own career focus on Turner, Manet and Cézanne (187). This hardly seems surprising, since it offers the artistic correlative of his bitter-sweet infatuation with the chaotic experience in which he is immersed.

The book offers an allegorical counterpart of this oblique relationship to Blake in its presentation of the hero's lovers. The eleventh to thirteenth chapters show Jimson reciting much of 'The Mental Traveller' to himself and relating it to his experience. In particular, the female principle of the poem – the 'woman old', the 'maiden' – is identified with the women in his life: 'Till he, that is Gulley Jimson, became a bleeding youth. And she, that is Sara, becomes a virgin bright' (52). Indeed, some of his most significant paintings have been depictions of these women, particularly of the Sara referred to here: some of the paintings – the 'bath' paintings, for instance – sound as if they are influenced by impressionism, since they obviously recall the work of Pierre Bonnard. But Blake's female is not to be closely related to individual women, being a symbolic representation of what he calls 'Nature'. Jimson is certainly aware of other connotations of the female in Blake's work – among other things, he equates the male–female relationship in 'The Mental Traveller' with the artist's imaginative mastery of experience. But an important element in the book resides in the appreciation of women's beauty, and in the love (however flawed) of women as individuals. Such love, it becomes clear, has been at the center of Jimson's life, and the book contains many poignant passages where the old man reflects on this fact. Blake seems to operate in this novel as a symbol, for one who is far more submissive to 'Nature' than Blake, of a desirable pursuit of the ideal in art. Appropriately enough, though, the reader is well aware that the 'historical Blake soon disappears from Gulley's commentary' (190).

There are grounds for thinking of this problematic relationship between chaotic experience and a sage who represents an ideal as characteristically postmodern. The work of Cary's friend Iris Murdoch offers a case in point.[4] She is frequently discussed as a postmodern artist these days: even as a postmodernist. Yet her life-long meditation on Plato, and her commitment to the search for truth and goodness, can make her look an unlikely candidate for such descriptions. But it is the search that is important to her: the idea of a secure possession of these things is a dangerous illusion. As Peter Conradi puts it, 'There are short glimpses of clarity and insight, but the single Big Truth is always illusory' (*Saint and Artist* 372). Furthermore, Murdoch makes it difficult for the reader of her works to arrive at a Big Truth about her fictional meanings, through her manipulation of point of view and the unreliable narrator. In the case of Cary, the gap between the long, italicized quotations from Blake and the experience and practice of the artist is patent, sometimes painfully so. This type of gap is different in kind from that which we perceive between myth and reality in modernist works such as Eliot's *Waste Land* or even Joyce's *Ulysses*. Both of these use the mock-heroic device of contrasting the unheroic present with the aura of the past, and one may discern a parallel between that aura and the authority invested by Cary and Murdoch in Blake or Plato. Nevertheless, Eliot's use of myth seeks to tell a central truth about all human experience, past or present, and Joyce's references to the *Odyssey*, while they ironically underscore his valuing of the facticity of modern life, also imply a humanist reading of the Greek epic. Things are not so secure with Cary, and his obtrusive foregrounding of the gap between experience and interpretation makes him a remote forebear of postmodernist writers such as Pynchon or Iain Sinclair. Interestingly, Oedipa Maas, the heroine of Pynchon's *The Crying of Lot 49*, regards Blake, along with Berkeley, as one of her most important points of reference, although there is undoubtedly an uncertain hint of irony in this fact: a suggestion of a mental imposition on experience, in line with her famous question, 'Shall I project a world?' This, however, is precisely illustrative of the general point.

In this neo-Romantic period of the 1940s, Blake is also important to the work of Dylan Thomas and Kathleen Raine. Thomas's work is indebted to Blake, to the Wordsworth of 'Intimations of Immortality', and of course to Yeats, for images of innocence and experience, of a redeemed and miraculous nature, and of the poet as visionary. Indebtedness of this kind is obvious in, for instance, 'Fern Hill'. Dylan Thomas's admiration for Blake is well-attested and is a determinant in the development of a symbolism of contraries which operates at several levels: there is an opposition between what is creative and what deadening. But there may also be a very Blakean opposition between the contrasting manifestations of what is sacred or creative, which may seem cruel and violent as well as kind. There is a corresponding contrast in the attitudes of the speaker, which may be rebellious or tender. As a critic, Kathleen Raine reads Blake as a visionary re-interpreter of an ancient mystical tradition incorporating the truths of neo-Platonism, the Kabbalah, and philosophical alchemy. While her own poetry is gentler and less assertive than that of Blake, it is clear that she sees herself as being in the same tradition. The postmodern is a period of increasing uncertainty and moral relativism, and it is striking to see the way in which Blake appears at this stage already to be accounted a sage in possession of insights which are still relevant. At the same time, Blake is often associated with, or at least conscripted in support of, bohemian wildness, in a late-Romantic fashion which does not accord with current scholarly interpretations. These, on the whole, are more aware of Blake's seriousness about the political.

Although an account which includes the word 'bohemian' might also be offered of Blake's role in the work of Robert Duncan and Allen Ginsberg, it would be qualified by the word 'Beat'. They share with Dylan Thomas a confidence about harnessing Blake's influence to a late Romantic agenda of their own, but unlike Thomas, they can also be seen as late Modernists, responding to (among other things) the influence of Pound and Williams on the poetic line. They are avant-garde poets, believers in the unsullied freshness of their vision, and cannot be assimilated to that category of postmodernism which embodies irony about form and convention, or anxiety about the role of their many mentors. Not surprisingly, Blake's influence has to compromise with elements of an American modernist inspiration. In Duncan's work, as befits one who was associated with Black Mountain and was an avowed admirer of Charles Olson, there is a palpable emphasis on experience and process. As Robert J. Bertholf puts it,

> while Blake evolves a complicated system with a cast of characters, divisions of those characters, a symbolic landscape, and a host of derived associations which define, in mythological form, his vision of mythological reality, Duncan evolves a poetry of process in which the drive of the imagination to propose approximations of eternal images takes precedence over the approximations which illustrate that process. (94)

The general tenor of Duncan's poetry is consonant with Olson's idea of 'Projective Verse' which comprises an emphasis on the poet's direct transfer of energy onto the page. Accordingly, Duncan can refer to '[t]he design of a poem' as 'constantly under reconstruction', something where 'thot shows its pattern', 'a proposition / in movement' (*Derivations* 9). We discover in the same place that this process is embodied in 'alternations of sound, sensations', and the reference to sensations seems appropriate to the model of experience implied elsewhere by Duncan. Thus, in 'Variations on Two Dicta of William Blake', when he meditates upon the assertion that 'Mental things alone are real', and invokes Olson as an example of a poet whose work illustrates the truth of that assertion, he introduces him in relation to the 'change in pulse' which occurs when the heart receives an 'answer', and goes on to describe how words can 'awaken / sensory chains between being and being'. He also recalls that 'like stellar bees my senses swarmed' (*Roots* 51). This emphasis on the senses within the general depiction of experience as process is not notably Blakean, and in fact Duncan explicitly revises Blake's dictum about 'Mental things' by adding his own qualification that 'There is no mental thing unrealized'. This reformulation, while its precise philosophical bearings might be inexplicit, certainly shifts the terrain from the mental to a channel of transformation issuing in something relatively concrete and embodied, while at the same time taking Blake's more idealist formulation as its starting-point (50). The simile of the stellar bees implies a parallel notion: the bees are the senses, and the idea of their swarming vividly evokes their activity; but their 'stellar' quality connotes the mental in the form of the ideal and is a gesture towards Blake.

Anyone who knows anything about Allen Ginsberg knows that his sense of poetic vocation is founded on the relationship with Blake, in the sense that it was given decisive impetus by a visionary encounter which issued in a dedication of the self. In 1948, living in East Harlem while a student at Columbia, he heard 'the voice of Blake himself' while he was masturbating and reading 'Ah! Sun-Flower': Ginsberg realized that he himself was the sunflower, and this realization issued in a sense of the profound significance of his momentary existence as part of the 'spirit of the universe' (Miles 208). As a result, Ginsberg believed that 'from now on I'm chosen, blessed, sacred poet' (Portugés 23). Appropriately enough, his works are full of references to Blake, and a number of them catch something of the Blakean prophetic note.

Chief among these are 'Howl' and its brief sequel, 'Footnote to Howl', which was written contemporaneously. This contains the line 'Everything is holy! everybody's holy! everywhere is holy! everyday is an eternity! Everyman's an angel!' The reference to *The Marriage of Heaven and Hell*, and the idea of the immanence of eternity, are sure pointers to the influence of Blake. Most of the expansive lines in the 'Footnote' begin with the word 'Holy', and parallelism of this kind, combined with a long and relatively loose line, is reminiscent of Blake and of the prophetic poetry of the Bible which both Blake and Ginsberg are imitating. But this fact should serve to remind us that this stylistic influence is also transmitted to the twentieth century via Whitman. Indeed, it is significant that in *Howl and Other Poems* a tribute to Whitman ('A Supermarket in California') follows immediately after the 'Footnote', beginning with the famous words, 'What thoughts I have of you tonight Walt Whitman' (29). The statement in 'Footnote' that 'The bum's as holy as the seraphim!', while not itself notably Whitmanesque in style, is more akin to Whitman than to Blake in its trenchant assertion of the democratic. Furthermore, apart from biblical parallelism there is another feature of Ginsberg's style which is reminiscent of Whitman, namely the accretion of details, sometimes approximating lists. A useful example can be found in Ginsberg's Moloch, whom Ostriker describes as 'a broadly Urizenic figure' (121). This is apt, and there are similarities even in the lists of Moloch's attributes and connections provided by Ginsberg:

Moloch whose mind is pure machinery! Moloch whose blood is running
   money! Moloch whose fingers are ten armies! Moloch whose breast
   is a cannibal dynamo! Moloch whose ear is a smoking tomb! [...]
Moloch whose love is endless oil and stone! Moloch whose soul is
   electricity and banks! Moloch whose poverty is the specter of genius!

Moloch whose fate is a cloud of sexless hydrogen! Moloch whose
name is the Mind! (21–2)

Just as in Blake, there are plenty of contemporary phenomena which
count as Urizenic. If we know the Bible, we know that Moloch 'is the
Canaanite god of fire to whom children were offered in sacrifice', and we
may infer that for Ginsberg, as for Blake, Moloch 'represents the obsessive
human sacrifice of war' (Ostriker 120, 121). But unlike in Blake there is
little attempt to specify the characteristics of Moloch as a personification,
and there is no Fall narrative. In sum, this quality of the accretion of
lists contrasts with Blake's structured allegorical landscape, which, as in
Duncan, is absent.

There are other stylistic features which contrast with Blake, and these
might be pointedly illustrated by some lines which actually refer to him:
near the beginning of 'Howl' Ginsberg is qualifying 'the best minds
of [his] generation', the 'angelheaded hipsters burning for the ancient
heavenly connection to the starry dynamo', and notes that (among many
other things) they 'passed through universities with radiant cool eyes
hallucinating Arkansas and Blake-light tragedy among the scholars of
war, / who were expelled from the academies for crazy & publishing
obscene odes on the windows of the skull' (9). This is very characteristic
of Ginsberg: it offers Burroughs-like kennings with narcotic connotations,
but is also slightly reminiscent of symbolism in its deliberately surprising
suggestiveness: what is it to 'hallucinate Arkansas'? Perhaps a memory of
a rustic home. What is 'Blake-light tragedy'? This seems slightly harder
to identify. None of these stylistic features is especially reminiscent of
Blake, but they do suggest that counter-cultural area where Modernism,
surrealism, symbolism and the influence of popular culture join to promote
a demotic version of the drug-inspired bohemian late-Romantic sage.

Somewhat unexpectedly, perhaps, given the genuineness of his
indebtedness to D.H. Lawrence, and the seriousness of his interest in the
visionary powers of the imagination, there is a strong case for seeing Ted
Hughes's *Crow* (first edition 1970), as a significantly postmodern response
to Blake. In the quasi-mythological and decidedly unmelodious 'songs' in
Crow, in which there is an element of the parody of Genesis, it is possible
to discern a similarity with another such parody, Blake's *The Book of
Urizen* (1794). Furthermore, the famous dust jacket illustration by Leonard
Baskin is arguably intended to function as a kind of 'illumination'. As
David Trotter notes, *Crow* 'might almost be part of the "Bible of Hell"
announced by Blake in *The Marriage of Heaven and Hell*: a counter-myth,
Creation and Fall seen from a different point of view' (200–1). This is by

no means a far-fetched suggestion. Hughes's interest in mythology and in philosophical alchemy (alchemy interpreted as spiritual symbolism), although it owes something to his reading of Jung, makes Blake a sympathetic forebear. Such a suggestion would be supported by works such as *Cave Birds: An Alchemical Cave Drama* (1978), which presents the reconciliation of the sexual contraries by reference to the idea of an alchemical marriage: that is, to the many symbols of the marriage of opposites which are to be found in the alchemical tradition, a tradition upon which Blake was drawing in *The Marriage of Heaven and Hell*. This book also intersperses the text with illustrations by Baskin.

The postmodernity of Hughes's *Crow* would reside in the combination of two factors which Trotter discusses in terms of a quality he calls 'anti-pathos': first, and more simply, there is the shocking squalor of what Hughes offers as a creation myth; secondly, as Trotter nicely puts it, Hughes's aim is 'to put about as many stories as possible, or as many versions of one story, rather than to describe a first-coming creator and so nurture the pathos of origins' (202). This aim seems postmodern, and might be seen in the light of concepts such as Lyotard's idea of the death of grand narratives. And arguably the connection to Blake is one which makes us aware of the postmodernism in Blake: it is notoriously difficult to isolate an original structure for Blake's myth. Here we have one of those indications as to why Blake remains such a congenial figure in the postmodern.

Later references to Blake seem increasingly dark, harnessing Gothic elements in his work to our own postmodern Gothic. The occasional references to Blake in the gloomier sort of graphic novels and thrillers offer a handy example. Thomas Harris's *Red Dragon* (1981) includes the incident where a killer called Dolarhyde, who thinks that he is possessed by Blake's image of the Red Dragon from Revelation (*The Great Red Dragon and the Woman Clothed with the Sun*), devours the original watercolor. In another best-selling novel, Michael Dibdin's clever Gothic-influenced thriller, *Dark Spectre* (1995), Sam, a disturbed Vietnam veteran, founds a society of drifters called The Sons of Los, and teaches them to murder at random, on the theory (which he thinks Blakean) that those they happen to choose are damned. Both these novels are arguably offering slightly more than a superficial reference to something almost manichean in Blake's vision. Furthermore, as Shirley Dent and Jason Whittaker remark, Blake has 'come to signify in the popular imagination a shorthand for a particular type of evil: a demented, perverse but highly intelligent, even empathetic, evil associated particularly with psychopaths and serial killers' (165). This, of course, is only one of the things that Blake can mean today, but the fact that there is some truth in the remark demands understanding. It looks as if, in a society which is increasingly paranoid about the extent to which it is influenced by dark forces of multinational capital, or the extent to which it is coming adrift from any center of value, or simply about the persistence of evil and suffering in a society of plenty, Blake is seen as offering appropriate imagery – even if, as with Dibdin, the implied view of him is not unambiguously complimentary. It should, of course, be remembered that Dibdin's title refers ironically to his hero, who is alienated from the feminine; and given his war experiences it is clear that an accusatory finger is being pointed at society and the state. But the title also refers critically to the dark unconscious of the 1960s: the reference to Manson is no less obvious for being inexplicit. The implication is that Blake's antinomianism is too easy for us to appropriate, and that this may have its dangers. Blake, it is suggested, offers a well-intentioned analysis of evil, and one where postmodernity finds his mistrust of authority congenial; but his liberating message may lead to a malleable ethics and offer a hidden opportunity for unhinged malevolence.

Red Dragon raises similar questions, in so far as the ingestion of a Blake painting can figure the incorporation of authority. But it also offers a reflection on the status of works of art, since the authority of a Blake painting derives from its high-art status and is inseparable from its aura. The novel self-consciously obtrudes these concerns by exploiting the implications of Dolarhyde's profession as film developer. He chooses his victims from home-movies he has developed, and subsequently splices in footage of their slaughter and also of himself with a copy of Blake's *Red Dragon*. Furthermore, he is described as hoping that 'he could maintain some aesthetic distance, even in the most intimate moments' (77). As Nicholas Williams points out, this episode 'forms part of a reflection on the competing claims of high art and mass reproduction' ('Eating' 155). Indeed, it could be said that Dolarhyde performatively undermines the claims of high art for autonomy even as he paradoxically submits to them, while at the same time he demonstrates that the kinetic affect of popular art (he masturbates while watching his film) is deferred and complicated by the demands of the aesthetic. As Williams puts it, this indicates a double failure: Dolarhyde can neither maintain 'aesthetic distance' nor 'intimacy', a fact which is predicated on a view which shows 'high' and 'low' art approximating each other, not least in the problems of representation which confront both.

Williams also notes that the eating of a Blake figures the consumption of art. He brings to bear two complementary frameworks of interpretation, that of Bourdieu, who links the consumption of high art to the class-based prestige it confers on the consumer, and that of Michel de Certeau, who, by contrast, emphasizes the active role of appropriation (140–7). Williams does not privilege one view over the other, drawing illumination from Derrida's discussion of the way the eater both incorporates and learns from the other that is eaten. He notes that both views involve sacrifice, either by the 'propitiation of the faceless god of necessary social structures (Bourdieu)', or by the destruction of 'the oppressive high art text (Certeau)' (146). In this perspective, the undoubted 'superficiality' of Harris's references to Blake are not only understandable, but necessary, since notwithstanding the broad outlines of Gothic imagery the most important thing is the art-work's symbolic status in these transactions (147). Nevertheless, Blake turns out to be a very fitting object of consumption in the light of his own incorporation of Milton via his foot, which permits him both to expand his own 'productive poetic vision' and to prepare for the self-annihilation which will unite him with Milton (149).

Blake has made his way into non-anglophone cultures, also, sometimes as part of the wider phenomenon of what I term 'postcolonial romanticisms'.[5] As part of this voyage he has been adopted by the Asian culture which, more than most, may lay claim to having entered the postmodern: that of Japan. He has long enjoyed popularity there, partly because of his supposed mysticism, which strikes a chord in a nation imbued with Buddhism. He makes a strange, poignantly discordant appearance in a work which bears the imprint of postmodernity, not least because of the way that it handles what it presents as Blake's 'wisdom'. Kenzaburo Oe's *Rouse Up O Young Men of the New Age* (1983, trans. 2002) offers the first-person narrative of a novelist who has a mentally and physically disabled son. The painful, moving and awkward episodes he has to recount are interwoven with his earnest reading of Blake, which is clearly motivated by a desire to learn, but also comprises a stranger element, whereby some hidden sympathy is suggested between the events which currently preoccupy him and the particular lines of Blake he is studying. This is another example, then, of the postmodern adoption of Blake as sage, but it also raises characteristically postmodern questions about the grounding of interpretation, and in a characteristically postmodern way: the question is raised whether the narrator is imposing a subjective interpretation, and the sublimity of some of Blake's lines contrasts piquantly with the pathos and ordinariness of the lives depicted. Yet the book also raises political and moral questions about the post-war development of Japanese society: how can a society which has been steeped in militarism, and which is strongly influenced by a traditional male warrior-code, come to accept the humanity of his touchingly comical, lugubrious and tender son, whom for most of the book he calls 'Eeyore'? Who, then, are 'the young men of the new age', and in what manner will they 'rouse up'?

The Gothic strain is also present in Iain Sinclair's books, *Lud Heat* (1975) and *Suicide Bridge* (1979), but arguably they conform more truly to the narrow definition of postmodernism proposed above, in embodying postmodernist blends of Burroughs-like prose and post-Olsonian poetry, which make extensive and significant use of Blake. Hand and Hyle, for instance, re-appear as sinister agents of late capitalism. There is a significant thread of parody in these books, for instance of the popular occult, which helps to validate the description 'postmodernist'. Thus it is maintained in *Lud Heat* that the Hawksmoor churches in London are linked by sinister lines of force, and that this sinister character can be gauged in part from the Egyptian motifs to be found in them. (Blake's negative symbolism of Egypt is cited in evidence.) Apart from referring to these connections in his text, Sinclair provides a useful map (8–9). Dent and Whittaker put it well when they say that Sinclair overlays 'a hieratic chart across London and thus uses Blake's systems of configuration of Albion, such as Los's naming of cities and attributing parts of the body and country to points of the compass, in an attempt to extrapolate a mysterious code' (61). The dark London of Sinclair's work is a place of mysterious evil forces which have found a new and congenial home in the postmodern, but which Blake understood in a way which is still relevant. On the other hand, the bizarre pseudo-scientific and occult connotations of Sinclair's map suggest a contrast with Blake: as if, where Blake offers the truth of vision, Sinclair is parodying the work of those who actually believe in the objective truth of occult forces such as he describes. But because of the eccentricity of such a view, the result is to make his map seem like a subjective imposition, on the lines of Slothrop's map of London in Pynchon's *Gravity's Rainbow*, which in any case is probably an influence. Pynchon and Sinclair are in the same postmodernist universe, where the map becomes a figure for paranoid interpretation. On the other hand, the fact that Blake's own mapping activities can be an influence on Sinclair's in itself suggests that they look sufficiently arbitrary and subjective themselves to be a congenial source for this kind of postmodernist topos. Jim Jarmusch's film *Dead Man* (1996) provides a close analogy in its playing with arbitrary-seeming interpretation. It offers another version of Blake as sage in a chaotic world, this time associating him with shamanic wisdom. But reality is mysterious, and the chief protagonist in a sense becomes Blake, the poet and painter, because his own name happens to be William Blake.

blake and theory

Whether motivated by an interest in Lyotard on the sublime, or deconstruction, or chaos theory, or the work of Walter Benjamin, contemporary theoretical treatments of Blake have stressed the plurality of meanings and the effects of difference in his work. As for deconstruction, while it is something of a solecism to equate poststructuralist theory with postmodernism, there is a cogent argument that the work of Derrida, in particular, has been a major instigating factor in the development of the late twentieth-century/early twenty-first-century postmodernist sensibility and a major influence on the criticism which appreciates and promotes postmodernism in art. While not definitively deconstructionist, Nelson Hilton's *Literal Imagination* (1983) is congenial to that trend in the importance it accords to polysemy. Peter Otto's *Constructive Vision and Visionary Deconstruction* (1991) points to Blake's deconstruction of tyrannous unities, but believes that ultimately an important difference between Blake and Derrida resides in the former's unironic rousing of the faculties to act. My own *William Blake* (1985) brings together deconstruction and Marxist criticism in a manner broadly analogous to the contemporaneous 'deconstructive materialism' of Marjorie Levinson in her work on Wordsworth and Keats.[6] I note the way in which Blake's works make reference to a number of discourses which are to some extent incommensurate with each other: antinomian Protestantism, mainstream dissenting Protestantism, Enlightenment liberalism, Romantic aesthetics (for example, of the sublime). One may offer a description of this confluence in terms of ideology, and note the likely connections of Blake's family with radical Protestant traditions. At the same time, however, the result of this uneasy confluence is undecidability, for instance in the interpretation of 'London' (Larrissy, *Blake* 42–55). This situation is later addressed by Livingston, when he says (referring to the use of the words 'mark' and 'marks') that for Blake's narrator 'the marking isn't so simple. It marks victims, but everyone is a victim (and an oppressor)' (180). In my own account, such undecidability can be described in terms of deferral and *différance*, and leads to formal effects whereby 'the clash of styles foregrounds style itself' (*Blake* 105). This last remark is indebted not just to the author's development of thoughts about difference, but also to his use of an unjustly neglected essay which reads Blake in terms of Bakhtin and Russian Formalism: Graham Pechey's '1789 and After: Mutations of

"Romantic" Discourse'. My own book asserts that Blake apprehends not only undecidability, but also the multiple indebtedness which gives rise to it, within his own texts. This apprehension, it is claimed, is the source of ambivalence about the 'bound' and the 'bounded', which can represent form (understood as created by some tradition) either as expressive or as limiting (*Blake* 70–109).

Nicholas Williams offers an original development of some of these topics in the conclusion to his *Ideology and Utopia in the Poetry of William Blake* (1998). In my book, I had observed that the phrase 'we impose on one another' from *The Marriage*, addressed to the Angel, could be taken to imply that imposition 'is a feature of all discourse including Blake's' (*Blake* 9). 'Imposition' can thus be related to 'difference', inasmuch as it seems to deny objective grounding to propositions. Williams conducts the thought-experiment of interpreting Blakean 'imposition' not in terms of the aggressivity of opposing 'stances' or 'world-views', but of Lyotard's aesthetics of unpresentability. As world-views, even discourses of utopia degenerate into narrow 'ideological programs' (*Ideology* 219). But 'if opposed in a mutually defining, though not mutually imposing, aesthetics of unpresentability, they [...] revive the utopian dynamics at the heart of even our most resistant present moment' (219). This formulation seeks to encompass a sense of the way in which Blake encourages a productive openness, an avoidance of foreclosure. It suggests a parallel with Livingston's approach to Blake: applying the analogy of chaos theory, he asserts that 'The force of Blake's often-repeated instructions on how to "see the World in a Grain of Sand" [...] is again to resist the reduction of the universe to individual particles or discreet singular units [....] Blake proposes a "scaling" and plural universe of worlds within worlds' (79). The perception of such a universe may open 'a liberatory path [...] that performs difference on what was otherwise the same' (73).

There is another aspect of Blake's work which can be aligned with difference, namely his printing method. Stephen Leo Carr has argued strongly for the significance of the facts of variation in different printings, in terms both of different ordering of the plates and different approaches to coloring. He has connected this variability to Derrida's concept of *différance*, especially in point of the way that notion comprises the concept of 'iterability': the capacity for a use of words or signs to be repeated, which entails that it can never be exhaustively explained by reference to an original context (187). Robert Essick and Joseph Viscomi have both disagreed with this analysis, not on theoretical grounds, but on the evidence of Blake's actual production and its context. Essick suggests that the variability is not as significant as the continuity, and refers to remarks such as 'My Designs unchangd remain' (*Notebook* 87). Both Essick and Viscomi cite the frequency of variation in eighteenth-century prints, though Essick concedes that the 'degree of variation' is greater in Blake (202). This seems to me to be an important concession. Furthermore, one might ask if prints, rather than books, are the closest analogy with Blake's works of composite art. If one is prepared to concede significant variability in Blake, then it becomes interesting to ponder Stephen Leo Carr's suggestion that Walter Benjamin's essay, 'The Work of Art in the Age of Mechanical Reproduction', is illuminating (188). (Naturally, Carr is not claiming a literal or historical relationship to Benjamin's study, with its references to photography and cinema.) In my essay, 'Spectral Imposition and Visionary Imposition' (1999), I suggest that variability in Blake is an attempt to overcome 'the loss of aura in repetition' associated with 'mechanical reproduction' (75). Here, perhaps, is another example of Blake's attempt to overcome the effects of 'commerce'. Since those days, his works have joined the ranks of the most auratic in our culture, as Nicholas Williams notes ('Eating' 145). Indeed, that is part of the point of eating a Blake in Harris's *Red Dragon*. The irony is that Blake's works may be co-opted for an exclusive and disempowering view of art, when he himself was trying to 'open up the scope of artistic production in his time, to retain the right of production for a broad variety of people and approaches' ('Eating' 150). At the same time, it is to be hoped that one of the chief points to be gathered from a study such as this is the way in which Blake is indeed apprehended as attempting what Williams describes.

notes

1. See *The Postmodern Condition: A Report on Knowledge*. The point about Kant is developed in an essay included in the appendix, 'Answering the Question: What is Postmodernism?' (71–82).
2. These points are well supported by a reading of the essay 'The Instruments of Mental Production' (*Stubborn Structure* 3–21). Adams's reference to Frye is on page 8 of 'Blake and the Postmodern'.
3. See Maurice Merleau-Ponty, 'On the Phenomenology of Language' and 'From Mauss to Claude Lévi-Strauss' in *Signs* 84–97, 114–25.
4. See Peter Conradi, *Iris Murdoch: A Life* 295, on Murdoch's friendship with Cary, and on their circle.
5. This was the subject of a conference in the School of English, University of Leeds, April 2005. Also worth mention is the Blake in the Orient conference held at Kyoto University in 2003, which included papers by Keiko Kobayashi and Barnard Turner on Blake and Oe.
6. For thoughts on 'deconstructive materialism', see Marjorie Levinson's *Wordsworth's Great Period Poems: Four Essays* 10.

works cited and suggestions for further reading

Adams, Hazard. 'Blake and the Postmodern' in *Essays for S. Foster Damon*. Ed. Alvin H. Rosenfeld. Providence: Brown University Press, 1969, 3–17.

Bertholf, Robert J. 'Robert Duncan: Blake's Contemporary Voice' in *William Blake and the Moderns*. Ed. Robert J. Bertholf and Annette S. Levitt. Albany: State University of New York Press, 1982. 92–110.

Byron, George Gordon, Lord. *Byron's Letters and Journals*. Ed. Leslie Marchand. 12 vols. London: Murray, 1973–82.

Carr, Stephen Leo. 'Illuminated Printing: Toward a Logic of Difference' in *Unnam'd Forms: Blake and Textuality*. Ed. Nelson Hilton and Thomas Vogler. Berkeley and Los Angeles: University of California Press, 1986. 177–96.

Cary, Joyce. *The Horse's Mouth*. 2nd ed. London: Michael Joseph, 1951.

Conradi, Peter J. *Iris Murdoch: A Life*. London: HarperCollins, 2001.

——. *The Saint and the Artist: A Study of the Fiction of Iris Murdoch*. 2nd edn with new foreword by John Bayley. London: HarperCollins, 2001.

Dent, Shirley and Jason Whittaker. *Radical Blake: Influence and Afterlife from 1827*. Basingstoke and New York: Palgrave Macmillan, 2002.

Didbid, Michael. *Dark Spectre*. London: Faber and Faber, 1995.

Duncan, Robert. *Derivations: Selected Poems 1950–1956*. London: Fulcrum Press, 1968.

——. *Roots and Branches*. London: Jonathan Cape, 1970.

Essick, Robert. 'How Blake's Body Means' in *Unnam'd Forms: Blake and Textuality*. Ed. Nelson Hilton and Thomas Vogler. Berkeley and Los Angeles: University of California Press, 1986. 163–76.

Frye, Northrop. *The Stubborn Structure: Essays on Criticism and Society*. London: Methuen, 1970.

Galperin, William H. *The Return of the Visible in British Romanticism*. Baltimore: Johns Hopkins University Press, 1993.

Ginsberg, Allen. *Howl and Other Poems*. San Francisco: City Lights Books, 1956.

Hamilton, Paul. 'From Sublimity to Indeterminacy: New World Order or Aftermath of Romantic Ideology' in *Romanticism to Postmodernism*. Ed. Edward Larrissy. Cambridge: Cambridge University Press, 1999. 13–28.

Harris, Thomas. *Red Dragon*. New York: Dell, 1981.

Hilton, Nelson. *Literal Imagination: Blake's Vision of Words*. Berkeley and Los Angeles: University of California Press, 1983.

Hughes, Ted. *Crow: From the Life and Songs of the Crow*. London: Faber and Faber, 1973.

Larrissy, Edward, ed. *Romanticism to Postmodernism*. Cambridge: Cambridge University Press, 1999.

——. 'Spectral Imposition and Visionary Imposition: Printing and Repetition in Blake' in *Blake in the Nineties*. Ed. Steve Clark and David Worrall. Basingstoke: Macmillan; New York: St Martin's Press, 1999.

——. *William Blake*. Oxford: Blackwell, 1985.

Levinson, Marjorie. *Wordsworth's Great Period Poems: Four Essays*. Cambridge: Cambridge University Press, 1986.

Levitt, Annette S. '"The Mental Traveller" in *The Horse's Mouth*: New Light on the Old Cycle' in *William Blake and the Moderns*. Ed. Robert J. Bertholf and Annette S. Levitt. Albany: State University of New York Press, 1982. 186–211.

Livingston, Ira. *Arrow of Chaos: Romanticism and Postmodernity*. Theory Out of Bounds Series, vol. 9. Minneapolis and London: University of Minnesota Press, 1997.

Lyotard, Jean-François. *The Postmodern Condition: A Report on Knowledge*. Trans. Geoff Bennington and Brian Massumi. Manchester: Manchester University Press, 1986.

Merleau-Ponty, Maurice. 'On the Phenomenology of Language' and 'From Mauss to Claude Lévi-Strauss' in *Signs*. Trans. Richard C. McCleary. Evanston: Northwestern University Press, 1964.

Miles, Barry. *Ginsberg: A Biography*. London: Virgin, 2000.

Oe, Kenzaburo. *Rouse Up O Young Men of the New Age!* Trans. John Nathan. New York: Grove Press, 2003.

Ostriker, Alicia. 'Blake, Ginsberg, Madness, and the Prophet as Shaman' in *William Blake and the Moderns*. Ed. Robert J. Bertholf and Annette S. Levitt. Albany: State University of New York Press, 1982. 111–31.

Otto, Peter. *Constructive Vision and Visionary Deconstruction: Los, Eternity and the Productions of Time in the Later Poetry of William Blake*. Oxford: Clarendon Press, 1991.

Pechey, Graham. '1789 and After: Mutations of "Romantic" Discourse' in *1789: Reading Writing Revolution*. Ed. Francis Barker, et al. Colchester: University of Essex, 1982.

Portugés, Paul. *The Visionary Poetics of Allen Ginsberg*. Santa Barbara: Ross-Erikson, 1978.

Sinclair, Iain. *Suicide Bridge: A Book of the Dead Hamlets: May 1974 to April 1975*. London: Albion Village Press, 1979.

——. *Lud Heat and Suicide Bridge*. London: Vintage, 1995.

Trotter, David. *The Making of the Reader: Language and Subjectivity in Modern American, English and Irish Poetry*. Basingstoke: Macmillan, 1984.

Viscomi, Joseph. *Blake and the Idea of the Book*. Princeton: Princeton University Press, 1993.

Williams, Nicholas M. 'Eating Blake, or An Essay on Taste: The Case of Thomas Harris's *Red Dragon*'. *Cultural Critique* 42 (1999): 143–70.

——. *Ideology and Utopia in the Poetry of William Blake*. Cambridge: Cambridge University Press, 1998.

index

Individual Blake works are listed separately